Figurations and Sensations of the Unseen in Judaism, Christianity and Islam

Bloomsbury Studies in Material Religion

Bloomsbury Studies in Material Religion is the first book series dedicated exclusively to studies in material religion. Within the field of lived religion, the series is concerned with the material things with which people do religion, and how these things – objects, buildings, landscapes – relate to people, their bodies, clothes, food, actions, thoughts and emotions. The series engages and advances theories in 'sensuous' and 'experiential' religion, as well as informing museum practices and influencing wider cultural understandings with relation to religious objects and performances. Books in the series are at the cutting edge of debates as well as developments in fields including religious studies, anthropology, museum studies, art history, and material culture studies.

Christianity and the Limits of Materiality, edited by Minna Opas and Anna Haapalainen

Materiality and Place in Italy, Francesca Ciancimino Howell

Figurations and Sensations of the Unseen in Judaism, Christianity and Islam

Contested Desires

Edited by
Birgit Meyer and Terje Stordalen

BLOOMSBURY ACADEMIC
LONDON • NEW YORK • OXFORD • NEW DELHI • SYDNEY

BLOOMSBURY ACADEMIC
Bloomsbury Publishing Plc
50 Bedford Square, London, WC1B 3DP, UK
1385 Broadway, New York, NY 10018, USA

BLOOMSBURY, BLOOMSBURY ACADEMIC and the Diana logo
are trademarks of Bloomsbury Publishing Plc

First published in Great Britain 2019
Paperback edition published 2021

Copyright © Birgit Meyer, Terje Stordalen and Contributors. This Work is licensed under the
Creative Commons License.

This work is open access and available on www.bloomsburycollections.com. It is funded by
the University of Oslo and Utrecht University.

Cover image: Sunrise (detail), Monir Shahroudy Farmanfarmaian.
Courtesy of the artist and The Third Line, Dubai

This work is published subject to a Creative Commons Attribution Non-Commercial
Licence. You may share this work for non-commercial purposes only, provided you give
attribution to the copyright holder and the publisher. For permission to publish commercial
versions please contact Bloomsbury Academic.

A catalogue record for this book is available from the British Library.

Library of Congress Cataloging-in-Publication Data
Names: Meyer, Birgit, editor. | Stordalen, Terje, 1958-editor.
Title: Figurations and sensations of the unseen in Judaism, Christianity and
Islam: contested desires / edited by Birgit Meyer and Terje Stordalen.
Description: 1 [edition]. | New York: Bloomsbury Academic, 2019. |
Series: Bloomsbury studies in material religion; 8 |
Includes bibliographical references and index.
Identifiers: LCCN 2019002828 | ISBN 9781350078635 (hardback) |
ISBN 9781350078642 (epdf) | ISBN 9781350078659 (epub)
Subjects: LCSH: Arts and religion. | Spirituality in art. |
Aesthetics–Religious aspects–Judaism. | Aesthetics–Religious
aspects–Christianity. | Aesthetics–Religious aspects–Islam.
Classification: LCC NX180.R4 F54 2019 | DDC 201/.67–dc23
LC record available at https://lccn.loc.gov/2019002828

ISBN: HB: 978-1-3500-7863-5
PB: 978-1-3502-2575-6
ePDF: 978-1-3500-7864-2
eBook: 978-1-3500-7865-9

Typeset by Deanta Global Publishing Services, Chennai, India

To find out more about our authors and books visit www.bloomsbury.com and
sign up for our newsletters

Contents

List of Figures	vii
Notes on Contributors	xi
Preface *Birgit Meyer and Terje Stordalen*	xv
Introduction: Figurations and Sensations of the Unseen in Judaism, Christianity and Islam *Birgit Meyer and Terje Stordalen*	1

Part One Reconfiguring the Image Question

1	Imagining Solomon's Temple: Aesthetics of the Non-Representable *Terje Stordalen*	21
2	Seeing with the Ear, Recognizing with the Heart: Rethinking the Ontology of the Mimetic Arts in Islam *Wendy M. K. Shaw*	37
3	The Hypericon of the Golden Calf *Yvonne Sherwood*	57
4	Idolatry beyond the Second Commandment: Conflicting Figurations and Sensations of the Unseen *Birgit Meyer*	77

Part Two Genealogies of Figuration

5	Beyond 'Image Ban' and 'Aniconism': Reconfiguring Ancient Israelite and Early Jewish Religion\s in a Visual and Material Religion Perspective *Christoph Uehlinger*	99
6	Visual Images in Medieval Jewish Culture before the Age of Art *Kalman P. Bland*	124
7	Real Absence: Imagining God in Turco-Persian Book Arts, 1300–1600 CE *Christiane J. Gruber*	132

Part Three Figurations and Sensations – Lives and Regimes

8	Aesthetic Sensations of Mary: The Miraculous Icon of Meryem Ana and the Dynamics of Interreligious Relations in Antakya *Jens Kreinath*	155

9 The *Ahl-i Beyt* Bodies: The Mural Paintings of Lahijan in the Tradition of
   Persian Shiite Figurations *Pedram Khosronejad*   172

10 Photographic Practices and the 'Aesthetics of Withdrawal' among
   Muslims of the East African Coast *Heike Behrend*   185

11 Moulded Imaginaries: Icons, Idols and the Sensory Environments of
   Eastern Orthodox Christianity *Sonja Luehrmann*   198

Part Four Desires for the Unseen: Art and Religion

12 From Ponte Sant'Angelo to Basilica di San Pietro: Figuration and
   Sensation in Bernini's Pilgrimage Route in Rome *Øyvind Norderval*   213

13 Figuration and 'Aesthetics of the Sublime': Aspects of Their Interplay in
   Christian Art *Else Marie Bukdahl*   229

14 Seeing, Hearing and Narrating Salome: Modernist Sensual Aesthetics
   and the Role of Narrative Blanks *Ulrike Brunotte*   245

15 The Art of Incarnation: Loss and Return of Religion in Houellebecq's
   Submission *Christiane Kruse*   260

Afterword: The Visual Culture of Revelation *David Morgan*   275
Notes   283
References   295
Index   327

Figures

1.1a, b	Reconstructions of (a) the front (opening to the east) and (b) the floor plan of the Solomonic Temple as imagined in 1 Kings 6–8	29
1.2	Relief on the Sarcophagus of Ahiram, King of Byblos (Phoenicia), around 1000 BCE	30
2.1	Madhu Khazanad, 'Plato puts the animals to sleep with the music of the spheres', from a 1593–5 manuscript of the *Iskandarnameh* (1194) from the Khamsa by Nizami of Ganj	38
3.1a	*The Adoration of the Golden Calf*, Nicholas Poussin, 1633–4	60
3.1b	*Dance around the Golden Calf*, Emil Nolde, 1910	60
3.2	*Agnus dei*, Francisco de Zurbarán, 1635–40	67
3.3	*Der Götze Moloch mit 7 Räumen oder Capellen*, 1738	68
3.4	*The Worship of the Golden Calf* by a follower of Filippino Lippi (1457–1504)	73
4.1a, b	Screenshots from 'Black Magic Woman', performed by Azizaa	94
4.2	*By All Means Satan Will Die*, Kwame Akoto 'Almighty'	96
5.1a	Enthroned god on the bifacial seal of Elishama' ben Gedalyahu, c. seventh century BCE	107
5.1b	Bronze figurine of a sitting god from Hazor Str. XI, eleventh/tenth century BCE	107
5.1c	Pair of male and female hybrid figures on an ink drawing on Pithos A from Kuntillet Ajrud, c. 800 BCE	107
5.1d	Terracotta group showing a bearded god enthroned, a stone erected in front of him, and an unbearded (female?) figure standing at his right, flanked by two quadrupeds. Judah, late eighth century BCE	107
5.1e	Two divine (?) figures, situated in a mountainous area, eighth-century-BCE incised pottery sherd from Jerusalem	107
5.2a	Anthropomorphic deities standing on bulls, as represented on stamp seals from eight-century-BCE Samaria	109
5.2b	Engraved bronze plaque showing a worshipper facing a long-robed, winged deity standing on a bull; Tel Dan, eighth century BCE	109

Figures

5.2c	Bronze statue of a bull from a rural sanctuary in the Samarian hill country, c. eleventh century BCE	109
5.3a	Enthroned god (labelled 'Zeus', possibly referring to Samarian Yahweh) on the obverse of a bronze obole from the Nablus/Shechem area, fourth century BCE	116
5.3b	Male god sitting on a winged wheel on the reverse of a Yehud silver drachm of unknown provenance, fourth century BCE	116
6.1a	Sarajevo Haggadah, ca. 1350 CE. Adam and Eve eating the forbidden fruit and being expelled from the garden (Genesis 3)	126
6.1b	Sarajevo Haggadah, two pictures concluding the story of the flood and Noah (Genesis 6–8)	126
6.1c	Sarajevo Haggadah, opening the story of Joseph and his brothers; Joseph having a dream and telling it to his father (Genesis 37)	126
7.1	Muhammad as a young boy is recognized as a prophet by the Christian monk Bahira, Rashid al-Din, *Jamiʿ al-Tawarikh* (Compendium of Chronicles), Tabriz, Iran, 1307–8 CE	136
7.2	The Prophet Muhammad, accompanied by soldiers and mercenary angels, embarks on his campaign against the Banu Qaynuqaʿ, Rashid al-Din, *Jamiʿ al-Tawarikh* (Compendium of Chronicles), Tabriz, Iran, 1314 CE	139
7.3	The Prophet Muhammad ascends through the heavens on the back of his human-headed flying horse, named al-Buraq, and accompanied by angelic troops as he approaches an opening in the sky, Nizami, *Makhzan al-Asrar* (The Treasury of Secrets), Tabriz, Iran, 1505 CE	142
7.4	The Prophet Muhammad ascends through the heavens on the back of al-Buraq, as he approaches an opening in the sky pulled apart by an angel in the upper left corner, Jami, *Yusuf va Zulaykha* (Joseph and Potiphar's Wife), Qazvin, Iran, ca. 1550–1600 CE	144
7.5	The Prophet Muhammad kneels as he speaks to God, represented as a large flaming bundle, Jami, *Yusuf va Zulaykha* (Joseph and Potiphar's Wife), Qazvin or Shiraz, Iran, 1570–1 CE	146
7.6	The Prophet Muhammad genuflects in the highest heaven while in the gold-and-red presence of God, anonymous, *Miʿrajnama* (Book of Ascension), probably Herat, modern-day Afghanistan, ca. 1436–7 CE	150
8.1	Map of Hatay	156

8.2	Wish Tree at the Meryem Ana Makamı in İskenderun, 2015	159
8.3	Meryem Ana Evi in Antakya, 2012	160
8.4	Miraculous Icon of Meryem Ana in Antakya, 2012	161
8.5	Miraculous Icon of Meryem Ana with the Hand of Fatima in Antakya, 2015	162
8.6	Orthodox Christian woman venerating the Miraculous Icon in Antakya, 2015	164
9.1	The Prophet Muhammad's Mi'raj, Seyed Davar Kiya Shrine, Lahijan, Iran, 1997	178
9.2	Imam Hoseyn holding his infant son Ali-Asghar in his arm while preparing for the final battle, Aqa Seyed Ibrahim Shrine, Babajan Dareh, Lahijan, Iran, 1997	179
9.3	Passing the *Sirat* Bridge, Aqa Seyed Ali Shrine, Mot'alegh Mahaleh, Lahijan, Iran, 1997	179
9.4	Front-door mural painting Seyed Ali Kiya Shrine, Rankouh, Lahijan, Iran, 1997	180
9.5	Lion guarding decapitated bodies, one of the episodes of the Battle of Karbala, Aqa Seyed Muhammad Shrine, Pincha, Astaneh Ashrafiyeh, Iran, 1997	181
10.1a	Women carrying *shiraa*, around 1900	189
10.1b	Woman with face mask, Zanzibar, 1905	189
10.2	Sultan Sayyid Said, Fort Jesus, Mombasa	191
10.3a, b	Bakor Studio, Lamu, c. 1970	195
10.4	Bakor Studio, Lamu, c. 1970	196
11.1	Icon of the Hieromartyr Nikolai Riurikov. Tsarevokokshaisk workshop, 2007	207
11.2a, b	Father Riurikov, early (a) and late (b) photo	208
12.1	Ponte Sant'Angelo and Hadrian's mausoleum, Rome	217
12.2	The angel with the superscription I.N.R.I., Ponte Sant'Angelo, Rome	218
12.3	Overview from St. Peter's basilica towards Ponte Sant'Angelo and Hadrian's mausoleum, Rome	221
12.4	The baldachin and the papal altar, St. Peter's basilica, Rome	224
12.5	The Cathedra, St. Peter's basilica, Rome	226
13.1	*The Deluge. Visions of the End of the World*, Leonardo da Vinci, 1514–15	232

13.2	The 14 pictures from *The Stations of the Cross*, Barnett Newman, 1958–66	238
13.3	*The First Station of the Cross*, Barnett Newman, 1958	239
13.4	Altarpiece, Fyllingsdalen Church, Norway, Hein Heinsen, 1980	242
13.5	Altarpiece, Old Holte Church, Denmark, Hein Heinsen, 2012	243
14.1a, b	Interpretation of Richard Strauss's opera 'Salome', Deutsche Oper, Berlin, 2016	257
14.2	Interpretation of Richard Strauss's opera 'Salome', Deutsche Oper, Berlin, 2016	258
15.1	*Adoration of the Magi*, Giotto, 1304–6	262
15.2	*Saint Luke painting the Madonna and Child*, Raphael (workshop)	264
15.3	*Rest on the Flight to Egypt*, François Boucher, 1737	268
15.4	*The Birth of Venus*, Alexandre Cabanel, 1863	271
15.5	*Olympia*, Edouard Manet, 1863	271
16.1	*The Resurrection of Christ* from *The Passion of Our Lord Jesus*, Albrecht Dürer 1511	279
16.2	*The Mocking of Christ* from *The Passion of Our Lord Jesus*, Albrecht Dürer 1511	281

Contributors

Heike Behrend (PhD in Anthropology) was Professor of anthropology at the Institute of African Studies, University of Cologne, Germany. She has conducted intensive ethnographic research in Kenya and Uganda in the field of violence, war and religion as well as in media anthropology. She has published extensively on photographic practices in Eastern Africa and worked as a curator of the exhibition *'Snap me One': Studio Photographers in Africa* (1998) in Munich and Amsterdam (together with Tobias Wendl) and *Studio Photography as a Dream Machine* in Tokyo (2010). Her latest publications are *Contesting Visibility: Photographic Practices along the East African Coast* (2013) and *Trance Mediums and New Media: Spirit Possession in the Age of Technical Reproduction* (2015), co-edited with Anja Dreschke and Martin Zillinger. Since her retirement in 2012 she lives and works in Berlin.

Kalman P. Bland (1942–2017, PhD in Near Eastern and Jewish Studies, 1971) was a professor at the Department of Religious Studies, Duke University, United States of America. His publications include two monographs, *The Epistle on the Possibility of Conjunction with the Active Intellect by Ibn Rushd* (1982) and *The Artless Jew: Medieval and Modern Affirmations and Denials of the Visual* (2000). At the time of his death, in July 2017, he was working on medieval animal fables, their transmission from East to West, their politics and their implications for the orientalist biases of Euro-American historiography.

Ulrike Brunotte (PhD in Religious Studies, Literary Studies and Philosophy, 1993, habilitation in Cultural Studies, 2000) is Associate Professor at the Faculty for Arts and Social Sciences at Maastricht University (Netherlands). She is also Adjunct Professor at the Humboldt-University of Berlin, Germany. Her fields of interest are as follows: role of gender in orientalism, colonial discourse and anti-Semitism, masculinity studies, genealogy of *material turn* in religious studies, ritual and performativity. Recent publications include 'From Nehemia Americanus to Indianized Jews. Pro- and Anti-Judaic Rhetoric in Seventeenth-century New England', *Journal of Modern Jewish Studies*, 14 (2), 2015; *Dämonen des Wissens: Gender, Performativität und materielle Kultur im Werk von Jane Ellen Harrison* (2015); *Orientalism, Gender, and the Jews: Literary and Artistic Transformations of European National Discourses* (2015, co-edited with A. D. Ludewig and A. Stähler).

Else Marie Bukdahl (PhD in Art History, 1980) is Adjunct Professor of art and technology at the Institute of Communication, University of Aalborg, Denmark, and a member of the Royal Danish (from 1985) and Norwegian (from 2006) Academies of Sciences and Letters. She is also President Emerita of the Royal Danish Academy of Fine Arts (1985–2005). Bukdahl is widely published in the field of art history, theory of art, and art criticism, and over the last decades she has been deeply involved in cross-disciplinary explorations in international settings, especially in the People's Republic of China and the United States of America. Her most recent book is *The Recurrent Actuality of the Baroque* (2017).

Christiane J. Gruber (PhD in Islamic Art History, 2005) is Professor of Islamic Art in the History of Art Department at the University of Michigan, Ann Arbor. Her primary fields of research include Islamic book arts, paintings of the Prophet Muhammad, and Islamic ascension texts and images, about which she has written two books and edited several volumes of articles. Her third book, entitled *The Praiseworthy One: The Prophet Muhammad in Islamic Texts and Images*, will be published in January 2019.

Pedram Khosronejad (PhD in Social and Cultural Anthropology, 2007) is Farzaneh Family Scholar and Associate Director for Iranian and Persian Gulf Studies, School of International Studies/School of Media and Strategic Communications, Oklahoma State University, United States of America. His research interests include cultural and social anthropology, the anthropology of death and dying, visual anthropology, visual piety, devotional artefacts, and religious material culture, with a particular interest in Iran, Persianate societies and the Islamic world. He is also the chief editor of *Anthropology of the Contemporary Middle East and Central Eurasia* (ACME). His next monograph is on *Tombstone Sculptors in Iran: Their Lives and Techniques in Bakhtiari Territories* (2018).

Jens Kreinath is Associate Professor of Sociocultural Anthropology at Wichita State University. He conducted research on Christian-Muslim relations in Hatay, the southernmost province of Turkey, with a focus on saint veneration at shared pilgrimage sites. His research interests include religious minorities in the Middle East, visual anthropology, semiotics of ritual, and aesthetics of religion. Kreinath co-edited *Dynamics of Changing Rituals* (2004) and *Theorizing Rituals* (2006–07), and edited *The Anthropology of Islam Reader* (2012). Most recent publications include articles in *Interreligious Studies and Intercultural Theology* (2017), *Religions* (2018), *Society and Religion* (2018), *History of Religion* (2019), *Journal of Ritual Studies* (2019).

Christiane Kruse (PhD in Art History, 1994; Habilitation, 2002) is Professor of art history and visual culture studies at Muthesius Kunsthochschule Kiel, Germany. Her fields of research are as follows: Bild-Anthropologie, Bildwissenschaft, art and pictures in visual culture, Rezeptionsästhetik und -theorie. Recent publications include *Taking Offense: Religion, Art, and Visual Culture in Plural Configurations* (co-edited with Birgit Meyer and Anne-Marie Korte, 2018); *Fassaden: Zeigen und Verbergen von Geschichte in der Kunst* (co-edited with Victoria von Flemming, 2017).

Sonja Luehrmann (PhD in Anthropology and History, 2009) is Associate Professor of anthropology at Simon Fraser University, Vancouver, Canada. Her research focuses on religion, materiality and lived ideology in Soviet and post-Soviet Russia, most recently with a project on anti-abortion activism and Soviet memory in the Russian Orthodox Church. She is the author of *Secularism Soviet Style: Teaching Atheism and Religion in a Volga Republic* (2011), and editor of *Praying with the Senses: Contemporary Orthodox Christian Spirituality in Practice* (2018).

David Morgan (PhD in Art History, 1990) is Professor of religious studies and Chair of the Department of Religious Studies at Duke University, United States of America. Morgan holds an additional appointment in art, art history, and visual studies at Duke University and an adjunct appointment in the Department of Religious Studies at the University of North Carolina at Chapel Hill. His scholarship has focused on the history of religious material culture in the modern era. His books include *Visual Piety* (1998), *The Sacred Gaze* (2005), *The Lure of Images* (2007), *The Embodied Eye* (2012) and *The Forge of Vision: A Visual History of Modern Christianity* (2015). His latest book, *Images at Work: The Material Culture of Enchantment*, appeared in 2018. Morgan is an editor of the journal *Material Religion*, co-edits a book series on the material culture of religion, which is published by Bloomsbury. He is an elected member of Clare Hall, Cambridge University.

Birgit Meyer (PhD in Anthropology, 1995) is Professor of religious studies at Utrecht University, Netherlands. Trained as a cultural anthropologist, she studies religion from a material and postcolonial angle, seeking to synthesize grounded fieldwork and theoretical reflection in a multidisciplinary setting. Recent publications include *Sensational Movies: Video, Vision and Christianity in Ghana* (2015), *Creativity in Transition: Politics and Aesthetics of Cultural Production across the Globe* (2016, co-edited with Maruška Svašek), *Taking Offense: Religion, Art and Visual Culture in Plural Settings* (2018, co-edited with Christiane Kruse and Anne-Marie Korte) and *Sense and Essence: Heritage and the Cultural Construction of the Real* (2018, co-edited with Mattijs van de Port). She directs the research programme *Religious Matters in an Entangled World* (religiousmatters.nl).

Øyvind Norderval (Cand. theol., 1978) is Professor of early church history and early ecclesial creed, Faculty of Theology, University of Oslo, Norway. Norderval has published in the field of early church history and dogma and also on issues in recent and contemporary church history and politics. His most recent engagement has been with Roman Catholic Counter-Reformation ideologies and strategies, and its connection to Jesuit theology and aesthetics of baroque art. His last publication was 'The Eucharist in Tertullian and Cyprian', in *The Eucharist – Its Origins and Contexts: Sacred Meal, Communal Meal, Table Fellowship in Late Antiquity, Early Judaism, and Early Christianity* (2017, edited by Hellholm, Norderval et al.).

Wendy M. K. Shaw (PhD in Art History, 1999) is Professor of the art history of Islamic cultures at the Free University Berlin. Her work focuses on the impact of coloniality on art-related institutions and premodern discourses of perception, with emphasis on the Ottoman Empire and regions of Islamic hegemony. She has authored the books *Possessors and Possessed: Museums, Archaeology, and the Visualization of History in the Late Ottoman Empire* (2003), *Ottoman Painting: Reflections of Western Art from the Ottoman Empire to the Turkish Republic* (2011) and *What Is 'Islamic' Art: Between Religion and Perception* (Cambridge: Cambridge Unviersity Press, 2019).

Yvonne Sherwood is Professor of Religious Studies at the University of Kent, UK. She has degrees in English Literature, Jewish Studies and Religious Studies (Hebrew Bible PhD 1995). She was the Speakers Lecturer at the University of Oxford in 2015;

was awarded an Honorary Doctorate from the University of Oslo in 2017; and was a visiting fellow at the Centre for Advanced Studies, Ludwig-Maximilians University Munich in 2018. She is the author of four monographs, six edited collections and over seventy articles and book chapters. Publications include *Biblical Blaspheming: Trials of the Sacred for a Secular Age* (Cambridge University Press, 2012) shortlisted for the American Academy Awards for Excellence Book Prize; The *Invention of the Biblical Scholar: A Critical Manifesto* (with Stephen D. Moore; Fortress: 2011); *Derrida and Religion: Other Testaments* (with Kevin Hart; Routledge: 2004); and *The Bible and Feminism: Remapping the Field* (Oxford University Press: 2017). Her current research projects are on the politics of migration and the figure of the 'resident alien'; blasphemy; sacrifice (especially the sacrifice of Abraham/Ibrahim); genealogies of religion and the secular; and colonial Bibles.

Terje Stordalen (Dr. theol., 1998) is Professor of Theology (Hebrew Bible/Old Testament Studies) at the Faculty of Theology, University of Oslo. He is also Obel Visiting Social Science Professor at Aalborg University, Denmark, and he headed a cross-disciplinary and international research group at the Centre for Advanced Study, Oslo, in 2014–15, where the work on this volume first started. He has published widely on Hebrew Bible issues (lately especially on the book of Job), and on biblical texts in cross-disciplinary perspectives, for instance in *The Formative Past and the Formation of the Future* (2015, co-edited with Saphinaz Naguib) and *Levantine Entanglements: Dynamics of the Local and Global in a Contested Region* (forthcoming in 2020, co-edited with Øystein S. LaBianca).

Christoph Uehlinger (Dr. theol., 1989) is Professor of history of religions/comparative religion and former (founding) Director of the Department of Religious Studies, University of Zürich, Switzerland. Among his publications is *Gods, Goddesses, and Images of God in Ancient Israel* (Minneapolis: Fortress Press & Edinburgh: T&T Clark, 1998; German original 1993, 6th ed. 2010), co-authored with Othmar Keel. He has initiated and (co-)edited several collaborative volumes on ancient Near Eastern visual/material culture and religion, including *Images as Media* (OBO 175, 2000) and *Crafts and Images in Contact* (OBO 210, 2005), and is the senior editor of the *Orbis Biblicus et Orientalis* series. His special research interests include the history of religion in the Southern Levant, the interface of religion and visual/material culture, and the aesthetics of religion.

Preface

This volume reflects the intellectual exchange between the two editors and their networks, starting with the international workshop in Oslo, *Religion Across Media: Theoretical Perspectives and Case Studies* (convened by Knut Lundby, Oslo), where Birgit Meyer was the keynote speaker and Terje Stordalen was the head of the host network (*Religion in Pluralist Societies*, UiO) and a contributor. The initiative resulting in this specific volume started during the academic year 2014–15, under the auspices of the Centre for Advanced Study, at the Norwegian Academy of Letters and Arts, Oslo. Terje was heading the research group Local Dynamics of Globalization in residence at the Center for Advanced Studies (CAS) that year. Birgit was a senior member of the group, and she took initiative to convene the international workshop named *Contested Desires* (22–4 April 2015). Most of the contributors of the present volume were already participating in this event. The contributors met again during a workshop held at the Leibniz Zentrum Moderner Orient (ZMO), Berlin (14–16 March 2016). We are thankful to the CAS and the ZMO for their hospitality and support, and for accommodating the cross-disciplinary conversations on which a project as ours depends. Comments and suggestions by Hans Belting, Vigdis Broch-Due, Finbarr Barry Flood, Øystein S. LaBianca, Adrian Herman, Amr Ryad, Richard Shusterman and Jojada Verrips helped us to sharpen our ideas. For the workshop presentations to transform into the contributions presented here required enduring engagement on the part of the contributors and a willingness to engage with our editorial comments and criticisms. We are grateful that our colleagues embarked on this joint interdisciplinary project with so much enthusiasm. We thank Kari Zakariassen and Pieter van der Woude for their assistance in various phases of the project.

For Birgit, the work on this book project is grounded in the research programme *Religious Matters in an Entangled World* (www.religiousmatters.nl) in the Department of Philosophy and Religious Studies at Utrecht University, which has been made possible thanks to two generous awards by the Netherlands Foundation for Scientific Research (NWO) and the Royal Netherlands Academy of Arts and Sciences (KNAW). We are grateful for the contribution of the University of Oslo (Oslo University Library as well as the Faculty of Theology) towards publishing this volume in OpenAccess format. Finally, heartfelt thanks to Amy Whitehead, chief editor of the Bloomsbury Studies in Material Religion series, and to Lucy Carrol, Camilla Erskine and Lalle Pursglove at Bloomsbury Publishers for their marvellous encouragement and support.

Amsterdam/Utrecht and Oslo/Aalborg, March 2019
Birgit Meyer and Terje Stordalen

Introduction: Figurations and Sensations of the Unseen in Judaism, Christianity and Islam

Birgit Meyer and Terje Stordalen

The excellence of divine things does not allow them to be offered to us uncovered, but they are hidden beneath sensible figures.

Meister Eckhart

Judaism, Christianity and Islam are commonly perceived to have more or less uneasy relations to images, especially images representing the divine. They all tend, at least nominally, to privilege verbal over pictorial media, preferring the spoken, sung or written word, and have often been understood to embrace a more-or-less rigid aniconism. However, when inspecting actual practices in these religious traditions across history, a more nuanced and complex picture emerges. Different trajectories within Jewish, Christian and Islamic traditions appear to embrace specific regimes that mould and direct the senses: embodied habits, standards for figuring, seeing, displaying and sensing the professed unseen through what we could call, with Meister Eckhart, 'sensible figures' (1936: 649, n745). Such regimes are not everywhere the same, and they are rarely explicitly formulated as such. But they are nevertheless there, silently bearing witness to the utter inadequacy of the convention to single out word and text as *the* canonical media of the so-called Abrahamic religious traditions. And yet, a lingering aniconism has so far been the conceptual and normative backdrop and common denominator also in academic study of these three traditions. Intended as a corrective of such bias, this volume calls for new analytical perspectives and for studying specific figurations and sensations of the unseen across various strands of Judaism, Christianity and Islam.

The fact that this volume assembles scholarship on Judaism, Christianity and Islam does not rest on a claim of an underlying similarity with regard to monotheism and a presumed aniconism under the label of the Abrahamic traditions (see Uehlinger, 102). On the contrary, we seek to problematize that claim – and its politics of use in various scholarly, religious and societal arenas – by confronting it through detailed case studies. Our intention is to open up scholarly inquiry towards the perplexing variety of practices of imagining and picturing the unseen – via internal and external, figural and non-figural images as well as words and sounds – within and across these traditions. Assembling cases from different strands in Judaism, Christianity and Islam and from the afterlives of Christian images in the spheres of art and literature allows us to get varieties into the picture, while certain general issues with regard to the question of how to study the complexities of imagining and accessing the unseen also come into view. Our intention is decidedly non-normative on the issue of whether and how legitimately to represent the divine, in that the contributions explore debates about the representability of God but refrain from stating whether the positions taken are defendable or not.[1]

The unseen is marked as unavailable to direct sight. Subject to manifold restrictions, its representation is a complicated and contested matter. Desires to render the invisible as visible and tangible, for sensing the unseen, are paradoxically confirmed as well as contested and controlled by the various visual regimes in vogue, which are entangled with broader sensational or aesthetic regimes. This yields a wide spectrum of stances and habitual attitudes, from appraisals of iconic images that represent the divine, to their dismissal as 'idols', from the embracing of visual signs alluding to the divine without suggesting likeness, to an indifferent attitude towards visual forms. Practices within Judaism, Christianity and Islam offer intriguing cases for a rethinking of the complex nexus of religion and pictorial media. Such a conceptual reconfiguration needs to be multidisciplinary and must move beyond taking unqualified notions of aniconism as the normative and conceptual default in these religions.

Beyond aniconism

As pointed out by Milette Gaifman (2017) in her introduction to a recent special issue on aniconism, the term itself is of relatively recent origin. It was coined by classical archaeologist J. W. Overbeck in 1864 in relation to primordial Greek art, which he presumed to lack anthropomorphic representations of the gods. For Overbeck, aniconism implied a non-existence of images – imagelessness (*Bildlosigkeit*) – which was due to the prevailing idea that 'unseen forces could not be envisioned as anthropomorphic and hence could not be represented in images' (Gaifman 2017: 337). They could, however, be represented through natural symbols. Interestingly, Gaifman suggests to 'deploy "aniconic" to describe a physical object, monument, image or visual scheme that denotes the presence of a divine power without a figural representation of the deity (or deities) involved' (ibid., see also Uehlinger, 122). In this understanding, aniconic representations are part of a religious visual and material culture and are to be analysed as such.

However, especially in relation to Judaism, Christianity and Islam, the term aniconism has been mainly employed by theologians and other scholars of religion, echoing the standpoints of religious elites, to denote a normative interdiction to represent divinity in *any* material or visual form. In this sense, it is part of theological and ideological apologies that reject the use of images as a fundamental feature of these three traditions. It is mobilized, for instance, by Calvinists, Puritans or Pentecostals against the use of images in the Catholic and Eastern Orthodox traditions, as well as in other religious traditions outside of the Abrahamic spectrum. And so aniconism means de facto anti-iconism and is employed as a synonym of the so-called Second Commandment that is evoked in a normative manner so as to insist on a historical and normative image ban (*Bilderverbot*) with regard to images of God, and even of all living beings, and to legitimate the fight against 'idolatry'. Notwithstanding fundamental critiques and the pioneering works in the study of religious images and material culture by scholars as David Morgan (e.g. 1998, 2012, 2015, 2018), Brent Plate (2015) and Sally Promey (2014),[2] the use of aniconism along these rather crude and extreme lines also extends into contemporary research on Judaism, Christianity and Islam and other fields, as many instances – for instance, the strategic references to the Second Commandment in the work of W. J. T. Mitchell and Bruno Latour (see the chapters by Sherwood and Meyer) – testify.

Our volume takes issue with this stance and seeks to open up broader perspectives. Three key points stand out. *One*, a normative view of Judaism, Christianity and Islam as being radically aniconic does not live up to historical evidence. It overlooks that the so-called aniconic passages in biblical literature are surrounded by less restrictive passages, and situated in archaeologically documented practices of rich use of pictorial media for cultic purposes (see the chapters by Stordalen, Uehlinger, Sherwood). Catholic and Orthodox traditions negotiate and employ images for making the invisible visible (see the chapters by Luehrmann, Norderval, Kruse), while in Judaism and Islam there have been and still are practices of depicting the divine (Bland) or the Prophet Muhammad and other motifs (Gruber, Khosronejad). This being so, scholars of religion should be wary to reproduce (in part partisan) normative theological claims as factual descriptions, and rather ground their analysis in historical, archaeological, art historical and anthropological records.

Second, our volume is up against the narrowness of an 'epistemic regime' (Uehlinger, 121) grounded in a presumed aniconism and image ban. The transmission of these arguably theological or emic concerns into the study of religion limits the scope of questions to be asked about the use and value of images, focusing all attention on the issue of the legitimacy of images employed to represent divinity. Once we are prepared to move beyond the conceptual deadlock of the Second Commandment, try to 'escape the straitjacket of modern preconceptions' (Bland, 128) with regard to Judaism and Christianity (see the chapters by Sherwood, Bland, Meyer) and discard the assumption of a timeless overarching image ban pertaining to Islam (Shaw and Gruber, see also Flood 2013), many more facets of the ways through which the unseen is imagined, imaged, sensed and experienced emerge, foregrounding multiple sensations in a multisensory and even synaesthetic manner, rather than focusing on visuality and seeing alone. Doing so requires a critical reflection on the implications of the long dominant mentalistic bias that ensued a problematic indifference towards other than verbal media and a strong focus on signification and hermeneutics in the study of religion as well as in post-Enlightenment conceptualizations of culture and society.

Third, a refutation of the notion of aniconism in the sense of anti-iconism as inappropriate may ensue a too narrow take on images as mere material representations or on images as the sole possibilities through which the presence of the unseen can be evoked. While several authors explore the use of images in the three traditions, it is not our concern to stubbornly spotlight a lingering 'iconism'. As argued, for instance, by Wendy Shaw, in the Islamic tradition an elaborate concern with images and visuality only emerged in the thirteenth century, whereas before that time Islamic scholars were above all interested in musical aesthetics as the prime form of mimetic representation. This indicates that in trying to understand how the unseen becomes tangible and experienced, it is advisable to acknowledge that there is more than 'the image question' alone (even though contemporary commotions around images of the Prophet Muhammad evoke strong negative responses by certain Islamist strands). Moreover, our volume seeks to complicate a simplistic, common-sense take on images as merely 'giving something to see' (Behrend, 185). The contributors do so by attending to the ways in which images are employed to conceal as much as they show, depicting the 'real absence' of an unseen God (Gruber) and producing 'iconoclastic icons' of forbidden photographic portraits via an 'aesthetics of withdrawal' (Behrend) or an 'aesthetics of the non-representable' according to which the empty seat in Solomon's Temple remains in the dark (Stordalen), or invoking a sense of a sublime via abstract forms and light (Bukdahl).

In sum, the basic idea of this volume is that a focus on figurations and sensations of the unseen allows to expand the rather narrow scope of questions arising around the legitimate use of images and the so-called *Bilderverbot*, towards a broader exploration of sets of practices through which humans mediate and sense the unseen, and struggle over legitimate ways in doing so. These struggles occur among learned elites in these traditions, as well as between clergy and common people (as in Kreinath's chapter on struggles about the recognition of Marian apparitions, or in Khosronejad's chapter about the existence of popular murals of Saints in Qajar Iran that clash with Sunni and Shiite theologians' interdictions of depicting human beings) or in colonial settings in which Western missionaries dismiss African worship of (non-figural) gods and spirits as idolatry, analysed by Meyer. Once scholars do not take aniconism as the conceptual and normative default in the study of Judaism, Christianity and Islam, more complex and productive questions arise. Grounded in Jewish studies, biblical studies, Islamic studies, religious studies, anthropology and art history, the contributors to this volume address these questions through detailed explorations that seek to complicate facile ideas about a presumed prevailing image ban.

Religion and the unseen

'Were one asked to characterize the life of religion in the broadest and most general terms possible, one might say that it consists of the belief that there is an unseen order, and that our supreme good lies in harmoniously adjusting ourselves thereto' (James 1917: 53). We agree with William James that the dimension of an unseen order – imagined in whatever ways – is at the core of Judaism, Christianity and Islam, and arguably of other religious traditions as well. Religion involves an awareness of a professed unseen that is taken to be existent and yet requires special forms to become manifest to common human sensation. Religion is about human attempts to render the invisible as *somehow visible* and the elusive as *somehow tangible* through forming and promoting embodied practices that shape what and how people see and sense (Orsi 2012: 147). We stress 'somehow' in order to highlight that the recognition of a trace or representation of a religious unseen that cannot be seen as such is subject to *inner images* in the religious imagination that may or may not be expressed in material form, and yet populate the imagination and are vested with value and meaning. And it would equally neglect the significance of figurative language and music. Why this is problematic is forcefully argued by Wendy Shaw, who calls attention to the antique concept of mimetic representation 'using any artistic intermediary – words, sounds, physical images – to signify and communicate realities beyond our physical experience' (42). Hence she cautions against the strategic, modern invocation of a normative idea of the image in relation to the presumed reservations regarding visual representations of the Prophet in Islam (which is ironic in itself, given that the image is all but taken for granted in the context of the study of Christianity). At stake here is an understanding of figuration as operating in the interface of images, words and sounds, understood as a process of imaging and shaping an unseen dimension and rendering it tangible through pictorial, written, spoken and sounding figures (see also Weigel 2015: 20–6).

This understanding resonates with and is informed by Niklaus Largier's reading of Erich Auerbach's notion of 'figura' as 'an expressive form' or 'sensory *Gestalt*' that is activated in the imagination and induces a realistic experience. While Auerbach developed figura in relation to practices of reading in classical biblical literature, Largier (2012, 2018, see also Meyer 2015: 156) extends it to a broader medieval mode of apprehension. Moving beyond a focus on the representation and signification achieved by pictorial, textual and aural signs, this mode involves a composite of perception, affects and concepts and takes figures as reality-producing, performative forms. Figures do not merely represent, but enable perception, sensation and understanding, and in so doing take part in effecting reality. This dimension is illustrated poignantly in Christiane Kruse's elaboration on incarnation as a meta-pictorial metaphor, through which the word was *shown to become* flesh in painting, rendering an image as a real human figure with a living soul in medieval and early modern painting. The break with this realistic embodiment in the art theory of the seventeenth century, as she shows, yielded ever more realistic, physiological representations of flesh, yet banished the soul; this disenchantment triggered a desire for a revival of religion as articulated by Joris-Karl Huysmans and Michel Houellebecq.

In our view, this take on figuration resonates with current critiques of a modernist, arguably Protestant overemphasis on representation and signification as the core of religion, and fits in well with attempts to recapture the material and corporeal dimensions of religion so as to grasp how imaginations of a religious unseen are vested with reality and truth (e.g. Meyer 2012; Orsi 2016; Vásquez 2011; Grieser and Johnston 2017; see also Belting 2001). Here is, in a nutshell, how we would operationalize figuration. We take as a starting point an understanding of images as involving an internal and external dimension. As Hans Belting put it succinctly, 'The picture is the image with a medium' (2011: 10; see also Mitchell 2008: 16–18). In German, both picture and image would be called *Bild*, and in our use of the term image we retain this understanding of it being constituted by a material, external and a mental, inner image. Material images invite their beholders to lift the mental image from its material carrier in the act of looking, and in this way an image seen in the world is incorporated and becomes part of and stored in a person's imagination. People may thus recognize God, Mary, Jesus, Muhammad or the devil *in* a painting or poster representing them, and beholders may even – to their delight or dismay – sense these pictorial figures to become real in and via that representation (Morgan 1998). The image they see is, as it were, lifted from the medium of the painting or poster in the act of looking, and incorporated, feeding the imagination (and possibly hijacking it and leading it astray). Inner, mental images may be externalized as and recognized in not only material images but also via other media such as words and sounds. We refer to this spiralling process in which material images and other media trigger inner images, and inner images are expressed via various material media, as figuration. Or more precisely, as transfiguration, in that inner images may be rendered via non-pictorial external media and vice versa. Religions shape the figuration of the unseen, by identifying key tropes or what Meister Eckhart appropriately called 'sensible figures', governing their representation via particular media – in short, by embedding such a figuration in a sensational regime.

The various chapters in this volume situate the use of inner and/or external images and other media in different sensational regimes, through which the unseen becomes imaginable and experienceable. For instance, through a study of historical mural paintings in Iran, Pedram Khosronejad identifies a complex Shiite visual aesthetic in which 'visualization and seeing are central to the recollection of holiness and saintly power' (184). Sonja Luehrmann describes how in Eastern Orthodox Christianity, in order to prevent the imagination from going astray, strict aesthetic and liturgical conventions were followed for the production and use of particular icons. While here recurrent material images are employed to ensure an asceticism of the imagination, Ignatius of Loyola, as Norderval shows, developed a technique of 'spiritual exercise' that aimed at achieving a plastic experience of 'being in spiritual contemporaneity with the locus where everything happened in the story of Jesus' (213) that became central to Jesuit piety. The spiritual exercises, in sync with baroque architecture and painting, were to overpower the imagination, to revel 'in the imagining of the unimaginable' (Wölfflin quoted in Norderval, 215). And while Brunotte points at the role of the imagination to fill the 'narrative "blanks" and uncertainties in the canonical biblical stories and in ancient historical documents' (245) by religious commentators and artists – yielding the iconic figure of Salome – Bukdahl notes that 'artists from Leonardo da Vinci to Wassily Kandinsky have always been aware that the language of form can communicate experiences and knowledge that the written and spoken word are either unable to express adequately, or simply cannot capture' (229). By contrast Christiane Gruber points at the elaborate 'visual "figures of speech"' with regard to an ineffable divine that Safavid artists struggled to evoke in their paintings. Metaphorical representations of God as light abound and are transfigured into art. All these examples point at processes of (trans-)figuration at work, in which material images are attributed with different values and shift into different figural forms. Religious traditions mould and shape the imagination of their adherents via multiple, intersecting media, and differ with regard to the trust they put in the imagination and the usefulness or danger of material images.

Importantly, the use of such intersecting media and their sensible figures in deploying authorized figurations of the unseen depends on incorporated sensational regimes that become part of people's habitus and part of a shared tradition. Such regimes involve particular 'sensational forms' through which the unseen is rendered available for common sensation, and through which the transcendent becomes available in the immanent (Meyer 2012, see also Kreinath). Sensational forms are sets of authorized practices that shape the perception by cultivating the inner and outer senses and shaping certain sensibilities. The regimes employed around the veneration of icons in the Eastern Orthodox tradition, Loyola's spiritual exercises or Sufi mystic imaginations of God yield distinctive, shared experiences and sensibilities through which the unseen becomes real for beholders, but may also be subject to contestations. This becomes especially marked in Kreinath's exploration of marked differences between the aesthetic regimes and related bodily sensations for Orthodox clergy and lay Christian and Alawite women in Hatay, Turkey, who experience Marian apparitions as real – much to the dismay of the clergy. Across the contributions, yet marked more or less explicitly, we find an understanding of sensation as an experiential embodied practice that yields a sense of attachment and commonality and is central to religious modes of perceiving the world and rendering the unseen as somehow visible and tangible. Religious sensational regimes produce the reality effects of religious figurations (see also Largier 2017, 2018). These figures, as the chapters by Brunotte and Kruse show evocatively, do not respect the boundaries set by the presumed vanishing of religion in the slipstream of secularization, but populate secular imaginaries and long for vesting them with new life and truth.

Contested desires

Scholarly research on aniconism and iconoclashes were occasioned, in the first place, by a series of events bearing witness to strong emotional forces triggered by conflicting regimes of depicting (or de-picturing) what should remain unseen (or seen in another way). Brunotte (247) aptly observes how Oscar Wilde recognized the potential of literary eroticism to stage a fusion between metaphysical longing and sexual desire, a staging that Brunotte pursues into opera performances of Salome. Several contributions in this volume explore elements of desire both in attempts to render the unseen to be seen and sensed, and in desires to direct and restrict such sensation. Strikingly, in the material explored by Luehrmann, a strong argument for the legitimacy in producing representations of the divine is carefully paired with an equally strong restriction on how to produce these representations and how (not) to use them. This volume originated under the premonition that the contrastive desires to portray *and* to avoid portraying that which is counted as unseen are fundamentally drawing from the same source of energy: the power generated by a sense of similarity and simultaneous difference between sensing representations of the unseen and interacting with that which these representations are held to represent. In other words, the field circumscribed in this volume is a field of perennially contested desires.

Several chapters in this volume reflect on a desire to display what cannot, or should not, be represented, *and* a simultaneous anxiety to mark a sense of distance between the representation and that which it represents. As we show above (and below), in some cases, this tension is explicitly verbalized, as in Bukdahl's analysis of the application of Kant's category of the sublime in production and analyses of European art. Correspondingly, several authors in the volume identify artistic strategies like the employment of light, darkness or emptiness in attempts at formulating artistic conventions to capture that which professedly can be figured, but not pictured with material images (Stordalen, 33–5; Gruber, 133; Norderval, 225–7; Brunotte, 246–7; and for popular regimes, cf. Kreinath, 168). In other contributions, configurations of the same tension are expressed much more subversively, as in the 'aniconic' gist of ornamentalizing photography in the Islamic East African coast (Behrend, 194–6), or in the staging of an exchange between the invisible (but audible) prophet and the very visible (and sensual) Salome in Strauss's opera (Brunotte, 245). Meyer (89–90) records how the missionary attempts at repressing material aspects of indigenous religion actually *produced* the reality of idols that the missionaries thought they had come to dismantle – yet another pointer to the paradoxical forces of hiding and showing at work under the surface discourse even in one of the most anti-iconic arguments produced in Christian religion.

Perhaps the most fundamental insight on the contested desires of figurations of the unseen emerges in the contributions of Sherwood and Uehlinger. Sherwood traces the paradoxically ambivalent reception of the icon of the destruction of the golden calf. It occurs as a negative image (one to be defined *against*) and a positive one (to be defined *with*). In subtle ways, Sherwood claims, this reflects that in the trajectories supporting this narrative it is always difficult to know at what point *latreia* (legitimate adoration using material objects) becomes *eidolatreia* (illegitimate adoration of idols). She then makes the point that these conflicting biblical traditions of figuring out the materiality of the divine silently transferred into European philosophy, and still haunt attempts at dealing with material representations of deity. These contested desires for divine transcendence and materiality are still very much in vogue also in contemporary scholarship (cf. also Meyer, 80–4). Uehlinger's chapter details how this is very much the case in intellectual traditions like biblical scholarship or archaeology of early Israel, both of which have contributed to producing a more nuanced primary record into impressions of dominantly aniconic texts, aniconic ('Israelite') environments and a vindictive image ban in biblical literature and material culture.

Similar critique of blind spots in scholarly reproductions of desirable past 'aniconism' is launched for instance in Stordalen (21–3), Shaw (38–43). Bland (131), Gruber (132–3) or Luehrmann (210), and Kruse (272–4) chronicles a corresponding longing for a desired past in which the balance of the seen and unseen was stable and productive. In sum, the volume represents a collective archaeology of knowledge (Foucault 1969) into the various academic disciplines that have dealt with figurations and sensations of the unseen in monotheistic and scripturalizing religions. The result is a view of how one of the professedly most characteristic features of this object of research – its perennial tendency to desire *and* contest figurations of the professedly unseen – came to influence also the research itself, as it depended upon analytical categories, theological concepts and philosophical reflections that were ultimately formulated under the regime of these same contested desires. We regard this as one of the more fundamental insights of this volume, and perhaps the one that most needs to be explicated, since it is likely to be subject to the same discourse of collective neglect and forgetfulness that has allowed the crude simplification of aniconic Abrahamic religion to live on, despite solid historical and conceptual refutation.

Overview of the volume

Part One: Reconfiguring the image question

The first part of the volume holds contributions that identify gaps in conventional analysis of pictorial media in the three monotheistic religions. Based on these gaps the chapters in this part present new analytical strategies for re-interpreting religious strategies for figuration and sensation.

In Chapter 1, Terje Stordalen first recounts how recent scholarship on the Hebrew Bible/Old Testament generally agrees that early Hebrew religion was not aniconic in the sense of absence of all pictorial media. Still, certain trajectories of biblical literature unquestionably do promote worship without pictorial representations of the deity, and Stordalen takes on one of the most central passages: the narrative of the Solomonic Temple in 1 Kings 6–8. The chapter pursues the question of whether the view that there existed an imageless cult reflects a general preference for verbal over non-verbal media (what Stordalen calls 'a logocentric ideology'). The story of the temple invites the reader to imagine traversing a long-lost temple of the past. This imagined itinerary is expected to activate all forms of human sensation, including seeing iconic representations, smelling incense and sensing spatial dimensions. However, when it comes to the focal point of the plot, all sensation comes to a halt, including the hearing of words. Rather than indicating a general distrust of pictorial media, this narrative reflects a regime of sensation that relied on the interplay of verbal and non-verbal media but did not trust any medium when it came to representing the deity. For that purpose, this regime resorted to emptiness and void in all registers of sensation, a strategy that reflects a particular aesthetics of the non-representable. So, this essay opens to the call for a more nuanced consideration of the roles and interplay of different media in religious sensation, and for seeing such interplay as part of larger strategies and regimes of sensation.

In Chapter 2 Wendy Shaw sets off registering the rich representations of secular and religious visual representations in Islam throughout the centuries. She points out that the framework of 'prohibition' that is currently employed should not be taken as indicative of an overarching image ban. Almost no aniconic discussion is recorded until the thirteenth century; in the first centuries of Islam there was simply a disinterest in pictorial media for displaying the sacred. Shaw then sets out to explore a neglected interaction between arts and music in Islamic tradition, examining a late-sixteenth-century Mughal illustration in a manuscript of Nizami of Ganj's twelfth century Book of Alexander. Nizami's description of Plato playing the organ before Alexander represents and consolidates a vast literature on religious musical aesthetics. Shaw argues that the modern emphasis on the visual over musical arts reflects different receptions of the late-antique concept of mimesis, which laid the groundwork for both European and Islamic artistic practice. She points out the inadequacy of modernist ontologies of sensation for perceiving the roles of pictorial and other non-verbal media in traditional Islam.

Modern Muslim and non-Muslim scholars alike risk missing the key role of sound in strategies for apprehending the divine in premodern Islamic philosophies and cultures – a role, we might add, that is still echoed in traditional Islamic recitation and prayer.

Adding further to that critique, Yvonne Sherwood, in Chapter 3, takes on the one item that most of all has become the topic for aniconism in the modern world: the golden calf, known first from the biblical story of Moses (Exodus 32) and then from innumerable receptions in art, religion and philosophy throughout the ages. According to Sherwood this figure has served as a 'hyperaniconic hypericon': an icon of the destruction of an icon, encapsulating an assemblage of knowledge, aesthetics, ethics and politics. It also became the figurative representation of the victory of the text over all pictorial media. That victory was, however, ambiguous. European modernism read the story of the destruction of the golden calf both positively and negatively: as an image to identify with and as an image against which to be identified. According to Sherwood, this double response mirrors the split function of the Bible in modernist stories about European foundations and values. On the one hand, the Bible stands as an ancient contrast to secular modernity. In this reading the destruction of the calf supports a modernist indictment of a jealous monotheistic deity with a very vindictive attitude to images. On the other hand, the smashing of the calf emerges as an early sign of the triumph of *Geistigkeit* over sensuality. For instance, to Kant and Freud the destruction of the calf represents the higher (proto-Christian, proto-universal) strand of the Old Testament: 'the heights of sublime abstraction'. We would argue that the continued preoccupation with the golden calf in European cultural history also echoes the perennial desire to figure the unseen out, also in terms of materiality, and the contesting impulse that such figuring will never represent the reality it professes to reflect.

Rounding off this part's reflection on the interactions between religion and programmes for sensing pictorial media, Chapter 4 holds Birgit Meyer's call for re-conceptualizing these interactions from a position 'beyond the Second Commandment'. The chapter makes a call for analytical scholarship to leave behind the idea that the interdiction of representational images of the divine is the normative default in the Abrahamic traditions. Meyer finds that this radical idea originated in Calvinist religion and critiques the apparently unwitting lingering of this legacy in Western secular scholarship. As a replacement for this idea, Meyer argues to open up towards a broader analysis of a range of strategies and visual regimes devoted to figurations of the unseen. The first part of the chapter offers a critique of Bruno Latour's dependence upon Calvinist interpretation of this commandment, echoed also in the work of W. J. T. Mitchell. The second part turns to the German strand of art history known as *Bildwissenschaft*, which is seen to offer important alternative takes on images and the theologies in which they are embedded. This helps understand how religion generates a sense of presence through images. Taking these approaches as a point of departure, the third part studies clashing figurations of the unseen in the export of the notion of idolatry produced by German Protestant missionaries to the Ewe in West Africa. The indigenous deities of the Ewe, which traditionally became tangible through other objects than images, were recast in Protestant religion as idols, and so dismissed as demonic. Having been *produced* through charges of idolatry, these recast indigenous figures continuously require to be pictured. Meyer claims that even the study of rejections of images requires a sound understanding of the use and appeal of pictorial items – a claim that should be taken seriously also by current-day scholarship addressing the presence of figurations in trajectories of the three monotheistic religions, and the various regimes of sensation they become subject to.

Part Two: Genealogies of figuration

The chapters in this part of the volume portray moments in the early and subsequent history of pictorial media and aniconic ideologies in the three (nominally) monotheistic and scripturally oriented traditions. Not only do each of these traditions include strands that explicitly endorse the use of images (see Parts Three and Four). Also, in their historical past Judaism, Christianity and Islam were more tolerant towards the use of images than is commonly known. Theologians representing various periods and traditions in these religions engaged with and reflected about images in ways that point to the fundamental inadequacy of simple modernist dichotomies between verbal and pictorial media. For this reason, these chapters all extend beyond simply historically recording past figurations and sensations; they also all substantiate the claim that new analytical approaches are needed in order to do justice to these complex histories.

That claim is particularly explicit in Chapter 5, holding Christoph Uehlinger's plea for reconsidering ancient Israelite and early Jewish figurations in a visual and material religion perspective. Combining a religio-historical and critical theoretical perspective, the chapter starts by recognizing a powerful conceptual matrix that has directed most modern reflection on these issues, namely, the assumption of the nexus between the rejection of cultic images, the practising of 'aniconic' service and belief in the deity's invisibility. This matrix, Uehlinger argues, became part and parcel not only of theologies in the three religious traditions but also of Western (now secular) thought. The chapter goes on to demonstrate that early Hebrew religion was never uniformly an imageless cult for a single deity – certainly not in local and probably also not in official practices. This portrayal, which seems fairly clear in the primary historical records, has been blurred by biblical and other scholarship relying too much on the heavily ideological representations of the past rendered in biblical literature. The vision of imageless cult now dominating a large strata of biblical literature came into being only in the Persian and later times, as elite strategies for generating religious distinctions and identity in the Persian (and Hellenistic) province(s) of Yehud. Uehlinger details seven stages that produced the matrix related at the opening of the chapter, a process developing from ancient distinction to identification, via Protestant iconoclasm and scripturalism, into modernist biblical scholarship and present-day archaeology. The chapter concludes with six theses sketching the changes necessary for analytical studies to move from the iconism/aniconism paradigm into studies of aesthetic formations in the perspective of visual and material culture. Thus, taking the discussion on 'biblical aniconism' as its example, this chapter amply discloses the complex intertwining not only between historical source records and religious ideologies but also between scholarly exploration of those source records and modernist ideologies unwittingly relying on the reception history of those very religious ideologies.

Departing from the medieval illustrated Sarajevo Haggadah – a manuscript possibly commissioned by a Jewish patron in Spain for the purpose of Haggadah celebration – our late and deeply missed colleague Kalman Bland, in Chapter 6, invites his readers into a fascinating comparison of three inherently dissimilar perspectives on the reality and validity of visual art in premodern Jewish culture. The first is that of Franz Kafka, a quintessential modernist, who denies the facticity of the visual arts in Judaism. Kafka's notion of an aniconic Judaism fails to account for a phenomenon like the Sarajevo Haggadah – and many more examples of the kind. The second perspective is that of the tenth-century Islamic Brethren of Purity, who open-mindedly affirmed the universal distribution of visual arts in all cultures, including Judaism, and who saw visual arts as forms of magic. The third perspective is that of medieval Jewish philosophy (Maimonides, Judah al-Ḥarizi and Profiat Duran) and rabbinic law (Rabbi Meir of Rothenberg and Maimonides). These all affirm the validity of Jewish visual art, highlighting its pedagogic, aesthetic and psychological benefits while underscoring its neutralization of magical or metaphysical implications. The Sarajevo illuminations reveal a medieval Jewish method for tickling the fancy, refreshing the sensorium and taking delight in the surprises of visual experience. Evidently, this practice of figuration and sensation disproves common expectations of a general Jewish 'artlessness', and of crude interpretations of the so-called biblical image ban.

Chapter 7 holds Christiane Gruber's analysis of the attempts of Persian and Turkish artists in the fourteenth to seventeenth centuries CE to represent God, or at least to convey a sense of the divine – thus challenging common assumptions about the totalist aniconism of Islamic traditions. Depending upon a rich variety of traditional Islamic exegetical, theological and poetical texts that describe God as theophanous, radiant, fragrant, cloud-like and transcendent, painters developed their own lexicon of forms to contribute to the broader discourse on God's nature. Gruber is able to demonstrate that painters used calculated devices and visual cues, such as light, veil and olfactory metaphors as well as colour symbolism, to convey the deistic sum (*tawhid*) of God in pictorial terms. One might say these painters articulated a medieval Islamic regime for representing the deity, and for piously seeing these figurations and employing them as religious items. In so doing, artists underscored and reaffirmed the apparent paradox that a numinous presence can be marked as much by its omnipresent reality as by its ostensible absence, what Gruber calls 'real absence'. Both strategies illustrate the interplay of art images and human imagination in the never-ending struggle to represent the unseen.

Part Three: Figurations and sensations – lives and regimes

Part Three is dedicated to anthropological explorations of the actual use of pictorial media in different trajectories of the Abrahamic traditions. The four studies document a fascinating variety and creativity in religious involvement with images, with local and temporal variations. They also spotlight how images may be used to subvert or challenge modes of religious authority that are primarily based on verbal media and conceptual reasoning. In so doing these chapters add weight and urgency to the call made in the previous parts: to develop more many-faceted analyses of the roles of pictorial media in actual practices in these monotheistic traditions.

In Chapter 8 Jens Kreinath offers an anthropological study of the aesthetics of representations of St. Mary in Muslim–Christian coexistence and exchange in the region of Antakya (Turkey), which holds remains of Jewish culture and religious belief as well. Kreinath argues that a key for understanding the dynamics of Christian–Muslim relations in specific localities of this region are the aesthetic sensations of St. Mary's appearances in dreams and healings. These are experienced by Christian and Muslim women alike after they have made vows at Marian sanctuaries. Kreinath's argument makes a distinction between the clergy and common believers in their ritual interactions with Marian icons. While the interactions of the Orthodox Christian clergy at first seem very similar to those of lay Christian women, the aesthetics of bodily sensations in Marian apparitions distinguish between lay and learned members of religion. The aesthetic regime regulating the sensations of these women is common also to Arab Alawite women, as seen in their practice of vows and wishes at Marian shrines and the experience of Marian apparitions and healings. In this case, a popular regime of sensation connects individuals across religious denominations, and it serves to distinguish within one and the same religion. This testifies not only to the need to study aesthetic regimes but also to the potential power of collective experience in such regimes.

In Chapter 9 Pedram Khosronejad reflects on Iranian folk narration and popular literature of the story of Twelver Shiism. This story appeared for the first time as illustrations in royal books of the Timurid Dynasty (1370–1506), but one particularly important testimony of the justification of the role of figurative art in Iran are religious mural paintings. It was only during the late nineteenth century that Qajar painters depicted figures of the Prophet Muhammad and other Shiite saints on a massive scale intended to be seen and used by the public. Khosronejad documents and illustrates this history and also demonstrates visual strategies and religious roles of these Persian Shiite figurations. The mural paintings illustrated in the chapter show the representations of holy figures in Persian Shiite visual culture, and the importance of their roles in devotion – topics which have until recently received little attention. In so doing, the chapter adds to the argument promoted throughout this volume.

Heike Behrend offers an analysis of restrictive and affirmative practices of photography on the East African coast (Chapter 10). The medium of photography was from the beginning contested among Muslims on the coast, because photography practices of the colonial state became associated with 'unveiling'. Thereby it collided with the aesthetic regime of the veil, yielding an aesthetics of withdrawal that was at the time dominant. So the original discontent with photography came from its being understood to violate traditional boundaries of public/private, male/female and of inside/outside. This perceived violation notwithstanding, many Muslim women and men eventually did make use of photography, albeit with caution, as a mode of self-representation to enhance their visibility and as a medium of exchange. It was only following the rise of reformist Islam in the 1980s that Muslim scholars increasingly invoked the 'Islamic interdiction of images' extended towards practices of using visual media such as photography and video. This dismissal was paired with a gendered concept of purity and seclusion. However, the use of photography continued, being particularly sensitive to one aspect of the aesthetics of withdrawal, namely, that by the very act of showing, photography also hides something else. At the end of her chapter Behrend explores ornamentalization of photography that play with regimes of aesthetic withdrawal, yielding 'iconoclastic icons' (cf. Sherwood, above). In this East African case, the prompt for such iconic aniconism comes from the similarities *and* differences associated with the aesthetics of the veil and the camera, respectively.

Sonja Luehrmann (Chapter 11) taps into the apparent paradox in Eastern Orthodox Christianity that sustains an elaborate theology of the icon and a simultaneous suspicion against imaginative evocation of mental imagery of the divine. The debate about the boundaries between icon veneration and idolatry is explored through nineteenth-century Russian Orthodox polemics against Roman Catholic spiritual exercises as these are echoed among post-Soviet Russian iconographers and lay believers. Luehrmann interprets religious art and worship environments as sensory regimes helping believers experience their faith as grounded in sense perception. The desire to distinguish iconography from other forms of visual representation becomes especially evident when iconographers create new motifs, such as depictions of newly canonized victims of Soviet anti-religious repressions. By tracing the choices iconographers make in creating new images within an existing visual canon, Luehrmann argues that religious image practices are always about constraining and guiding the imagination as much as enabling it. Displaying this double concern in the one Abrahamic trajectory that is most explicitly embracing the use of pictorial media for veneration, Luehrmann is able to give a lucid demonstration of the necessity to study these traditions taking full account of their internal complexities.

Part Four: Desires for the unseen – art and religion

The chapters in this part study aesthetic programmes in European arts, either in the use of art for religious purposes or in the recurrence of religious motives in secular European art and literature. These examinations demonstrate how European art discourse is often very sensitive to the complex roles of figurations, sensations and pictorial media in religious experience and imagination. They also document instances of multifaceted interplays between religion and art, based specifically in human sensation of the artwork. As such, they verify and illustrate the call produced throughout this volume for reconfiguring the intellectual analysis of the roles of pictorial media within strands of religion that are so often branded as 'aniconic'.

In Chapter 12 Øyvind Norderval explores the aesthetic regimes of baroque religion by reading Gian Lorenzo Bernini's architectural plan for the pilgrim's entry to the Vatican city alongside Ignatius Loyola's *Exercitia Spiritualia*. The goal of Loyola's spiritual exercises was to lead the believer to have a sense of being imaginatively situated onto the very *locus* where the sacred story took place. Bernini's design of the route to the Vatican followed an overall scheme founded on that programme, developed from the idea of the basilica over St. Peter's grave as the goal of pilgrimage to Rome. The route starts at the bridgehead of Ponte Sant'Angelo and ends up in the high choir of St. Peter's basilica, at the cathedra. Jesuit theology played a key role in the Roman baroque, in which Bernini worked. Norderval asks whether it is also possible to find a close relationship between Jesuit mysticism and Bernini's art. Engaging in an in-depth analysis of interaction between Loyola's text and artistic forms of expression in Bernini's project of the pilgrimage route, Norderval argues to see the pilgrimage route as a materialization of Ignatius's *Exercitia*. The route employs sculpture and architecture so as to evoke spiritual sensation and emotion, thus offering an excellent example of the possible roles of figurations and sensations in Roman Catholic religion.

Chapter 13 holds Else Marie Bukdahl's reflections on strategies across centuries of European art for representing that which ultimately is held to be non-representable. Artists of the Middle Ages, the Renaissance and the baroque often portrayed the divine by using abstract artistic effects. At the end of the eighteenth century, Immanuel Kant connected Edmund Burke's definition of 'the sublime' with the Second Commandment, taking this interdiction to express the highest insight on the matter of representing the deity. Further interpretations of Burke's and Kant's definitions of the sublime appeared in the nineteenth and twentieth century. Precisely because the sublime is associated with depictions of the sacred, and hence with a central problem in art for religious purposes, its reappearance in modern art gives rise to some of the most extreme innovations in visual art, as illustrated in recent Danish art for ecclesial use. In this line of strategies, the sublime is often represented by non-figural art where light plays a central role.

In her contribution in Chapter 14 Ulrike Brunotte considers the reception of the biblical figure of Salome in art and especially in opera. As it turns out, the very name Salome is not mentioned in the biblical stories of the death of John the Baptist; her dance lacks a narrative description and is oblivious of the 'seven veils'. These narrative 'blanks' provided spaces for the imaginative involvement of later recipients of the story, first, by religious commentators and, then, by artists. The figure of the 'dancing Salome' became an icon in Renaissance/baroque art. In the nineteenth century she was revived through narrative folk stories and literature. Since the fin de siècle dance, Oscar Wilde's play and Richard Strauss's opera, Salome is so centrally embedded in modern visual regimes that she can be defined as 'a sign of the visual as such'. Wilde's play started the production of an aesthetic spectacle of symbolist and biblical metaphors. In an opening scene of Strauss's opera, Salome's visual-bodily attraction is contrasted with the fascination of the disembodied 'holy' voice of the prophet who announces the message of God from the depths of the cistern. This dramatic configuration incorporates the interplays between words, figurations and sensations thematized in this volume. Brunotte explores the sensual mediations of the sacred in this interplay between the embodied and the disembodied voice, the visible and the invisible (but audible).

In the last contribution of the volume Christiane Kruse takes inducement from Michel Houellebecq's novel *Soumission* (*Submission*), which deals with the search for cultural identity in the aftermath of modernist secularization. The novel depicts an Islamic government taking over France in 2022, a shift substantiated by the claim that the atheist humanist thesis 'there is no God' would be utterly presumptuous, rendering the human to serve as the divine. This professedly arrogant humanism is in the novel paired with the Christian creed, that God did, indeed, become human, incarnated into human flesh. Kruse explores the role of European art in comprehending painting as, precisely, 'incarnation'. The Italian humanist painter Cennini used the term *incarnazione* to denote the coming-into-being of a bodily image. Flesh is seen as the interphase of body and soul, and the painting of the flesh thus explicitly echoes the dogma of God becoming human. With the rise of positivism and the epoch of naturalism in the arts in the nineteenth century, spirit and soul are driven out, as it were, from painted flesh. Now the human skin is perceived merely as a membrane between outer appearance and inner physiology. The protagonist of *Soumission*, François, follows in the footsteps of Zola's contemporary Karl Joris Huysmans (author of the *Décadence* and subsequently a convert to Catholicism) into a monastery in Rocamadour, home of a black Madonna statue. Facing the sculpture, he feels reduced to his sheer physical existence, abandoned by his spirit. François loses his faith, according to Kruse an indication that the moderate Islam unfolded in the novel is equally devoid of metaphysical depth, having made the natural sciences their prime witness for the existence of God.

Part One

Reconfiguring the Image Question

1

Imagining Solomon's Temple: Aesthetics of the Non-Representable

Terje Stordalen

Logocentrism and aniconism

The contributions in this volume encircle an age-old question: How does one represent that which is conceived to be non-representable or not suitable for exposure? The conventional wisdom is that ancient Hebrew religion (as well as later Jewish traditions and their Christian and Islamic cousins) simply avoided pictorial representations of the divine – due to a preference for verbal over iconic media.[1] This view relies on a surface reading of the passage known in Reformed and Anglican traditions as the Second Commandment: 'You shall not make for yourself an idol, whether in the form of anything that is in heaven above, or that is on the earth beneath, or that is in the water under the earth. You shall not bow down to them or worship them [...]' (Deut. 5.8, cf. Exod. 20.4-6).[2] Moreover, the conventional view rests upon a particular perception of this command, illustrated by one commentator in this way:

> Images are forbidden because they are inadequate, and thus false, representations of Yahweh's identity (Childs, *The Book of Exodus*, 409; idem, *Old Testament Theology in a Canonical Contest*, 66–8). [...] Yahweh has revealed himself to his people through the word, not in a specific form (Deut. 4.12, 15-19). This dynamic of the God who speaks and whose words act, cannot be confined to a static representation. (Hartley 1992: 312)

This quote, with its internal reference to earlier exegesis, is an example of how the myth of biblical logocentrism is propagated in biblical studies.

The concept of 'logocentrism' goes back to the German philosopher Ludwig Klages of the 1920s, who saw a distinction between logocentric (shallow) and biocentric (deep) consciousness (cf. Kasdorff 1969: 69, 155). Recent intellectual exchange on logocentrism is more marked by Derrida's use of the word in his attack on a Platonic strand of thought in de Saussure (Derrida 1976: 6–26, etc.). Both Klages and Derrida used the concept to criticize dominant tendencies in classical Western philosophy, which explains why few current philosophers employ this term as a self-designation.

Within theology, however, several studies positively identify themselves as logocentric (like, recently, Gäde 2010). Indeed, George Aichele (2001: 29–30) identified widespread thought patterns in theological scholarship that come close to the philosophy that Derrida called 'logocentric'. A plausible reason for the more positive standing of the concept in theology is the fact that Christ is envisioned as the incarnated *logos* (Greek for 'word', 'concept', 'reason') in the prologue to the Gospel of John. So, in theological language 'logocentric' might translate as 'oriented towards the divine origin of the incarnated Christ', or similar.

Derrida attacked idealistic philosophy, which he saw as a 'logocentrism which is also a phonocentrism: absolute proximity of voice and being, of voice and the meaning of being [...]' (Derrida 1976: 11–12), and in addition understood written text as 'the signifier of the signifier' (i.e. signifier of voice), a 'nonexterior, nonmundane [...] interpreter of an originary speech itself shielded from interpretation' (pp. 7–8). In logocentrism as perceived by Derrida, there goes an immediate line from a text back to a spoken word, back to being and truth. Similarly, in Christian logocentric theology, the medium of revelation (signifier of the signifier) would be the Bible, heard as the *viva vox evangelii* (the living voice of the gospel) (Gäde 2010: 132). There goes a similar line from the textual witness of revelation, back to the actual revelation, which again aligns with ultimate truth. This displays Christ as *logos asarkos* (non-incarnated word), pre-existent, non-created and with divine qualities (Ibid., 134).

Logocentrism proposes that mental representations of the *logos* are more immediate and true than material representations: 'There is [...] a good and a bad writing: the good and natural is the divine inscription in the heart and the soul; the perverse and artful is technique, exiled in the exteriority of the body,' and '[t]he good writing has therefore always been *comprehended*' (Derrida 1976: 17, 18). The implication is that 'good' writing is the only acceptable material ('bodily') medium suitable for representing the logos. Adjacent to such preference for comprehension and *logos* and the concomitant devaluation of matter lies the tendency to prefer verbal over non-verbal representations of the logos, which brings us to aniconism.

The term aniconism can be used in a narrow as well as a broad sense. In the narrow sense, aniconism names a view that avoids iconic representations of deity, especially for cultic purposes (Gaifman 2017: 338). Most experts today hold that this is the kind of aniconism promoted in the Second Commandment (see next section). In a broader and more general sense, however, aniconism denotes a general distrust in pictorial media. Perceiving biblical aniconism through the lens of logocentrism, the implication clearly would be that of a general, rather than a narrow, sense of aniconism. Perhaps this helps explain the staggering resilience of the untenable view of ancient Jewish culture as generally aniconic.

The above combination of logocentrism and aniconism has generated what Birgit Meyer in this volume calls the *mentalistic* view of religion. This perception of religion privileges words, teaching and ideas and tends to overlook or downplay the role of pictorial and other non-verbal media in defining and interpreting religion. Such a logocentric interpretation of aniconism should be recognized as belonging to the *modern* era, although it is often transcribed back into deep posterity by modern interpreters, for instance, in their interpretation of the Second Commandment:

> The prohibition of images in ancient Israel has led to [...] the obvious dearth of the plastic arts within Jewish (and, indirectly, Muslim) tradition. [...] The theological reason is expressed well by Craigie: 'To attempt to represent and limit God by human form in wood or stone would be to undermine the transcendence of God' ([1976] 135). (Christensen 2001: 89)

This quote illustrates the mode of existence for this knowledge in biblical scholarship: commonly shared but rarely actually examined. The wide presence of pictorial media in the Iron Age Southern Levant has been richly documented over the last five decades, not least by Othmar Keel (1972) and his students (see next section). However, the common view still is that the religious practices enshrined in biblical texts (possibly by a learned minority) were different from those reflected in the archaeological record of the period (which are sometimes classified as 'Canaanite'). Thus, the view of words and texts as privileged media in *biblical* religion strangely seems to remain largely intact.

This chapter sets out on a case study examining the presumed biblical distrust in non-verbal media for representing the presence of the deity, focusing on a passage that should represent such distrust in a typical way. One challenge for making this examination is that the disciplinary machinery, and its corpus of knowledge, is tilted towards neglecting reflections of non-verbal religion in biblical texts. This void is not simply generated by the contents of the sources. It would, for instance, have been possible to explore the use of pictorial or performative media in biblical religion through the way these are reflected in biblical sources (Stordalen 2012, 2013). The near complete lack of such research renders scholarship unable, for the time being, to speak with confidence about whether the biblical ban on images did, in fact, imply a religious practice that excluded a prominent role for all other media (cf. Otten 2007: 33f). The time is more than ripe for a case study exploring the perceived relation between verbal and non-verbal media in one biblical passage. First, however, a brief recourse to the historical context.

Early Jewish aniconism in recent scholarship

The assumption that early Jewish societies were aniconic (in the wide sense) is clearly exaggerated. This view relies on much later rabbinic ideals: Jewish art in late antiquity was quite heterogeneous (Levine 2012). Likewise, medieval Jewish art featured a number of pictorial representations (Bland 2000, and see Bland's entry in this volume). This is now commonly accepted by experts in the field, and the general public could see a documentation, for instance, in the New York Metropolitan Museum of Art, Essays section (Boehm and Holcomb 2008).

Over the last five decades a parallel reorientation has taken place in research on pictorial media in early Israel. The reorientation relied on comparative research in ancient Levantine archaeology, Near Eastern iconography and biblical studies – as illustrated by Christoph Uehlinger in this volume (cf. also again Mathys 2013). The archaeological record of the Iron Age Southern Levant (Edom, Moab, Ammon, Israel, Judah, Philistia) is rich in pictorial representations (Keel and Uehlinger 1992).

Domestic religion was not aniconic, neither in the broad nor in the narrow sense. It was dominated by the use of figurines in various forms – certainly in the Iron Age, but to some extent also later. Particularly important were the Judaic Pillar Figurines (Kletter 1996), a form that was indigenous and characteristic to these territories (see Wilson 2012). The archaeological record also holds pictorial representations – like those in Kuntillet Ajrud (Meshel 2012). These and similar finds re-opened the question of whether there may have been iconic representations of deity even in official Hebrew religion, such as in the Temple of Jerusalem (see Uehlinger 1997). The claim for aniconism (in the narrow sense) in the Jerusalem Temple was usually backed by reference to the narrative of King Josiah's reform in 2 Kings 22–3. Recently, however, there has been a discussion of the historical value of this passage (Uehlinger 2005; Stordalen 2014). Today, therefore, even scholars who defend the conventional view of an aniconic cult in Jerusalem admit that the earliest form of aniconism probably did not promote an aniconic programme or reform. Programmatic aniconism, intolerant to all images of deity, is a fairly late conviction of a religious minority.[3]

To make a long story short, religion in the classical Hebrew era was not uniformly aniconic. Faith practices in households and local sanctuaries were hardly ever so, and it seems probable that the view of a normalized aniconic official religion was generated by later scribes. Aniconic ideals were predominant in the group behind the so-called deuteronomistic trajectories of the Hebrew Bible, and over time this group would dominate the redaction and reception of the collection.

Aniconism in context

Before coming to the actual case, we also need to consider the distinction between ideals and practices. The first may be governed by more or less utopian ideas. The second may aim to promote certain ideals, but will, in practice, be conditioned by historical, social and material circumstances. Take as example the most programmatically aniconic passage of deuteronomistic theology, a passage where Moses reinterprets what happened during the giving of the Torah – according to Knut Holter (2003), an elaborate attempt at interpreting the Second Commandment:

> [T]he LORD spoke to you out of the fire. You heard the sound of words but saw no form; there was only a voice. […] Since you saw no form when the LORD spoke to you at Horeb out of the fire, take care and watch yourselves closely, so that you do not act corruptly by making an idol for yourselves, in the form of any figure. […] (Deut. 4.12-16)

How would such a theological conviction be lived out in real life? That is a different question than asking what may have been the ideal world of someone reading (or writing) this passage. The deuteronomists did not live in a vacuum. Although their preferred service was that of a single deity worshipped without the use of images in a single central temple, they lived among people that had different ideals and practices (cf. above). More importantly, they shared concepts and sentiments, landscapes, institutions and installations with their less-than-deuteronomistic neighbours. They would have been familiar with, respectful of and perhaps positive to religious emotions, practices and motives that fellow Israelites celebrated using cultic figurations. For instance, burials in the local environments of deuteronomistic scribes would often involve the use of figurines representing the dead kin, the deity and so forth (cf. Bloch-Smith 1992: 95–103). Are we to assume that deuteronomistic theologians would show disrespect for the dead kin of village peers, for instance, by refusing to take part in such funerals, not recognizing their validity, or by scorning the grief rituals? Moreover, to the extent that deuteronomists wished to interact with these neighbours (and deuteronomistic literature certainly leaves the impression that this is their intention), they would have to activate their command of general Hebrew linguistic, cognitive and other resources. So, in many ways they would be compelled to identify with their peers, at least in some measure.

In asking how deuteronomistic ideals were lived out in practice, we are asking for their cultural embeddedness. The interconnections of deuteronomistic theology are most visible in the Deuteronomistic History (DtrH; the sequence from Deuteronomy through 2 Kings in the Hebrew Bible). Although a deuteronomistic theological watermark is evident across the composition, the work incorporates and interacts with numerous sources, narrative cycles, characters and episodes that reflect views of Israel and Judah other than those preferred by the deuteronomists. Moreover, deuteronomistic theology constitutes itself as an interpretation of a past that was affirmatively shared with people from the former states of Israel and Judah. DtrH argues for re-conceiving a past that was already known by the addressee. Several passages promoting the deuteronomistic rhetorical strategy confirm this dilemma. For instance, the work starts with Moses giving one long speech (the book of Deuteronomy) in which he reinterprets the giving of the Torah at Sinai already narrated and experienced (also in the narrative world) in the books of Exodus, Leviticus and Numbers. In this process the *torah* is redefined, in content and in form: In Exodus, Leviticus and Numbers *torah* is basically oral lore curated by Aaronitic priests. In Deuteronomy it becomes a written scroll (the Torah of Moses), now in the hands of Levite priests. The religious well-being of the Israelites no longer relies on their listening to the advice and instruction of (Aaronitic) priests, but on keeping the stipulations of the Mosaic *book* to the letter (Vogt 2006). Similarly, the book of 2 Kings reports that during the reign of Josiah the priests discovered a book of Moses in the Temple. This scroll had (inexplicably) fallen into oblivion but was retrieved during a renovation of the Temple (2 Kings 22–3). Josiah's reform consists of putting back into force the professedly original stipulations of Moses, as recorded in this book. In the prism of memory studies, this is an argument to reformat the past so as to legitimize contemporary political action (cf. Stordalen 2014). In both cases DtrH confirms the theological importance of the very institutions it aims to change – the Torah and the Temple cult. And so, the deuteronomists must interact with the public perception of these institutions. They did not invent a version of Hebrew religion *ex novo*; they related to existing symbols, narratives, beliefs, groups, practices, institutions – and to the religious charge of these symbols and institutions.

So, again, how would deuteronomistic aniconism be lived out in real life? In particular, did the deuteronomistic ban on representative images entail a devaluation of alternative media and semiotic systems? A good place to probe this question is the part where the DtrH narrates the building and dedication of the Temple in Jerusalem (1 Kings 6-8) – a major religious institution with documented significance within and without deuteronomistic religion.

The Jerusalem Temple in deuteronomistic literature

Peter Vogt (2006: 227–31) argues that deuteronomistic theology marks a shift from the earlier cultic recognition of YHWH towards everyday recognition of the Torah of Moses. And indeed, when it comes to cultic practices and venues, deuteronomistic literature has somewhat of a blank spot as compared to priestly texts. While the book of Deuteronomy argues for limiting worship to a single, central temple (cf. Deut. 12), the emphasis is on abandoning local shrines. Not much is said about *how* to worship in that central place, except that tithe offerings should be brought (cf. Deut. 14.22-28 and 26.1-15) and seasonal celebrations be kept (Deut. 16.1-17). In the literary fiction of the book, Moses lived hundreds of years before the building of the Temple; so Deuteronomy consistently talks about 'the place that the Lord is going to choose for his name to dwell'. But even considering that this framing might dictate a distance to actual temple cult, the book leaves the impression that ceremonial details are not very important. Accordingly, as documented by Gary Knoppers, many scholars have seen some form of religious devaluation of the temple in deuteronomistic theology (Knoppers 1995: 230-1, n. 8-11).

This relative silence notwithstanding, there are in fact echoes of the Temple's significance in DtrH. Deuteronomy reflects an ideal sanctuary, featuring a ban on pictorial representations of the divine (as pointed out above).[4] These texts would be heard as statements on temple design and practice. Similarly, the book describes the ark of the covenant and artefacts and practices to occur 'before the Lord'[5] – which could well refer to the cultic venue. So, there *is* a sanctuary implicitly reflected or imagined in Deuteronomy, and the reflection suggests a centralized cult for one single god celebrated without iconic representations of the deity.

An important passage late in the DtrH (2 Kings 22-3) narrates how stipulations professedly given by Moses hundreds of years earlier were rediscovered and implemented under King Josiah in the seventh century BCE. Once again, the emphasis is upon that which is going to be abandoned. Still, here too the ideal service is an aniconic cult for one god in the Jerusalem Temple. The narrative tacitly admits that cult before Josiah was neither aniconic nor centralized, and it addressed several deities. The argument in DtrH is that cult before Josiah had been perverted because earlier rulers had disobeyed the Mosaic commandments. The reported reformation in 2 Kgs 23.4-20 is violently iconoclastic, and this passage was an inspiration for later iconoclastic incidents.

In between the stories of Moses and Josiah sits the narrative of the construction of the Solomonic Temple in Jerusalem (1 Kings 6-8). An audience immersed in the universe of DtrH would easily say those Mosaic stipulations that had been disobeyed prior to Josiah were originally established in the Temple of Solomon – all the more so since the narrator of that passage has the Lord remind Solomon that the divine stipulations must be kept (1 Kgs 6.11-13). So, between the implicit ideal temple of Deuteronomy and the violent iconoclasm of 2 Kings 23, the story of the Solomonic Temple appears as a more tempered, and infinitely more detailed, middle ground. It is also the one text in DtrH that positively reports on the installations and activity in the Temple. Moreover, it is a story actively interacting with its cultural context and earlier sources relating to the Temple in Jerusalem. A reasonable interpretation is that the deuteronomists drew on to various theological and social ideals in order to generate 'enthusiastic support by all sectors of the people' (Knoppers 1995: 254) – possibly on a topic that was not on their own top-ten list (cf. Schweizer 2011). Looking for a text reflecting the playing out of deuteronomistic aniconic ideology in its real-life context (above), 1 Kings 6–8 is a very suitable candidate.

The story of the Solomonic Temple

Text and profile

The textual situation for 1 Kings 6–8 is complex (DeVries 2003: xlii–lx). These chapters contain source materials that were available to the redactor along with editorial comments and framings by deuteronomistic as well as by post-deuteronomistic hands. After the text had reached a stable stage there was a complex textual transmission, effecting a number of (smaller) differences between the Hebrew and the Greek versions. This means, we have two different versions, both featuring several voices. It is not uncommon in biblical literature that different voices in one text may express different focus and conflicting views.

So, how should we read such a text? I follow a triple strategy. First, I regard the Hebrew and Greek as separate versions that should not be mixed. Even though the Greek *could* be older in certain passages in 1–2 Samuel and 1–2 Kings (Schenker 2004, but cf. Pietsch 2007), in this case I stay with the Hebrew. Secondly, I agree with Hurowitz (1992: 106–8) and others that the story is generally coherent and follows expected narrative paradigms. This allows for a continuous reading of the story across different layers. Thirdly, I also agree with DeVries (2003: xliii–xlv, 89, 92–3) and others that it is possible to identify deuteronomistic comments in chapters 6 and 7. Similarly, the best part of the prayer in 1 Kings 8 (i.e. from 8.14 onwards, and possibly parts of vv. 1-11) has a deuteronomistic ring. On the other hand, the detailed descriptions of construction and decoration in the main trajectory of 1 Kings 6–7 indicate sources close to the Temple, with full knowledge of the Temple complex. These would presumably reflect priestly experiences and preferences. All this allows for reading the text as a fairly coherent building account, largely with a priestly-like profile, but with occasional contrastive deuteronomistic comments.

The narrative of the dedication of the Temple (1 Kings 8) is clearly fictional, with a deuteronomistic profile (cf. Knoppers 1995: 299). Contrastingly, the narrative of the building and decoration (1 Kings 6–7) makes the impression of being realistic – or 'factual' (Van Seters 1997: 56, cf. 55–7). And yet, it is not possible to draw an unambiguous blueprint of the Temple from the report (cf. Cogan 2000: 249-51; DeVries 2003: 89-93). A massive amount of scholarship has gone into attempts at figuring out the precise shapes and dimensions of the Temple, much of it by use of comparative textual and architectonic material. No definitive solution has been offered, but, for instance, the comprehensive study of Busink (1970) and the work of Bloch-Smith (1994) on Temple symbolism show that the contours of the Temple building and installations imagined on the basis of 1 Kings 6–8 are generally similar to those of contemporary temples (similarly Zwickel 2013). This confirms the impression of a realistic narrative.

It is difficult to date such a complex text, which must have been compiled over a long period of time. I am currently not discussing the age and character of any sources, only the date of the final story (before the text-historical developments).[6] The Hebrew text in 8.8 contains a remark indicating that the Temple was still intact by the time of narration. That would imply a date for (that part of) the account prior to the fall of Jerusalem (586 BCE). However, this remark is missing in the Greek version, and it is hard to tell the historical value of this remark. In any event, the DtrH as a totality was concluded at the earliest a few decades after the fall of the Temple (cf. events reported in 2 Kings 25). So, at the time of the complete work, at least, the story of Solomon's Temple was that of a lost past – to be experienced not by sensation, but only through imagining one's being in the building on the basis of this narrative account. The text invites its audience to proceed from a textual description of a lost physical arrangement and perform an *imagination* of visiting the Solomonic complex. Extending this invitation to imagining, this story nicely illustrates the complex relations between text, physical matter, sensation and imagination being explored in this volume.

Narrative and framings

In general, the account 'follows the path that a visitor to the building might take and notes items observable on such a tour' (Cogan 2000: 248). Scholars reading the narrative in light of comparative material end up imagining the Temple somewhat in the fashion illustrated in Figures 1.1a and b. Assuming that ancient readers used a similar reading strategy, the itinerary they imagined would be like this: First, one entered two courts (not rendered in the figures): an outer great court (1 Kgs 7.12), accessible by males (cf. 2 Kgs 12.4; 23.2); and an inner court (1 Kgs 6.36, etc.), for common priests to conduct offerings (1 Kgs 7.38-39). In the inner court there was a huge bronze vessel formed like a lily and standing on twelve oxen (7.23-26) along with additional decorated items (7.27-47). Passing through the court one came to the house proper: the *hechal* – palace – of the deity. It had an imposing façade opening to the east (Figure 1.1a), featuring two large pillars named *Jachin* and *Boas*, richly decorated (1 Kgs 6.3; 7.12-21; Figure 1.1b: G and H). Past the pillars and through the vestibule (A), the plot opened to the great hall (B) known in English as *The Holies* (1 Kgs 6.17; 8.8-10). Access here was probably limited to priests in service (cf. Lev. 4.5-7, 16; Num. 31.54). The imagined past itinerant, however, was not restricted by this limitation, and hovered into the hall lined with cedar and cypress wood. The walls had 'carvings of gourds and open flowers' (1 Kgs 6.18) and 'engravings of cherubim, palm trees, and open flowers, in the inner and outer rooms' (v. 29) – and so had the doors (vv. 32-35). The hall also featured an altar (6.20), lampstands and a 'table of the Presence' (7.48-51).

(a)

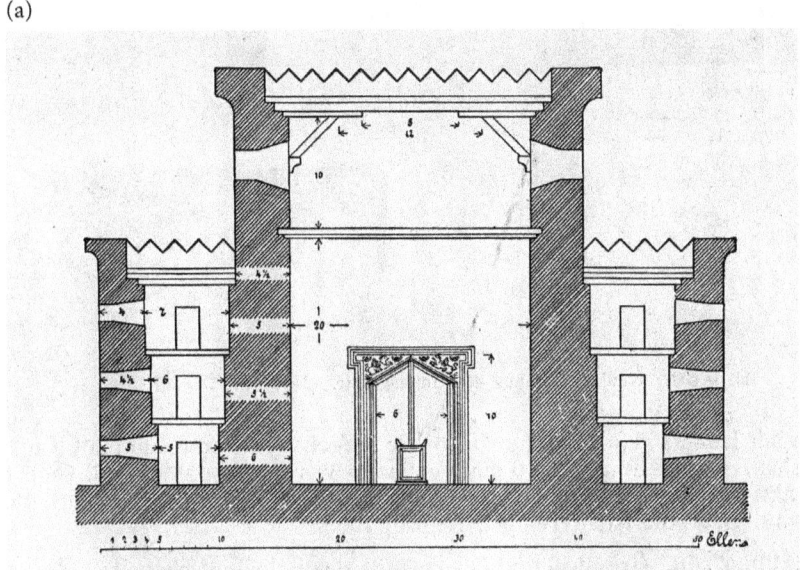

(b)

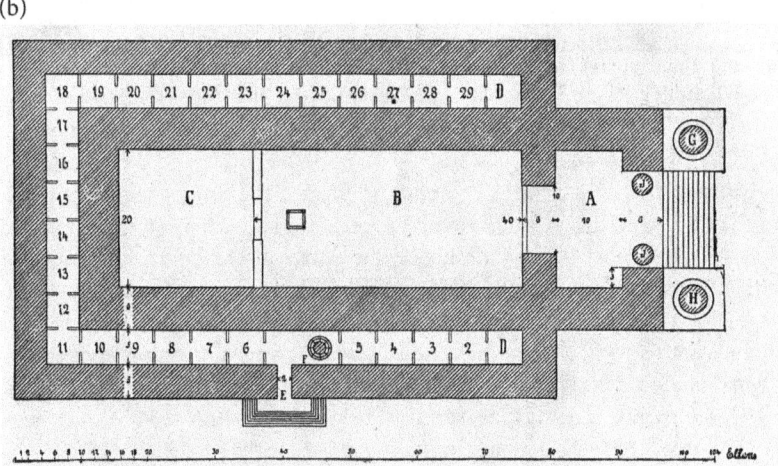

Figure 1.1a, b Reconstructions of (a) the front (opening to the east) of the Solomonic Temple and (b) the floor plan of the Solomonic Temple as imagined in 1 Kings 6–8. Illustrations from Greßmann, H. (1909). *Altorientalische Texte und Bilder zum Alten Testament, Band II: Bilder*, p. 38, Figs. 58 and 57.

Passing through the hall, the itinerant reached the Holy of Holies, in Hebrew, *debir*, the temple cella (1 Kgs. 6.19, 27; 8.6; Figure 1.1b: C). This was the focal point of the entire architectural complex, the place that would normally house a cult image of the deity to whom the temple was dedicated (Köckert 2009: 371–2, with much literature). The cella of the imagined Solomonic Temple was magnificent: 'Solomon overlaid the inside of the house with pure gold [...] drew chains of gold across, [...] overlaid the whole

Figure 1.2 Relief on the Sarcophagus of Ahiram, King of Byblos (Phoenicia), around 1000 BCE. Beirut National Museum. Photo: O. Mustafin. Wikimedia Commons.

house with gold […] even the whole altar that belonged to the inner sanctuary he overlaid with gold' (1 Kgs 6.21-22). Moreover, there were two large cherubim of olive woods '[…] in the innermost part of the house; the wings of the cherubim were spread out so that a wing of one was touching the one wall, and a wing of the other cherub was touching the other wall; their other wings toward the centre of the house were touching wing to wing' (6.27). Such mixed creatures are protecting divine abodes throughout ancient Near Eastern temple architecture and iconography (see Freedman and O´Connor 1995, cf. Figure 1.2, see more below, cf. also Figure 5.3b), and they are known also from the tent sanctuary in priestly literature (Exod. 25.18-19, etc.).

Underneath the cherubs sits the ark of the covenant (6.19; 8.6-21), and the cherubs and the ark could be seen to form a joint complex. The ark is known throughout biblical literature, and its symbolism and significance are complex (see Zobel 1974; for Deuteronomy see Wilson 2005). In priestly literature the ark has two winged cherubs on top, conceived of as a throne seat and serving as a meeting place between God and Moses (Exod. 25.19-22; 37.8-9, cf. Lang 1995). Much of this is reflected in DtrH too, but often in its pre-deuteronomistic sources. In some passages the ark represents the presence of the Lord (cf. Judg. 20.27; 1 Sam. 4.3-5). This is the case also in the opening of 1 Kings 8: the ark entering the cella means the glory of God taking possession of the house (8.10-11). There is a divine name associated to the ark: 'The LORD of hosts, who is enthroned on the *cherubim*' (1 Sam. 4.4; 2 Sam. 6.2; 2 Kgs 19.15). This suggests that the cherubs on top of the ark were forming a royal seat, not unlike what is illustrated on the Phoenician Ahiram Sarcophagus, from around 1000 BCE (Figure 1.2). It stands to reason, therefore, that the arrangement to be imagined at the heart of the Solomonic Temple is the ark underneath an empty seat, now formed by the wings of the two giant cherubs in the room (cf. Köckert 2009: 390–5). Tryggve Mettinger (1995) coined the phrase 'empty space aniconism' to denote this programmatically empty seat.

Corresponding to the empty seat, there is a symbolism of darkness (and hence: invisibility). While there are ten lamps standing in the great hall (B) (1 Kgs 7.49), the cella (C) is lacking in light. There are doors between the great hall and the cella (1 Kgs 6.31-2). Possibly for this reason, only the poles of the ark inside the cella (pitched towards the door) are visible from the hall (1 Kgs 8.8, but only in the Hebrew, see discussion of this entire complex in Schenker 2006). This dim cella corresponds to the convention that theophanies (incidents of divine self-revelation) occur in cloudy darkness.[7] The motif of darkness also resonates with the possibly old poetic dedication of the house in 8.12-13 (my translation):

The Lord said, he would live in a dark cloud.[8]
I have verily built you a lofty house, a place for you to dwell for all time.

The dedication identifies the temple as a permanent place of theophany (lofty enough to house even the clouds), and the architecture secures the expected dimness at the site (cf. similarly Sweeney 2007: 132–3).

So much for the main account of the story. Let me now turn to the comments interacting with the main story. The redactor of 1 Kings seems not entirely comfortable with all the conventional symbolism. At salient points a deuteronomistic voice interferes with the report, framing and limiting the significance of the generous presentation of pictorial media in the Temple. For instance, in 6.11-13 the redactor slips in a note declaring that the Lord will only reside in the Temple if the Israelites keep the Torah: the significance of the Temple is subordinated to that of the Torah (cf. Vogt 2006: 83–93, 227–9, etc.). Likewise, in 8.27 the deuteronomist lets Solomon make an important point; the Temple is not *really* the House of God, for God exceeds even the heavens; only the *name* of God can reside in the Temple. This reflects a tendency to envision a programmatically transcendent deity (Weinfeld 1972: 191–9, etc.). While the scholarly concept of transcendence applied here needs to be qualified (Wilson 1995), the remark clearly challenges conventional sanctuary theology, where the Temple as such signals the presence of the deity (as in Psalm 46.5-6, cf. Hurowitz 2005: 97–8).

Approaching the focal point of the Temple complex the deuteronomistic redactor is not primarily concerned with the dim *debir* or the empty cherub seat. It is the box underneath that catches attention: 'There was nothing in the ark except the two tablets of stone that Moses had placed there at Horeb' (8.9). With DeVries (2003: 123–4) I find here a deuteronomistic voice. Relying on ancient Near Eastern temple convention one could speculate that the deuteronomist had first penned out the presence of a statue or other significant representative items associated with the ark, and then underscored the deletion by stating what was (not) inside. In any event, the two tablets, holding the Decalogue, and so also the Second Commandment, sit in the place where a culturally literate audience would expect to find some material representation of the main divinity of the Temple. In the deuteronomistic narrative, these tablets are the second set that Moses received at Horeb, inscribed by God Himself (Deut. 10.1-5). They shall also be our main focus as we move on to consider relations between verbal and non-verbal media in the Solomonic Temple.

Logocentric imagination of the Temple?

The text invites the audience to imagine visiting the Solomonic Temple. Would this imagined visit reflect a preference for verbal over non-verbal semiotic systems when it comes to representing deity? Scholars answering this in the affirmative point to the fact that the imagined cella features a void rather than a representative image (Mettinger 1995). Also, the two tablets at the focal point have been seen as a programme of sacred words in the centre (cf. Weinfeld 1972: 208–9, etc.). And yet, on closer inspection, none of this seems to be defendable.

First, the reader is invited to imagine a building complex loaded with decoration and symbolic artefacts. The account taps into common ancient Near Eastern symbolism (cf. Hurowitz 2005: 73–8, etc.) that was multi-medial – primarily various pictorial media, but also with verbal elements. The interplay between these different media produced the desired effect (for the general phenomenon, see Larsen 1979; Reade 1979). Secondly, the imagined Temple is dominated by the symbolism of graded holiness centred on the cella (Hurowitz 2005: 88–90, etc.). This was a spatial-architectural semiotic system, which was particularly prominent in Hebrew priestly theology (Jenson 1992). Hence, the reader's perception of a programmatic absence of God relies almost entirely on non-verbal communication.

Finally, there are the two tablets in the ark. Apparently, their most significant aspect was *not* their semantic qualities. The tablets did not contain the entire Torah – only the Decalogue. In Deuteronomy, Moses wrote a book while sojourning in the Transjordan, and he commissioned the Levites responsible for the ark (Deut. 31.9) to place that book 'beside the ark' (Deut. 31.26) – not within it. This Mosaic book is the focal point of deuteronomistic theology (Vogt 2006), but in the Temple narrative it is not mentioned at all. If the tablets in the ark signify the Mosaic Torah, they do so in a sort of symbolism that is clearly not simply verbal. More importantly, there were other texts holding the Decalogue, but none are imagined to be handled with the same reverence as the tablets. And the reason seems obvious: the tablets in the ark had been written by the finger of God (Deut. 9.10) – yet another idea that the deuteronomists shared with their religious environment (cf. Exod. 31.18). What singled the tablets out from all other documents holding the Decalogue were their artefactual qualities: they enshrined the prints, as it were, of the finger of the deity. They had been in closer material contact with the sacred than even Moses himself had been. He, according to biblical lore, got to see the Lord (Exod. 33.18-23, cf. 34.33-35), but the tablets had been touched by the finger of God. They are the closest one comes to a material representation of deity in deuteronomistic literature. And they sit at the centre of the Solomonic Temple.

In short, 1 Kings 6–8 invites its audience to imagine being in the Solomonic Temple, and the ensuing imagination does not at all seem to be imbued with a disdain for matter or a preference for verbal communication. The pictures on walls, doors and pillars, the spatial symbolism encircling the sacred focal point, the huge cherubs forming an empty seat with a petrified 'fingerprint' of the deity in a box underneath – all this confirms the religious validity and significance of non-verbal sensation, experience and performance. The narrative invites the audience to imagine engaging one's sensory capacities: a bodily recognition of grades of holiness, perhaps a smell of incense and burnt offerings, a gaze at the bronze pillars, the rich illustrations, the gold works, the cherubs and the ark. If they were reading the entire DtrH the audience might also imagine hearing a recitation from the book of Moses in the outside court, perhaps once every seventh year (Deut. 31.9-11). But it seems unlikely that imagining this incident, somewhat removed from the centre of the plot, should signal to the implied itinerant that listening to words is more important than all other sensation at the place. So, despite passages like Deuteronomy 4 (above) and the hard-line reception of this passage in modern scholarship, the story of the Solomonic Temple, as commissioned by the deuteronomists, relies heavily on pictorial, spatial and other non-verbal semiotic systems in its attempt to account for the absence–presence of the sacred. In its interaction, positively and negatively with all these systems, the story of the Solomonic Temple presents itself as a historically credible example of how the deuteronomistic ban on images might have played out in culturally embedded, real-life contexts.

Aesthetics of the non-representable

If the arrangement of the imagined Solomonic Temple does not reflect a preference for verbal over non-verbal media, then what is it that motivates the programmatic absence and void at the heart of the Temple complex? Taking a lesson from Jacques Rancière (2004), I do presume that a given group of people typically develop regimes that (a) guide the forging of specific artistic strategies and artefacts, (b) give standards for how such artefacts were to be sensed and experienced, (c) promote specific ways of understanding the reality or significance of the art/artistic artefacts, and (d) disciplines the use and perception of art into promoting certain political interests. Since these points reflect only parts of Rancière's argument on the aesthetic regime of art, I have here opted to use the name regimes of sensation for such socially sanctioned formations of matter, practices and ideas.[9]

Several of the contributions to the present volume attest to the development of (quite distinct) regimes of sensation designed to represent that which is thought to be in some sense non-representable. This is the case, for instance, with the aesthetics of withdrawal from public view in Eastern Africa (Behrend), the recognizing by the heart in early Islamic tradition (Shaw), the restraining of media in order to discipline the sensorium in Orthodox Christianity (Luehrmann), or the aesthetics of representing religious realities as sublime in European art (Bukdahl). These are regimes of sensation with a desire to display what cannot, or should not, be represented *and* a complimentary anxiety to communicate precisely a sense of distance between the representation and that which it represents.

It seems to me, the imagined Solomonic Temple in 1 Kings 6–8 offers one variation of such a regime. For instance, the programmatically empty cherub throne and the play of light versus darkness immediately seems comparable to the artistic strategies that Bukdahl in her chapter in this book identifies as strategies for displaying the sublime in European art (See esp. pp. 234–6). Deuteronomistic theology emphasized the transcendence of the deity. Even after God's name takes possession of the Temple the divine persona is still so distant that Solomon has to call upon God's eye to keep observing from a distance:

> But will God indeed dwell on the earth? Even heaven and the highest heaven cannot contain you, much less this house that I have built! Regard your servant's prayer and his plea [...] that your eyes may be open night and day toward this house, the place of which you said, 'My name shall be there,' that you may heed the prayer that your servant prays toward this place. (1 Kgs 8.27-9)

The passage illustrates a recurring oscillation between words and concepts on the one hand and tangible materialities and practices on the other. In a peak of abstraction, Solomon defines divinity through *via negationis*, a strategy shared across several layers of ancient Hebrew literature (cf. Labuschagne 1966). This concept of deity animates the entire deuteronomistic theology. However, when naming his hope for a lasting divine *presence*, Solomon uses categories of body, practice and space: God's eyes and ears ensure divine presence at the place where God could not dwell, provided God's servants pray directed to that place.

This configuration carries over into the imagined Temple as a totality. A continuous presence of the ear of the deity is presumed in arrangements for prayer and offerings throughout the court and in the great hall. Similarly, the awareness of the divine eye is suggested in the system for graded holiness and control of access around the Temple. The presence of the deity is explicitly indicated through the guarding cherubs all around the place. And yet, when the imagined itinerant reaches the focal point of the complex, materialities and practices as well as words dissolve into a void in so many registers:

1. In the central cella there is an empty seat for the Lord, a seat that is hardly visible due to the darkness.
2. There are no words. In Deuteronomy 4, the absence of divine form is compensated by a presence of divine speech. Similarly, in priestly literature the voice of God speaks to Moses from between the cherubs (cf. Exod. 25.22; Num. 7.89), but in 1 Kings 8 nothing occurs in the *debir*. It is possible that a similar notion of silence was entertained in the most elite priestly circles (Knohl 2006).
3. Underneath the seat is a box enshrining petrified prints by God's finger: marks left from a long past epiphany. While documenting a past material presence of the deity, the tablets simultaneously denote the historical distance and thus the absence of the divine finger in the Temple.
4. And alas, by the time the DtrH is finished, the Temple, the cherubs, the ark and the tablets were all gone. What was left was the readers' imaginations of the place where the echo of God's absent-presence used to dwell.

Why should there be a regime of sensation so bent on demonstrating the shortcoming of material representations of the deity? It seems impossible at the present to give a commonly acceptable answer. What seems to be clear is that ancient Near Eastern deities were not perceived to be statically chained to their cult images: deities could abandon their temples as well as statues; iconic gods were as transcendent as aniconic ones. And yet, rituals for dedicating a statue as a cult image were very strong, establishing wide-ranging connections between the deity and the statue. This entailed potential danger for both parties. The deity could suffer humiliation (by the statue being captured or neglected). The community could risk having their relation to the deity severed through violence against the image (cf. Köckert 2009: 372–4, 380–1, 402–6). It seems possible that Hebrew religion in the Persian age, having experienced the destruction of the Temple and now being bent on protecting the sovereignty and elusiveness of the deity, would perceive all direct representation of the deity as a potential threat.

But it must be emphasized that in the Solomonic Temple imagined in 1 Kings, the hesitation to represent the deity in commonly accessible forms applies to all media, not just cult images. Words are no more capable of representing sacred presence than non-verbal media. At the centre of the Temple all representation dissolves into silence, invisibility, emptiness and historical absence. It is striking, indeed, that deuteronomistic theology, which made the *written* word (inevitably an artefact that could be ruined or lost) its focus, also moulds this story where neither speech nor tablets are in the end representing divine presence for the audience of the story. It is as if the deuteronomists attempt to protect the deity from the potential exposure brought even by their own bookish and verbal religion.

Conclusion

It is commonly agreed that the view of ancient Hebrew (and early Jewish) religion as uniformly rejecting the use of pictorial media is exaggerated. This chapter, however, targeted those parts of biblical Hebrew literature that most programmatically do represent an apparent ban on cultic images: the so-called deuteronomistic texts. Most biblical scholars think that at least these layers of biblical literature express a general preference for verbal over non-verbal media when it comes to representing the sacred.

Now, deuteronomistic theology was, of course, culturally embedded, and the task of editing the story of the Solomonic Temple (1 Kings 6–8) placed one deuteronomistic scribe at an intersection with priestly theology, encountering commonly shared cultural and religious preferences, inherited materialities and the social memory attached to these materialities. The story in 1 Kings 6–8 is also one of few passages in the entire DtrH that is sufficiently detailed to sustain an analysis of how the deuteronomistic ban on images would play out in architectural reality. The analysis suggests that deuteronomistic ideology was more tempered, nuanced and sensitive to situation than is commonly expected.

1 Kings 6–8 represents a regime of sensation grappling with how to represent what was perceived as non-representable, namely divine presence. In its struggle to relay this dimension, the text invites the audience to engage the interplay of textual and material media in order to produce a mental image that would represent the unseen in acceptable ways. The carrying medium is the text with words and concepts, but the text points to

spatial, architectural and symbolical media, as well as to sensations and emotions these might trigger. When it comes to the central point, the precise representation of the deity, this regime does not trust any medium. Instead, the strategy is to represent a simultaneous void in several registers. The central chamber of the Solomonic Temple is characterized by silence (no speech), invisibility (darkness), emptiness (the seat) and two artefacts (the tablets) enshrining a past material presence as well as its absence in the present.

It seems to me questionable whether this regime of sensation could even be classified as aniconic. Admittedly, there is a programmatic absence of iconic representation of the deity, and in that narrow sense the regime is perhaps aniconic. But there is a simultaneous absence of words and light, and yet we would not say the plot is anti-verbal. The empty seat is a void in only one of several coordinated media registers in the imagined Solomonic Temple.

There is, of course, no doubt that deuteronomistic literature emphasized the role of writings and books as compared to other strata of contemporary religion. However, the DtrH engages non-verbal semiotic systems also outside of the Temple narrative, for instance, when relating to people 'coming before the Lord' at the elected place, at specific times, with specific purposes and specific gestures (e.g. in Deut. 26.1-16; cf. 2 Kgs 19.14-34). Such recognition of the religious significance of time, space and materiality was no deuteronomistic characteristic: it is more intensely reflected in other strata of the Hebrew Bible. And yet, its presence also in deuteronomistic literature needs to be taken into account when drawing a profile of deuteronomistic religion and theology.

2

Seeing with the Ear, Recognizing with the Heart: Rethinking the Ontology of the Mimetic Arts in Islam

Wendy M. K. Shaw

The more one looks at the painting of *Plato at the Organ*, attributed to Madhu Khazanad in a late-sixteenth-century Mughal manuscript of the Book of Alexander (*Iskandarnameh*, 1194) of Nizami of Ganj (1141–1207 CE), the stranger it gets (Koch 2010: 286) (Figure 2.1). In a layered anachronism, a twelfth-century Persian poetic depiction of the ancient Greek sage Plato (428–348 BCE) plays a European organ, probably one of the earliest organs collected by ambassadors of the court of Akbar in the Portuguese colony in Goa in 1581. Scattered around him, animals lie belly up, tongues hanging out, in a sleep so deep they have been mistaken for dead (Wade 1998: 153). Illustrating, and thereby emphasizing, this tale from Nizami's rendition of the Alexander romance, this painting examines a relationship between painting and music central to aesthetic concerns in Islam processed through new European encounters. The painting thus engages one of the most ubiquitous questions of contemporary understandings of Islam: Does Islam prohibit the image? And who has the right to decide?

Despite frequent discussions of the Islamic image through the framework of 'prohibition', innumerable secular and religious visual representations reflect the absence of any overarching ban. Almost no discussions of the image emerge until the thirteenth century. In contrast, treatises about music abound. The modern emphasis on the visual over the musical arts reflects different relationships with the late-antique concept of mimesis as it laid the groundwork for both European and Islamic artistic practice. Islam emerged through engagement with the late-antique culture into which it was born and with the translation of ancient philosophy with which it was fed. Reflecting multiple sources, Nizami's poem consolidates a vast literature on musical aesthetics. Its painted interpretation four centuries later reflects an evaluation of European visual practices through the lens of established Islamic mimetic norms. Interpretation of poem and painting as a theorization of mimesis suggests that, in placing emphasis on the image, modern Muslim and non-Muslim scholars alike miss the important role of sound as a means of apprehending the divine in premodern Islamic thought and cultures.

Figure 2.1 Madhu Khazanad, 'Plato puts the animals to sleep with the music of the spheres', from a 1593–5 manuscript of the *Iskandarnameh* (1194) from the Khamsa by Nizami of Ganj. © The British Library Board, OR 12208, f. 298r.

Islam is not characterized by an image prohibition

The association between Islam and a dogmatic prohibition of images emerged in nineteenth-century Europe in an effort to define Islam coherently. This often coincides with modern puritanical interpretations of Islam claiming authority from the first thirty years of Islamic practice. Despite confirmation by these apparent antagonists, the rich legacy of images populating the lived history of Islam contradicts this assertion. More interesting than the binary distinction between permissibility and sanction, however, is the fact that the image in early Islam was understood through a broader category that included music and which was informed by late-antique concepts of mimesis. Modern European oculocentric understandings of aesthetics lose this sonic aspect of mimesis. This disjunction, along with the conflation of presumed Judaic and Byzantine iconoclasms, lies at the root of the assertion of an image prohibition in Islam.

The persistence of the trope of prohibition emerges from the direct interpretation of sources without attention to their historiographic interpretive utilization. The Qur'an warns against idolatry, but does not mention images as such. Rather than looking at the history of images in the Islamic world, modern scholarship on the image in Islam generally cites the record (Hadith) of sayings and deeds (*sunnah*) of the Prophet Muhammad as establishing a normative prohibition (Lavoix 1859; Arnold 1928; Creswell 1946; Paret 1976/7; Naef 2003; Ibric 2006; Watt 2002). Several Hadith underscore the effect of the image on an individual engaged in prayer, indicating no restriction outside of sacred space. Another oft-cited Hadith accuses the artist of the sin of *shirk*, placing another in the place of God. Here, however, the replacement is not the idol, but the artist who makes the claim of creating, one of the powers understood as unique to God.

These sources suggest concern about images which cannot amount to a prohibition without the intervention of law. Islam does not consist merely of foundational texts. Rather, it emerged historically across centuries of interpretation. The scholarly use of 'scripture' as directly establishing norms overrides this historical process. It presumes a relationship with the historical legacies of the prophet analogous to the premise of *sola scriptura* in Protestant thought, and ignores the historical nature of Islamic discourse as differentially integrated into practice (Fudge 2006).

Islam can be traced to the lifetime of the Prophet Muhammad (c. 570–632 CE) who initiated the religion through Qur'anic revelation, but the social praxis of Islam depends on historical processes. The Qur'an was first compiled in 653 CE, and was not reduced to a single canonical form until the late eighth century (Neuwirth 2003). Additional components of Islamic law developed in the ninth century: the compilation of widely accepted Hadith compilations; legal procedures governing the evaluation and interpretation of Qur'an and Hadith in light of precedent and contemporary conditions; and the proliferation and then reduction of schools of law legitimated under competing Islamic caliphates, resulting in four dominant Sunni rites as well as diverse (minoritarian) Shiite rites. During the same period, mystics began to draw on the visionary aspect of Muhammad's revelation as an example for mystical approaches to faith. Often grouped under the label 'Sufism' (*tasavvuf*) these practices offered multiple regulated intrinsic approaches to spirituality, practised thought and ritual, which served as an everyday interpretive medium between the Qur'an and the world. By the twelfth century, Sufi leaders emerged at the core of powerful public foundations which gathered the faithful in spiritual practice, became linked with guilds, and created networked structures of knowledge and power that at times coincided and at other times collided with state power. By the thirteenth century, Islam functioned as a complex system of mutually recognizable, interconnected and yet distinct systems of interpretation that traversed a vast geography from Andalusia to Central Asia, incorporating numerous systems of power, ethnicities and languages, and in close and generally peaceable contact with numerous religious groups living under Islamic suzerainty. Then came the Mongol invasions.

Mongol tribes who challenged the Abbasid Caliphate in the thirteenth century undermined existing systems of power. Their alliance with Persian lords, some of whom were Shiite, led to new systems of governance. For traditionalists, this was a disaster. Yet new rulers brought new practices, fostering the rise of figural painting not only on walls (common under the Umayyad, Abbasid and Fatimid Caliphates), but also in books. The earliest manuscript paintings to survive include a thirteenth-century illustrated volume of the Arabic translation of Dioscorides's 'On Pharmacy and Medicine' and 'The Assemblies of al-Hariri' by Yahya ibn Mahmoud al-Wasiti.

The earliest injunction against painting in Islam occurs in this context, in the *Riyadh al-Salihin* of al-Nawawi (1234–78), a follower of the Shafi'i legal rite. He says,

> The authorities of our school and others hold that the making of a picture of any living thing is strictly forbidden and that it is one of the great sins because it is specifically threatened with the grievous punishment mentioned in the Hadith. [...] The crafting of it is forbidden under every circumstance, because it imitates the creative activity of God. (Ahmed 2015: 49–50)

He uses the following Hadith from the compilation of al-Bukhari to support his assertion:

> The image-makers will be punished on the Day of Resurrection and will be told, 'Give life to that which you have created'. (Hadith 2151; www.ahadith.com)

Al-Nawawi's interpretation contrasts that of the ninth-century Persian scholar al-Tabari, who interpreted the same hadith as referring to objects that 'one consciously worships instead of God, which makes one an unbeliever' (Ahmad and Glidden 1968: 254). Al-Nawawi further indicates that a sign or image of an object without the breath of life (*ruh*) cannot in any case be embodied, and is therefore sanctioned; a sign of an object with *ruh* can only be sanctioned if it clearly cannot be embodied.

Although al-Nawawi's interpretation became widespread following modern publication of his text, it seems not to have been widely influential in his own or subsequent eras. The implementation of scholarly *fatwas* depended on state enforcement. Although like him, both the Great Seljuk Empire and Mamluk Sultanate at times gave precedence to Shafi'i interpretation, they patronized figural sculpture. Painting flourished in Timurid and post-Timurid states, including those of the Safavids, Ottomans and Mughals, all of which favoured the Hanafi rite (Gruber 2009; Gruber and Shalem 2014).

If al-Nawawi's denigration of the image had been widespread, it might have been corroborated by the other great naysayer of the era, Ibn Taymiyyah (1263–1328), a follower of the Hanbali rite, who wrote while under house arrest in Damascus following the Mongol invasions. Although not influential in his own era, his argument against Sufism proved inspirational for Muhammad ibn Abd al-Wahhab (1702–92), who inspired many modern puritanical Sunni movements (el-Rouayheb 2010). Yet Ibn Taymiyyah's interpretation resembles that of al-Tabari. The compilation of his judgements (*Majmu al-Fatawa*) relates that he commanded the destruction of 'two types of images: images which represent the deceased person, and images which are placed on top of graves – because *shirk* may come about from both types' (Ibn Taymiyyah). Even the contemporary Salafi scholar Sayyid Sabiq, an ardent follower of Ibn Taymiyyah, points out that if images were unlawful, the Prophet would have explicitly forbidden them (Kabbani 1995: 19).

This is not to say that Islamic contexts never restricted images. The earliest acts of idol destruction at the time of transition from Arabian polytheism to the monotheism of Islam were not repeated after the era of conversion. In many ways, these performances of destruction resemble Christian desecration of pagan images in ancient Rome. During the Umayyad period, doctrinal concerns rendered the display of the cross far more problematic than representational imagery, which at the time was no longer normative as many Christian sects took on varying degrees of iconoclasm (King 1985). Destruction often signalled conquest more than iconoclasm, befalling disputed Islamic texts as readily as Hindu idols (Flood 2009: 32–4). Image destruction, including cutting the throats of illustrated figures, occurred as discrete events, which reflect a concern with disempowering the image, but did not constitute a universal cultural norm (Flood 2002). As Isa points out, 'If the question of *taswir* had been as important as other problems, such as those of strong drink, marriage, divorce and inheritance, the Qur'an certainly would have dealt with it explicitly, as it did with other problems of conduct and worship' (Ahmad and Glidden 1968: 252). More than prohibiting images, it seems that most Islamic scholars simply did not care about them.

To say that Islamic cultures periodically considered the power of images is very different from asserting an overarching prohibition of the image in Islam. If the only overt rule against images emerged in the thirteenth century, are we to say that Islam did not precede this rule? Are we to say that the proliferation of images after this ruling was therefore not Islamic? Does Islam emerge only in the modern application of a thirteenth-century rule that makes a claim on the undocumented truth of the seventh century? The problem may be that we are asking for a ruling about something that *did not even exist as we know it*. In emphasizing the modern European norm of the representational image, we neglect the discourse of mimesis that did emerge in early Islamic discourses, not in relation to visual but in terms of musical representation.

The normative idea of the image requires a signifier (the image) which makes present the signified (something that is absent). The vehicle for this semiotic representation has been visual verisimilitude: the representation of an object through devices that fool the eye into believing that something is there when it isn't. Many of these devices, including foreshortening, modelling and perspectival spatial construction, developed during fourteenth and fifteenth centuries in Italy and, in subsequent centuries, came to define the image across Europe. They were still relatively new devices when artists in late-sixteenth-century India encountered them through images propagated by proto-colonial Catholic missionaries expanding the power of the Church through global outreach (Subrahmanyam 2010).

Coming at this moment of encounter, the unprecedented illustration of the poetic trope of Plato at the organ suggests a critical evaluation of European claims of the proselytizing power of the visual mimetic image. It sets these claims in comparison with a different mimetic norm pervading Islamic discourses, expressed through the emphasis on music and inherited from antiquity. In his examination of late-antique aesthetics, Stephen Halliwell proposes that the ancient concept of mimesis emerged in relation to the musico-poetic arts and only later became applied to visual arts. Mimetic representation thus suggests a family of concepts of representation using any artistic intermediary – words, sounds, physical images – to signify and communicate realities beyond our physical experience, what Plato calls the Real or Kant refers to as the Numen. He points out that the Greek tradition emphasizes the effects of mimetic artworks on their viewers or hearers and frequently 'characterizes and evaluates the kinds of recognition, understanding, emotional response and evaluation that such artworks can or should elicit in their audiences' (Halliwell 2002: 16–19).

> The history of mimesis is the record of a set of debates that form themselves around a polarity between two ways of thinking about representational art. The first of these places central emphasis on the 'outward-looking' relationship between the artistic work or performance and reality ('nature', as it is often though problematically termed in the mimeticist tradition), whereas the other gives priority to the internal organization and fictive properties of the mimetic object or act itself [...] encapsulating a difference between a 'world-reflecting' model (for which the 'mirror' has been a common though far from straightforward metaphorical emblem), and, on the other side, a 'world-simulating' or 'world-creating' conception of artistic representation. (Halliwell 2002: 23)

Whereas we, as modern subjects considering Islam, only recognize the first, 'outward-looking' aspect of mimetic practice, premodern Islamic commentators and theorists focused largely on the latter. This emerges less in discourses concerning the image than in the extensive discussions of the role of sound, particularly music, which transpire from the ninth to the thirteenth centuries and spiral into an episteme of mimetic representation underlying normative transmedial artistic expressions, spiritual and secular, across the Islamic world.

Modern considerations of this tradition tend to treat it as a secular practice outside of theologically guided Islam, asserting a deeply anachronistic distinction. For example, introducing his summary of Islamic thinkers on music, Fadlou Shehadi distinguishes between the Greek and Islamic traditions, saying, '[...] there is a mastery in the restatement of Greek thought, and much elaboration and refinement, but one still feels almost entirely in a Greek world. When Muslim thinkers concern themselves with the integrity of Islam, a different breeze is blowing' (Shehadi 1995: 2). Why presume a conflict if this was the very intellectual environment in which Islam developed? Recognizing that the Islamic philosopher al-Kindi (801–73) wrote during the same era that al-Bukhari initiated the arduous process of authenticating and compiling the Hadith which would become the foundation of a yet nascent practice of Islamic law, how can we consider that practice more authentically Islamic than the integration of

Greek philosophy into emerging practices of Islam? To do so would be as anachronistic as to argue that Mathias Grünewald's *Isenheim Altarpiece* is secular because it was not part of the world of the twelve apostles.

While modern puritan (*Salafi*) Muslims argue along such lines that an authentic Islam must be derived from the experience of the first thirty years of Islam and that subsequent practice constitutes inauthentic innovation, this mode of understanding Islam would have been unrecognizable to almost all Muslims before the twentieth century (Abou el Fadl 2007: 18). The coincidence between this puritan perspective and the orientalist drive to define an authentic Islam based on its scriptural sources, exemplified in the definition of an 'Islamic image prohibition' through direct recourse to the Qur'an and the Hadith rather than through Islamic discursive practice, has led to an understanding of mainstream, widespread Islamic practices that conceive of mimetic representation integrating audition (including music and dance) as heterodox to a presumed narrow orthodoxy which never existed until it was 're'-constructed in the contemporary era (Ahmed 2015: 73–97).

Music as mimetic representation in Islamic discourses

Although early Islamic writers never developed discussions of the image, they wrote extensively about music. Rather than providing a mimetic iconography in which visual images represent a reality beyond perception, as in our modern 'outward-looking' understanding of mimesis, Islamic discourses of music offer a detailed taxonomy of meaning grounded in reception – in the perception of a world through interiorization. This taxonomy of meaning can be understood as a semiotic process parallel to the type of meaning art history expects to glean from the iconographic analysis of the visual. Taxonomies of sound developed discursively across the writings of multiple thinkers and encompassed a wide range of experience. While these take form in a cosmology based on similitude, their effects encompass the therapeutic, spiritual, sinful, divine, rational and irrational. This baseline of meaningfulness pervades the thought both of proponents of music and of detractors. This basic understanding of the practice reflects an aesthetic culture exceeding the auditory. It suggests a mode of apprehending the world analogous to, but distinct from, the modern visually centred paradigm.

In a discourse initiated with al-Kindi's distinction between *musiqi* as theory and *ghina* as performance, ninth- to tenth-century discussions of *musiqi* developed a cosmology in which the strings of an instrument and eventually the musical modes played on it came to represent the temperaments and humours of the body, the four elements, the planets and the zodiac. Pythagorean in his understanding of music as analogous to the cosmos, al-Kindi stops short of his understanding of arithmetic as the universal principle. Rather, he understands the universe as stacked with theoretically significant correlations which the philosopher uncovers.

> [...] the *falak* is the proximate efficient cause of change in the sensible world. It affects the seasons, generation and corruption, the distribution and the combining of hot-cold, dry-moist. The last are related to the four elements: fire – hot and dry;

air – warm and moist; water – cold and moist, earth – cold and dry. In so far as the celestial sphere affects the epochs and seasons which in turn affect the character and mores of peoples. (Shehadi 1995: 26)

Musical therapy consisted of using select sounds to realign bodily humours in relation to celestial patterns. As discourses on music proliferated in the Islamic world, the understanding of music through layers of cosmic similitude prevailed even when writers disagreed concerning the details of analogies (Shehadi 1995: 63).

In his *Great Book of Music*, al-Farabi (c. 872–950) identifies three kinds of music as affecting the listener in varying proportions. Rather than imagining an iconography of representation of an object made present in the artwork, we can instead imagine sonic art that produces its meaning in the recipient. The most basic level of meaning induces pleasure, as in popular song. The second evokes images in the mind in a manner akin to poetry. Al-Farabi compares this with statues, which may simply be suffused with visual elegance or may also represent in the soul of the viewer the appearances of things, and their dispositions and character traits, much as the statues of ancient Greece and India did for the heroes they adulated and the gods they worshipped. In the case of melodies, the images suggested and the representations evoked in the listener are a function of the poetic power of words as married to the appropriate musical idiom which in turn enhances the effectiveness of the words. Thirdly, he describes the affective dimension of music beyond semiotic expression, which, applying to both humans and animals, can express delight, sadness, fear or anger (Shehadi 1995: 63). For al-Farabi, the essence of meaning does not emerge through the semantic interpretation of music unique to humans, but through an affectivity that acknowledges the intimate relationship between human beings and animals based on the possession of a similar soul.

This musical affectivity is underscored by an apocryphal anecdote related by biographers of the twelfth and thirteenth centuries (Guytas 1999). They relate that near the end of his life, al-Farabi came to the court of the Shiite ruler Sayf al-Dawla (r. 945–67). When he arrived at the court, the ruler was sitting with religious scholars (*'ulema*).

> Then he said to him, 'Would you like to eat?' Al Farabi said, 'No.' So he said to him, 'Would you like to drink?' Al-Farabi said, 'No.' So he said to him, would you like to listen [to some music]?' Al-Farabi said, 'Yes.' So Sayf al-Dawla gave orders for the singers to be brought in and each expert in this art came in with a variety of musical instruments. But each time one of them played on his instrument, al-Farabi found fault with him, saying, 'You have made a mistake!' Then Sayf al-Dawla said to him, 'Have you any proficiency in this art?' Al Farabi said, 'Yes.' He then drew from his waist a leather bag, opened it, and drew from it some reeds, which he put together. Then he played on them, whereupon all who were at the *majlis* laughed. Then he took them to pieces and put them together another way, and when he played on them, everyone in the *majlis* cried. Then he took them to pieces [yet] again, put them together differently, played on them and everyone in the *majlis*, even the doorkeeper, fell asleep. And al-Farabi went out. (Netton 1992: 6)

Al-Farabi becomes a mythico-historical character who conveys the meaning of music not as pleasure, but as an organizational principle resonating with the seat of emotions. The story describes how representation touches the auditor not through remote transmission of an external ideal, but by transposing the external ideal into the recipient of the art.

The fifth epistle of the Brethren of Purity, a semi-secret organization promoting spiritual knowledge in tenth-century Basra and Baghdad, shifts the emphasis of music theory from cosmology to theology. It categorizes sound, particularly music, as a direct spiritual mimetic language because it obviates the use of matter in its expression.

> [...] in every manual craft the matter dealt with consists of naturally occurring material, and that all its products are physical forms. The exception is music, for the 'matter' it deals with consists entirely of spiritual substances, namely, the souls of those who listen to it. The effects it has on them are also entirely spiritual, for melodies, consisting of rhythms and tones, have effects on the soul analogous to the effects of the art of those who work with the particular material associated with their crafts. (Wright 2010: 76–7)

This statement embodies precisely the type of world-constructing mimetic representation lost in the modern tradition, but fully at home within the Platonic and Neoplatonic realms of mimesis. For them this was indissoluble from practices of faith.

> With regard to the use of music by the custodians of divine ordinances in temples and places of worship, when reciting during ritual prayer, at sacrifices, when praying, supplicating, and lamenting, as the prophet David used to do when reciting his psalms, and as the Christians now do in their churches and the Muslims in their mosques, with sweetness of tone and a melodic form of recitation – all that is used for hearts to be softened and souls to be humble, submissive, and obedient to the commands and prohibitions of God almighty [...]. (Wright 2010: 82)

Rather than considering an iconography between the signifying artistic object and the signified event or object indicated in painting, such as that emphasized in European art history, the Brethren develop an iconography of affects from the music to the recipient in which the proportions of strings on an oud correspond to the rhythms of poetry, the forms of calligraphy and the proportions of the body. 'The attacks on these strings then have the status of pens; the ensuing high notes, that of letters; the rhythmic melodies, that of words; song, that of utterances; and the air conveying them, that of parchment' (Wright 2010: 117). Music takes on the role of both text and image in representing not only the human body but the human in relation to capacities beyond the human. The Brethren describe the proportions of the child by saying, 'it opens its hands and stretches [its arms] right and left like a bird stretching its wings' (Wright 2010: 146). The ideal measure of the human relation to music becomes equivalent to the animal whose capacities of flight and song exceed that of the human. Echoing the Vitruvian model taken up by Leonardo da Vinci in his famous drawing of man at the centre of the squared circle, the arm/wing soon becomes geometric ('when it stretches its hand out above its head, and a pair of compasses with one point on its navel is extended to its fingertips [...]' (Wright 2010: 146)). These in turn become a model for the distances between the stars and the planets, ultimately comparing God to 'a creator who has made them [the stars and the strings of the lute] and a skilled artificer who has constructed them and a benign composer who has organized them' (Wright 2010: 147). Similarly underscoring music as conveying emotions in the hearer, the eleventh-century theoretician of music al-Hasan al-Katib suggests that 'the meaning of the melody is the goal of the composer [...] just as with the speaker (of a language), these must resemble the various states and circumstances (of the soul)' (Shehadi 1995: 87).

Similarly, *Lightening Flashes Concerning the Refutation of Those Who Declare That Music Is Forbidden* by Ahmad al-Ghazali (1061–1123 or 1126) distinguishes between music for entertainment and that enabling proximity to the divine. While he emphasizes audition in a context of the correct time, the place, and companions he also notes that audition must be open not only to those already pursuing the path of knowledge, but also to those who might discover it by encountering audition (Robson 1938: 72). Just as one who is not yet pure can go into a mosque to seek purity, so can he who 'desires the purity of his soul, the cleansing of his heart and the serenity of his spirit by listening to wonderful things in speech and comprehending delicate things in poems which uphold the establishment of his relationship to the angels and the cutting off of his relationship to the devils' (Robson 1938: 73).

He describes audition as a mode of mimetic representation in which the divine becomes articulated in its recipient. Representation does not take place in a relationship where the other world is necessarily absent, but through the experience of audition across time which engenders divine presence in the perception of the listener.

> The audition of this party is a reference to the observation of strange secrets in the delicate poems which the *qawwal* recites while joined to the ecstasy which arises in the heart of the gnostic who works and the novice who is perfect. It induces them to put off resistance, to be drawn to the presence of the One, the Powerful and to ponder delicate things and secrets. And for the removal of these veils they have chosen audition with beautiful voices. [...] Then when there arises in him increase of arrangements of notes and spiritual analogies which are called music, [man's nature] prefers them to everything else. So when a person hears the analogies which pertain to notes which include the realities which pertain to taste and the truths which pertain to the Unity, the being inclines to all those, and every bodily member receives its portion separately. The hearing receives the things of the unrestrained analogies; the sight, the analogies of the movements; the heart, the delicate things of the realities; and the intellect, the inner consciousness of the unrestrained analogies. (Robson 1938: 71–3)

Engagement with the divine presence thus transpires not through the ear, but through the apprehension of sound as it enters the heart and transforms into the movement that often accompanies the practice of remembrance (*zikr*) undertaken in Sufi brotherhoods devoted to intrinsic rituals of worship. He offers a further iconography through the symbolism of the instruments in their relationship of similitudes.

The [form of] the tambourine is a reference to the cycle of existing things; the skin which is fitted on to it is a reference to general existence, the striking which takes place on the tambourine is a reference to the descent of the divine visitations from the innermost arcana upon general existence to bring forth the things pertaining to the essence from the interior to the exterior, the five small bells are a reference to the prophetical ranks, the saintly ranks, the apostolic ranks, the khalifate ranks, and the Imamate ranks, and their combined sound is a reference to the appearance of the divine revelations and unrestricted knowledge by means of these realities in the hearts of the saints and the people of perfection. And the soul of the reality is the form of the rank of the Truth, since it is He who sets the things in motion, brings them into existence, and enriches them. And the voice of the singer is a reference to the divine life which comes down from the innermost arcana to the levels of the spirits, the hearts and the consciences. The flute is a reference to the human essence, and the nine holes are a reference to the openings in the outer frame. [...] And the breath which penetrates the flute is a reference to the light of Allah penetrating the reed of man's essence. And their being moved in audition is a reference to the bird of human reality in the station of the eternal address, 'Am I not your Lord?' and to the excitement of the spirit on account of the cage of the body being broken and its return to the true home. [...] And the dancing is a reference to the circling of the spirit round the cycle of existing things on account of receiving the effects of the unveilings and revelations; and this is the state of the gnostic. The whirling is a reference to the spirit's standing with Allah in its inner nature and being, the circling of its look and thought, and its penetrating the ranks of existing things; and this is the state of the assured one. (Robson 1938: 98–100)

This iconography persists in the poetic imagery of the introductory lines of the *Mesnevi* of Jelal ad-Din Rumi (1207–73):

Listen to this reed flute as it tells its tales
Complaining of separations as it wails:

'Since they cut my stalk away from the reed bed
My outcry has made men and women lament

I seek a breast that is torn to shreds by loss
So that I may explicate the pain of want

Everyone who's far from his own origin
Seeks to be united with it once again. [...]' (Holbrook 2011)

Like the Brethren of Purity, who emphasize the intimate relationship between the proportions of music and calligraphic script, Jelal ad-Din Rumi uses the trope of the reed – raw material of both flute and pen – to indicate the conceptual indivisibility between sound and writing. This similitude emerges through the Qur'an, which describes itself as both spoken to the Prophet through the angel (Gabriel; Q 96.1) and written by the reed pen (Q 68.1-3). Signification does not rely on semiotic indivisibility between the signifier and the signified, described as the two sides of a leaf in the thought of Ferdinand de Saussure, instigator of modern linguistics. Rather than indicating an invisible signified, the sonic signifier functions as an expressive agent (de Saussure 1976: 30). The Brethren refer to this relationship also as an image, saying,

> when the meanings conveyed by melody and rhythm reach the mind via hearing, so that an image is formed there of the ideas that were contained within those rhythms and melodies, their existence [as vibrations] in the air can be dispensed with, just as writing on tablets can be dispensed with once the ideas written on them are understood and memorized. (Wright 2010: 126)

Here, mimesis does not transpire between the signifier and the signified, but through the direct incorporation of the signified by the subject through the vehicle of the signifier.

Critics of music share the same understanding of music expressed by its proponents. The preservation of Ibn al-Dunya's *Censure of the Instruments of Diversion* and Ibn Taymiyyah's *Letter on Audition, Dancing, Shouting, and Listening to the Recitation of Poetry* in a single 1391 manuscript suggests their limited circulation. Influential as the teacher of two Abbasid Caliphs as well as Ibn Taymiyyah, Ibn al-Dunya found music guilty by association with forbidden practices such as drinking, gambling and fornication (el-Rouayheb 2010). Ibn Taymiyyah finds music acceptable as entertainment for the young (as the Prophet allowed for his young wife Aisha), but censors pleasure-inducing music as increasing sensual appetites culminating with drinking and sexual intercourse. Ibn Taymiyyah uses the partial homology of *al-ghina* (song/entertainment music) and *al-zina* (fornication) to liken them as pleasures in the absence of reason, akin to drunkenness. Wine, music and the image similarly induce a state of drunkenness. He similarly condemns meditative audition practised by Sufis: the ecstatic state induced by music does nothing more than replace one passion with another, equally detracting from the meditation on God enabled through the Qur'an. Thus a taste for poetry and music would detract from the pleasures of the Qur'an, the only audition that clearly exemplified the Prophet (Shehadi 1995: 95–9).

Music's proponents acknowledged these dangers. The Brethren of Purity write, 'The reason why music has been proscribed in some of the prophetic laws is that people have made use of it in a way different to that of the sages, in fact, for idle entertainment, and to incite a craving for the pleasures of this world and its deceptive desires' (Wright 2010: 124–5). Although at the end of his treatise, Ahmad al-Ghazali (1061–c. 1123) notes that 'by common consent', instruments of diversion including the viol, lute (oud), Persian lute (*barbad*), reed pipe, except the tambourine, are prohibited, he initiates his discussions of the metaphysical benefits of audition by equating an absolute prohibition with blasphemous disrespect for the example of the Prophet. Noting those Hadith where the Prophet is said to have listened to music, he explains,

> He who says that audition is absolutely forbidden must acknowledge that the Prophet did what is forbidden, looked at what is forbidden, and confirmed others in what is forbidden. If that flutters in anyone's mind, he is an infidel by general consent, and the paths of the favours and the indication are closed to him. (Robson 1938: 70)

Despite their different evaluations, what becomes clear in comparing the discourse of the proponents and detractors of music is that music was understood as mimetic not in that it describes a world outside itself, as in our common understanding of mimesis (as outward-looking), but in terms of the effects it engenders in the auditor. Regarding music as mimetic combines the immaterialism of the thought of Plotinus with the idea of music as an affective agent permeating the thought of Aristotle. As Halliwell explains, in the writings of Aristotle, musical mimesis emerges as

> an intrinsic capacity of musically organized sound to present and convey (affective) aspects of character; the patterns of music have properties 'like' the emotional states that can, for that reason, be the objects of their mimesis. As evidence for this view, Aristotle cites music's power to put its audiences into states of mind or feeling that contain, or are characterized by, these same emotions, so that musical mimesis seems to be a case that covers what might now be distinguished, by some philosophers, as representation and expression [...] mimesis registers itself in its directness of effect upon listeners: 'our souls are changed [...]'. (Halliwell 2002: 159–60)

Rather than imagining direct lineages between these traditions, such resonances suggest a world view where scholars were simultaneously steeped in normative Islamic monotheism and truths offered in philosophy perceived as absolute that became integrated into the ritual practice and theorization of intrinsic approaches to Islamic faith.

From theology to poetry: Plato as musician in the *Iskandarnameh* of Nizami of Ganj

The 1194 *Iskandarnameh* of Nizami of Ganj (1141–1207 CE) incorporates the Alexandrian legacy into the Islamic sphere. It addresses the relationship between music and philosophy as it pertains to the wisdom of the ideal ruler in a story in the second part of the book, the *Iqbalnameh* (Book of Wisdom), which stages a row of poets sitting before Alexander. Soon Aristotle announces that he is the pathfinder for all rational knowledge, and all praise him, except Plato, 'the master of all arts', who goes out to contemplate hidden wisdom. The poem (rendered in translated prose) continues,

> [...] And as the star-watcher took his place in the cask (*Khom*) and followed the traces of the spheres and the ways of the stars, he made a model of the sound of the harmonies that he found there. As he discovered the proportions for each sound on his lute, he began in his hiding place to weave the lute. For singing he laid the leather over the gourd and unharnessed the strings, and after he had rubbed the gazelle skin with musk, he brought wet sound out of the dry wood.
>
> And so from his imagination and drafts did he create a form of organ [...]
>
> Plato had discovered a music, that nobody other than him knew. From dry wood he elicits sounds that attract the spheres with their moisture.

> When he moves his finger in one mode, all the animals fall immediately asleep. When he then plays another mode, he brings them from sleep to wakefulness [...].
> (Nizami and Bürgel 1991: 433–4, translation from German by the author)

Plato presents this music at the court. There, Alexander recognizes its superiority because it encompasses and yet also transcends the forms of knowledge that he offers. Alexander rewards Plato with a higher rank than that of Aristotle.

This emphasis on the organ contrasts the discussion of instruments like oud and reed flute dominating earlier musical treatises. This may allude to a wind instrument called an *urganon* referenced by al-Farabi. Alternatively, it may play upon the homologous collective name of Aristotle's six works on logic, the *Organon*. Anachronistically playing on Aristotelian logic transformed, as in a dream, into an instrument, Plato inverts it by engaging the emotions of the pure at heart, represented by the animals.

The story condenses numerous elements of the mystical descriptions of Neoplatonism expounded in earlier Islamic works with the Pythagorean equation of music with philosophy. This equation features in Plato's *Phaedo* where Socrates deems philosophy 'the noblest and best art' and is thereby inspired in a dream to make music immediately before his execution. In Nizami, Plato enters into a meditative state by seeking solitude in a wine flask, merging inspiration with drinking. The association with Socrates's death by poison recalls an analogy drawn by al-Ghazali, in which he explains that the consonants establishing the root form of the word for audition, *sama*, the letters *sin* and *mim*,

> indicate poison (*samm*) meaning that the inner nature of audition is like poison which causes one to die to the attachments of things which are other than Allah and causes one to reach the unseen stations. (Robson 1938: 103)

In Nizami, drinking and music, both poisons, function through their capacity to destroy reason, the logical discursivity of analytical thought. This destructive capacity enables presence of the divine.

Through the heightened state enabled through the poison/cure of the wine, Plato becomes able to hear the music of the spheres and, like the sages praised by Islamic philosophers, invents an instrument analogous not only through the sounds it produces but in the balancing of elements such as dryness and moisture. The resulting instrument affects the emotions so deeply that, like the reed flute supposedly played by al-Farabi at the court of Sayf al-Dawla, it puts not only humans but animals to sleep, addressing the most basic elements of the resonance between the cosmos and our sphere of life, echoing al-Farabi's emphasis on the highest, affective nature of music shared by man and animals (Shehadi 1995: 62).

The music Plato produces – representing philosophy itself – fulfils the role of the musician set out by the Brethren of Purity, who state,

> It is also part of the musician's skill to use the rhythms corresponding to [various] moments according to the [different] moods that correspond to them, that is, to begin at social invitations, feasts, and drinking parties with rhythms that reinforce

the moral qualities of generosity, nobility, and liberality, such as the first heavy and the like, and then afterwards to perform joyful, gay rhythms [...] and when there is dancing and ensemble-dancing. [...] At the end of the session, if he is afraid that those who are drunk might be noisy, rowdy, and quarrelsome, he should use slow, calm, and sad rhythms that quieten people down and send them to sleep. (Wright 2010: 161)

This picks up on Plotinus's description of such sleep as a form of waking from the delusion of materiality in which the body is normally stuck.

> Thus far we have been meeting those who, on the evidence of thrust and resistance, identify body with real being and find assurance of truth in the phantasms that reach us through the senses, those, in a word, who, like dreamers, take for actualities the figments of their sleeping vision. The sphere of sense, the Soul in its slumber; for all of the Soul that is in body is asleep and the true getting up is not bodily but from the body: in any movement that takes the body with it there is no more than a passage from sleep to sleep, from bed to bed; the veritable waking or rising is from corporeal things, for these, belonging to the Kind directly opposed to the Soul, present to it what is directly opposed to its essential existence. (Plotinus and Mackenna 1991: 196)

Both al-Ghazali and the Brethren indicate a similar shift from the material to the immaterial image. Thus al-Ghazali says,

> If you seek to open a comprehensive gate, verify the realities of the phenomena of every place. Then divest yourself of looking at the figures [ideas] whence comes all that constitutes the purest faith. [...] The farthest point reached by earthly lovers in their deserts is but the starting-point of the lover [i.e. the mystic] and of him whom realities enclose. (Robson 1938: 100)

Similarly, the Brethren portray an imaginary assembly of philosophers at a court discussing the relative merits of sight and hearing.

> When rational souls are free of the filth of bodily desires, abstain from natural pleasures, and are untarnished by materiality, they intone plaintive songs, recalling their exalted and noble spiritual world and yearning for it. But if [their instinctual] nature hears that [same] melody, it will reveal itself to the soul in the beauty of its forms and the splendour of its colours, in order to draw it back. (Wright 2010: 167)

In its ideal function, music thus affects the soul rather than simply pleasing it; it moves beyond matter to the immaterial.

This ambivalence towards materiality reflects a pervasive thread in the thought of Plato, Christianity and Islam. We see it in Book 10 of Plato's *Republic* in the description of how philosophy leads people out of their epistemic caves into the light of knowledge through material intermediaries; in the biblical injunction in the book of John often paraphrased as 'being in the world but not of it', and in the Qur'an's recognition of materiality as a means through which we recognize the divine that should not become a value in itself (Q 3.14, 10.24, 43.33-5). This tension between the value of materiality and its utility as a ladder to immateriality informs the imagery of the image permeating much of the Persian poetic tradition (Shaw 2019).

From poetry to painting

The manuscript painting captures the story at the scene in which Plato at his instrument puts the animals to sleep. The relationship between Plato's music and the stars may be indicated by golden dots on his armpit and foot, suggestive of constellations. The dots disseminate across the sleeping animals like the music of the spheres, putting them at ease. The figure sits in a landscape painting that incorporates European perspectivalism and naturalism in the clouds, while retaining the Chinese-influenced stylizations of mountains and post-Timurid detailing of leaves. The branching river framing the musician suggests the similitude between natural sound and music. The homologies of al-Farabi's *urganon* and Aristotle's *Organon* find a third companion in the European organ.

The composition suggests models from European prints showing animals around a central Orphic figure. The relationship with European models recurs in the paintings on the organ itself. On top, a scene of a supplicant woman holding a baby before a seated ruler suggests Solomon's wise decision not to split a baby. Underneath, a scene of Majnun (the symbolic beloved who becomes a hermit because of his separation from Leyla, but metaphorically also the divine) with the animals adds further confirmation to Koch's interpretation of the intertwined myths of Orpheus and Solomon. Yet the Orphic association with Plato cannot be reduced to a simple visual coincidence, as Pythagoreanism, and through it Platonism, finds its roots in Orphism, as discussed by Proclus, the translation of which into Arabic underscores its importance in philosophy under Islam (Brisson and Tihanyi 2004: 89–92). The incorporation of Orphic iconography inspired by European examples interprets the poem by reincorporating the Orphism of Plato, not part of the work of Nizami. This suggests an active interest in the philosophical legacy at the Mughal court beyond that filtered through historical literature.

In its sophistication, the image also offers a meditation on the relationships between image and music, as well as mysticism and philosophy emerging through increased contact with the cultures of Europe. This meditation parallels the discussion of European painting engaged by Abu'l Fazl in the 1590s in the *A'in-i Akbar* (Constitution of Akbar), comparing painting in the European tradition with writing. He says,

> A picture (*surat*) leads to the form it represents [*khu davand-i khvud*, lit. its own master] and this [*leads*] to the meaning (*mam*), just as the shape of a line (*paykar-i khatti*) leads one to letters (*harf*) and words (*lafz*), and from there the sense (*mafhum*) can be found out. Although in general they make pictures (*tasvir*) of material resemblances (*ashbah-i kawni*), the European masters (*karpardazan-i*

Firang) express with rare forms (*ba-shigirf surat-ha*) many meanings of the created world (*basa macant-i khalqi*) and [thus] they lead those who see only the outside of things (*zdhirnigahan*) to the place of real truth (*haqiqatzar*). However, lines [*khatt*, writing, calligraphy] provide us with the experiences of the ancients and thus become a means to intellectual progress. (Koch 2010: 277)[1]

The painting follows the example of the Brethren of Purity, who offer a summary of the potentially deceptive nature of the mimetic image as doubly removed from reality only to follow it with meditations on the greater perceptive value of hearing. Similarly, the painting incorporates European practices of visual verisimilitude in the drawings on the organ, only to frame them in terms of a more real, affective sphere of music. It indicates that music, in taking the soul from the body, represents the divine with greater realism than that offered in the European image as recently proffered in India by Catholic missionaries.

Across from the scenes juxtaposing Solomon and Majnun, the organ offers two more: at the bottom, a Mughal artist kneeling before a European who holds his paints for him; and above, the portrait that apparently comes out of this interaction, indicated by the repetition of the same hat, this time hovering at an angle above the head of the bald and beardless European. The hat seems to allude to a common trope of those associated with the 'school of love' (*madhab-i ishq*) in which a person wearing their hat at an angle (*kajkulahi*) indicated an openness to worldly pleasures and the seduction of beauty that reflected indifference to the mere appearances of moral uprightness and public propriety. One of the most famous occurrences of this trope occurs roughly contemporaneously with this painting, in the memoirs of the Sultan Jahangir (*Tuzk-i Jahangir*, 1569–1627), in a story about the interaction between Sayyid Nizam-ud Din Awliya, patron saint of Delhi, and Amir Khusraw, whose poetry exists in Persian, Ottoman and Mughal canons, and to whom North Indian Muslims trace their musical systems.

> One day, Sheykh Nizam al-Din Awliya had placed his cap to the side of his head, and was sitting on a terrace by the River Jumna observing the spectacle of the Hindu rituals and devotions. Just then, Amir Khusraw appeared. The Shaykh turned to him and said, 'Do you observe this congregation?' and this hemistich came to his tongue:
>
> For every people: it's path, it's *din*, and its prayer-direction [*qiblah*]![2]
>
> The Mir, without a moment's contemplation, and with all due decorum, addressed himself to the Shaykh with the completing hemistich: 'I have set my *qiblah* straight in the way of the crooked-hatted.' (Ahmed 2015: 203)

The visual application of the allusion to a European rearticulates the pairings of European and Islamic narratives of Orpheus and Plato, and Solomon and Majnun explored in the rest of the image. The application of crooked-hattedness to a European in this context underscores the incorporation of foreign practices as acceptable not simply through the toleration of the other, but its incorporation as no longer distinct from the self. Just as crooked-hattedness suggests a wisdom to move beyond the known, its application to the European suggests that the greater wisdom is not to stick to the narrow paths of cultural habit, but to embrace difference despite the apparent danger of change. Yet in emphasizing the story of Plato and the animals through a representation suggestive of European norms as outlined by Abu'l Fazl, the artist suggests that the basic forms of knowledge enabled through music – knowledge that is crooked-hatted in relation to the straightforward representation of the image – retain a capacity beyond the rationalism attributed to Aristotle, gently critiqued through Nizami's trope of the competition.

This reassertion of the mythic and spiritual in the face of the literal takes visual form in the inclusion of the rainbow-tailed *Simurgh*, the mythical bird that inspires the mystical quest described in Farid ud-Din's *Conference of the Birds* (1177). The animals bring to mind those anthropomorphized in *Khalila wa Dhimna*, adopted from the ancient Indian *Panchatantra* and translated into Arabic in 750 and into Persian by Rudaki (858–941). Deeply entrenched in the literary canon, the Brethren cited Rudaki's work anonymously in Persian, clearly linking the affectivity of music with sleep, death and the instinctual apprehension of animals used as metaphors for humans.

> The nocturnal lament of the lute string
> is sweeter to my ear than [the cry of] 'God is great!'
>
> If the plaint of the lute string – and do not think this strange –
> attracts its prey from the wide plains,
>
> With no arrow it yet from time to time
> pierces its body, the dart transfixing the heart,
>
> Now weeping, now grief-stricken,
> from break of day through noon till dusk.
>
> Although bereft of a tongue, its eloquence
> can interpret the lovers' story,
>
> Now making the madman sane,
> now casting the sane under its spell. (Wright 2010: 165)

Thus the 'nocturnal lament' of the string, inducing sleep as in Nizami's poem, also parallels death through the 'dart transfixing the heart' of 'prey'. If the animals in the painting appear dead – tongues hanging out, eyes wide open, and one near the top left even with the mark of an arrow on her flank – it may be because the sleep induced by a music resonant with divine ecstasy enables knowledge of that which surpasses life. The animals, merely pacified by the Orphic song in Ovid's rendition (Book 11), here gain his ability, unique among mortals, to cross the boundary between life and death through the 'spell' of music. The link with the animals comes full circle to the image of Plato performing music parallel with the image of Socrates making music as philosophy, 'the greatest kind of music', based on the myths of Aesop, which show the same natural order as evinced in the harmonies of music and the logical systems of philosophy (Northwood 2015).

This painting provides a visual response to the new techniques of painting made available through the recent introduction of European prints circulated by missionaries. It suggests that European visual mimetic methods be subsumed into a powerful existing mimetic practice in which transmedial sensory perception, image and sound, animal and human, body and philosophy, Muslim and European coexist through their essential similitudes. In other words, it refutes the alterity ascribed to Islam through a supposed iconoclasm which has dominated modern discussions of its arts. Rather, this image suggests a cohesive world view rooted in Islam, not as something essential and isolated in unique origins, but as something dynamic, multifaceted, intertextual and transcultural.

Far from representing only a geographically and temporally bounded Mughal perspective, its expressiveness can only function from within a powerful legacy of aesthetic discourse, primarily about music and itself rooted in the antique Greek philosophical tradition that developed in concert with the discursive procedures which define juridical Islam during the ninth and tenth centuries and established the basic codes through which mimetic representation in its multiple forms – poetic, calligraphic, visual, musical, architectural and cosmological – circulated in premodern Islamic cultures. Within this panoply of mimetic practices, the image was not banned so much as it was not central. Thus, in contrast to the iconoclastic controversy in the Eastern Orthodox Church centuries earlier, it did not engender extensive discourses.

By the twentieth century, when Muhammad Abduh travelled to Sicily, he could respond to the careful preservation of artefacts from the past by applying the same analogy between poetry and painting that al-Farabi had applied between poetry and music, explaining that 'portrayal is a kind of poetry which is seen but not heard, while poetry is a kind of picture which is heard but not seen' (Ahmad and Glidden 1968: 263). With this rendition of Horace's famous dictum 'Ut picture poesis' into Islamic culture, the incorporation of European understandings of mimetic representation initiated under the Mughals could be said to have come to full fruition. It is, of course, soon after that Western explanations of an Islamic painting prohibition coincided with the Salafi erasure of Islam as a trans-historical practice, and that an ever-shifting relationship with mimetic representation shut down under the increasing avalanche of images enabled in the twentieth century.

The sophisticated development of visual representation in the post-Timurid courts suggests that al-Nawawi's proscription of painting was not normative. Rather, the high cost of paintings, combined with the unimportance of the image in Islamic ritual practice, led to its rarity in the everyday life of Muslims, even as it functioned as a trope common in poetry indivisible from faith, including that of Amir Khosrau, Jelaleddin Rumi and Nizami of Ganj. To the extent that music had a visual counterpart, this found form in the rhythms of geometry, understood to follow the same Neoplatonic universal essences as music. Yet the materiality upon which geometry depended rendered it a weaker representational medium than music (Necipoğlu 1995). Not only was music extensively theorized early in the development of Islam as a mimetic tool in making the divine present in the heart of the believer, it remained central to Islamic intrinsic practice as it developed in numerous Sufi orders in Central, South and Southeast Asia across Africa and retained its centrality in multiple court cultures (Harris and Stokes 2017).

Epilogue

The problem with understanding a culture conceived as other, whether by time, space, religion or culture – and I would suggest that in the case of Islam, time reduces all of us moderns, including contemporary Muslims, to foreigners – is that it never answers back to the questions that we ask it. A supposedly singular Islam cannot function as an agent to tell us if the image was prohibited or not. As Emmanuel Levinas points out, often the expressions of the culture of an Other can, at best, enter into a conversation with the culture we define as our own, thereby producing an ethical relationship through which we consider, despite the inalienable boundaries produced between the analyst and the analysand: 'To approach the Other in conversation is to welcome his expression. [...] It is therefore to *receive* from the Other beyond the capacity of the I [...] this also means: to be taught' (Levinas and Lingis 1969: 51, emphasis in original). If modern culture engages with Islam through the notion of the prohibition, it does so through the demand of a visual analogue for normativity presumed through European experience. Instead of the answer it waits to see, it must listen. If we are to understand Islamic art, we must learn to see with the ear and recognize with the heart.

3

The Hypericon of the Golden Calf

Yvonne Sherwood

Introduction: Memes with legs (or hooves)

The golden calf is one of those few biblical memes that still has legs – or hooves (cf. Mitchell 2005: 87). Despite – or in fact because of – its emphatic destruction, the calf (or more accurately, its ghost or image) has trotted off the edges of the Bible into safer and more permanent cultural domains. The calf has become nothing less than a 'hypericon': the term W. J. T. Mitchell coins for those ambitious images that encapsulate an entire episteme or theory of knowledge and summarize a particular assemblage of knowledge, aesthetics, ethics and politics, such as the '*tabula rasa*' or Plato's cave (Mitchell 1994).

But the golden calf has always been a very peculiar kind of hypericon: a *hyperaniconic hypericon*. The calf survives as an image *and* an image of the destruction of the image. It lingers as a sign of presence and absence; representation and its erasure. Both poles are as extreme as could possibly be conceived. The calf materializes as a hyperimage; an image invested with such passion that we call it an 'idol': the term that we use for images with exceptional powers to mesmerize, that seem preternatural, supernatural, divine. The destruction of the calf is equally and oppositely emphatic. Moses burns it, grinds it to powder, dissolves it in water, and forces the creators to drink it and gag on it (Exod. 32.19-20). He then orders the sons of Levi to massacre three thousand people in retaliation, just in case the point was not entirely clear (Exod. 32.28). The annihilation is thorough, genocidal. The calf has become such a powerful cultural meme because it represents not just 'contested' but colliding desires.

The (destroyed) golden calf is often taken as a summary image of absolutism and a definitive media decision: from art to scripture. As the golden calf is pulverized, dissolved in water, and given to the sinful people to drink (Exod. 32.20), so the calf seems to dissolve into a *text* about the triumph of textuality. You can no longer see the golden, brazen calf, but you can read the written record of its erasure in any modern Bible. *The smashing of the cow is the victory of the text*, or so it is commonly believed. I say 'so it is commonly believed', because such an assertion relies on too sharp a division between 'word' and 'image', 'art' and 'scripture' (cf. Plate 2015: 277). 'The visible can be arranged in meaningful tropes; words deploy a visibility that can be blinding' (Rancière 2007: 7). Were we to actually read any of the words in the Bible, we would find some strange old words that have not yet thought of becoming an alternative to the image. Taking our cue from Hans Belting who writes of the 'image before art', we could think in terms of words before scripture, and before canons, codices and all the miracles of reproduction and circulation that came with print. In the Bible, words are often strange and graphic, figurative, personified, concrete, tangible *things* – with all the paradoxical powers of the thing (cf. Morgan 2015). Words look at you. They serve as witness, judge and memorial (Josh. 8.30-2; Josh. 24.26-7). Jesus as logos walks on earth. Wives suspected of sexual sins are forced to drink potions of words (Num. 5.11-31) just as the Nafana in Ghana make a soup from a tonic washed over slates inscribed with words from the Qur'an (Plate 2015: 78), and makers of the golden calf are forced to drink powdered grains of calf. Words are things, grains, matter – and *in the Bible*, not just in 'other religions'. The words that replace and archive the destroyed calf are not words that efface their own materiality, dissolving into the interiority of silent reading. They are tablet objects that preserve the petrified fingerprint of the deity (cf. Stordalen in this volume), words that are chiselled and carried on stone, broken and laboriously remade. Caveat lector. We should be extremely cautious about taking the public Protestant, modern *image* of the Bible as 'Word' (as we say in English) 'as read'.

The story of the calf in Exodus 32 is bookended by self-conscious texts about *writing*: the giving of the two tablets of stone, inscribed with the very finger of God (Exod. 31.18); and the laborious cutting of the second set of tablets, to replace the first set hurled to the foot of the mountain in Moses/God's fury (Exod. 32.19, 34.4). In the second version told in Moses's own words in the first person in the book of Deut. 9.8–10.5 (Deuteronomy being the *Deutero-nomos* or Second Law, the second casting), the subsuming of the image is even more complete as the figure of the calf is shattered into a little shard of words contained within the first-person words of Moses. As Terje Stordalen points out in his chapter for this volume, Deuteronomy redefines Torah as written, not oral, text (cf. Stordalen, 25). In line with this programme of textualization, it foregrounds the icon of the tablets, and dissolves the calf into the subclause 'then I saw that you had indeed sinned against the Lord your God by casting for yourselves an image of a calf [...]' (Deut. 9.16).

Absorbed back into ink on papyrus, or black-and-white print, the destroyed calf has supported the dominant modern image of the Bible as a monolith of logocentrism, a density of *text*. But ironically, in a reversal of the presumed desires of the biblical myth, the calf has persisted as an icon in contexts where the relevance of scripture has expired. As 'image', the calf floats eternally free of the brutally destroyed material (first casting). Thus it can be seen as an iconic figure of the *image*, the word we use for the 'phantasmatic, virtual, or spectral appearance' that can be miraculously lifted off the picture, and abstracted from its material form (Mitchell 2005: 85). There is something divine about the image: it lives eternally and does not depend on its material form. The very idea of the image recalls Paul's strange statements about the spirit that exceeds, out-lives, survives and even negates the letter, the flesh or the merely material form (e.g. 2 Cor. 3.6). For Paul, the true word is not merely, or not even, the covenant 'chiselled in letters on stone tablets' (2 Cor. 3.7), but the spirit which is compared to the glory and transcendence shown (or not) in Moses's and God's unseeable, unrepresentable face. The image, which does not depend on its material form, reflects the representational aporiae that haunt divinity in the Abrahamic religions. But it also begs the question: How can an image (or a god) possibly transcend material form, and imagine that it/he could live without a material form?[1]

Recasting the calf

The image of the calf and its obliteration seems to have had far more life in it than the texts about the calf. Long after the strangely conflicted words of the Torah have been forgotten, a host of artists including Nicolas Poussin, Raphael, François Perrier, Fillipino Lippi, Andrea Celesti, Emil Nolde and Damien Hirst – as well as protesters on Wall Street – have gone on making golden calves (Figures 3.1a, b).

The calf occupies the strange space at the intersection, not just of aesthetics, ethics and politics (according to W. J. T. Mitchell's definition of the hypericon), but *also* of the economy and markets. Damien Hirst's *The Golden Calf* – a bull dipped in formaldehyde, with its head crowned with a solid gold disc and its hooves and horns cast in eighteen-carat gold – was sold at Sotheby's for £10,345,250. No photograph could be included here due to exorbitant copyright fees. Its anti-typos was the papier-mâché golden calf made by Judson Memorial Church for the Occupy Wall Street protests, fusing the biblical calf with the *Wall Street Bull*, or the *Bowling Green Bull*. Ironically, no photograph could be included for this popular icon either, due to the labyrinths of copyright law currently in force. The calf has also functioned as a summary image of politics, separated into the starkly opposed forms of sovereign (divine/fascist) absolutism and the power of the crowd. It is impossible to know whether Nolde's *Dance around the Golden Calf* (1910) sides with 'the people', or the forces of censorship that will/must restrain them. Terror, freedom, revolution, eroticism and fanaticism find conflicted expression in the wild yellow naked women who are dancing and, in Moses's and God's view, acting 'perversely', and 'running wild' (Exod. 32.7.25). (The King James Bible has 'naked' instead of 'running wild'.)

Golden calves have often been caught up in an ongoing cycle of transgression/defiance and retribution; construction and iconoclasm. Nolde's *Dance around the Golden Calf* (1910) was publicly shamed by the Nazis in the 1937 Munich exhibition *Entartete Kunst* (Degenerate Art). Despite his personal appeal to the local Nazi party leader in Vienna, and his very public condemnation of 'Jewish art' and his support for National Socialism, Nolde saw a total of 1,052 of his works removed from museums and was banned from producing artworks even in private. This led him to produce secret watercolours which he called the 'Unpainted Pictures': a striking parallel to the unpainted and unspoken Gods produced (or not) by some strands of Jewish, Christian and Islamic art. In 1978, Poussin's *Adoration of the Golden Calf* hanging in the National Gallery in London was slashed with a knife. In 2011, it was sprayed with red aerosol paint. Perhaps the vandals were the old divinities, come back from the dead to wreak vengeance. Or perhaps they were 'freak acts of rage' – an outburst from a member of the always potentially unruly crowd (cf. Waters 2011).

The images most likely to stay with us, and haunt us, are the ones about which we are undecided and divided. The ghost calf has become such a haunting and resilient

Figure 3.1a *The Adoration of the Golden Calf*, Nicholas Poussin, 1633–4, National Gallery, London. Public domain, Wikimedia Commons.

Figure 3.1b *Dance around the Golden Calf*, Emil Nolde, 1910. Public domain, wikiart.org.

meme because it is so profoundly and productively divided. Its destruction has become, in Bruno Latour's terms, an iconic figure of 'Iconoclash'. Iconoclash, as opposed to 'iconoclasm', is when 'one does not know, one hesitates, one is troubled by an action for which there is no way to know, without further inquiry, whether it is destructive or constructive' (Latour and Weibel 2002: 14). The destruction of the calf can be celebrated, as when the Wall Street protesters call down divine wrath against the golden idols; or it can be invoked as the ultimate offence against freedom and freedom of expression. As modern thinkers have struggled to define their relations to the old gods and new political orders and 'freedoms', the destroyed calf has functioned positively and negatively: as an image to identify with and an image *against which* to define self-consciously *modern* religions and selves. The destroyed calf has become a pin-up image for aniconicity – and also, conversely, an icon of modernity's necessary coup against the old oppressive gods who so violently opposed our freedoms of expression. *Thus the destroyed calf came to embody Europe's tortured and divided relationships to its Christian foundation, and to 'religion'* (the word that modern thinkers inflected in very special ways).

Contested/conflicted modern foundation myths: Applauding and lamenting the destruction of the calf

We tell two equal and opposite foundation stories about religion. In one, religion serves as a *foundational allergy* for self-consciously 'modern' times. We are defined by freedom from religion and by rebellion against the old violent gods and the wars conducted in their names. But according to an opposite and equally strong (complementary) foundation myth, the modern 'West' identifies with, and appeals to, a loosely biblical Christian heritage on which (so the myth goes) our very identity depends. According to this extremely helpful myth, Christianity was uniquely placed to birth and sponsor modern dreams of freedom, which it had dreamt from the beginning. Christianity and higher religion helped to birth the founding freedoms, ethics and politics of the modern state.

The same double story that was told about religion was also told about monotheism. According to one foundation story, monotheism was seen as violent, intolerant and opposed (by definition) to plurality and creativity. It was by definition a despotic tyranny of the one. The modern subject had to struggle for his/her freedom against the monotheistic deity, like Prometheus stealing fire from the gods. But the late nineteenth century saw the emergence of a completely opposite narrative of 'ethical monotheism' (see further Vial and Hadley 2001). In this story the single god of monotheism became a figure and an ally for the individual human subject, not his opposite. God and human beings were linked in the revelation of eternal ethics. Our true religious foundation led inexorably to higher, ethical, spiritual religion, which transcended the 'gross' material,[2] and parochial elements of religion – or at least so we hoped and prayed. The Christian-biblical tradition was for ethics, rights and natural, universal religion. But it was also against.

Both foundation myths have been important. It has also been important not to be forced to notice the fundamental conflict between them. To a large extent, the conflict has been masked by a careful distribution of positive and negative forces between Christianity and 'religion' (cf. Anidjar 2006). In the most crude form of this distribution, positive forces have been attributed to Christianity and the New Testament while negative forces have been displaced onto 'religion' or, more specifically, primitive, parochial religions, such as Judaism and/or Islam, and the Old Testament and/or the Qur'an.[3] Recent belated and guilty attempts to rebrand the good Christian foundation as 'Judeo-Christian' and to speak of the three equal brothers in the 'Abrahamic' or Mosaic religions, can hardly paper over the fact that Judaism, Christianity and Islam have been anything but equal brothers and have had anything but an equal relationship to the 'fraternal' community of the modern state. In older, ruder versions of the foundation myths (the ones that were spoken out loud by all and that are still spoken out loud by some), the *valorized* foundation and the tradition that led inexorably to modern politics was *Christian*. It was defined *against* the shadowy 'Turk' or 'Moor', who served as a distant site of contrast. The Old Testament often became the lone source for the manifestly intolerant, insensitive, monotheistic, proto-fascist God, who destroyed all who offended him, like the poor creators of the calf. However, because the Christian Bible includes the Old Testament, some Old Testament scenes were caught up in the evolutionary trajectory, understood as the progress of the living spirit latent within the sometimes-dead letters of the text. Chief among these elevated Old Testament texts were those of the Hebrew prophets (widely seen as precursors of ethical monotheism and a truly spiritual religion that stepped up out of the bloody, messy material religion of the Jewish priesthood) and the so-called Second Commandment and the golden calf. Appropriately enough, the Hebrew prophets looked to the future of religion in matters of ethics. And the destroyed calf and the Second Commandment looked towards the future of religion in spirituality and aesthetics.

For many iconic *modern* thinkers, the shattered calf has signified *positively*. In *The Metaphysics of Morals* Kant offers what sounds like a philosophical commentary on the scene of the golden calf: 'Kneeling or prostrating oneself on the ground, even to express adoration of celestial objects, is contrary to human dignity; as is also the worship of them by images. For then you humble yourself not before an ideal, the handiwork of your reason, but before an idol' (Kant 1964: 436–7). In the *Critique of Judgment* he writes: 'Perhaps there is no sublimer passage in Jewish law than the command "Thou shalt not make to thyself any graven image, nor the likeness of anything which is in heaven or in the earth or under the earth"' (Kant 1951, 78). Terje Stordalen's chapter shows how willingly this Kantian reading of biblical aniconicity was taken up by biblical scholars, as an excuse for avoiding evidence of material religion in the biblical texts (cf. Stordalen, this volume). The destroyed calf and the Second Commandment become an icon of aniconic transcendence and a refusal of crude images for humanity and divinity. The ban on and obliteration of images saves humanity from bowing down in an inappropriate fashion and undermining the human autonomy that true divinity supports. In Kant's reading, the destruction of the golden calf is legitimate, necessary. It is an early sign of the triumph of *Geistigkeit* (abstraction or intellectuality) over sensuality and merely material religion. In this strong modern reading, the hypericon of the golden calf functions rather like the hypericon of the Platonic cave (*Republic* 514a–520a). Both hypericons dramatize revelation as liberation from wrong ways of seeing and emancipation from mistaking the shadow for the Ideal.

The divinely pulverized golden calf points to a transition in the 'moral and religious tone' in which we speak about true divinity in the rarefied atmosphere of self-conscious modernity. As William James provocatively observes, gods die due to changes in the 'mental climate' (James 2002: 264). Gods cannot live outside the atmospheres created by media and mediation. They are also susceptible to sudden or gradual death when those mediaspheres change. The kinds of gods that can no longer breathe in the changed atmosphere and tone of the modern era include the gods who have relied on too 'coarse signs of power' and those who have depended on ritual worship and 'vulgar forms'. As James puts it: 'Ritual worship in general appears to the modern transcendentalist, as well as to the ultra-puritanic type of mind, as if addressed to a deity of the most absurdly childish character, taking delight in toy-shop furniture, tapers and tinsel, costume and mumbling and mummery, and finding his 'glory' incomprehensibly enhanced thereby' (James 2002: 265). Gods caught up in such travesties are quietly forgotten, allowed to die in obscurity, or demonized – or they are actively fought off by tradition's more progressive strands.

Historically, the condemnation of ritual and material religion was inflected as particularly Protestant (and Protestant-secular), and clearly contrasted with the Catholic and the Jewish (Old Testament). Later, in another one of those highly awkward modern compromises, the divisions were patched over and the polemic against material religion and superstition became strangely and awkwardly inclusive. The campaign for truly spiritual religion was now a trademark of 'ethical monotheism' or that awkward amalgam the 'Judeo-Christian', even as the contours of the argument were still firmly defined by its Protestant roots. The calf episode could still be read as a mutiny against Judaism from within the Old Testament. But now it could also be read, conversely, as a shared epiphany of ethical non-material religion that was Judaism's particular gift to the world. The golden calf and the Second Commandment became the summary image of dignified modern religion: a religion of apophasis, negative theology; God-as-ethics; God-beyond-aesthetics; and a fusion of human and divine dignity that was truly 'divine'. For the German Jewish neo-Kantian Hermann Cohen god was the holy one, the 'beyond me', the archetype of human morality. The people's sin became a philosophical category mistake (Cohen 1995). Philosophical-theological aniconicity found its pin-up image in the calf.

At the same time, the destruction of the calf came to function, equally intensely, as an icon of religious, specifically monotheistic, violence, opposed by righteous human resistance. W. J. T. Mitchell provides one of the strongest and most graphic examples of this myth of divine *Bilderverbot* and human defiance. Conflating Eden and the calf as two versions of the same myth, Mitchell argues that God wants exclusive rights over representation and animation of 'the living'. He will not allow humankind to infringe on his exclusive copyright on life, any more than he will give them a permit to eat from the tree of knowledge and the tree of life. As Mitchell puts it, 'When God creates Adam as the first "living image" he knows that he is producing a creature who will be capable of the further creation of new images. This, in fact, is why the notion that the image is alive seems so disturbing and dangerous, and why God, having made Adam in his own image, goes on later to issue a law prohibiting the further creation of images by human hands' (Mitchell 2005: 93). Fearful of having unleashed the power to make an *eikôn* or *homosiosis*, God attempts to put the genie back in the bottle. He prohibits and destroys all works cast by (merely) human hands, making art one of those fundamental distinctions between the human and the divine. According to Mitchell, the destruction of the golden calf is a sign of God asserting *exclusive custody of the secret of life* (Mitchell 2005: 17) and launching a wholesale attack on 'the cult of images, *whatever they represent*' (Cesare Bori 1990: 19; Mitchell 2005: 17, my emphasis).

Mitchell's reading could have found far more biblical support than he realizes. His story of the absolute divine prohibition of life-drawing and life-making fits well with the established pattern in the Genesis myth. The Eden story is an aetiology of human limits. The myth begins by breaching and blurring the line between the human and the divine – and then redraws the line by stressing the limits of merely human life. The line must be drawn somewhere, but where? Where to draw the line between the merely human and the divine? According to Genesis, humans will suffer labour: hard work in unyielding soil and labour pains in childbirth. Humans will die; gods will not. And in Mitchell's supplement, gods will make line drawings and draw lines, and humans will not. In Gen. 3.22, a very anxious and not very monotheistic deity says to his shadowy heavenly companions: 'See, the man has become like one of us, knowing good and evil; and now he might reach out his hand and take also from the tree of life, and eat, and live forever', and the narrator concludes, '*therefore* the Lord God sent him from the garden of Eden'. The human is separated from the God by the boundary guarded by the cherubim: emphatically *not* cute Christmas card baby angels, but winged creatures with a human face and the body of a lion or bull. These bull–human composites, crossing the line between the human and the animal, police the boundary line between the human and divine and prevent all further nibbling from the fruit of the tree of life (Gen. 3.22-4).

Like that iconic text that we call the 'second amendment', the so-called Second Commandment has deeply contested meanings and desires. The Second Commandment is not the second commandment – in fact, not even a separate commandment – for Lutherans and Catholics, Eastern Orthodox churches and Jewish denominations. The Ten Commandments, including the highly disputed 'Second' Commandment, are given twice in Exodus 20 and Deuteronomy 5. As an iconic word against the image, the Second Commandment has completely eclipsed other biblical injunctions against images (e.g. Exod. 20.22-3; Exod. 34.17). Its interpretation is deeply contested. Everything depends on how you translate the word '*pesel*' ('idol'? 'image'? 'graven image'? or simply 'sculpture' or 'statue' as in modern Hebrew?); how you relate the creation of the *pesel* to worship of the *pesel* (is the worshipped image distinct from the image as such?); whether you put the injunction against the *pesel* together with the preceding injunction 'You shall have no other gods'; and whether you relate the prohibition to the next commandment, which follows directly after the prohibition of the *pesel* ('You shall not make wrongful use of the name of the Lord'). Is making a *pesel* equivalent to protecting the name of God? (Neh. 9.18 is already connecting the calf to blasphemy and the salvation/securitization of the divine name.) There are also many ways of playing out the centuries-old tradition of trying to work out the true relationship between God, the human and the image, in the vexed textual vortex between Eden and the golden calf. For example, 450 years before Mitchell, in his *Preface to the Lives of the Most Excellent Painters, Sculptors and Architects* (1550) Giorgio Vasari read Eden and the calf together to present God as the first artist and the first *patron* of human art. In the beginning 'the Most High [...] descended through the limpid air to the solid earth, and by shaping man, disclosed the first form of sculpture and painting'. The deity used earth because he wanted to 'endow [...] man with a bright flesh colour' but also because by using a mere 'clod of earth', the divine artist could '[...] demonstrate [...] in the imperfection of his materials, what could be done to improve them, just as good sculptors and painters are in the habit of doing [...]'. The modelling of the first man is the first art class: the production of 'a living example'. In Vasari's Renaissance hands, the deity's breath-infused human sculpture, Adam, becomes an animated figure to walk alongside – indeed in front of – Aphrodite of Knidos, Ovid's Pygmalion and Daedalus's statues. The work called 'the Man' eclipses the miraculous statues of Daedalus that, according to Plato, had to be nailed down lest they walk away (*Meno* 97d). Though

Vasari is forced to acknowledge the considerable 'fury' of God and Moses (to put it mildly), he anxiously qualifies this violence as a reaction against 'the golden calf *manufactured and adored* by his people'. Mere creation is not just innocent, but actively encouraged. *Adoration* is the sin. Images can be praised, and loved, and can move us deeply, but they should not be worshipped. (But where do we draw the line and how do we tell the difference?) Moreover, the forms used to embody divinity should be appropriately elevated (but again how high is high enough but not too high?). According to Vasari, 'Moses was greatly troubled at seeing divine honours accorded to *the image of a beast*' (my emphasis).

The *modernity* of Mitchell's interpretation is highlighted in stark contrast to Vasari's Renaissance reading. Mitchell turns golden-calf-making into a fundamental human right – a right that has to be asserted against retro violent deities who oppose it. The calf episode becomes a Feuerbachian drama of stealing back the powers that rightly belong to man but have been wrongly projected onto the divine. The calf-pulverizing God becomes the most perfect image of the rogue deity, against whom modernity rightly rebelled, founding its very modernity and secularity on the necessity of this rebellion. Mitchell's calf becomes the pin-up of secular defiance and the birth of modernity – a version of what Talal Asad calls the 'heroic secular' (Asad 2008). Divinity is seen as a force of regulation and management, and jealousy and violence. The biblical God has a Taliban-like attitude to images. He is the divine Salieri to humanity's Mozart. He is the most violent art critic; the most paranoid and damning reviewer of a work of art.

But this divine fury is all for nothing. Images and names will inevitably be taken in vain. God will not get what he wants. God is not omnipotent. He cannot enforce exclusive copyright to life. In this sense, god is not divine. The image is divine. God cannot control the life of images, any more than he can keep Adam and Eve in their 'herbaceous playpen' in Eden (Sawyer 2002: 52). In Mitchell's reading, the rebellious human figure becomes an anthropomorphized figure of the created object that refuses its passive objecthood and goes live. Adam and, especially, Eve have epistemophilia. They cannot but eat from the tree of knowledge. Similarly human beings have a bad case of technephilia, and compulsively go on making art.

Reading against the grain of the biblical text, Mitchell calls us to side with the people, now allegorized as nascent artists and progenitors of freedom who are 'running wild' (Mitchell 2005: 32). Liberalism has always had an anxiety about the demos/crowd and their potentially unruly freedoms. Assertion of the freedom to draw as one pleases, make what one wants or 'blaspheme' against the old gods has become one of the easiest and most comforting ways of affirming our founding freedoms. Freedom is most freely and easily affirmed as 'secular' freedom in contrast to divine/religious control over freedom of expression and art.

The Moh-Duns and living image: Good lamb versus bad calf

Crucial to the *official* epistemology of the tribe that Bruno Latour calls the 'Moh-Duns' (the 'light-skinned peoples living in the northern reaches of the Atlantic', 2001: 1) is 'the ability to extract the subjectivity of the knower from the material contingency of the object and from the physical and corporeal immediacy of the experience of cognition' (Masuzawa 2008: 657), so releasing the human agency that had been bound by 'fetishes' and 'despots' (Keane 2007: 49; cf. Latour 2011). According to Hans Belting, art came into being when the beholders 'seized power over the image', transferring agency from the image to its enlightened, contemplative consumer (Belting 1994; cit. Mitchell 2005: 95). We have already noted how the phantasmatic 'image' seems to mimic divinity in its transcendence of the merely material form. The image now takes up the same role as God in the modern drama of stealing back the powers. The image loses (or divests itself of) exceptional powers and becomes the object of a delicately adjusted aesthetic response (Belting 1994). Appreciation might be gushing, but it can be (perilously) separated from 'worship' by an element of critical distance. The enlightened and emancipated Moh-Dun responds to images with appreciation, rather than worship, and with particular forms of words: criticisms, papers, reviews and gallery guides, rather than chants, blessings and prayers.

But the Moh-Duns have never quite believed this, or believed this consistently. Having never been modern, having been predestined to fail at the impossible work of being modern, the Moh-Duns habitually speak as if 'works of art had minds of their own, as if images had a power to influence human beings, demanding things from us, persuading, seducing, leading us astray [...]' (Mitchell 2005: 7). Like the conflicted biblical texts on idols, they lurch between denouncing images as 'mere nothings' and condemning them 'as all-powerful forces, responsible [for] everything from violence to moral decay' (Mitchell 2005: 77).

The tensions around gods, images and objects have become more acute for self-consciously 'modern' thinkers – which is why the calf has continued to be such a resonant image. The act of thinking so self-consciously about the lines between the person, the thing and the God, and the subject and the object has *compounded* the Moh-Duns' problems with 'materiality' and the powers. 'On the one hand, a mere multiplicity of material representations of spiritual reality amounts to idolatry, a cult of many (false) gods; on the other hand, the equally multiple iconic/symbolic representations of the truly spiritual God do not seem to threaten the unity of that deity. But how do we tell the difference?' asks Tomoko Masuzawa (2008: 653). In order to attempt to tell the difference, the Moh-Duns went wild devising comparative tabulations of religions, which related to complex evolutionary schemes, which in turn were often based on tortuous distinctions between neologisms like 'totemism', 'fetishism' and 'animism', and good and bad relations between gods and objects/things. Key – and highly dubious – criteria for discerning bad signs included tautologous materiality folding back on itself, with absolutely no 'spiritual' surplus; and an inappropriate relationship between the subject and the object, involving the attribution of too much power to the object so that creations came alive and subjugated humans to their powers and demands. Other sure signs of a bad object were *extreme* worship, involving the *waste* of resources, especially human resources and category confusions: failing to distinguish between gods, animals and things. The bad object was the object that (seemed to) exert the kind of insistent wanting that we call a demand or a command, and that compelled obedience even unto death. It was also the object that wrongly mixed divinities and animals and things. But these

Figure 3.2 *Agnus dei*, Francisco de Zurbarán, 1635–40, Madrid, Prado Museum. Wikimedia Commons.

anxious distinctions have always been precarious. There is no firm conceptual ground from which to distinguish the good objects from the bad objects, the sheep from the goats, the wheat from the tares, the lambs from the calves, the 'sacred cow' from the *agnus dei* (Figure 3.2, cf. Figure 3.1a). The only sure way to distinguish between the good lamb and the bad calf is to invoke those other tortuous–simplifying schemas that moderns are so fond of: the ones that map levels of religion and spirit onto philological kinships. The (bad) calf is Egyptian-Jewish Semite; the (good) lamb is Christian-Greek.

For the Moh-Duns, a key summary image for extreme worship was the god Moloch, who became a doppelgänger for the golden calf. This god, who may have been conjured into being through a misreading of Lev. 18.21 (a prohibition against offering children and their blood 'to Moloch'[4]), developed into a figure for all extremely bad objects/idols which brazenly display their badness by feeding on human flesh and blood. Despite the fact that the name relates to the Hebrew word 'king' with no reference to any animal, Moloch has frequently been portrayed as a double of the calf (Figure 3.3).

Freud's divided calf

Even critics like W. J. T. Mitchell, who know (and indeed preach) that moderns have never been modern because they have more faith in 'vital signs' than they like to imagine, still tend to prefer a polarized either–or version of the golden calf (see Meyer in this volume). Either the transcendence of the merely (vulgarly) material is celebrated, as a sign of proto-modernity, or divine violence and prohibition is condemned. The calf is popular because the religious figure provides a kind of comfort or escape from

Figure 3.3 *Der Götze Moloch mit 7 Räumen oder Capellen* (The idol Moloch with seven chambers or chapels), Johann Lund, *Die alten jüdischen Heiligthümer*, p. 504, but attached to p. 639 (reprint 1738 – originally printed in 1704/11).

modernity's paradoxical conflicts and impossible positions. The calf goes both ways, but never both at the same time.

But there is one exception: Freud's strange book *Moses and Monotheism*, or *Der Mann Moses und die monotheistische Religion* (2001, orig. 1939), written at the end of his life, in Vienna and London. Freud's strangely haunting book is remembered for its two shocking theses: (1) Moses and monotheism were both Egyptian in origin – a thesis that came from the recently discovered story of Akhenaten's heretic monotheistic revolution in Egypt; and (2) the Israelites killed Moses. But the book is arguably even more striking for its tortured hypotheses about the relationship between religion (specifically Judaism and Christianity) and materiality: hypotheses conflict around the divided figure of the calf. Rather than reading the divine prohibition on images negatively like Mitchell, or positively like Kant, Freud reads the conflicted figure of the calf as Jewish and Christian, and a convergence of contested desires.

German source critics famously divided the Bible into different textual strands named, for example, 'J' (after Jahve or Yahweh), 'E' (after the 'Elohist') and 'P' (after the Priests). Freud takes his cue from source criticism: but his Bible is simpler. It is simply split between *two* groups of people, *two* religions and '*two conflicting religious impulses*' (2001: 52, 43, my emphasis). This is not really about sources, but about conflicting *impulses*. Like the psyche, the Bible becomes a site of antagonistic conflict between colliding and contested desires. One layer of the Hebrew Bible – let us call it Freud's 'J' source – records the religion of the 'savage semites' who worshipped Yahweh, a 'demonic' narrow-minded local god, imported from Midian (2001: 47). The other – let us call it Freud's 'M', or 'Moses', source – records the 'highly spiritualised' (2001: 47) pure monotheism which was imported to Israel from Egypt by the Egyptian Moses who learnt it from Akhenaten. This 'rigid monotheism on the grand scale' taught that 'there is only one God, he is the sole God, omnipotent, unapproachable; his aspect is more than human eyes can tolerate, no image must be made of him, even his name may not be spoken' (2001: 18).

Freud's point is that both religious impulses are 'alien' (2001: 44) to us, but differently so. The J-Semitic religion is too vulgar and crude. Its God is anthropomorphic and bound to ritual objects – crude artefacts like Moses's bronze serpent. But the other M-religion is too violent in its purity. No one – perhaps, even no God – can live with its austerity, particularly its austerity in relation to material forms. Pure aniconicity is always too much and too little for us. It is also arguably too much for the gods, who simply cannot live without form.

According to Freud's sensationally retold biblical history, it was inevitable that the people would rebel against the Mosaic prohibition on sensation. They did so in no uncertain terms by killing Moses and burying the traces and the corpse. The Mosaic religion of *Geistigkeit* and abstraction was buried under Yahweh religion, in practice and in the textual record. The single clue to all of this – the all-important trace or smoking gun – is the golden calf. The calf, which has always signified erasure and obliteration, now signifies for Freud the obliteration of M-religion, the religion of *Bilderverbot*. The 'people's defection from the new religion is also described in the text – only as an episode, it is true: namely in the story of the golden calf' (2001: 38, 43). Moses was killed and his pure aniconic monotheism was buried in the 'mausoleum' of the text (2001: 62). But ghosts haunt – and this seems to be particularly and uncannily true of ghosts without bodies. Eventually the crudely bodied and violent god Yahweh 'had to pay heavily for his usurpation' (2001: 50). The god without a body and an image returned and defeated him. 'The shadow of the god whose place [Yahweh] had taken became stronger than himself' (2001: 50). In what sounds like a parody of supersession, the shadow was more powerful than the body, and it preceded and exceeded it.[5] Indeed it was this shadow – and the light and energy of this shadow god – that had always mysteriously kept the people alive. The tradition of ethical and *geistig* (intellectual/ spiritual) monotheism was kept alive in the 'great and mighty tradition of the Prophets' and eventually resurfaced as the 'permanent content of the Jewish religion' (2001: 50).

But the supersession of J-religion or M-religion has never been perfectly achieved, says Freud. The two impulses are in permanent tension and rotation. Even as it becomes a manifesto of M-religion and ethical monotheism, Judaism retains the memory of a profound allergy to its central tenet. Judaism is 'alien' (44) to itself in its very purity. This is why it keeps on falling back into circumcision and other crude material rites. *But crucially Judaism is not alone and certainly not iconic in this for Freud.* In 1939, at least eleven years and worlds before the first public uses of the uncomfortable and guilty amalgam of the 'Judeo-Christian', Freud, who wrote *Der Mann Moses* as he was escaping the Anschluss, argued that *Christianity and Judaism were alike because both were uncomfortable amalgams of the two religious impulses and both were similarly split.* Reversing the drama of supersession, he aggressively presented Christianity as a regression – even as in his preface he recorded his former hope in, and then betrayal by, the Austrian Catholic Church:

> In some respects the new religion meant a cultural regression as compared with the older, Jewish one, as regularly happens when a new mass of people, of a lower level, break their way in or are given admission. *The Christian religion did not maintain the high level in things of the mind to which Judaism had soared* [my italics]. It was no longer strictly monotheistic, it took over numerous symbolic rituals from surrounding peoples, it re-established the great mother-goddess and found room to introduce many of the divine figures of polytheism only lightly veiled, though in subordinate positions. Above all, it did not, like the Aten religion and the Mosaic one which followed it, exclude the entry of superstitious, magical and mystical elements, which were to prove a severe inhibition upon the intellectual development of the next two thousand years. (2001: 88)

The first shall be last. The higher shall be lower. And vice versa. Again and again. In Freud's counter-usurpation or inverted supersession, Christianity is also lower than Judaism, and rather more Semitic and primitive than Aryan-Greek.

In Freud's reading, the golden calf becomes a conflicted figure for contested and conflicted religious impulses. Monotheism is presented as violent and intolerant *and* the source of eternal ethics and spiritual, intellectual religion. Aniconic monotheism is modern Europe's foundation – and it is forever 'alien' (2001: 44), ghostly as well as *geistig*. Unlike Kant, who would rather ignore the violence at the level of the crude biblical letter, Freud sees the advocates of pure monotheism, like Moses and Akhenaten, as by definition uncompromising, iconoclastic, destructive, and absolutely authoritarian (even fascistic). And the violent conflict finds its summary image in the (destroyed) calf. Prohibitions against plurality and the image lead to acts of iconoclasm, supersession and contrast: comparative religion with a bloody edge. 'We are purer than them.' And, conversely, 'We are less austere than them, more material, touchable, more incarnate, less removed.' For Christians and Jews, a purely *geistig* monotheism has proved far too difficult. It has been – and could only ever be – partially fulfilled. There is nothing here of the contemporary fantasies of separating good and bad images, good and bad religion, good and bad politics that we find in contemporary government agendas that try to separate the promise and values of religion from the danger. It was arguably quite difficult to entertain such fantasies in the age of Nazi Christianity.

The unstable biblical calf

Mitchell compares the calf to the ambiguity and fluidity of the duck-rabbit (Mitchell 2005: 189). But he doesn't know the half of it. It turns out, unexpectedly, that the duck-rabbit would be a perfect figure for the Exodus version of the calf narrative, which is surprisingly close to Freud. Like Freud, Nolde or Poussin – and unlike Kant or W. J. T. Mitchell – the old biblical myth is ambiguous, turbulent, anxious and resistant to polarization as a statement either for or against the calf. The old words do not share the same anxieties as modern thinkers. But it is as if, in a different register, they are trying to epitomize or anticipate or prophesy all our troubles with materiality and plurality, all our confusion about god, gods and things.

Beyond and above the technical fractures of source criticism, the biblical narratives of the calf are fractured between orthodoxy and heterodoxy, between monotheism and polytheism. They are divided between two 'impulses'. And they dispute the very sources of life. When the people see the calf, they say, 'These are your gods, O Israel, who brought you out of Egypt', or, *in an equally possible reading*, 'This is your god, O Israel, who brought you out of Egypt' (Exod. 32.4). Moses's brother Aaron responds by (a) building an altar before the calf and (b) making the proclamation: 'Tomorrow shall be a festival to the Lord' (Exod. 32.5). The calf seems to be more orthodox than heterodox; more monotheistic than polytheistic (to use anachronistic terminology). The vocabulary deliberately recalls the two golden calves that were erected by Jeroboam, the first king of the northern kingdom of Israel, at the northern shrines of Dan and Bethel, after Israel had split from Judah (1 Kings 25–33). Later overwriters and reinventors of tradition from the southern kingdom saw Jeroboam's innovations as an offence against the centralization of worship in Judah and Jerusalem and ostracized the calves as sin. The prophetic books of Amos and Hosea denounce Bethel (the house of God) as Beth-Aven or Beth-Al, the 'house of wickedness' or the 'house of nothing', and condemn the people for 'kissing calves' (Amos 5.5; Hos. 4.15; 10.5; 13.2). But as archaeological and biblical evidence clearly shows, Yahweh did not always clearly separate, or even desire to separate, himself from the Canaanite deities El and Baal, represented as a bull. Bull-calf terracottas from Bethel and Samaria, a bovine Yahweh and his Asherah from Kuntillet Ajrud, and the figure of a bull on a bronze plaque at Jeroboam's shrine at Tel Dan all suggest that the golden bull at Jeroboam's shrines and Aaron's golden calf may have been traditional and orthodox (cf. Smith 2016: 64–5).

The mass of text that precedes and follows the golden calf, but that is far less shiny and has been largely obliterated from cultural memory, attempts another technique for making the invisible God present: the temple and the tabernacle, the temple's portable, 'camping' form. When Moses goes up the mountain, God gives him six full chapters itemizing an inventory of all the contents of the temple/tabernacle (Exodus 25–31), and then this information is reiterated in Exodus 35–40. The two tablets, written with the very finger of God (Exod. 31.18) are a footnote or an extended colophon in comparison to all the words about the tabernacle, in all its exquisite details, including the frame, the curtains, the vestments, the table, the lampstands, the altar and the oil. The tabernacle is an unfeasibly portable, proleptic temple. The words about the tabernacle are more easily portable. They can be carried for posterity, independently of the temple/tabernacle's material form. The plans include the verbal blueprint for an ark of the covenant with a mercy seat supported by cherubim (like the cherubim that guard the Garden of Eden) modelled on the Assyrian–Babylonian human-headed winged bulls, the *lamassus* or *shedus*. The people willingly give all their gold earrings to make the calf – and then they do the same for the temple, which contains the bull-calves or cherubim. After the calf debacle, Moses commands the people: 'Whoever is of a generous heart bring the Lord's offering: gold, silver, and bronze; blue, purple and crimson yarns and fine linen: goats' hair, tanned rams' skins and fine leather; acacia wood; oil for the light, spices for the anointing oil and for the fragrant incense, and onyx stones and gems to be set in the ephod and the breastplate [...]' (Exod. 35.4-9) – and this is just the beginning of the list. The temple and tabernacle seem to be designed, by God, as vast grids to convert the dangerous force of art into labour: work that is productive and directed to a clear, single referential object that is not only constantly referred to, but worshipped, for worship as intensified reference is what temples and tabernacles demand. Moses makes an altar call; a call, quite literally, for the materials to make the altar. Exod. 35.4-19 reads like an extravagant wish list for a funding campaign. The result is that 'everyone whose heart was stirred' or 'everyone whose spirit was willing' brought 'brooches and earrings and signets and pendants; all sorts of gold objects' (Exod. 35.22), including the gold from Egypt. The people bring more gold than they ever brought for the calf. And/but not everyone comes, but only those who have a willing heart. We can sense the mimetic rivalry, the anxiety and the traces of competition and dissent. The reference to 'those that were willing' implies those that were unwilling. The massive inventory of precious stones and metals, fabrics, yarns, skins, oils, spices, leathers and costly woods anxiously announces: 'We will crush that calf to little pieces. Our temple will be more glorious and more extravagant than the calf (and/but it will contain bull-calves).'

The calf is destroyed – and the bull/calf returns and remains as an orthodox prop and support for the temple – in the same composite text. And the calf is and is not *cheiropoeitos*, made by human hands. Aaron makes it, and the calf makes itself. The first textual casting of what happened states: 'He [Aaron] took the gold from them, formed it in a mold [alternatively "cast it with a graving tool"] and cast an image of a calf; and they said "These are your gods/This is your god who brought you out of Egypt"' (Exod. 32.4). When Aaron stands accused, he re-casts the story of creation as the story of autogeneration in which the calf is *acheiropoeitos* – not made by human hands. He now says to Moses: 'I said to them, "Whoever has gold, take it off" so they gave it to me, and I threw it into the fire, and out came this calf!' (Exod. 32.34). 'The calf made itself.' In *The Worship of the Golden Calf* by a follower of Filippino Lippi

Figure 3.4 *The Worship of the Golden Calf* by a follower of Filippino Lippi (1457–1504), National Gallery, London.

(1457–1504), the calf not only lives, but miraculously boings and bounces across the skies (Figure 3.4).

Uncomfortable with the uneasy biblical balance between the calf as automaton and the calf as a work of human manufacture, the Qur'an pushes the calf firmly into the realm of human making and deception (just as Deuteronomy anxiously buries, in subclauses, the making of the calf). Only the tiniest hint of the true supernatural remains. The calf is allegedly made from the dust trodden on by the angel Gabriel, so perhaps it contains a few particles of the right kind of divine magic. But for the most part, it is a work of human hands. The maker of the calf is not Aaron (Harun) but a man of unknown (foreign?) origin, called Samiri. He makes a hollow statue of a calf and, as the wind blows through it, it seems to make a lowing sound, which manages to convince the credulous people that it is alive (Q 20.88). The deception uncannily anticipates those modern gestures of disenchantment that claimed that miracles and movement were special effects produced by 'frauds' of 'Glasses, Speaking Trumpets, Ventriloquies, Echoes, Phosphorus, Magick Lanterns' and machines (Trenchard 1709; cit. Schmidt: 93). In the Qur'an, the calf episode becomes a neater tale of idolatry or shirk (شرك), and the graciousness of Allah. 'Did they not see that it could not return to them any speech and that it did not possess for them any harm or benefit?' (Q 20.89). The people repent and are spared the biblical bloodbath. Most importantly, the calf has no (or hardly any) *real* life in it.

The biblical account is far more ambiguous about animation and the sources of life. Just as the calf has become a meeting point for foundation myths that must be kept apart (serving as an emblem of divine violence and bad religion; and an emblem of good, higher religion, above crude images) so it troubles moderns by embodying the paradox of *le fait*, which means both 'what nobody has fabricated' and 'what somebody has fabricated': the manufactured thing (Latour 2011). In Latour's terms, the calf is a fact object *and* a fairy object. It really is, and its life is nothing but our projection. It is a 'thing', with all the ambiguities of the 'thing', and its mysterious occluded powers. As David Morgan astutely points out,

> In many languages, the pronoun for a thing is an 'it'. An it, or id [the It, *das Es*], signifies some entity other than I, or ego. It often operates grammatically in the passive voice in order to signal, and at the same time also conceal, agency. 'It was said that you committed the deed'. As an 'it', a thing dwells in obscurity [...] thingness refers to an identity and precise agency that remains hidden. (Morgan 2015: 255)

The amorphous raw material, the nameless thing, the object-in-waiting, becomes a calf – a discernable object that we can name. But the calf retains its thingness. What is it? It is said that Aaron made it, and it is said that it made itself. Which is worse? Or to put it another way, which is the best way to terrify those who attribute powers to false gods and objects? Should we say: 'You made it and therefore it cannot be god' (the way of demystification)? Or should we say: 'Beware of it, beware of its very real powers over you'? Are false gods nothing, impotent, mere objects – in which case why do we trouble ourselves about them? Why are there so many passages in the Bible that reduce the idol to something like the modern category of the 'fetish', 'materiality at its crudest and lowest' (cf. Masuzawa 2008: 657) and protest (too much) that the other gods are really nothing but lumps of wood or stone (e.g. Isa. 44.9-20; cf. *Genesis Rabbah* 38)? And why is the biblical discourse on idols so 'astonishing[ly] fluid' (Halbertal and Margolit 1988: 250)? The Hebrew term translated as idolatry is *avodah zarah* ('strange worship'). But the point at which worship becomes 'strange' is contested – as is the question of whether this desire for strange worship comes from outside, from foreign influence, or from inside (even from Yahweh's own command). In this composite syncretistic tradition, it is impossible to pinpoint the exact point at which *latria* (worship) becomes *idolatria*. Denunciations of the merely material and affirmations of the real life of the religious object/god sometimes coincide. The first-century apocryphal text, the Wisdom of Solomon, awkwardly combines the solid thump of polemic (idols are nothing, vain illusions) with premonitions of later theories of the complex sources for idolatry in the ancient equivalent of psychology, sociology, politics, statecraft and art. Idols are created (or create themselves) from our desire for beauty, from our grief and mourning, and from realpolitik (the need to disseminate physical figures of the king). Idols are not mere lumps of wood and stone. On the contrary, they are symbols and indices of deities and desires – including the desire for beauty and the desire to commemorate and immortalize. Instead of functioning as empty material forms, idols are full of signification and significance, and, even in the pre-secular world of the Bible, 'the gods' are already only the half of it.

The Hebrew Bible regularly relates the making and worshipping of other gods to 'harlotry': the strongest possible metaphor or more-than-metaphor for the seductive–demonic power of art. Making gods and physical forms is as compulsive as sex and as resistant to prohibition. The people are frantic to create images. They just cannot stop doing it. Like sex, the act is addictive and (re)productive. The intense desire of art finds its iconic expression in the calf. As with prohibited ('adulterous' or 'harlotrous') sex, it is the other gods that hold the passion/temptation of art. According to the Bible's own witness, the true God seems to be the one who *lacks* these special powers. The invisible God labours to make himself present in the massive edifices of temples (or tabernacles); in a people; in his own partly materialized body; in the Torah (cf. Scarry 1985) – and in destructive acts of iconoclasm against other gods. (He *is* because he was able to make them as if they were not.) But the books of the Prophets are full of passages declaring how much more sensational and desirable the other gods (like Baal or the Queen of Heaven) were, by contrast. Only those who are 'willing' donate to the temple (Exod. 35.22), whereas everyone pitches their gold into the calf. God's preferred forms of presencing (like writing, or the temple) are often portrayed as very labour intensive and precarious. They take so much effort to make/inscribe, and they are regularly destroyed or lost. It is good that the temple is archived in words in scripture, because those same scriptures speak at length about the destruction of the first and second temples. Texts like Jeremiah 36 and 2 Kings 22–3 agonize over lost and burnt scriptures. Condemned to die outside the promised land, Moses sends a piece of writing to go with the Israelites and help them remember, but the recorded oral song foretells the forgetting of the Exodus story and the betrayal of Yahweh by 'making him jealous with strange gods' (Deut. 32.16). Words are not only curiously material. They are often strangely weak. At times, the Bible seems uncannily close to post-Christian times as it presents its own words as a monument to forgetting – an artefact that stands unread.

The 'regimes of sensation' (cf. Stordalen in this volume) in the biblical archive are far more complex than we remember. Even for gods, transcending the body and material form is hardly an easy task. There are many strangely conflicted passages in the Bible that deserve re-reading as a witness to the tortured positions taken on and by God's body and the materialization of divinity. Stordalen gives us a brilliant re-reading of the deuteronomistic temple: the house of God where God is and is not at home; or is at home as trace, name, the material record of the point of contact. At the centre is the empty seat above the ark, the box of sacred things, including the 'petrified fingerprint of the deity'; the tablet as a record of the point of touch. Though the regimes of sensation in the book of Exodus are not the same, the golden calf is god, and is and is not alive. And the calf episode is followed, almost immediately, by a passage about God's passing by which dramatizes, with perfect awkwardness, the Bible's literally shifting position on imaging the divine. In Exod. 33.18-23, God tells Moses that he cannot see his face, but only glimpse his back as he 'covers [him] with [his] hand until he has passed by' (Exod. 33.22). The profoundly awkward portrayal of God's figure can be read as a figure of the intersection of two fundamentally incommensurable biblical positions on images. On one hand – that is, according to the tradition that can show God's hand – the biblical tradition is radically and shockingly anthropomorphic. God clearly has a body, and has had one long before the over-exaggerated newness of the divine incarnation in Christ. But God uses his body parts (his back and hands) to *conceal his body* in faithfulness to the opposing tradition: the prohibition against visualizing the divine. Try to imitate the position of God's body at home, using your own human body and a willing friend or family member. Try to put your hands in front of someone else's face, pass them, then show yourself from the back, without your face being seen. It would be easier for Francis Bacon to paint this split and contorted figure, than for us to copy it. The impossibly contorted position taken up by God's body can be seen as an agonized figure of conflicting traditions of figuring the divine. Like the empty seat above the petrified fingerprint, God's contorted 'body' in Exodus 33 is an iconic figure of contested figuration. Like the calf, it is a shattered and eternally enduring presence–absence; a figure of temptation–prohibition; and a profoundly conflicted answer to the question of materializing the divine.

4

Idolatry beyond the Second Commandment: Conflicting Figurations and Sensations of the Unseen[1]

Birgit Meyer

The production and use of images in the Abrahamic traditions is usually debated against a backdrop of aniconism and the interdiction of representational images of the divine as the normative default. Although these monotheistic traditions grapple with the legitimacy of images in manifold ways, it is problematic to take this as the backdrop for scholarly research. Focusing on figurations and sensations of the unseen, this volume aims to broaden the scope of scholarly inquiry towards a wider set of practices through which humans mediate the unseen. While many contributions explore negotiations of the making, value, use and legitimacy of images *within* Judaism, Christianity or Islam, this chapter calls attention to the *margins* of Christianity, where 'idolatry' charges arise with regard to the cult objects and images in indigenous religious traditions. Charges of idolatry, of course, do not necessarily indicate a clash between aniconism and the worship of things framed as 'idols'. Rather, such charges involve conflicting ways to figure and sense the unseen. Throughout the history of Christianity, non-Christian cult objects have been – and still are – dismissed and renamed as idols, and their worship as false. Across the world, Catholic and Protestant missionaries legitimized the iconoclastic acts with regard to indigenous religious traditions by referring to the biblical interdiction to make and worship idols (most prominent being Exod. 20.4-6; Deut. 5.8-10).

As a compound of the classical Greek terms *eídōlon* (image, in the sense of phantom) and *latreía* (worship), the term idolatry refers to the worship of idols. The scandal to which the dismissive term idolatry refers is the worship of a god or gods, whereas God is the one and only to be worshipped – and not through an image. The question whether and how images can play a role in the Christian tradition has been hotly debated and has yielded a distinction between idolatry and iconoduly. As a compound of *eikôn* (image, in the sense of a figure or portrait) and *douleia* (service), it signifies the veneration of images. Of course, the qualification of an image as icon or idol depends on the perspective of beholders, and their visual regimes. Idolatry became a resilient generic term to acknowledge and dismiss indigenous worship practices, reframing them in the context of a conventional exegesis of the Old Testament, according to which the God of Israel furiously called for the destruction of the gods of neighbouring peoples and punished his people for making idols such as the golden calf (Sherwood 2014). Rejections of such things as idols are inextricably linked with biblical interdictions to make and use images – often referred to in the shorthand of the Second Commandment. However, as I will argue in this chapter, it would be reductive to take this commandment as a frame for analysing the clashing figurations of the unseen that are covered – and even covered up – by the term idolatry.

Through my research on nineteenth- and early-twentieth-century Protestant missionaries of the Norddeutsche Missionsgesellschaft (NMG) among the Ewe in today's Ghana and Togo, I found that the missionaries associated non-Christian practices of worship with idolatry, fetishism and the devil, the master of deception and sensuality. Taken up by African converts, the repercussions of this iconoclastic preaching are still felt today in Southern Ghana, where human-made sculptures, masks and objects used in religious devotion, and the spectre of idolatry and fetishism hovering around them, are still rigorously and zealously debated. Pentecostals, in particular, dismiss such material forms as idols and even contest their value as cultural heritage. As the focus of my historical and ethnographic research over the past twenty-five years, this frontier area of European imperial outreach offered me a critical vantage point to rethink key concepts and approaches in the study of religion from a material angle. Gradually I recognized – also in my own work – a Protestant-Calvinist inclination to privilege 'inner' mental processes of meaning making, while the 'outward' forms (images and objects included) and practices through which meaning was established and performed were secondary.[2] Here I do not aim to give a detailed historical analysis of actual encounters between missionaries and indigenous populations around charges of idolatry and the destruction of so-called idols in Southern Ghana (for this see Meyer 1999, 2010). Instead I take this setting as a suitable horizon for reappraising the role of images – and cult objects in general – and the complexities regarding the figuration and sensation of the unseen in the study of religion and culture from a position 'beyond the Second Commandment'.

Scholars studying religion limit their analytical options if they take biblical passages conveying interdictions with regard to the making of images at face value, as if these references would prove the aniconic nature of Christianity – and for that matter Judaism – as a norm and explain, or even legitimize, its stance against idolatry. Although religious studies scholars tend to emphasize their distance from Christian theology, arguably the study of religion has long been indebted to a post-Enlightenment Protestant legacy, which shows in the tendency to privilege text and word above images and other religious media (see also Uehlinger in this volume; Asad 1993). Even historically and theologically, the normativity of aniconism in Christianity is questionable. Yet the legacy of Calvinism, which fully realizes and mandates this assumption, has infused much of the modern, secular study of religion. This limits conceptual approaches in analysing the modes of imagining and imaging the unseen. A full conceptual appraisal of images and figurations of the unseen and of the relation between religion and art in the framework of religious studies is still to be developed (e.g. Mohn 2013),[3] and this volume is part of that endeavour.

The need to reappraise images from a position beyond the normativity of the Second Commandment emerges against the lingering legacy of this Calvinist attitude towards images. This attitude became engrained not only with text-centred scholarly presuppositions in the study of religion, but also with mainstream understandings of modern society as shaped through the disenchantment of the world and the iconoclastic attitude towards cult images famously attributed to Calvinist reformers by Max Weber. The historiography of this legacy engaged in this chapter enables movement beyond its restrictions. An alternative conceptual approach to religion and images acknowledges the constitutive, world-making role of pictorial media and the visual regimes in which they operate, shaping lived experience in the midst of competing and contested processes of figuration and the triggering of sensations. The rejection of (certain) images on the part of believers and theologians indicates a particular *visual regime* – that is, embodied, habitual practices of looking, displaying and figuring. Visual regimes involve specific, restrictive attitudes and practices towards the use and value of images. Restrictions on the use of images in representing the divine – and the demonic – can best be analysed in the context of clashes and contestations over different, co-existing figurations and sensations of the unseen in historically situated power constellations. Doing so requires a broad framework distinguishing the stances of various religious visual regimes to images, ranging from outright interdiction (*Bilderverbot*), to disinterest, to their positive appreciation as harbingers of divinity (see also Jakiša and Treml 2007: 42). Also, it has to be taken into account that restrictions with regard to physical images are not necessarily extended to inner, mental images in believers' imagination.

This chapter has three parts. Seeking to move towards a standpoint 'beyond the Second Commandment', in the first part I critique Bruno Latour's emphasis on the Calvinist interpretation of this commandment, echoed in the work of W. J. T. Mitchell. Latour's neglect of alternative visual regimes narrows modernity to a field continuously trespassing the Second Commandment which triggers acts of iconoclash. If his work is helpful to grasp the energy invested in the destruction of images, art history engages the constructive negotiation of images for religious purposes. The second part turns to the German strand of art history known as *Bildwissenschaft*, which, I argue, offers stimulating insights into alternative takes on images and the theologies and contested desires in which they are embedded. These insights are also helpful to develop an understanding of how religion generates a sense of presence through images and, by implication, other material forms. Taking these Europe-grounded approaches as a point of departure for the study of an export of the notion of idolatry by NMG missionaries to West Africa, the third part addresses clashing figurations of the unseen. It shows how the indigenous deities recast as Christian idols and dismissed as demonic continuously require to be pictured.

Latour and the Second Commandment

Different Christian traditions number the Decalogue differently. Some do not even recognize the Second Commandment as a separate commandment (see Sherwood in this volume).⁴ Far from incidental, the enshrinement of the interdiction against carved images as a separate commandment laid the groundwork for anti-Catholic fervour and extensive iconoclastic destruction in sixteenth-century Germany, Switzerland, England and the Netherlands. Insisting on a sharp division between matter and spirit, iconoclasts regarded paintings and sculptures (or carved images) as unsuited to represent and convey a sense of the divine (van Asselt 2007). At stake are complicated theological questions concerning the representability and, by implication, accessibility of the divine; the status and value of matter and of the gendered body as suitable harbingers of divine presence; and the role of humans in this process (see Brunotte 2013). As pointed out by David Morgan, a major disagreement between Protestants and Catholics concerned divergent understandings of 'the shape of the holy' and the related authorized manners in accessing the power of the sacred (Morgan 2015: 16–23).

The predominance of aniconism in Christian Old Testament theology has been challenged and deconstructed since the 1970s, when the rise of iconographic approaches to the Hebrew Bible literature went hand in hand with a rehabilitation of religious history as a study field. This was an important move in disentangling normative theological claims about the meaning of the Second Commandment from actual practices with regard to carved images in ancient Hebrew culture (see Uehlinger in this volume). As Stordalen argues in his contribution, the idea of a necessary aniconism may even prove to be a projection of modernist, logocentric readings of the Old Testament sources back onto biblical Hebrew theology, rather than a genuine reflection thereof (see also Sherwood in this volume). Similarly, scholars of Christian visual culture have refuted stereotypical ideas of Protestantism – even its strictest versions – as aniconic, pointing out that Reformed Christianity assigned a role to and reformed images (e.g. Koerner 2004; Morgan 1998, 2015; Promey 2011). Nonetheless, these normative claims have a life of their own and were periodically actualized in the context of clashes around the legitimacy of visual, material means in re-presenting God. And they are still lingering on, most blatantly in current Pentecostal theologies that fiercely dismiss idolatry, which is held to thrive in Catholicism and indigenous cults alike (also in Ghana where Pentecostalism is highly prominent).

Intriguingly, the Second Commandment is also a favoured point of reference for scholars outside of theology and Christianity who are interested in the complexities of human–image relations in modern societies, such as Bruno Latour. Latour made me think about human–image and human–object relations in new ways, freed from fixed and purifying asymmetries that distinguish modern Westerners from their primitive Others (Meyer 2012: 21–3). I agree with him that contemporary modern society is inflected with stances and attitudes towards images from the religious past, including aniconism and iconoclastic attitudes. And I value his introduction of the notion 'iconoclash' to designate a stance on the part of idol smashers to affirm the existence and power of idols in the act of destruction.

Yet his invocation of the Second Commandment comes with its own problems. In his influential introduction to the *Iconoclash* volume and exhibition at the Zentrum für Kunst und Medien (ZKM) in Karlsruhe (2002), Latour sketches a scenario in which reality and fabrication are fundamentally opposed. Obviously, it is directly indebted to biblical prophetic parodies on how idols are produced and therefore cannot be gods.

At stake is the 'digging for the origin of an absolute – not a relative – distinction between a pure world, absolutely emptied of human-made intermediaries and a disgusting world composed of impure but fascinating human-made mediators' (2002: 14). This problematic, modern distinction, he claims, cuts across the spheres of religion, art and science. In this crazy scenario, images feature as the return of the repressed; against all iconoclastic impulses they appear to be unavoidable and necessary – epitomes of contested desires that are prone to be made and destroyed over and over again. Behind the human struggle against – as well as with – images stands a larger project to grasp an objective reality presumably untainted by human mediations. Latour wants to solve the deadlock produced by the modern opposition between the real and the fabricated in science, art and religion with a plea to acknowledge mediation, and hence the capacity of the human hand to make reality, to create a world, to fabricate the divine. Though I very much agree with this larger point (and endorse an understanding of religion as a practice of mediation, Meyer 2012, see below), I nonetheless find problematic the overall scenario sketched by him, which revolves around the Second Commandment. He asks:

> Are we sure we have understood it correctly? Have we not made a long and terrifying mistake about its meaning? How can we reconcile this request for a totally aniconic society, religion and science with the fabulous proliferation of images that characterizes our media-filled cultures? (2002: 18)

Obviously, this 'we' *includes* those who maintain a rigid position associated with the Reformed tradition that counts the commandment as the second (in itself an index of a modern interpretation). It *excludes* those who have long acknowledged the impossibility of obeying the commandment in full or insisted on alternative interpretations; who developed sophisticated theologies of images as mediating the divine through which it becomes possible to maintain icons and still reject idolatry (in the Orthodox traditions, see Luehrmann and Kreinath in this volume); or who at least condoned the use of images for didactic or celebratory purposes (as, for instance, the Roman Catholic and Lutheran traditions). His statement that art historians and theologians 'know' that 'many sacred icons that have been celebrated and worshipped are called *acheiropoieta*; that is *not* made by any human hand' is correct. However, it reduces the spectrum of possibilities in making the divine present to the case of the *acheiropoieta*, which is one among others. As the next section will show, art historians *also know* that painters negotiate the possibility to represent the divine via paintings. Latour's claim that for 'religion in general' the idea 'to *add the hand* to the pictures is tantamount to spoiling them, criticizing them' (2002: 16, italics in original) cannot be maintained. Outside of the Reformed tradition, there is abundant evidence of sophisticated theologies of the image – and mediation in a broader sense – that develop models for how to think and sense divine presence through certain figural forms, whether they proclaim a likeness with the divine or only allude to it indirectly (see below). Tremendous energy went into keeping open the possibility to make and use images, notwithstanding strict interpretations of the Second Commandment and the spectre of idolatry. A more inclusive 'we' would have brought all these co-existing traditions of mediating the divine – including Catholic, Orthodox and Lutheran traditions – into the picture, showing that iconoclastic and iconodule stances and acts have always coexisted, even in modernity.

An interpretation of the commandment as 'a request for a totally aniconic society' – which Latour presumes as the dominant meaning – is only one possible interpretation. Of course, certain religious protagonists legitimize(d) their iconoclastic acts through iconophobic interpretations (though rarely advocating full aniconicity), as did foundational Enlightenment philosophers following Kant who regarded the *Bilderverbot* as the ultimate sublime passage in the Torah (see also Bukdahl in this volume).[5] Yet Latour reaffirms this position as universal. Asking whether 'we' understood it correctly or not, he echoes stereotypical views of the role of images and objects in Christianity and Judaism that ignore the nuanced analysis as developed in biblical scholarship since the 1970s, let alone acknowledge the complex aesthetic practices with regard to images in the context of which the Second Commandment arose (see the chapters by Uehlinger, Stordalen, Sherwood in this volume). The commandment has all too often been invoked by scholars to support 'the myth of aniconism', which should, however, not be taken at face value with regard to the Abrahamic traditions (Freedberg 1989: 54–81) but rather be deconstructed.

In Latour's plot, according to which the Second Commandment calls for an aniconism that is impossible to be maintained, humans face a maddening double bind:

> Human hands cannot stop toiling, producing images, pictures, inscriptions of all sorts, to still generate, welcome, or collect objectivity, beauty, and divinities, exactly as in the – now forbidden – repressed, obliterated old days. How could one not become a fanatic since gods, truths and sanctity have to be made and there is no longer any legitimate way of making them? (2002: 22)

Here he alludes to a happy past – prior to the Reformation and the rise of modernity, or even a past before the rise of monotheist Judaism – preceding the interdiction of image production. But in the aftermath of Mosaic law, the instigation of the Second Commandment has triggered a fanatic attitude which yields an iconoclash, understood by Latour as an aggressive energy with regard to images, unleashing 'an action for which there is no way to know, without further inquiry, whether it is destructive or constructive' (2002: 14). And so, in his reading,

> the second commandment is all the more terrifying since there is no way to obey it. The only thing you can do to pretend you observe it is to *deny* the work of your own hands, to *repress* the action ever present in the making, fabrication, construction, and production of images, to *erase* the writing at the same time you are writing it, to *slap* your hands at the same time they are manufacturing. And with no hand, what will you do? With no image, to what truth will you have access? With no instrument, what science will instruct you? (2002: 23, italics in the original)

Latour, in venturing an interpretation that is cruder than the strictest Reformed theology, overlooks the complex debates and theologies about the relations between humans, God and images in the various Christian traditions that developed alternative interpretations of biblical passages about image restrictions. Seeking to critique mainstream understandings of the modern, Latour vests his interpretation of the commandment with an exaggerated authority that reaches even beyond the sphere of (Reformed) Christianity. His idea that the Second Commandment would prohibit any human fabrication – not just images in the common sense[6] – in the framework of religion and in society in general is misguided. Paradoxically, this idea affirms the modern drive towards purification that Latour relentlessly wished to critique. A less rhetorically charged position would immediately open up alternative interpretations and possibilities in the Christian archive, as 'we have never been' under the sway of the Second Commandment in the strict sense just as 'we have never been modern'.

A similar critique can be made with regard to W. J. T. Mitchell, who refers to the Second Commandment throughout his book *What Do Pictures Want?* (2005). He regards it as

> not some minor prohibition. It is the absolutely foundational commandment; the one that marks the boundary between the faithful and the pagans, the chosen people and the gentiles. Its violation (which seems all but inevitable) is the occasion for terrible punishment, as the episode of the golden calf suggests. (2005: 246)

Over and over he stresses the authoritativeness of the interdiction to 'make an image of anything' (2005: 133). Like Latour, he states that this commandment 'has never been well understood, and certainly never obeyed literally'. And yet he claims that the Abrahamic God takes it more seriously than all the other commandments, even as more important than the interdiction to kill (2005: 133). While he grants that it is 'an impossible commandment' that has never been, and can never be, followed 'literally', he is struck by the fact that there are commentators (he refers to our contributor, the late Kalman Bland, explicitly) who, in arguing against claims of a presumed aniconicity of the Abrahamic traditions, chose to 'ignore the literal meaning completely' (2005: n23). To me, it is quite puzzling that Mitchell insists so strongly on a 'literal' (as he understands it) reading of Exod. 20.4 in order to underpin his plea for humans to move against it and reclaim from God their capacity to make pictures. As argued by Sherwood (in this volume), Mitchell's is in fact a typically modern reading that founds modernity and secularity in the human rebellion against the interdiction to make images. So while Latour sees modernity as caught up in a double bind of image making and image rejection, for Mitchell modernity offers the possibility to be liberated from the sway of the Second Commandment. Notwithstanding these differences, both share a rather narrow, ultra-Calvinist reading of this commandment that staggers their critical project.

If we agree that 'we have never been modern', it is time to fully take into account that the break assumed between modernity and the medieval world is not as rigorous as assumed, just as the difference between modern Europe and the non-Western world cannot be mapped on a narrative of Western superiority that legitimated imperialism. In order to develop more subtle approaches for the study of the role of images with regard to the unseen, sustained interdisciplinary inquiries are necessary. Trained in anthropology and religious studies, I find it productive to engage with critical scholarship in Old Testament theology and art history. Taking into account the expertise of the former in the context of this book project triggered my critical reading of Latour and Mitchell. In the next part, I focus on debates about the use of images and theologies of mediation in the Christian tradition as they have been traced, in particular, in the German strand of art history called *Bildwissenschaft*. Doing so unpacks multiple genealogies of modernity and attitudes to images outside the Calvinist legacy. It thus opens the full archive of the Christian traditions and their multiple attitudes to images.

Images as media of the unseen

Gottfried Boehm, one of the architects of *Bildwissenschaft*, states explicitly that he does not explore the interdiction of making carved images in the narrative of the golden calf with the aim to trace the *origin* of image wars from the Byzantine struggles to the Reformation and modern political forms of iconoclasm (1994: 329, see also 1997). Like Latour and Mitchell, he proposes a modern reading of this interdiction. But rather than taking it as the Mosaic origin calling for a radical aniconism that still echoes in modern societies, Boehm investigates it as a resource to gain philosophical insights into the nature of images and their power. Situating the narrative of the golden calf in relation to the idea of God-likeness of humans (Gen. 1.26-7), according to which the latter are an image of God, he argues that the main point of the Second Commandment is that the analogy between humans and God is not reciprocal: humans are images of God, the first image maker and artist, but they should not depict Him in a visual form. From whence does this interdiction emanate? Boehm argues that it is due to the capacity of the image 'to render present an impalpable and distant being, to vest it with a presence that is able to fill the sphere of human attention entirely. The image owes its vigour to its capacity to convey a similarity, it generates a sameness with the represented' (Boehm 1997: 330, translation mine).[7] In Boehm's reading, the so-called *Bilderverbot* recognizes this capacity, which he regards as the very reason for the interdiction for humans to make images of God.[8] Boehm acknowledges that there is need for a historical investigation of the concrete theologies developed by the enemies and friends of images. While I have reservations regarding his ahistorical approach to the *Bilderverbot*, I regard the fact that he takes this interdiction as a starting point for understanding *what an image is* as a productive starting point.

Boehm conceptualizes the image not as a static form, but as a tangible outcome of a process of *Gestaltwerdung* (taking shape, formation) through which the likeness of a representation (*Darstellung*) with what it represents (*das Dargestellte*) is constituted. Evoking likeness involves a continuous balancing between the image and its referent. As long as a distinction can be maintained between the image as a representation and its referent, there is 'iconic difference'. But in conveying a likeness with something, images have the potential to *become* what they represent and thus to *make* reality – hence their perceived power and danger. When the 'iconic difference' between representation and reality is dissolved, they cease to be images. Becoming real, the image destroys itself, as it were, through an inner iconoclasm. So according to Boehm's philosophical analysis of the *Bilderverbot*, the image, by its very nature, contains an iconoclastic potential from within. His understanding of the image as continuously balancing between its intrinsic iconic and iconoclastic dimensions is important for my purposes. Acknowledging an intrinsic iconoclasm as part of the reality-making potential of images means acknowledging the power of images to become what they depict, to render present something which is not there – including a presumed unseen divine sphere.

Pursuing Boehm's idea, it could be argued that the loss of a discrepancy between an image and its referent is what defines an idol. This raises the question of how and under what circumstances an image may become an idol – and for whom. Obviously, in many religious and secular settings, images are experienced to become real, in the sense that the mediating nature of the image is overlooked in favour of its referent. A qualification of an image as idol refers to an incapacity to observe a difference between a representation and its referent. Still it remains to be seen – and this has to be subject to detailed scrutiny – whether what outsiders see as an idol to be smashed would at all be understood as such by its users. Idols are always a figment of accusation. It is likely that those destroying an image in an iconoclastic act actually produce it as idol – echoing the logic of 'iconoclash' coined by Latour – whereas its users may be aware of the iconic difference that defines an image according to Boehm, and develop attitudes and theologies that mediate divine presence and yet retain that difference.

While I find Boehm's approach to the image insightful and stimulating, as an anthropologist studying religion my interest is not with the image as such. Nor do I share his generalizing take on images, which appear to be situated outside of actual social configurations. My basic premise is that human relations to images are constituted in the framework of specific, socially situated *visual regimes*, including those offered by religious traditions across time and space. What images should and should not depict, whether they are regarded as making real what they represent, whether they are venerated, worshipped or taken as illustrations, how they are valued, which sensations and emotions they arouse, how and where and for which purposes they are produced and reproduced, and why they are broken, are questions that must be subject to detailed investigation. To pursue such investigations, art historical work has much to offer for the contemporary study of religion, which still struggles to find a more adequate and productive conceptual access to images 'beyond the Second Commandment'. A particularly useful resource are studies of images before 'the era of art' (Belting 1990), that is, the modern era that entailed the compartmentalization of religion and art in separate domains, the rise of the museum and the emergence of art history and the study of religion as separate disciplines. Many images analysed by art historians working on ancient and medieval Europe had the status of cult images. Work on these images can be an inspiring resource for scholars in religious studies who are interested to move beyond a predominantly textual orientation of the discipline and to flesh out an approach to images as prime media of religion, next to and intersecting with objects, bodies, sounds and texts (Meyer 2012).

In *Bild und Kult* Hans Belting offers a detailed analysis of the rise of the cult image in sixth-century Christianity (1990: 101–30, 164–84). In my view, this point in time may prove to be a more apt starting point for understanding the valuation of the image in Christianity than a turn to ancient Hebrew religion, or a conjuring of the Second Commandment as a timeless law. The 'theologies' around the image that were developed especially in the debates unleashed by the Byzantine image war by John of Damascus and others (1990: 170–84, 559–61) could not be grounded in an existing apology of images as a religious medium in the Christian tradition; a theological appraisal of the image had to be authorized against the backdrop of the recognition of Christ as the sole revelation of God through whom the word became flesh (in the sense of incarnation, see Kruse in this volume). In a detailed analysis Belting traces how the icon was constituted as conveying the presence of God – a view that was always haunted by the fear or suspicion that it might be seen as a substitute of God and thus slip into an idol. His book tracks subsequent theologies of cult images and the contestations generated by them, including the debates around the 'true portrait' of Christ (the iconic print of his face in the cloth offered to him on his way to the cross by Veronica, see also Kruse 2003: 269–306), the use of relics, the role of altar images in evoking the divine, the emergence of private devotional images (*Andachtsbilder*) up to charges of idolatry in the context of the Reformation and the subsequent Catholic responses to these critiques.

Inspired by Belting's approach, Christiane Kruse (2003) offers a fascinating exploration of the negotiation of the potential and limits of painting by artists, scholars and theologians from the Middle Ages up to the baroque. The human imagination was regarded as indispensable to picture in the mind, through mental images, the life of Christ and the acts of God as narrated in the Bible, but it was potentially deceptive at the same time. The status of paintings of Mary, Christ and God, with regard to the adequacy and implications of their devotional use, was up for serious debates. On the one hand, they were rejected for being mere illusions that had no likeness to the presumed real, yet absent original. On the other hand, they were appraised as pictorial media that could render the divine visible as and via a painted image. The condition for the visibility of the unseen was its mediation. Kruse convincingly argues that in the debates about the capacity of paintings to show what is held to be invisible to the naked eye and can only be imagined, text and image were taken as distinct, but interrelated, media, each having their own properties, possibilities and limitations. Images were made in order to allow their beholders to see what the biblical text could not convey (but only by triggering their inner imagination). What I find particularly fascinating is Kruse's point that paintings were acknowledged as *media*, and hence understood as indispensable to picture the divine by imaging an imagined likeness, grounded in and at the same time supplementing and surpassing the biblical text (see also Hecht 2016).[9]

It would lead too far to attempt to summarize these and other theological-philosophical negotiations and debates here. At stake in these theologies is the acceptance of images as mediators of the unseen, cherished and authorized against the backdrop of lurking challenges of idol worship according to which images become what they represent. For my purposes here it is sufficient to note that such a detailed tracing of what I call 'image-theologies' opens up the archive of the Christian past in a highly illuminating way, to which scholars of religion interested in the image as a central medium of religion, like myself, can relate easily and build upon (Meyer 2015a, b: 31–21, 197–8). The approach offered by Belting and Kruse is relevant because it alerts us to multiple types of images – and types of behaviour and attitudes with respect to (even the same) images – in co-existing and subsequent (Christian, Western) visual regimes that, taken as a whole, lead far beyond the scope of the Second Commandment. Taking this diversity of images and the visual regimes with their 'semiotic ideologies' (Keane 2018) into which images are embedded into account opens up a broader scope of possibilities in the religion – image nexus. A visual regime evolving around idolatry and iconoclash is just one – contested – possibility among others.

As pointed out in my earlier work, Belting's 'anthropology of images' (2001) can fruitfully be incorporated into the study of religion so as to refine our approach to images and transcend the textual bias – without, of course, claiming that images are more immediate and privileged media of the divine than words, objects or sounds. For Belting, a painting, sculpture or other external pictorial representation is a material medium that, by virtue of its technological affordances, renders present a mental image or figure in the imagination. Involving a referential relation between a physical depiction and something which is not directly visible by itself, the image has a close affinity with religion, in that both can be understood to mediate absence into presence. Using the notion 'iconic presence' (2016), Belting points at the capacity of images to render present the represented 'in and as a picture' (2016: 235) for their beholders. Iconic presence also pertains to religious pictorial media, as 'pictures represent deities who have no direct presence in the physical world; these deities are not held to be absent (let alone non-existent), but in need of a picture in order to become visible' (ibid.).[10] The specific image-theologies woven around and legitimating images of deities, of course, are to be explored through detailed research. For the users and beholders of images, these images may be mediators, but they may also be taken as true incarnations of the divine or, at its flipside, as problematic idols. The important point here is that an approach to images as material signs which mediate between the physical world and a professed unseen is above all important as an analytical distinction for scholarly research.

Religion necessarily requires mediation in order to figure out the unseen. From this perspective, religion is conceptualized as a set of ideas and practices that pertain to a realm held not to be directly tangible, but requires certain authorized practices and forms through which it becomes somehow palpable in the immanent. I understand the multiple media employed to generate the presence of the professed unseen as tangible signs that mediate and materialize a transcendent dimension which, in turn, can only be experienced and communicated through these signs (Meyer 2012; see also Mohn 2013: 207). This occurs through multiple media – including, but not limited to, images – authorized in a religious tradition. Images are particularly powerful media to achieve this because they 'promise' to evoke the represented and render it present. At the same time, they are prone to fabricate it, thereby ceasing to be images and becoming the 'real thing' for their beholders, or according to the latter's iconoclastic critics. Religious visual regimes, with their specific modes of figuration and embodied sensational practices, make the invisible visible and the absent present in one way or the other. They shape what and how people see, involving them in 'looking acts' (Morgan 1998: 8) without which nothing would be seen at all.

So in order to study the image–religion nexus beyond the Second Commandment it is advisable to engage with a long history of competing, partly overlapping, image-theologies that negotiate whether and how images (and which ones) can be employed in mediating the unseen in the Christian traditions, and beyond. It is difficult to miss the irony of the fact that scholars working on images in the period from late antiquity to early modernity appear to be more versed in the theological–philosophical debates surrounding these images, than scholars in the study of religion with their strong attention to words and texts. However, the research conducted in the context of *Bildwissenschaft* on 'images before the era of art' primarily focuses on the history of art and religion in Europe. The conceptual approach to images as media of an unseen can, in my view, be fruitfully employed with regard to other settings. But the specific shape of image-theologies, especially those inflected with an idolatry discourse in the frontier areas of European imperial and missionary outreach, is up for further research. In the third and last section of this chapter, I will turn to the export of the notion of idolatry to the West African coast. Inspired by the work of Boehm, Belting, Kruse and others, I will sketch the co-existing, competing and yet intersecting theologies with regard to images, as well as objects and bodies, in this setting.

Producing idolatry

The various iconoclasms and ensuing theological debates in the various Christian traditions are often framed as a matter of the past, having come to an end with the Peace of Westphalia in 1648. In the public outcry over the iconoclasms committed in the name of Islamic State in such world heritage sites as Hatra, Mosul and Palmyra, the sixteenth-century iconoclasms in the aftermath of the Reformation usually were remembered as ambivalent: as somewhat shameful because of the violence involved in the smashing of idols, but as nonetheless a useful step in the rise of an understanding of images as (mere) representations that befits not only radical Calvinists, but also secular, civilized modern people. However, what is often overlooked when pondering the iconoclastic past of Christianity is the steady export and affirmation of the iconoclastic attitude that characterized Christian missionaries' attitudes in preaching the gospel in the frontier zones of European expansion from the colonization of America throughout the world up to our time. Nowadays this attitude is often carried on by Pentecostals across the globe.

Protestant mission activities took off on the West African coast on a massive scale in the nineteenth century. Missions endorsed the long-standing theological discourse on idolatry, thereby transmitting it into the context of the colonization and missionization of Africa. This discourse incorporated the notion of the fetish that had emerged in the aftermath of late-fifteenth-century contacts between Portuguese traders and Africans, and that had become a key term for European traders, missionaries and scholars to debate the vesting of human-made artefacts with supernatural powers. Rather than referring to a long-standing, historically authentic African attitude to images and objects, the term 'fetish' indicates a mimetic appropriation of Catholic sacred objects – statues of Mary, crucifixes – by Africans from sixteenth-century Portuguese merchants. This implies that, paradoxically, Africans only *became* fetish and idol worshippers and adepts of Satan as a consequence of their contacts with Catholic traders and missionaries (Kohl 2003: 19–20). While, in the sixteenth and seventeenth century, Catholic missionaries sought to make Africans replace their cult objects – disqualified and renamed as idols and fetishes – with Christian sacred objects, Protestants polemically designated Catholicism itself as fetishist and dismissed both indigenous African priests and Catholic priests as frauds. This stance flowed into eighteenth-century Enlightenment critiques of religion, according to which both were equally superstitious and irrational. The *Bilderverbot* was framed as mirroring a sublime capacity (of Jews, Muslims and Protestants) to imagine the divine negatively, through the interdiction of picturing it (as suggested by Kant, see above, and Bukdahl in this volume). The fetish – as idol – was associated with a view of Catholicism as backwards and of Africa as dark and primitive. Serving as an inverted mirror to assert Western superiority, the notion of the fetish blinded enlightened scholars to recognize the ideas and practices with regard to objects and images behind – and gradually enmeshed with – the terms fetishism and idolatry in African people's own understanding (Böhme 2006: 178–86; Kohl 2003: 18–29, 69–91).

Missionary preaching – both Catholic and Protestant – popularized the entangled notions of fetish and idol, which were employed to attack indigenous religious practices; their consistent use 'created a social reality that was reproduced over and over again throughout the nineteenth and twentieth century' (Leyten 2015: 106).[11] Such verbal attacks were also made by the missionaries of the NMG. Active among the Ewe, these missionaries conveyed a total package consisting of a new lifestyle, with a new Western material culture, education and religion in the name of the Second Commandment. They typically condemned what they regarded as pagan worship of idols and inscribed the Ewe into the Christian script according to which they were the cursed sons of Ham who had broken away from, and were to be led back to, the monotheistic Ur-God.

According to the dictionary of the Ewe language by the former NMG missionary and later professor of African languages Diedrich Westermann, the generic (Northern) Ewe term for god, *trɔ̃*, was rendered as the translation for *Götze* (German for idol), and the newly coined term *trɔ̃subɔla* (*subɔ* meaning 'serving', also rendered as worshipping) designated *Götzendienst* (German for idolatry) (Westermann 1906: 86). As noted, in missionary preaching, idol and fetish were used as synonyms, and the custodians of the gods were consistently called *Fetischpriester* (German for fetish priests, or even *Fetischdirnen*, German for fetish harlots). While Westermann's dictionary renders *dzo* (fire, magic) as *Fetisch*, and *dzosasa* as *Fetischdienst*, the missionaries also translated *dzo* as *Zauber* (German for charm), which they took as a special trait of the Ewe – perhaps rightly so, as up to our time the Ewe are renown (and feared) by other people in Southern Ghana for their powerful charms. 'Heathendom', with its local gods, spirits, charms and practices, was framed by the missionaries and their African converts as an abode of the Christian devil – termed *Abosam*, after the horrible bush monster Sasabonsam (Meyer 1999: 77–8) – whom the Ewe were considered to worship, albeit without being aware of it.

Exploring these encounters and the local appropriations of Christianity that came out of them through historical and ethnographic research, I noted that the notions of the idol and the fetish have always indicated a minefield of contestations between missionaries and Ewe. Converted Africans were asked to renounce their idols and destroy them – a performative act required over and over again to affirm the uncompromising striving for purity of missionary Protestant Christianity (cf. Keane 2007). With the establishment of colonial rule, people increasingly turned away from indigenous religious traditions towards Christianity. While there were many reports about people 'sliding back to heathendom', often because they did not find the new faith sufficiently effective in combatting evil, indigenous cults were increasingly abandoned. Many cult images and objects were destroyed or handed over to missionaries who would take them home to Europe and exhibit them as material testimonies of the idolatry they sought to eradicate (Leyten 2015).

It is difficult to reconstruct Ewe religious ideas and practices at the time, as they were mainly described from a missionary perspective. Next to reports, intended for a broader German-speaking audience in support of the NMG, in which the terms idol and fetish were continuously used as markers of heathendom, the missionaries also produced linguistic and ethnographic work. Especially important is the work of the missionary Jacob Spieth, who wrote extensively about Ewe religion (1911). According to Spieth, for the Ewe the invisible, spiritual world was the bearer of life that had preceded the physical world, in which it became clothed in solid matter. The physical was understood as entangled with the invisible, spiritual dimension (1911: 4–5). Typical for a Protestant missionary, he paid little attention to the material and ritual dimension through which the gods and spirits became tangible for people. The *legba* figures that act as messengers between the sphere of humans and gods were anthropomorphic images, albeit with a high degree of abstraction. But most of the *trɔwo* of the Ewe in the late nineteenth and early twentieth century were not represented via physical (carved) images, and conversely images were not understood to be the privileged media through which they appeared. In this sense, the *trɔwo* did *not* conform to the notion of idol – in the sense of an image representing its referent by suggesting a likeness that is taken as real and worshipped as a god – by which they were dismissed through missionary translation and preaching. *Trɔwo*, such as the sky, rivers, mountains, termite mounts, pieces of iron and the like, were not represented through images that suggest a presumed likeness, but were held to be – temporarily – present in power objects such as bundles or pots containing herbs, bones, liquids and other substances. They would also take hold of people's bodies through possession, and appear in people's dreams. Rather than corresponding to the idealtype idol, these power objects may come closer to the understanding of the fetish, in the footsteps of Charles de Brosses, as 'neither emblematic nor symbolic, neither figurative nor representational' and thus 'a thing in itself' (Morris 2017: 147, see also Pels 1998).

Popular missionary framing of Ewe religion as idolatrous was not only derogatory, but exaggerated the role of images in existing Ewe religious practice. At stake is a more complicated idea about the gods and spirits becoming present through material forms and human practices and thus of an alternative ontology or theology that regarded matter and spirit as irredeemably entangled, rather than opposed. The point was not to create and worship images that suggest a likeness with a god, but to make objects in which gods could dwell, and to allow human bodies to be permeable so that gods could get in. Of course, this is not to claim the non-existence of iconographies of the spiritual, as the *trɔwo* were recognizable in their physical manifestations during possession (with humans acting as their image through embodiment). The imagination of the unseen was figured and sensed through other means than images alone.

And yet the idolatry discourse proved to be resilient and productive. It would be wrong to merely understand it as a missionary misrepresentation of Ewe religion. The latter being dynamic and flexible, the notion of idolatry *produced* new ideas and practices. The Catholic use of images for devotion may even have formed a source of inspiration for embracing images more strongly as religious media. The point is that there are good reasons to argue that in the course of the twentieth century images became more important media for rendering spirits present. This can be inferred from, for example, the deployment of the Mami Water cult, which entails colourful images and carvings of this spirit represented as a European woman with a fishtail (e.g. Wendl 1991; Meyer 2015b: 210–16).

When I started my ethnographic research in the late 1980s, to my initial surprise I noted that the missionary understanding of local gods and spirits as idols was still alive and kicking. Pentecostal Christianity – with its strong reliance on the Holy Spirit and the framing of the body as prime medium to sense divine presence – qualifies local traditional cults as dirty and polluting instances of idolatry. In the same vein, family gods are dismissed as demonic and people are called upon to get rid of them, or at least to protect themselves against their influence. Former devotees of local gods – or people experiencing encounters with these gods in their dreams – are exorcized, so as to be 'delivered' and 'born again'. This negative take on indigenous traditions is enhanced by the popular video film industry (Meyer 2015b, see below), that also features the dangers of idolatry and shows in vivid images how the 'powers of darkness' that operate through local gods are at work and seek to harm people. For Pentecostals, idolatry is real – and taken to evolve around physical images. They promote an inverted image-theology that, in contrast with the careful attempts to retain images notwithstanding the interdiction of worshipping idols in the Christian tradition as documented by Belting and Kruse, reproduces African deities as idols that are to be destroyed.

Take, for instance, a Pentecostal booklet *100 Facts against Idolatry* (2009) by the Nigerian Born Again overseer of the Mountain of Fire and Miracles Ministries Dr D. K. Olukoya that was a popular read in Ghana around 2010 (when I bought it in a Christian bookshop). The author explains that Nigeria – and for that matter Africa – served idols for far too long and that God laments this situation:

> What is the greatest problem of the Blackman? It is idolatry. Idolatry has led to divine punishment extended even to future generations. Idolatry is a system devised by the devil to control the land, the family and the people. It is an abomination. It is a form of contention and rebellion against God. It promotes false worship, deceptions as well as animal and human sacrifice. (Olukoya 2009: 7)

The passage is immediately followed by a quote of Exod. 20.2-5, which is explained by a harsh statement:

> God hates idolatry with perfect hatred. He sees idolatry as spiritual prostitution. Once there is idolatry there is divine wrath. People should recognize that idolatry is a kind of marriage covenant. Africa has the largest altars and the largest number

of idols. Africa has ignited strange fire and raised evil smokes to the devil, insulting God to His Face. (2005: 8)

A loud echo of nineteenth-century missionary preaching, the author goes even further in introducing an angry God who feels insulted and who curses idol worshippers, but is also prepared to have mercy on them, provided they leave their idols behind. Over the past years, the Ghanaian Osofo Kyiri Abosom (translated as 'pastor hates idols', *abosom* being the term for gods in Twi, which like the *trɔwo* of the Ewe were framed as idols; see, for example, Leyten 2015: 78–80) has been destroying shrines across Ghana, both upon invitation of custodians, who want to get rid of the responsibility of taking care of the spirits and their paraphernalia, and as part of a broader assault against pagan idols in the framework of spiritual warfare.[12] His destructions are broadcast via his commercial TV channel; certain scenes show him with an axe in his hand slaying idols in their head, reminiscent of the iconic video-recorded assaults of IS (see https://youtu.be/Jpk3M8iZvcQ).

Even though not all Born Again Christians would speak about idolatry as harshly as these pastors, their anti-idolatry stance is widely shared. Indigenous traditions are understood as dangerous dwelling points of the powers of darkness that threaten to attack people and keep them in their grip. Many Pentecostals are therefore reluctant to acknowledge images of local gods – for example, sculptures, masks, paintings through which gods are (increasingly) understood to materialize as idols – as well as traditional drum rhythms and dances as valuable forms of cultural heritage. In so doing they challenge the policy of the postcolonial state to promote a positive appraisal of the past and the recognition of its moral and aesthetic values, which, however, no longer takes seriously as really existing entities the spirits and gods associated with this past (De Witte and Meyer 2012; Meyer 2015b: chapter 7).

What, then, is idolatry for Pentecostals? The point here is to grasp the complex ways in which, in their inverted image-theology, the divine and the satanic, anti-idolatry and idolatry are clearly separated while one side always presupposes the other which is included and rejected at the same time. What fascinated me in my research from the outset is the persistent talking about the idols that true Christians are to leave behind, which yet become manifest in their world of lived experience, especially through dreams, but also through possession. As I argued extensively, the figure of the Christian devil served as both a principle of rejection and inclusion, allowing for the 'pagan' gods and spirits and their material forms to remain present, albeit as evil forces. He is a boundary figure who includes non-Christian spiritual entities into the Christian universe, and at the same time is to be cast out ('You devil, go away from me!').

Over and over again, I was told that 'the spiritual' (in Ewe: *le gbɔgbɔme*) is entangled with 'the physical' (in Ewe: *le ɲutilame*), implying that spiritual forces act in the physical world, but cannot be seen via the naked eye, and thus depend on a superior spiritual eye to be discerned. This is the prime capacity of Pentecostal pastors, as well as of indigenous priests. Spirits, I learnt, move about and are able to inhabit any form, which means that anything inhabited by them can become an idol (and even objects which do not offer figural representations). This means that, for Pentecostals, idols are not limited to particular traditional shrines and traditional sculptures – which often do not claim to refer to a spirit through likeness, but surreal abstraction. The category of idol also came to include masks and figurines made for decorative purposes as well as mass-produced sculptures and posters depicting Jesus, Mary and Saints (Meyer 2010). Many Pentecostals reject such images for being idols (or, if they have them, explicitly characterize them as merely decorative). Nonetheless the spiritual unseen – battleground between the powers of darkness and divine power – speaks to their imagination very much. There is a continuous engagement with the invisible, spiritual dimension of idolatry, which is invoked by a great deal of Pentecostal pastors in an obsessive manner, thereby continuously recalling that from which Born Again Christians are asked to turn away. In so doing, the Pentecostal imagination is geared to the unseen, keen to get revelations about the operation of hidden, occult forces in the material world. Paradoxically, the zealous rejection of idolatry demands its constant imagination and figuration. This occurs through vivid narratives – sermons, testimonies, rumours – that are transfigured into paintings, posters and movies. Picturing the occult, through words and images, is itself understood as an iconoclastic act, through which what remains invisible to the eye is dragged into the limelight of the Holy Spirit and exposed.

As I showed in my book *Sensational Movies* (Meyer 2015b), the locally produced films that were highly popular between the 1990s and early 2000s tied into the common understanding of the spiritual and physical realms as invisible, yet effectively entangled. A particular type of movie, which I circumscribe as 'film as revelation', set out to audio-visualize the occult. I traced the transfiguration of narratives about occult powers into moving images (Meyer 2015b: chapters 4 and 5), which yielded spectacular, albeit recurrent and stereotyped, depictions of idols. Suggesting that video film-makers act as modern high priests of the imagination, I looked at their movies as displaying a Pentecostal visual regime in action. The films are dismissed by traditional priests and intellectuals as misrepresentations of indigenous religion, but have a resilient impact on how Christians imagine African gods. My point here is that the notion of idolatry, rather than simply rejecting (and misrepresenting) indigenous worship practices, triggers the imagination and evokes a desire for figurations of the unseen which pretend to reveal how the powers of darkness operate, and which are ultimately defeated by divine power (preferably represented through light, fire and the like). Local movie productions offered highly sensational audio–visual figurations of the unseen, thereby creating ever more image-like idols for the screen that populate viewers' imagination of how the spiritual and the physical are folded into one another.

While the movies have lost popularity by now, the imaginations of the occult shaped by them live on even in attempts to recapture indigenous religion in a positive manner. For example, in a recent video clip by the Ewe artist Azizaa (Ewe for 'little people' in the bush, or dwarfs) titled 'Black Magic Woman' (https://www.youtube.com/watch?v=bf eGpcmfMBA), two aggressive Pentecostal pastors are charmed to follow the lady they try to convert into the bush, where she turns out to be a priestess seated on a stool and is accompanied by other priests and spirits, and a drum with eyes (see Figure 4.1 a,b). The scene could have come straight out of a Ghanaian movie. So here an attempt to challenge the Pentecostal dismissal of indigenous cults as idolatry resuscitates the very same images employed to depict the occult unseen in the Pentecostal imagination.

Figure 4.1a, b Screenshots from 'Black Magic Woman' (performed by Azizaa).

So, having reached the end of the third part of this chapter, let me briefly rehearse the trajectory. The central concern of this chapter is to further a scholarly approach to images – their appraisal as well as their rejection – from a position beyond the Second Commandment. As pointed out, Latour's reference to the Second Commandment as a law prescribing an aniconism which is impossible to realize, and which triggers iconoclastic outbursts, has certain limitations. Neglecting alternative stances to images, his scenario of modernity is of little help to grasp the ways in which the various Christian traditions have found ways to reconcile a religious use of images with (a softer interpretation of) this commandment. To achieve this, art historical works along the lines of Boehm, Belting and Kruse offer important insights, in that their approach to images as mediators of a professed (religious) unseen helps to unpack the complex image-theologies developed in the Christian traditions. Clearly, idolatry is in the eye of the beholder. Many users of images, who understand them to generate divine presence, may well maintain (albeit implicitly) a view of images as media, rather than as a divine thing that is worshipped as such. The Protestant missionaries of the NMG, however, did not appreciate such subtle image-theologies (which they would associate with Catholicism and find basically idolatric). Approaching Africa as the land of idols, they communicated the Christian notion of idolatry along with the figure of the devil in their sermons. This clearly misrepresented the views of the Ewe, according to whom gods and spirits could inhabit natural sites, objects, people and, to some extent, images, but for whom images were not the preferred media for rendering the unseen present for humans. The assault of idolatry not only triggered the destruction of the material culture related to particular indigenous deities (or their transfer to European ethnographic museums). It also proved a productive discourse that constituted a new social reality, in which these deities became evermore like idols. The inverted image-theology of the Pentecostals generated a constant rejection of indigenous gods as idols, entailing a profuse call on believers to imagine the powers of darkness, which are to be exposed through figuration in words and images. Clearly, the fight against idols does not lead beyond the visual but relies on it. Reflecting on the steps taken in this trajectory, I conclude that charges of idolatry and subsequent iconoclasms in the Christian context can only be fully understood if the full scope of attitudes to images – from iconophobic to iconodule stances – is taken into account. Even the rejection of images requires a sound understanding of their use and appeal.

Epilogue: 'By all means Satan will die'

Luther's fellow campaigner in Wittenberg, Alexander von Bodenstein, alias Karlstadt, preached fiercely against idolatry. In his polemical text *Von abthung der Bylder* (1522) he explained that *Ölgötzen* (statues, figures, idols) and *Bilder* (images) should neither be worshipped nor feared. He rejected the argument made in defence of their use – also by Luther – that they were the books of the illiterates and could serve as mere illustrations. For Karlstadt, images were deceptive and dangerous. Beholders would take them into their hearts and feel love towards them. But he admitted that, having been raised in a Christian world in which images were venerated, he feared to get rid of them:

> Therefore I am afraid to burn an idol. I am frightened that the stupid devil would hurt me, although I (on the one hand) have the Scripture and know that images can do nothing and have neither life, blood nor spirit. And yet, on the other hand fear holds me captive and makes me be afraid of a pictured devil, a shadow or the sound of a light leaf, and I dodge what I should manfully go for (e.g. burning images). (Karlstadt 1522: 23, translation mine)[13]

What I find particularly intriguing in this statement is Karlstadt's association of images with the devil, a terrifying figure whose existence was beyond doubt. His statement fits in with Reformed polemics against Catholicism as misguiding believers to worship

Satan. With Boehm we could say that Satan is held to efface the iconic difference, thus allowing the image to become an idol. Prone to lure beholders into deceptive illusions, images were dismissed by Karlstadt as a potentially demonic, scary and difficult to get rid of medium, while the biblical text was the privileged medium of God.

Contrast this take on the danger of images with the painting titled *By All Means Satan Will Die* (Figure 4.2) by the Ghanaian artist Kwame Akoto alias Almighty God. Akoto, a Born Again Christian, is a famous popular artist who has his workshop at Juame junction in Kumasi (Meyer 2015a: 348–9; Ross 2014). He paints signboards, portraits and all sorts of motifs from the Christian imagination, including the Sacred Heart of Jesus, witches and the devil. In the painting Satan is depicted standing in the bush in a reddish gown with a third eye on his forehead and his eyes covered by sunglasses. He stands in the light, shining. His wings mark him as the fallen angel of light, Lucifer. Two men with rifles aim at him, one rifle touching the devil's nose. While certainly agreeing with Karlstadt's anti-idolatric stance, as a painter Akoto uses the image as a medium to confidently assert the sure future death of Satan, and perhaps even as a means to kill him. Nothing can better illustrate the paradoxes entailed in the figuration of the unseen produced under the banner of a rejection of idolatry, looked at from beyond the Second Commandment.

Figure 4.2 *By All Means Satan Will Die* (painting by Kwame Akoto 'Almighty', collection Birgit Meyer).

Part Two

Genealogies of Figuration

5

Beyond 'Image Ban' and 'Aniconism': Reconfiguring Ancient Israelite and Early Jewish Religion\s in a Visual and Material Religion Perspective

Christoph Uehlinger

I Introduction: Questioning a powerful conceptual matrix

Prohibitions against the production and worship of images representing one's own or other deities (often referred to in the singular as 'image ban' or *Bilderverbot*) – as much as their seeming corollary, the so-called aniconic worship of a single supreme deity – are commonly held to be distinctive characteristics of ancient Israelite and Judahite, Jewish and Islamic religion. The two aspects (the normative rejection of a given ritual practice and the realization of its opposite as alternative practice) are often considered as two faces of a coin. Yet the relation between the two is much more complicated. The terms image ban and aniconism are problematic and both certainly need to be properly defined and qualified.[1] Scholars such as Tryggve Mettinger (1995, 2006), Brian Doak (2015), Milette Gaifman (2012) and others have recently offered important contributions to that end, focusing on first-millennium-BCE Israel, Phoenicia and Greece. The present chapter aims at continuing this conversation while putting it into a wider horizon, both disciplinary and theoretical.

Neither programmatic prohibitions of cultic images nor de facto abstention from producing and using them in cultic rituals or imageless rituals are exclusive to early West Semitic traditions, Judaism and Islam (see the essays collected in Gaifman and Aktor 2017);[2] however, they distinguish these traditions from many others past and present. Moreover, both scholars and the wider public associate these traditions with the concept of monotheism. To be sure, none of the traditions studied by Mettinger, Gaifman and Doak should be considered monotheistic in any way. But the history of Western Asiatic and Mediterranean religion\s since late antiquity seems indeed to privilege an elective affinity of sorts between the belief in a single, invisible, transcendent deity on the one hand ('monotheism') and the injunction not to represent that deity in a cultic image on the other hand. Monotheistic theologies have developed sophisticated arguments regarding the presumed inadequacy of any kind of visual, let alone anthropomorphic or theriomorphic (i.e. human, animal or hybrid), form to convey an appropriate representation of the deity (God, capitalized) or to appropriately mediate a presence which is considered all-encompassing, transcendent or both.

The matrix

Much in the way of an irreducible matrix, these three aspects (rejection of cultic images, 'aniconic' ritual practice and theological assumptions about the deity's/God's invisibility) have long been construed to define a kind of *system* of belief and behaviour, in which each reinforces the others and is itself stabilized by them.

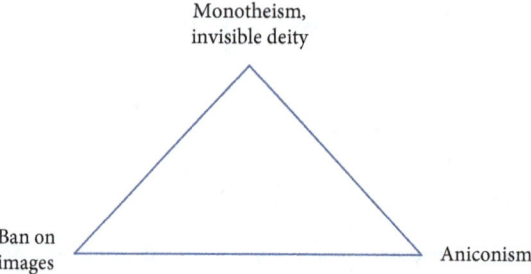

A further characteristic of the so-called Abrahamic religion\s (on which this volume concentrates) is their heavy reliance on the transmission of the deity's will, revealed as 'divine word' by prophetic messengers, and ultimately the scripturalization and canonical fixation of that will. Reading from scripture and listening to the divine word forms an important part of Jewish, Christian and Islamic ritual, so that in the believers' understanding such reading and listening may be experienced as a process of actual communication mediating divine truth and presence. Framed in such a way, listening to the divine (or divinely inspired) word of the invisible deity may be considered a powerful corollary, and even qualitative improvement, of aniconic worship as such. In a second diagram, each angle again reinforces the other two and the three aspects together again form a kind of system.

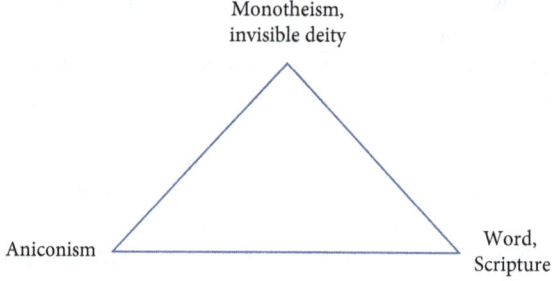

Once the two triangles are assembled, listening to the divine word (recited or otherwise framed in ways that underline its otherworldly origin) appears to be a strong opposite, and perhaps the ultimate alternative, to encountering the divine in one or several cultic images (cf. Otten 2007). Combining the two triangles produces a diagram of even higher systematic ambition and epistemic strength. This diagram reflects a foundational matrix of normative assumptions about how to relate to the one, invisible, transcendent, but all-communicative God.

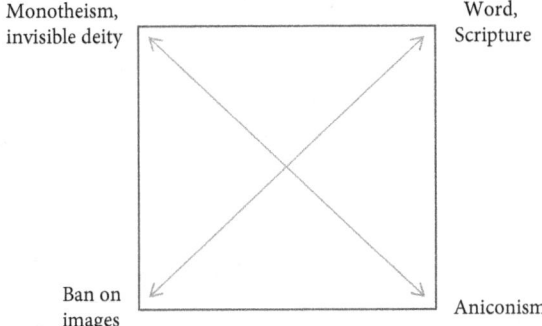

The argument presented so far will sound familiar and appear plausible to many modern Westerners, religious or not. This only indicates how much they have been socially and culturally conditioned by a religio-philosophical tradition shared by many Jews, Christians and Muslims since late antiquity and the Middle Ages. The conceptual dichotomy of right and wrong, religion and idolatry, word and image (the latter often extended from cultic image to icon, and even to image tout court) has shaped confessional polemics since the early modern period, provided a powerful instrument to classify and conquer non-European societies, and efficiently infiltrated Western philosophy – not least when the latter sought to emancipate itself from the constraints of religion (cf. Sherwood and Meyer, this volume). The matrix is meant to visualize an epistemic formation; it does not necessarily reflect actual practices. It is a heuristic tool to visualize how conventional modernist discourse on religion, and the discourse of religious studies perpetuating their Protestant ascendancy, construe the relationship of image and word, or the ambiguity of the former versus the validity of the latter, when considering 'Abrahamic religion\s'.

The four corners of our matrix operate in different ways in various manifestations of the three religions, particularly in their ritual traditions. Both Jewish and Islamic religion usually reject cultic images, which they attribute to the 'nations', 'pagans' or 'polytheists'; their rituals do not generally make use of images to represent the deity, who is thought to be one and invisible; and they turn to reading from scripture when searching for the deity's will. The situation appears much more complex when we consider the variety of Christian religious traditions. Building on ancient Jewish discourse rejecting 'pagan idolatry', Byzantine iconoclasts and Calvinist Protestants could label 'idolaters' their opponents who valued the use of images in worship; in these instances, the matrix may serve to define a pattern of division *within* the varieties of Christian traditions and their way to distinguish in their midst 'true' from 'false' religion, or faith from heresy.

That Christianity as such (in toto) should range alongside Judaism and Islam in a discussion of imageless worship is therefore all but obvious. If it does so, nevertheless, this is largely due to the weight of Protestant assumptions in the contemporary discourse on 'Abrahamic religions'. If Protestant religious reformers of the sixteenth century claimed to recover the original purity of early Christian ritual from its distortion by Papist idolatry, they also considered reading, listening to and explaining scripture (*Sola Scriptura*) to be the most important element in the worship of the true God. It is along similar lines of thought that modern scholars of religion classify Protestant Christianity, particularly the Reformed and Calvinist traditions, among the 'aniconic' and even iconoclastic, thus ranging them close to Judaism and Islam in their rejection of cultic images and the valuation of scripture as the sole (or most eminent) medium through which the faithful may encounter God.

Abraham

From a historical, non-theological point of view, many aspects of the development of image-related ritual and theological discourse (that is, iconophile and iconolatrous positions) in early, medieval and early modern Byzantine, Catholic and Oriental Christianities may be regarded as creative receptions, perpetuations and reinterpretations of pre-Christian ('pagan') traditions and ritual practices. One would be hard-pressed to range these traditions among the anti-iconists. Early Islam originated in the late-antique Middle East as a kind of reformation movement directed against both domestic 'idolatry' and various forms of Jewish and Christian religion. Invoking Abrahamic descent (*dîn Ibrahim*) and the tradition remembering Abraham smashing idols worshipped by the society he had been born into served Muhammad to claim ritual and genealogical precedence over Jewish and Christian claims to true religion; a similar argumentative strategy had already served Paul to claim religious superiority for early Christian versus Torah-obedient Jewish faith.

Should we then consider the matrix described above to represent something distinctively 'Abrahamic' in the first place? Or does that label only serve as a convenient pretext for lumping together three religions which, after all, differ considerably, internally and among each other, in their interpretation of a putative 'image ban', 'aniconism' and the pre-eminence of the revealed word? From the point of view of a historian of religion\s, the label 'Abrahamic' is problematic if it obscures the many differences among the streams, sub-streams and confluents of the three traditions. Their many entanglements, and the variety of practices with regard to images particularly within the Christian traditions, cannot easily be homogenized in a simple genealogical model as implied by the 'Abrahamic' metaphor. Historians of religion\s should therefore critically assess rather than step in and follow this 'Abrahamic' genealogical discourse, which is of very recent conjuncture and, in my view, of little analytical use.

Biblical tradition concerning Abraham (most prominently, Genesis 12–25) does not relate Abraham to specifically 'aniconic' forms of worship, nor to any kind of 'image ban' (the latter is brought much later into the biblical narrative, when Moses and Israel meet Yahweh at Mount Sinai, Exodus 20). It was Jewish Midrash which first associated the divine call experienced by Abraham at Ur with a rejection of idolatry, that is, the illegitimate form of worship which it attributed both to Abraham's forefathers and to his mighty opponent, the legendary Mesopotamian king Nimrod. In ancient Jewish 'rewritten Bible' and Midrash (e.g. *Book of Jubilees* ch. 12; *Genesis Rabbah* ch. 38; cf. Levenson 2012: 117–23), Abraham is said to have destroyed the idols of his family before emigrating west, towards the land that God would show him. This narrative tradition seems to have been largely ignored in (Western) Christian sources, but well-received in early Islam, which added stories relating the purification of the Ka'aba that extended Ibrahim's iconoclastic fame to his son Ishmael (Lowin 2011). If there is anything explicitly 'Abrahamic' in the rejection of cultic images, it may be located among the traditions of late-antique Judaism, early Islam and possibly 'oriental' Christianities, but not in Western or Orthodox 'mainstream' Christianity.

Moses

Biblical tradition and Western Christianity associate the rejection of idolatry with Moses rather than with Abraham. As in the case of Muhammad's reformation, this concerns both the rejection of other gods, the gods of others, and the claim to know how to appropriately worship one's own deity. These motifs are part of a cluster of religious innovations and attitudes conveniently synthesized by Jan Assmann in his concept of a 'Mosaic distinction' (Assmann 1996). Moses's farewell speech and legacy to Israel (Deuteronomy 4) provides the most articulated biblical argument justifying what was meant to become a Yahwistic proprium, namely abstention from figuring Yahweh, let alone any other deity, in material form. Beyond the Torah of Moses, certain strata of biblical writings take issue with 'idolatry', whether in historiography, prophetic critique or parody mocking the production of cult images in Babylonian religion (Jensen 2017). From a historical point of view, these trajectories of biblical material represent the earliest preserved example of 'anti-idolatrous' discourse from the world of Eastern Mediterranean and Western Asiatic religions. Within that material, the prescriptive texts embedded in the Torah of Moses, and among them, especially, the so-called Second Commandment, have made the strongest impact on religious history due to their emblematic link with the Sinai covenant scenario. It therefore seems legitimate to investigate the origins and developments of that prescriptive tradition, in order to historicize its genealogy, break the conceptual spell it exerts on modern scholarship and consider theoretical alternatives.

The present chapter is written with such a double interest in mind, religio-historical and theoretical. Just as the religion or religions of 'Ancient Israel' have not always been monolatric, let alone monotheistic, they have not always been 'aniconic'. Since the biblical tradition stands at the background of most concerns with the figurative representation of the divine that are the focus of this volume, it seems worthwhile to give a brief account of how and under what circumstances these prohibitions may have emerged from (and in opposition to) earlier and more traditional religious custom. In section II, I briefly review current religion-historical knowledge on how Yahweh was represented in Israelite and Judahite religion, especially in cultic settings, prior to the Babylonian destruction of Jerusalem in 586 BCE and the so-called exilic period. Section III will outline how critical scholarship evaluates the antiquity and emergence of the various biblical forms of a ban on cultic images, both of Yahweh and of other gods in post-exilic times. The relevant disjunction occurred under particular conditions of social change and shift of power during the latter part of the first millennium BCE. I contend that it is possible to explain it in purely historical terms.

Section IV combines a historical and a theoretical concern. I shall ask under what conditions the Torah's normative stance against cultic images could be adopted and appropriated by much later readers of the Bible, modern scholars included, who read it as a faithful description of ancient Israelite actual religious practice, and how this (after all, quite erroneous) perception could contribute to the scholarly construction of ancient Israelite and Judahite religion as essentially different and distinct from the religions of their Levantine neighbours. Modern scholars of the twentieth century have construed theoretical assumptions and categories out of a 'taking-for-granted' reading of normative biblical texts, thus producing ahistorical and apologetic representations of ancient Israel's religion that reflect religious inhibitions and theological bias of their own present rather than the plain sense of the biblical texts themselves. Historians of religion should ask under what circumstances religion-related scholarship can be affected by the theological, religious or cultural bias of its sources even when it claims to practice so-called historical-critical methods of inquiry.

Section V will hint at an alternative approach on how to deal with ancient Israelite, Judahite, but also Jewish, Christian and Islamic religion\s in ways that do not from the outset place them in opposition to other religions. I shall suggest that instead of perpetuating ill-defined and biased concepts such as 'image ban' or 'aniconism', scholars of religion should give preference to second- and third-order categories and a religious aesthetics approach that reach beyond the iconic/aniconic dichotomy. Only then will we be able to address and analyse the varieties of religious traditions and their internal diversity, their ritual practices and their manifold views on mediation in a less biased and more properly descriptive, analytical, comparative and explanatory perspective.

II Representing Yahweh in ancient Israelite and Judahite religion\s

In this section I briefly present the current state of research on ancient Israelite and Judahite religion\s, before reviewing the most salient lines of debate regarding the use of cultic images or 'aniconic' media representing the divine in various ritual settings of the monarchic period (roughly tenth/ninth to sixth centuries BCE).

Primary versus secondary data

Among the many shrines and sanctuaries of the time, the main temple of Jerusalem and the question of whether and how Yahweh (the main deity in Israel and Judah and divine patron of the Davidic dynasty ruling in Jerusalem) was represented in this temple occupies a central position in the biblical record and in the scholarly discussion. Historians of religion should resist the scriptural Jerusalem-centred perspective, a product of scribes and schools based in Jerusalem whose ideological agenda stressed the city's pre-eminence. A more balanced view can be achieved on the basis of archaeological data, which most contemporary historians consider as 'primary evidence' for historical inquiry, and by reading much of the relevant biblical literature somehow against its grain. Ranging biblical literature second in a historical inquiry is necessary for two reasons: first, because, unlike archaeological data, biblical texts represent a stream of tradition and are often far more difficult to date; second, because reading a text against its grain is an hermeneutically tricky operation, in which the modern historian must navigate carefully between uncritical naïveté and wishful imagination. Lucid scholarship acknowledges that when archaeological data (which are external to the religious discourse) and biblical texts (which stand at its roots) are correlated, be it to call on like-minded witnesses or to use one against the other as a corrective, wishful imagination is perhaps the most difficult to resist and to control even when commenting on archaeological primary data. The latter, to be sure, do not speak by themselves. They are generally addressed through a critical lens of inquiry that is itself full of assumptions already shaped by biblical material – and by the matrix discussed in section I.

This said, critical scholarship has over the last few decades come to a certain consensus regarding the status of ancient Israelite and Judahite religion\s in their Southern Levantine context. Israelite and Judahite religion\s are increasingly viewed as subsets of West Semitic religion; they may have differed in details of practice and belief from the religion of their neighbours (Phoenicians and Philistines, Arameans, Ammonites, Moabites and Edomites) as much as they shared many common assumptions with them. Current scholarship stresses aspects of diversity much more than claims of essential distinctiveness or tends at least to interpret the latter in terms of the former (Uehlinger 2015).

Religion or religions?

Departing from twentieth-century models considering diversity (and distinctiveness) mainly in 'national' terms (an anachronistic concept still in use in much contemporary scholarship), current research construes diversity by stressing varieties of social, regional, economic and ecological settings and regimes which would have shaped ancient religion and culture as much as ethnic concerns (Stavrakopoulou and Barton 2010). Not surprisingly then, contemporary scholarship has come to address 'the religions of Ancient Israel' in the plural (Zevit 2001), introducing ever finer distinctions among religious customs and practices within Israelite and Judahite society according to their location and functionality vis-à-vis particular micro-environments, social locations, networks of commercial or political interaction, and so on. That the religion of a Jerusalem-based court or temple scribe would be the same as that of a townsman living in the Judahite countryside, let alone that of officials, traders, landowners or herdsmen from other regions of the northern hill country and beyond cannot be taken for granted anymore. Ironically, even the most naïve reading of the Hebrew Bible would have allowed such a seemingly trivial insight which, however (perhaps under the impact of the national paradigm and the modern search for religious and national cohesion, in Israel as in many other modern Western societies), was resisted rather strangely in most twentieth-century reconstructions of ancient Israelite religion.

Yahweh or Yahwehs?

Taking stock of religious diversity in ancient Israel and Judah also affects our understanding of the main deity worshipped in various regions and of the various ways that deity was represented and worshipped in different cultic settings. A major blow against a too-homogeneous view of ancient Israelite religion came from the discovery, in 1976, of inscriptions mentioning 'Yahweh of Samaria and his Asherah' and 'Yahweh of Teman (or Yahweh of the southern steppe) and his Asherah', alongside figurative drawings on *pithoi* and walls at an ancient way station called Kuntillet Ajrud, located in northern Sinai on the overland road connecting Gaza and Beersheba to the Red Sea (see Meshel 2012 for a final report on the data). A concept used to acknowledge the newly attested situation is 'Poly-Yahwism' or the notion of a 'splintered divine' (Allen 2014): there was more than a single Yahwism, and more than a single Yahweh. The scholarly task is, on the one hand, material, descriptive and analytical: what forms and locations of worship of a deity named Yahweh do we actually know, and on what grounds? Another question is more theory oriented: Should we consider these different forms varieties of a single deity (the same, if 'splintered', Yahweh), or would it be theoretically more appropriate to construe various forms and locations of Yahweh, co-existent at one given time, not only as varieties of the same Yahweh but as several distinct Yahwehs? While the first option represents the majority approach in current scholarship, the latter option is gaining support and credentials. The underlying question is of course to what extent historical research on that issue should or should not continue to be affected by assumptions about divine identity, which are by definition of a theological nature. Stepping out of deep-rooted assumptions (not to say, prejudice) is definitely a very difficult and challenging task.

Turning now to the question how various forms of Yahweh (or various Yahwehs) were represented in ancient Israel and Judah between the tenth/ninth and the sixth centuries BCE, the following, necessarily brief, observations may give a rough idea of the potential variety we should expect once all relevant data are taken into account.

Varieties of Yahwist iconographies

According to ancient Hebrew and other inscriptions, archaeological findings and biblical texts, Yahweh was worshipped during the so-called monarchic period at many different locations, including Beersheba, Bethel, Dan, Gibeon, Hebron, Jerusalem, Penuel, Shechem, Shiloh, Samaria and others. As mentioned, some inscriptions construe a particular relationship between the deity and a region (e.g. 'Yahweh of Teman') or place (e.g. 'god of Jerusalem').

As early as 1906, the German scholar Gustav Dalman suggested that an image of Yahweh enthroned could be identified on a seventh-century-BCE Judahite seal acquired in Jerusalem (Figure 5.1a; Dalman 1906). In the 1970s, Swedish biblical scholar Gösta Ahlström pointed to a bronze figurine from early Iron Age Hazor (Figure 5.1b; Ahlström 1970/71). Following the discoveries at Kuntillet Ajrud and their preliminary publication, scholars quickly attempted to identify 'Yahweh and his Asherah' among the drawings discovered at that site. Due to the nature of the evidence and religious assumptions about Yahweh (a male single or a male with a wife?), the

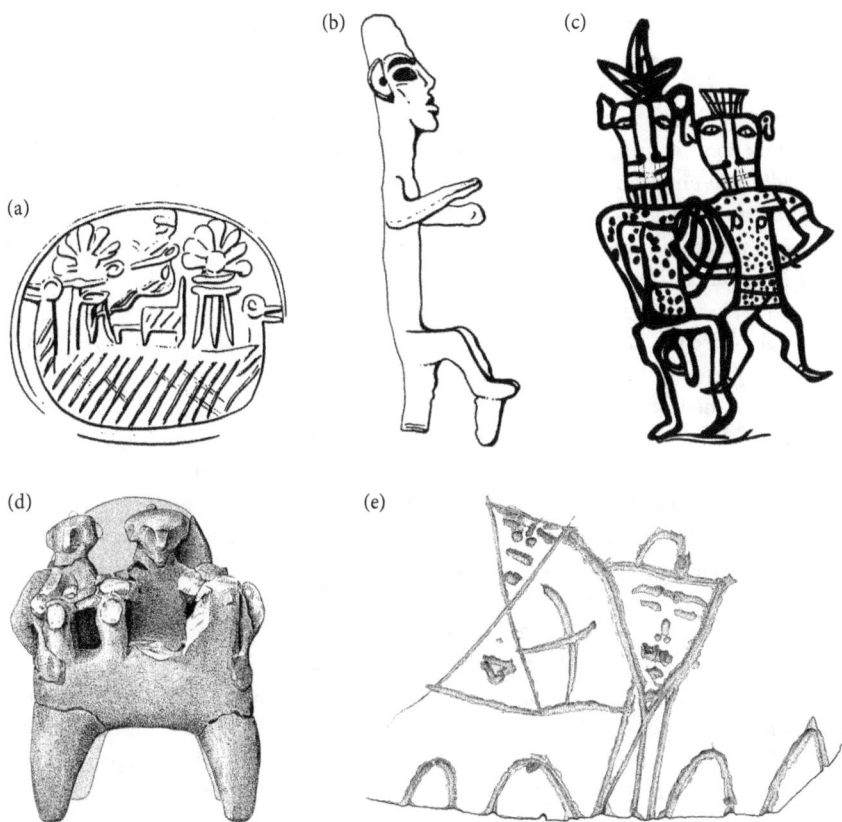

Figure 5.1a Enthroned god on the bifacial seal of Elishamaʾ ben Gedalyahu (owner's name inscribed on the verso), acquired in Jerusalem, c. seventh century BCE (after Keel and Uehlinger 1998: 308, fig. 306a).

Figure 5.1b Bronze figurine of a sitting god from Hazor Str. XI, Iron Age I, eleventh/tenth century BCE (after Keel and Uehlinger 1998: 117, fig. 141).

Figure 5.1c Pair of male and female hybrid figures on an ink drawing on Pithos A from Kuntillet Ajrud, c. 800 BCE (after Meshel 2012: 166, fig. 6.20; courtesy Zeʾev Meshel, University of Tel Aviv).

Figure 5.1d Terracotta group showing a bearded god enthroned, a stone erected in front of him, and an unbearded (female?) figure standing at his right, flanked by two quadrupeds. Judah, late eighth century BCE (Jeremias 1993: 46, fig. 1; courtesy Orbis Biblicus et Orientalis).

Figure 5.1e Two divine (?) figures, situated in a mountainous area, scratched on an eighth-century-BCE pottery sherd from Jerusalem (Gilmour 2009: 91, ill. 4; drawing Dylan Karges, Cobb Institute, Mississippi State University, reproduced courtesy Garth Gilmour, Jerusalem, and Palestine Exploration Fund).

ensuing discussion concentrated more on finding Asherah (a cult symbol or Yahweh's female *paredros*?) among the findings of Kuntillet Ajrud rather than identifying a picture of Yahweh himself. One drawing, however, which shows a hybrid figure combining anthropomorphic, leonine and, for some scholars, bovine features (Figure 5.1c), was soon addressed as a possible representation of Yahweh, and the smaller and slightly feminized figure construed as Asherah (Gilula 1979). The hypothesis has been repeatedly deconstructed and rejected (iconographically speaking, both figures represent variants of a quite well-known apotropaic figure called Bes), but it continues to fuel the scholarly imagination (see again Thomas 2016). Once set to look out for figurative representations of 'Yahweh and his Asherah', scholars have pointed to further potential referents: an eighth-century-BCE terracotta group from the Judean hill country representing a pair of deities, one of them enthroned (Figure 5.1d); two crude figures scratched on an eighth-century-BCE potsherd from Jerusalem (Figure 5.1e); and so on. All these suggestions have remained controversial, to say the least, and none of the suggested artefacts can as yet be proven to represent Yahweh.

Biblical historiography attests two major iconographic traditions for the representation of Yahweh. One, associated with Bethel, Dan and the northern kingdom of Israel (Samaria), is based on bovine iconography, in which a bull can be construed either as the symbolic representation of the storm god himself or as an attribute animal serving as a pedestal of sorts and carrying the anthropomorphic deity on its back (compare Figures 5.2a, b; on the latter item the deity's gender remains uncertain, see Ornan 2006). Bull statues (Figure 5.2c) are probably related to this tradition. Their interpretation as pedestals for an invisible god is motivated by religious inhibition and should be rejected as an instance of wishful thinking. Another tradition, genealogically related to Phoenicia and Canaanite heritage, stresses the notion of divine kingship through the concept of a throne guarded by a pair of winged sphinxes, or cherubim. Since the biblical account of Solomon's Temple in Jerusalem includes a description of giant cherubim in the Holy of Holies, a biblical epithet of Yahweh addresses him as 'riding on cherubim', and Ezekiel 11 describes Yahweh leaving his temple on cherubim, many scholars construe the cherubim throne tradition as peculiar to the Jerusalem Temple (cf. Stordalen, this volume, Figure 1.2). Scholars who consider the so-called image ban tradition a product of post-exilic Judahite scribes are generally inclined to postulate the existence, in the pre-exilic Temple of Jerusalem, of a cultic image representing Yahweh anthropomorphically sitting on a cherubim throne (e.g. Niehr 1997; Römer 2015: 141–59). Admittedly though, this theory lacks full iconographic confirmation and is to some extent no less wishful than its alternative, a deity who in the worshippers' imagination was invisibly enthroned above the cherubim, a view defended by Othmar Keel (2001; 2007: 292–307) and many others (see the discussion by Stordalen, this volume).

Religious iconography from Iron Age Israel and Judah attests to further potential alternatives, for example, an anthropomorphic god standing or riding on a horse (at Tel Moẓa, inter alia) rather than a bull. Scholars have attempted to relate Yahweh to an anthropomorphic heroic figure known as 'Lord of the ostriches' (Keel and Uehlinger 1998: 140). Whether any one of these iconographic types relates to a form of Yahweh or to another deity is unclear; but what is obvious from these and other images is the actual existence of a variety of divine representations in Iron Age II Israel and Judah, including undoubtedly anthropomorphic ones.

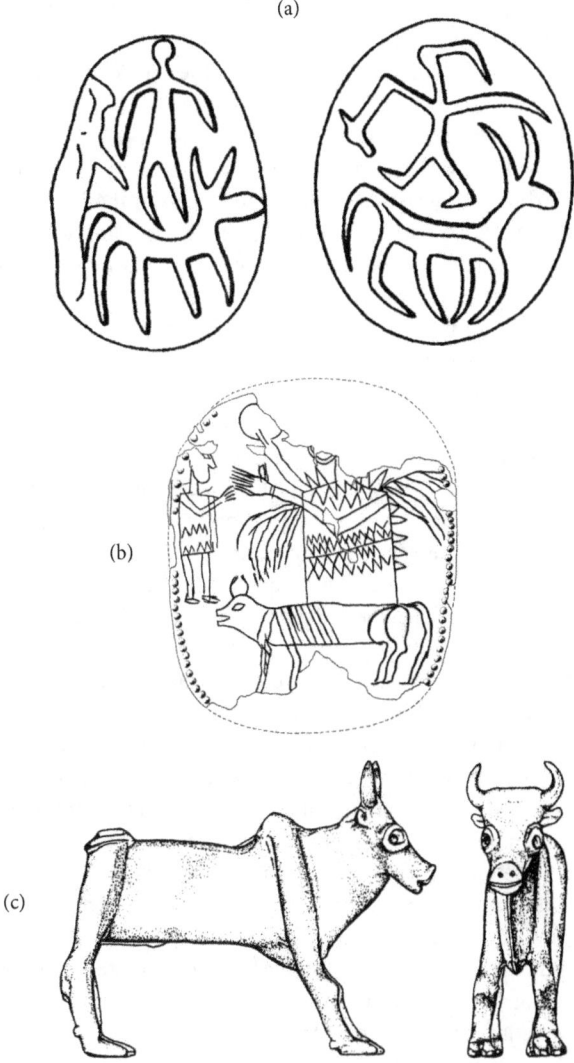

Figure 5.2a Anthropomorphic deities standing on bulls, as represented on stamp seals from eight-century-BCE Samaria (after Keel and Uehlinger 1998: 193, fig. 207a–b).

Figure 5.2b Engraved bronze plaque showing a worshipper facing a long-robed, winged deity standing on a bull; Tel Dan, eighth century BCE (after Biran 1999: 54, fig. 14; courtesy Nelson Glueck School of Biblical Archaeology, Jerusalem).

Figure 5.2c Bronze statue of a bull from a rural sanctuary in the Samarian hill country, c. eleventh century BCE (after Keel and Uehlinger 1998: 119, fig. 142).

To these anthropomorphic and/or theriomorphic options, one should add a number of non-figurative items, among which is the *maṣṣebah*, or standing stone, attested as a probable representation of Yahweh (and possibly other deities, including ancestors) by archaeological findings and by biblical texts (Mettinger 1995; Bloch-Smith 2015). Another non-figurative representation mentioned in the Hebrew Bible is the so-called ark of the covenant, which is said to have contained sacred stones (or the tablets inscribed by the finger of God) and to have rested under the wings of the Jerusalem cherubim until the first temple's destruction. Since the Hebrew word for 'ark' (*aron*) means 'box, container, cupboard', this tradition has been connected by some scholars with miniature shrine models in stone or terracotta unearthed at various ancient Canaanite, Israelite, Judahite (and Transjordanian) sites (see Garfinkel and Mumcuoglu 2016). Such miniature shrines have rarely been found with actual content (to the notable exception of a much older, sixteenth-century-BCE example from Ashkelon which contained a metal bull figurine), but those found at Israelite and Judahite sites have puzzled archaeologists and their public, raising the question 'To What God?' they may have been employed in ritual (see Mazar and Panitz-Cohen 2008). Scholars sticking to the 'aniconism' paradigm of Israelite religion occasionally construe such shrines (when considered Israelite) as essentially empty and thus 'aniconic', which viewed from a distance seems rather implausible and yet another instance of wishful imagination.

To sum up, there is ample evidence, both primary and secondary, for figural (anthropomorphic, theriomorphic) and non-figural ('aniconic') representations of deities in ancient Israelite and Judahite religion. The question whether any one (or which ones) of the many options should be positively identified as a visual and material representation of the god Yahweh remains as yet unresolved. But the more the data attest to practices, representations and conceptualizations in line with other Southern Levantine codes and customs, and the more the variety as such increases, the more the theory according to which Yahweh would have been worshipped in exclusively aniconic forms (as forcefully argued by Na'aman 1999 and Mettinger 2006) loses plausibility as an explanatory model. We may thus state as an intermediary conclusion that Yahweh was probably worshipped in ancient Israel and Judah under various forms and representations, among which are anthropomorphic and theriomorphic statuary in some places, and non-figurative material representations in others (Berlejung 2017). In this regard, the local, regional and institutional varieties of his cult would not have differed much (and certainly not in essence) from that of any other major deity in the Southern Levant.

III The emergence of the biblical ban on cultic images

If ancient Israelite and Judahite religion\s were less distinct from neighbouring religions than what conventional wisdom has assumed, one needs to explain the genealogy of a discourse of distinctiveness with which this volume is concerned and whose roots can be found in the Hebrew Bible. In this section I outline how the emergence of the so-called biblical image ban may be understood from a strictly historical point of view. The prohibition is generally viewed through the focal lens of the so-called Second Commandment of the Decalogue (itself embedded in two distinct literary contexts, Exodus 20 and Deuteronomy 5); but the Torah of Moses contains a number of additional texts prohibiting the production and use of cultic images. Again, there is more variety than often assumed, and the prohibitions are less encompassing than what the term image ban suggests, since these texts are exclusively concerned with cult-related imagery, never with images as such in a general sense. This holds true even for the Septuagint, the third-century-BCE Greek translation of the Torah (Tatum 1986). Important studies on the emergence of the biblical 'image ban' include articles by Herbert Niehr (2003) and Matthias Köckert (2007), among others.

The aim of this section is first to clarify the meaning and purpose of the various prohibitions found in the Torah of Moses. In earlier research (Uehlinger 2003), I argue that the variety of formulations reflects a process of increasing exclusion of figurative materials from ritual environments in which Yahweh would be worshipped in post-exilic Judah. My ambition here is to provide a religio-historical explanation which circumscribes and contextualizes the emergence of the biblical prohibitions as part of a historically contingent social process. Whatever its impact on later developments in Jewish, Christian and Islamic religious traditions, neither the process nor its consequences should be reified by historians of religion as a static, 'original' and once-and-forever feature of biblical religion. Methodologically speaking, this section deals with what I have called secondary sources in the previous section, since the relevant 'image ban' texts are all part of the biblical tradition. To analyse them in a historical perspective and to align them in a diachronic sequence is fraught with difficulties. The hypothesis cannot be securely tested against primary evidence for several reasons: first, it is hard to tell from artefactual evidence whether a particular commandment or prohibition was known in a specific context, let alone whether it was followed or not; second, it is virtually impossible to tell from the absence of particular artefacts in specific contexts (in this case, figurative imagery from a cultic context) whether this is the result of a normative injunction of this or that biblical commandment; thirdly, the archaeological record offers an inevitably incomplete documentation, as underscored by every new discovery. Still, I consider my historical reconstruction a plausible scenario for two reasons: internally, it tries to make sense of the variety of formulations, taking into account both a certain expansion in emphasis and a tendency to unify the issue of cult-related imagery; externally, I contend that I could demonstrate from archaeological evidence that at any stage in the postulated development of the prohibitions, the features at issue were actually available as real options (if only to be rejected by the biblical authors) to the post-exilic Judahite (Jerusalemite) society whose ritual regime these texts were probably meant to discipline.

Jerusalem versus Bethel

The starting point of our historical account is the conquest of Jerusalem in 587 BCE by Babylonian invaders who destroyed not only large parts of the city but also the royal palace and the temple adjacent to it. An earlier conquest in 598 had already led to the partial plundering of the temple, affecting particularly its ritual vessels. If the pre-exilic temple housed a cultic image of Yahweh (a hotly debated question which I tend to answer positively, see above), 598 would have offered the first opportunity for the

Babylonians to remove it together with the ritual vessels; but there is no clear evidence for such an operation, which would no doubt have required considerable attention on behalf of the conquerors. It seems safer to hypothesize that if the Jerusalem Temple housed a cultic image of Yahweh, it did so until the destruction of 587, when the image would have been destroyed together with its architectural envelope (Anthonioz 2015). Although one should not imagine post-587 Jerusalem devoid of any ritual activity addressed to Yahweh (Keel 2007: 784–6), the latter probably did not (no more?) involve a figurative cultic image. Limited ritual activity at best may have existed at Bethel, Jerusalem's rival sanctuary sixteen kilometres to the north which by the time had lost much of its former prestige. Biblical writers condemn Bethel and its figurative bull symbolism, whether in the book of the Israelite prophet Hosea (which by the sixth century would be preserved and rewritten by Judahite scribes) or in deuteronomistic historiography (cf. 1 Kings 12; 2 Kings 23), and finally in the latter's retrojection back to the times of Moses (Exodus 32). The 'Golden Calf' episode at the foot of Mount Sinai represents the ultimate disqualification of Bethel's cultic tradition and figurative bull symbolism, rejecting it as the most intolerable of Israelite idolatries (see further Sherwood, this volume).

'Image Bans' in the Torah

Apart from the latter narrative, one may distinguish three different strands in the literary development of 'image ban' texts in the Torah of Moses: One strand prohibiting the production of 'gods of silver' and 'gods of gold', preserved in the opening of the so-called Book of the Covenant, emphasizes the precious metal required for the production of cultic images, whether to be used for the worship of Yahweh or of other deities next to him (Exod. 20.22-3). Interestingly, this prohibition is preceded by a memento: 'You have seen [sic] that I spoke to you from heaven' (v. 22a), a statement which in its present context qualifies Yahweh's first encounter with Israel at Mount Sinai a few verses earlier. What Israel saw was not Yahweh, but His speaking from heaven. Together with Deuteronomy 4, this is one of the foundational texts establishing the dichotomy between the true (and ultimately transcendent) God who communicates with his people by words of heavenly origin, and other gods whose material preciousness cannot qualify them as real gods.

A second strand of prohibitions derives from the Decalogue, delivered a few verses earlier in Exodus 20 and repeated in Deuteronomy 5. Within the Torah's overall narrative, these words are of the highest authority since the narrative implies that Yahweh spoke directly, without any intermediary, to the people of Israel gathered at the foot of Mount Sinai. The version of the 'image ban' known as the Second Commandment represents a secondary addition to an earlier version of the Decalogue, as even a modern translation may show:

Exodus 20 // Deuteronomy 5

(v. 3/7)   You shall have no *other gods* before (or: facing) me.
(v. 4/8)   You shall not make for yourself a cult image (Heb. *pesel*),
            (or/and) any likeness of anything that is in heaven above,

or that is on the earth beneath,
or that is in the water (reaching even) under the earth.
(v. 5/9)   You shall not bow down to *them* or serve *them*,
for I, the LORD, your God, am a jealous God [...].

The plural pronouns in v. 5/9 ('them') have their referent in v. 3/7 ('other gods'), which implies that in an earlier version of the Decalogue v. 5/9 must have followed immediately after v. 3/7. The original intent of vv. 3/7 seems to have been to ensure the exclusive and solitary worship of Yahweh by excluding any kind of divine company, whether permanent or visiting. V. 4/8 adds a particular specification, excluding the production of a cult image (note that the standard translation 'graven image' is misleading here, since *pesel* includes any kind of material and is not limited to sculpture). The insertion of v. 4/8 has a double raison d'être: it excludes the production and worship of cult images per se, whether of Yahweh or of other gods, requiring no cult image at all; at the same time, it apparently implies that a cult image of Yahweh would be considered as representing 'another god', too. The latter, rather sophisticated argument would not have been necessary, had the issue of whether and how to figuratively represent Yahweh already been settled by the time of redaction. The emphasis on *no cultic image at all* (meaning: whether of other gods or of Yahweh) implies considerable debate on the issue among post-exilic Yahwists in Jerusalem (and possibly Samaria as well). As for v. 4b/8b, this seems to be a further extension of the prohibition: it excludes the production even of votive figurines (e.g. of animals or human worshippers, well attested in earlier Israelite and Judahite sanctuaries), that is, images which would not have become the focus of worship anyway but which as donations contributed in their own way to the material production of divine presence.

A third strand extends the former's concern with statuary to relief sculpture and even plain standing stones (Lev. 19.4, 26.1), that is, cultic objects known from local shrines and sanctuaries in the countryside that had once been considered perfectly fit for Yahwist worship but which anti-ruralist polemics of a new, post-exilic priestly elite would now disqualify by turning them into features of Canaanite backwoods rituals (Bloch-Smith 2015). Scribes and priests of the same pedigree would now underline their 'aniconic' Yahwism by promoting an anti-iconic, even iconoclastic, attitude against rural sanctuaries (Exod. 23.23-4; Num. 33.52-3) very much in line with the anti-Canaanism of Deuteronomy 12.

A more reflective and eminently theological synthesis of the various strands too briefly summarized here can be found in Deut. 4.1-40. This rhetorically sophisticated and compositionally complex chapter presents itself as an emphatic reminder to Yahweh's original revelation, here located at Mount Horeb, and adds dramatic narrative visuality to the memory of Israel's encounter with God. A large quote of the text will provide some sense of the chapter's rhetoric intensity.

Deuteronomy 4

[11] You came near and stood at the foot of the mountain, while the mountain burned with fire to the heart of heaven, wrapped in darkness, cloud, and gloom. [12] Then

the LORD spoke to you out of the midst of the fire; *you heard the sound of words, but saw no form; there was only a voice.* [13] And he declared to you his covenant, which he commanded you to perform, that is, the ten commandments; and he wrote them upon two tables of stone. [...]

[15] Therefore take good heed to yourselves. Since *you saw no form* on the day that the LORD spoke to you at Horeb out of the midst of the fire, [16] beware lest you act corruptly by *making a graven image (pesel, lit. cultic image) for yourselves,*

> *in the form of any figure,*
> *the likeness of male or female,*
> [17] *the likeness of any beast that is on the earth,*
> *the likeness of any winged bird that flies in the air,*
> [18] *the likeness of anything that creeps on the ground,*
> *the likeness of any fish that is in the water under the earth.*
> [...]

[23] Take heed to yourselves, lest you forget the covenant of the LORD your God, which he made with you, and *make a graven image (pesel) in the form of anything* which the LORD your God has forbidden you.[24] For the LORD your God is a devouring fire, a jealous God.

Scholars have long noticed that this chapter represents a *summa* of sorts of all previous reflections on how the Israelites could experience actual divine manifestation and communication (Yahweh himself speaking) and yet survive; under what conditions they would have been able to remain in their land instead of being led into exile, where they were exposed to the idolatrous cult of the material non-gods (fetishes *avant la lettre*) of foreign nations; how they were allowed to return and under what conditions the returnees would prosper in the country restored to them. With regard to this volume's central topic, it is striking to see how all this is conditioned upon the central obligation of an imageless worship of Yahweh. All emphasis is put on communication with Yahweh and the very possibility of divine presence, a presence that does not tolerate material mediation by any figurative image, but which can only be imagined and remembered in terms of fire. Fire is difficult to grasp and thus somehow immaterial, but as visible and radiating energy it is the symbol par excellence to which the faithful may associate the memory of hearing words of divine origin.

In a brilliantly perspicacious article, Matthias Köckert (2009) has demonstrated that even such a relatively late deuteronomic (fourth century BCE) text, for whose author an icon-related worship of Yahweh seems totally unacceptable, presumes the memory (which it construes and deconstructs in the very process of remembering) that pre-exilic Israel and Judah had not worshipped Yahweh aniconically, that is, the way this chapter and the Decalogue prescribe as ultimately normative:

Deuteronomy 4

[25] When you beget children and children's children, and have grown old in the land, if you act corruptly by *making a graven image (Heb. pesel) in the form of*

anything, and by doing what is evil in the sight of the LORD your God, so as to provoke him to anger, ²⁶ I call heaven and earth to witness against you this day, that you will soon utterly perish from the land which you are going over the Jordan to possess; you will not live long upon it, but will be utterly destroyed. ²⁷ And the LORD will scatter you among the peoples, and you will be left few in number among the nations where the LORD will drive you. ²⁸ And *there you will serve gods of wood and stone, the work of men's hands, that neither see, nor hear, nor eat, nor smell.*

So the Torah of Moses spells out (more lucidly than conservative scholars are ready to admit) that Israel's pre-exilic cult of Yahweh included the use of figurative images and must have been far from 'aniconic' in essence and in principle.

IV A hermeneutical pause: How come that modern scholars read prescriptive Torah as a template of actual 'Israelite religion'?

Sections II and III above can be read as summaries of two subsequent stages in the development of ancient Israelite, Judahite and ultimately early Jewish religion, to sum up: from Israelite cult practices which allowed for both iconic and aniconic representations of Yahweh (and of other deities and divine intermediaries) to the implementation of an 'aniconic' official worship of Yahweh in post-exilic (Persian period) Yehud, where Yahweh would now be progressively conceived as the one 'God of Heaven'. It is important to recognize that in fourth-century-BCE Samaria (Figure 5.3a) and Yehud (Figure 5.3b) Yahweh could still be anthropomorphically represented on coinage (Wyssmann 2013; De Hulster 2013). But the regime of his main temples was different, so that the official cult of Yahweh would henceforth operate on largely 'aniconic' assumptions. In this aesthetic regime, the significance and presumed augmented reality of Yahweh (or God) would no more be mediated by a statue or any other *direct* material representation (not even a standing stone, which would have been considered archaic and despised as 'Canaanite'); yet there were *indirect* indexes of presence (most notably, furniture and ritual vessels).

Following the rhetoric of Deuteronomy 4, Yahweh's word encoded in the Torah of Moses should now be regarded as the canonical medium. Yet considering what we know of post-exilic religion from extra-biblical data, it would be short-sighted to simply take the 'logocentric' perspective of Deuteronomy 4 at face value. Religious aesthetics has taught us to keep logocentric pretensions at critical distance and to consider the variety of sensory mediations even in the context of aesthetic regimes which celebrate the pre-eminence of a revealed Word or Scripture. Post-exilic Judahite religion may have been increasingly shaped by theological concerns preserved in deuteronomistic strata of the Hebrew Bible, but biblical tradition was by no means the only, nor probably the most, significant resource to give meaning and significance to late Judahite and early Jewish religion. That religion now centred increasingly

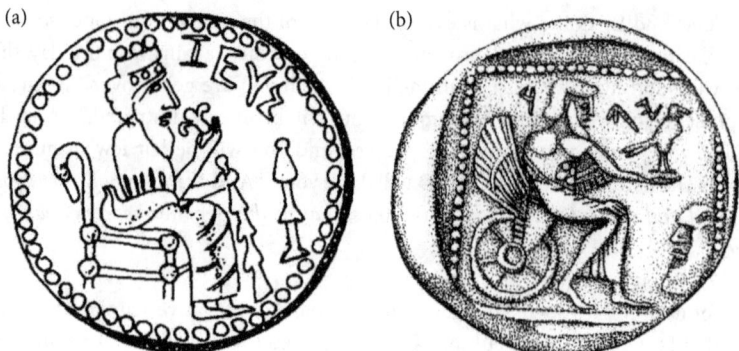

Figure 5.3a Enthroned god (labelled 'Zeus', possibly referring to Samarian Yahweh) on the obverse of a bronze obole from the Nablus/Shechem area, fourth century BCE (after Meshorer and Qedar 1999: 51, no. 40; courtesy Israel Numismatic Society).

Figure 5.3b Male god sitting on a winged wheel on the reverse of a silver drachm of unknown provenance, fourth century BCE; the legend has been read as Aramaic *YHD* (for Yehud) and as Paleo-Hebrew *YHW* (for Yahweh) respectively (after Gitler and Tal 2006: 231, fig. XVI.25; courtesy Haim Gitler, Israel Museum, Jerusalem).

around the rebuilt Temple of Jerusalem, a sacrificial economy which, together with the temple's sheer architectural materiality, its environments and the experience of crowds moving through them, would have represented the most tangible (and eminently sensual) aspects of lived religion for most visitors of ancient Jerusalem. A priest-run liturgy seems to have operated in a very peculiar kind of monumental 'empty space' (or *Leerstelle*) – empty in the sense that it did not contain what one would normally have expected in a building of the kind. That the temple did not house a statue was known to Jews and non-Jews alike, although the details of the Holy of Holies remained unavailable to the average visitor, for whom monumental architecture, purity concerns and sacrificial preoccupations, and feasting with a crowd or with one's family were far more important experiences. To be sure, this temple was different from the pre-exilic one, even if the scripturalized imagination of the Solomonic Temple provided a frame for experiencing the post-exilic temple to those who mused on that text (cf. Stordalen, this volume). Still, visiting the Jerusalem complex[3] remained a heavily multisensory experience, not least in terms of visual, material and spatial formations. Its multi-sensoriality would even increase during the Hellenistic and Roman periods, reaching its apogee with the huge renovation and extension of the so-called Second Temple by King Herod the Great. Even a cursory reading of this temple's enthusiastic description by Jewish historian Flavius Josephus demonstrates that 'aniconism' and multi-sensoriality do not mutually exclude each other at all. That this temple's statue-less character (assumed by all and known to some, but experienced inside by only a very few) was part of a peculiar visual and material regime which still allowed for an intense sensory experience has rarely been discussed by biblical scholars and historians of religion, many of whom tend to take early Jewish 'aniconism' as a pretext to switch from the visual to the auditory, or from image to scripture.

Stages in the evolution from prohibition to positive identity marker

In sum, historical-critical scholarship of the twentieth century construed a representation of ancient Israelite and Judhaite religion as 'aniconic' and monolatric from the very beginning. Yet, biblical literature is full of references to ancient Israelite and Judahite 'idolatry'. On the background of the archaeological record, these references may be requalified as distant and somehow distorted memories of previous religious diversity. Why would modern scholars ignore this evidence and reconstruct 'ancient Israelite' practices as having been in line with deuteronomistic interpretations of the Torah? How could biblical scholars produce such disingenuous readings of what their primary object of study actually says?

The main reason, in my view, lies in the normative power of prescriptive Torah, or rather in the assumption of biblical scholars and historians that what the Torah defines as an *ideal* and required ritual regime should be regarded as the *actual*, and under normal circumstances *usual*, form of ancient Israelite and Judahite religion. Such a view can hardly withstand the testimony of archaeological and historical evidence, nor that of critical biblical scholarship. Bluntly put, I suspect that 'ancient Israelite religion' as construed by twentieth-century theologians, biblical scholars and historians of religion owes more to modern synagogue and church education than to biblical, let alone historical and archaeological, data.

The basic hermeneutic problem at stake seems to be the epistemic mutation of positional, explicitly normative prescriptions of biblical texts into seemingly factual statements and rather unengaged assumptions by Biblicists and archaeologists alike. Is it possible to explain such a mutation? Since it affects the episteme, it must be related to the different epistemes' contexts. I suggest that instead of focusing our attention exclusively on the question how to construe and imagine ancient Israelite religion\s from primary and secondary data, we give equal attention to the contexts in which this (re-)construction and imagination took shape in history and takes shape today, and to the religious, institutional and/or scholarly agendas the various (re-)constructions and imaginations were and are meant to serve. Among the many different contexts that one might consider, largely disconnected from each other though genealogically related as members of a widespread family, let me single out the following.

Stage 1: The (hypothesized) context from which the earliest biblical prescriptions against the use of cultic images originated – real-life controversies in post-exilic Judah over an issue which particularly priests (many of whom had returned from Babylonia or were descendants of returnees) must have considered of the highest concern, namely how to serve Yahweh and communicate with him in his rebuilt temple.

Stage 2: The context (preserved by and available through the Hebrew Bible) in which the dominant outcome of the debates was fixed in prescriptive law (the Decalogue, the Covenant Code and other biblical law codes), supporting narrative (such as the story about the 'Golden Calf', Exodus 32; see Sherwood in this volume) and historiography (such as the tradition about Jeroboam's bull images in 1 Kings 12, for which see Berlejung 2009) by fifth-to-fourth-century temple scribes. The latter would increasingly read and rewrite these materials in terms of a coherent 'system', the Torah of Moses, to which traditionists would soon attribute the highest authority (Moses being elevated to the status of the most eminent prophet, or more than a prophet). This process leading from social controversy through normative regulations to ultimately canonized scripture must be considered the first phase of a substantial transmutation, out of which the *idea* that Yahweh (God) cannot be rendered in a cultic image because He did not want to render himself visible in such a way emerged as a *fundamental religious principle*, a principle which incidentally allowed to distinguish rather easily the one true God (and one's own religion) from those of all others (the 'nations').

Stage 3: The many contexts in which this systemic idea and religious principle would be adopted by Christians as part of their own religious heritage – a transference and adaptation into new social and cultural environments by a multi-ethnic and heterogeneous movement that was an extremely challenging task. The fundamental religious principle that (the Christian) God could not be worshipped in the form of a cultic statue allowed strong dissociation from Greek and Roman ('pagan') religion, but it collided with another, typically Christian principle (divine incarnation) and the notion that Christ himself could be regarded both as God's *logos* and *eikôn*. The issue became pressing when the Church acquired hegemonic power. Yet despite the many controversies, which led to just as many pragmatic and theological accommodations, the religious principle defined in the Decalogue was preserved as one of the most binding parts of Holy Scripture.

Stage 4: The context of religious controversies in Western Europe, which from the late medieval to the early modern period led to Reformation, occasionally accompanied by iconoclastic events, and the confessionalization of European Christianity. The binary dichotomy of true worship of God versus idolatry read out from scripture provided a convenient blueprint for dissociating especially Calvinist Protestantism from Papist Catholicism (which being the most proximate was also construed as the most perverse variety of idolatries by polemicists who had little concern for the Eastern European Orthodox traditions).

Stage 5: The context of modern biblical scholarship owes as much to Protestant scripturalism as it does to antiquarianism, Enlightenment and romanticism. Protestant scripturalism not only invented new ways of disciplining ritual, but also allowed pious Protestants to imagine themselves as 'the true Israel' – which in turn meant that enlightened Israel should be construed according to rules defined by modern Protestants. Antiquarianism opened new ways to historicize religion, including the religion of ancient Israel. Enlightenment favoured an understanding of religion in heavily intellectualized terms of abstract philosophical principles, a context in which the prohibition to figuratively represent God enjoyed obvious plausibility. Romantic distinction and essentialization of *Volksgeist* led to the idea of the faithful among ancient Israelites as those whose religion stood out from antique heathenism and prepared humanity for recognition of the one true God. Needless to say, these various constructs had little or nothing to do with the long-gone controversies which had produced the biblical texts in stages 1 and 2; but they provided the intellectual framework through which ancient Israel was reinvented.

Stage 6: Add to this the context of nineteenth- and twentieth-century biblical scholarship, which in times driven by a spirit of resolute modernity extended and modernized traditional ecclesial interpretation. Steps in, at the end of the nineteenth century, the typically modern, quasi-colonial discipline of biblical archaeology, which allowed Bible-inspired scholars to recover from the ground what former scholars had only imagined in their minds. In a context enriched by comparative history of religion\s, anthropology, but also radical dialectic theology, scholars versed in biblical studies and archaeology would produce a new episteme, in which the distinction between Israelite religion and Canaanite idolatry provided the blueprint for classifying and organizing the new material evidence from the past according to pre-established categories. This stage has been crucial for the epistemic transmutation postulated in this section, since the most robust resistance offered against new views on the histories and religion\s of ancient Israel and Judah in contemporary scholarship comes from scholars still operating according to the 'biblical archaeology' paradigm.

Stage 7: The modern archaeology of Israel/Palestine should be mentioned as yet another stage and background to our discussion. Secularization notwithstanding, many current debates in the archaeology of Israel/Palestine during the first millennium BCE relate to issues of national, political and religious identity in one way or another. The spectrum of scholarly positions on how to correlate archaeology and the Bible is wide, but defenders of a 'biblical archaeology' approach, in which one of archaeology's essential roles is to confirm and illuminate the Bible (which is thus legitimized to provide the default script for whatever archaeology has not yet brought to light), still represent a significant faction. This is important for my argument insofar as such an approach endorses and promotes the Mosaic principle of Israelite distinctiveness, re-inscribing the biblical dichotomy of Israelite versus Canaanite culture and religion (which for the first millennium BCE is differentiated into Israelite versus Phoenician, Philistine, Aramean, Ammonite, Moabite, Edomite) into artefactual data and thus reifying putative 'national' identities. This epistemic regime has produced scholars who will read the difference of Edomite versus Judahite religion into the terracotta statuary from Ḥorvat Qiṭmit versus the standing stones from Tel Arad (see Uehlinger 2006 for a critique), who wonder how a Judahite temple with cultic figurines can have existed in the ninth century BCE a few kilometres west of Jerusalem (Tel Moẓa, see Kisilevitz 2015 for a preliminary report),[4] or who look at empty miniature shrines made of clay and stage them as models for the 'aniconic' Temple of Solomon and 'the earliest archaeological evidence of the worship of the Lord of the new nation in Judah' (Garfinkel and Mumcuoglu 2016: 210).

Needless to say, this short summary of epistemic transmutation represents an oversimplification and would require refinement for all stages (see Levenson 2011 for a similar, much more detailed argument). Stages 6 and 7, which are closest to us, are perhaps the most delicate to describe, and I should stress that the evaluation given here concerns significant factions within highly contested, controversial fields which are also characterized by increasing methodological sophistication and intellectual brightness. My comments will hopefully not be read as a disrespectful bashing of colleagues whose work I highly appreciate even when disagreeing over models of interpretation. The aim of this all-too-brief genealogy of 'aniconic Ancient Israel' is to provoke reflection on the impact of epistemic regimes on our understanding of texts, traditions and material culture.

V From the iconism/aniconism divide to visual/ material culture and aesthetic formation

This section considers the theoretical challenge posed by the epistemic permutations summarized above, and sketches a possible way out of the apparent dilemma by suggesting a more robust engagement with recent theoretical advances in the study of religion\s. From the analytical and evaluative mode adopted in the previous section, I now switch to a more directional stance by offering a few briefly commented theses.

Thesis 1: Biblical texts prohibiting the production and use of cultic statuary stand at the origin of both religious and scholarly discourses on 'image ban' and 'aniconism'. Historians of religion should not read such texts at face value, but with attention to their variety, taking into account the socio- and cultural-historical contexts and controversies in which they were first formulated, however hypothetical, elusive and hard to recover these ancient contexts may be for modern scholars.

Texts which stand at the beginning of complex and elaborate discourse traditions (such as the 'image ban' discourse) are particularly likely to imply and reflect debates and controversies on the very issues they pretend to settle when referring to a divine or otherwise authorized authority. A major problem in the interpretation of biblical texts (here, prohibitions of cultic images) is the notorious difficulty to precisely date them in time and locate them in space and society. However, this should not be taken as an excuse to privilege de-contextualizing and ahistorical, over-generalizing modes of interpretation.

Thesis 2: By extending the prohibitions' scope of application from focal cult images through votive imagery to any kind of figurative representation in a cultic setting, post-exilic Judahite priests and scribes developed a particular aesthetic formation, whose perpetuation installed a new religious habitus ultimately leading to an epistemic regime that would posit itself as presenting a fundamental alternative to other ('idolatrous') regimes.

Although the principle that the 'God of Israel' should not be represented figuratively may have been debated as late as the second century BCE, it became constitutive of official early Jewish religion since at least the third century BCE, to the extent that external observers would know and comment about this particularity of Jewish ritual. The particularity would become habitual over time, and thus enjoy an ever-stronger plausibility. It is possible to demonstrate that whenever Judaism was construed in strong opposition to pressures from outside or alternatives within, such as during the so-called Maccabean crisis, under Roman imperial rule or during the Jewish Wars, the 'idol-less' Temple could easily become an emblem to enhance social cohesion and a sense of distinctiveness. In contrast, when the Jewish minority living in late-antique

Galilee enjoyed relatively good relations with its Christian neighbours and enjoyed a high degree of self-administration and participation in the overall framework of Byzantine society, religious distinctiveness may still have been an issue but did not need to be expressed through the radical avoidance of all visual imagery, as the famous mosaic floors from late-antique Galilean synagogues demonstrate (Levine 2013 and cf. Bland, this volume).

Thesis 3: Much like the data studied by anthropologists, historical data related to ancient religious practice and belief (and thus also the biblical prohibitions of the production and use of cult images) need to be studied as closely as possible 'from within', according to their (hypothetically retrieved) meaning, significance, pragmatic functionality for particular social groups and their specific religious ideology and interests.

For the social historian a text is a product of labour performed by someone occupying a particular position in the social fabric he or she once belonged to. The re-reading and re-working of texts by later generations were yet another kind of such labour. To get a sense of the social fabric in which these processes of writing and reading, rewriting and re-appropriating occurred, one must study the relevant society in its different stages from its primary evidence, based on as many media as possible (texts, images and other artefactual data). Needless to say, such evidence must be situated in ancient ecology, geography, economy, politics and so on. One cannot, however, overestimate the huge gap in terms of epistemic regime between the biblical texts' ancient *Sitz im Leben* (a somehow old-fashioned term which includes both the social location of texts and their social relevance to particular groups) on the one hand, and their modern location in the Bibles of believers or the computers of scholars, on the other.

Thesis 4: The ultimate aim of religio-historical research is not the most subtle (re-)construction of an ancient religious regime as such and according to its own logic, but its historical explanation in terms of social history and functionality, including ideology. While dense description is predicated on the interpretation of a maximum of relevant data, explanation requires engagement with theory.

The critical historian studying the evolution of ancient 'image bans' from targeted prohibitions to generalized, habitual *apriori* cannot limit him- or herself to mere exegesis of biblical texts. There is one option which remains closed to him or her (as a historian), namely to consider the 'meaning' of a particular text or discourse tradition as a 'message' for his or her own world view or belief. The critical historian will be curious to learn under what conditions and medial circumstances a restricted prohibitive discourse could turn into a disciplining discourse which today shapes the ritual regime of major religious traditions. Even more relevant in theoretical terms, he or she will need to critically reflect to what extent his or her own assumptions, research questions, terminology and so forth are tributary of the religious discourse tradition he or she wants to unravel.

Is it possible to step out of the pitfalls of a normative tradition which has so strongly impacted Western theological and philosophical thinking as the discourse on 'aniconism' and the *Bilderverbot*? As argued above, the very concept of 'aniconism' is heavily indebted to the mistrust developed in Western intellectual history against the visual and material mediation of the divine, the transcendent, the ultimately true and real. In order to escape from this conceptual deadlock, one needs theory; alternative ways of approaching the data, ways that do not carry the weight of normative epistemic bifurcations such as the ones lying at the basis of the matrix exposed in section I above.

Thesis 5: Much terminology employed by scholars (theologians, biblical scholars, historians of religion\s, anthropologists) to interpret and explain the religious phenomena discussed in this chapter is closely related if not directly borrowed from the emic terminology of the religious traditions concerned. That the same terminology has also been largely received into secular ideologies confirms rather than weakens the point. Since first-order terminology tends to simply duplicate religious discourse in a way or another, it is unlikely to produce plausible and robust theoretical explanations. This also applies to the domain addressed and debated under the labels of 'image ban' and 'aniconism'.

Although the term aniconic can be construed to 'describe a physical object, monument, image or visual scheme that denotes the presence of a divine power without a figural representation of the deity (or deities) involved' (Gaifman 2017: 337), an analytical terminology built on dichotomies and normative alternatives (as implied by both 'image ban' and 'aniconism') is in my view rather unhelpful to explain the phenomena and controversies discussed in this chapter in theoretically robust terms. An alternative approach should rest on concepts and a theoretical framework that overarches, or encompasses, so-called aniconic and iconic ritual regimes, allowing to analyse them with the very same questions regardless of their apparent antagonism.

It has long been shown that the binome 'iconic versus aniconic' does not need to be construed in a dichotomic way. The variety of artefactual data from many religious traditions rather invite to regard the two terms as extreme positions on a spectrum of materializations, many of which cannot be properly described as fully iconic or totally aniconic (Uehlinger 1996; Schipper 2013; Aktor 2017). It is here that visual and material religion enter the debate, allowing to make an additional step forward in terms of theory and focus: after all, both the so-called iconic and the aniconic object occupy a particular position in ritual space, can be seen and manipulated in this or another way, may serve to mediate an entity that would otherwise be considered physically absent, and so on. As an example from the history of early Jewish religion after the exile, I may refer to Bob Becking's convincing demonstration on how the temple vessels presumed to be those employed in the pre-exilic temple could materialize continuity and the presence of Yahweh in the post-exilic sanctuary of Jerusalem (Becking 2013). Applied in such a nuanced way to close readings of the data, sophisticated theory may enable scholars to analyse, compare and explain within a consistent framework of second-order concepts and explanatory models objects of study which first-order classifications would regard as essentially heterogeneous and disjunctive.

Thesis 6: Religion engages people to act as members of communities and, in ritual performance, to engage in particular settings which activate, exacerbate or curb sensory experience according to specific, group- and/or tradition-related rules. Focusing on the issue whether and how the presence of a not-to-be-seen deity might or should not be mediated through material objects and a particular visual representation is but one aspect of that larger condition. What has been described as 'image ban' and 'aniconic' ritual may be peculiar ways to regulate mediation and the participants' sensory experience, but they do not render the ritual setting itself opaque to such experience. 'Aniconic' as much as any other setting or regime can and should be analysed in terms of sensory formation or bodily-and-material culture.

To dissociate oneself from emic or first-order terminology when analysing material, visual, sensory ritual formations allows the critical scholar of religion to approach them in a way which is both epistemically less enmeshed in the data and theoretically more robust. As Urmila Mohan and Jean-Pierre Warnier rightly underscore (with reference to theoretical work by Michel de Certeau), in religion 'the religious subject is produced and marched in the name of a Real that is produced as such by an Imaginary giving shape to given discourses, bodies and material things' (2017: 377). 'Aniconic' ritual (or 'worship') fully conforms to that rule. It does not force its participants to act as if they were blind and does not eliminate media, the material and the sensory from ritual experience – it simply regulates them in particular ways, no more and no less. 'Aniconic' ritual offers multisensory and at times synaesthetic experiences as much as any other ritual regime. Regardless whether a deity is objectively presentified in a statue or not, his or her hold on participants *is* materially and visually mediated in ritual space in a way or another, and 'aniconic' ritual practice inevitably produces as much as it follows a particular order (an etiquette) of interaction with the deity, and among participants. To analyse this regime and its effects on socially constructed experience and imagination (or, when socially and culturally condensed, the imaginary) is the task of the critical study of religion. Scholars have efficiently conceptualized this task in terms of visual and material religion (Morgan 2010, among others), aesthetic or sensory formation (Meyer 2009, among others, and Promey 2014), religious aesthetics (Grieser and Johnston 2017) or bodily-and-material culture of religion (Mohan and Warnier 2017). Putting the body at the centre of religious experience, Mohan and Warnier suggest to shift the study of religion 'away from the verbalized creeds, doctrines and texts towards the consideration of the bodily-and-material cultures that are prominent in most' (if not in all) in order to 'understand how the bodily-and-material cultures of religious practice contribute to producing the devotee and obtaining compliance' (Ibid.: 369). It is my conviction that to dispose of the dichotomic language game of 'image ban' and 'aniconism' and to address ancient Levantine ritual – as documented in archaeological evidence, inscriptions and biblical texts – in terms of religious aesthetics, sensory formation and/or bodily-and-material culture will open new perspectives for the critical, historical study of ancient Israelite and Judahite, early Jewish and early Christian religion\s – and the study of their many diverse appropriations in subsequent periods and further traditions alike.

6

Visual Images in Medieval Jewish Culture before the Age of Art

Kalman P. Bland

Historical research is akin to the exploration of alien, often impassible, territory: in both cases, investigators require expert help with logistics and navigation. On this expedition, I have relied on an unusual combination of suppliers and navigators, all of them splendid: Hans Belting, Franz Kafka and the *Ikhwān al-ṣafā*, the Brethren of Purity. Belting, our contemporary, is a quintessential art historian. Kafka is a quintessential modernist. The Brethren are quintessential premodernists. Their differences are striking. Kafka (1883–1924) was Jewish, lived in Prague and wrote celebrated fictions in German. The Brethren were Arabophone Muslims, cosmopolitan philosophers and intellectuals, tending towards Ismāʻili inflected Shiite loyalties. They flourished in the tenth century, living most probably in Iraq, in the southern city of Basra (see El-Bizri 2008; Callataÿ 2005; Hamdani 2007). Although striking, their differences are inconsequential compared to their commonalities. Like Kafka, the author of unforgettable animal fables, including *The Metamorphosis*, 'A Report to an Academy', and 'Investigations of a Dog', the Brethren were masters of the genre. Witness their unforgettable fable *The Case of the Animals versus Man before the King of the Jinn* (Goodman and McGregor 2009).

Kafka and the Brethren share a second trait: they were keen observers of visual art. They share an exquisite sensitivity to painting and sculpture with Hans Belting, author of *Likeness and Presence: A History of the Image before the Era of Art*. In the post-Reformation 'era of art', according to Belting, Christian images ceased being 'receptacles of the holy'. They were 'divested of aura', subordinated to 'the written word and interpretations of the preachers' and 'made subject to the general laws of nature, including optics'. Detached from the transcendence embodied in saintly beings and things, images ultimately devolved, becoming products of artistic 'imagination' and 'manifestations of art' (Belting 1994: 14, 458–9, 470–1). In Belting's pre-Reformation era of images, by contrast, paintings, mosaics, sculptures and architecture, at least the Christian ones, were understood to be agents exuding sacred power rather than mere expressions of an idea or displays of creative genius. In Belting's scheme of eras, where do Kafka and the Brethren fit?

Evidence of Kafka's engagement with the visual arts can be gathered from a book of personal recollections, *Conversations with Kafka*, written by his young friend, Gustav Janouch. One day, Janouch showed Kafka a portrait painted by the Czech artist Vladimir Sychra (1903–63). Janouch reports that Kafka was 'delighted with the portrait', and declared several times, 'The drawing is wonderful. It is filled with truth.' Janouch asked, 'Do you mean that it is true to life as a photograph is?' Kafka replied: 'What are you thinking of? Nothing can be so deceiving as a photograph. Truth, after all, is an affair of the heart. One can get at it only through art' (Janouch 1953: 87). Kafka's dual apotheosis of the human heart and art as the exclusive means of achieving truth exemplifies the post-Reformation, disenchanted, secularizing 'era of art'.

On yet another occasion, Janouch and Kafka were discussing illustrations drawn by George Grosz. Gazing upon one of them, Kafka remarked, 'This is the familiar view of Capital[ism] – the fat man in a top hat squatting on the money of the poor.' Noticing that the image did not depict the fat capitalist as a victim, Kafka was dissatisfied. He observed that 'the picture is not complete. For that reason it is not good. Capitalism is a system of relationships, which go from inside to out, from outside to in, from above to below, from below to above. Everything is relative, everything is in chains. Capitalism is a condition both of the world and of the soul.' Janouch challenged Kafka, 'Then how would you picture it?' Doctor Kafka shrugged his shoulders and smiled sadly. 'I don't know. In any case we Jews are not painters. We cannot depict things statically. We see them always in transition, in movement, as change. We are story tellers' (Janouch 1953: 86–7).[1]

Consider the set of visual images supplied here (Figures 6.1a–c).[2] They depict creation. They appear on the opening pages of an illuminated medieval Hebrew manuscript, in this case a Haggadah, the liturgical handbook meant for domestic use containing instructions, hymns, homilies, rabbinic prayers and biblical recitations for conducting the Passover Seder meal. Using Kafka's pronouncements as a framework for seeing them, what might we observe? Cognitive dissonance, anomaly and antinomy spring to mind. Since the language of the manuscript is liturgical, rabbinic Hebrew and the images read from right to left, the most likely provenance is Jewish. A modicum of research confirms the hypothesis: The illuminations were produced in late-fourteenth-century Spain, most likely commissioned by a wealthy Jewish patron living in the kingdom of Aragon, probably Barcelona, not too far removed from the cultural orbit of Provence. In 1492, the manuscript, like many of its kindred, accompanied its owners into exile. It may have spent some time in Venice before settling permanently in the Ottoman Empire, in the region surrounding the town called Sarajevo, from which it eventually took its name and where it survived first the Nazis and then more recent battles between Bosnia and Serbia (Roth 1962: 7–16).[3] Facts, however, do not easily trump preconceptions. It is a foregone conclusion that the painter was not Jewish, because, as Kafka declared, 'we Jews are not painters'. The same holds true for the patron who commissioned the Sarajevo Haggadah or used it to celebrate Passover. He or she is unlikely to have been recognizably Jewish, because, as Kafka asserted, visual images are 'static', as static as this figure resting on a bench, and therefore inimical to Jewish habits of mind that prefer telling stories with words, habits which presumably accord with the biblical injunction against idolatrous depictions of the sacred and conform to the

126 *Figurations and Sensations of the Unseen in Judaism, Christianity and Islam*

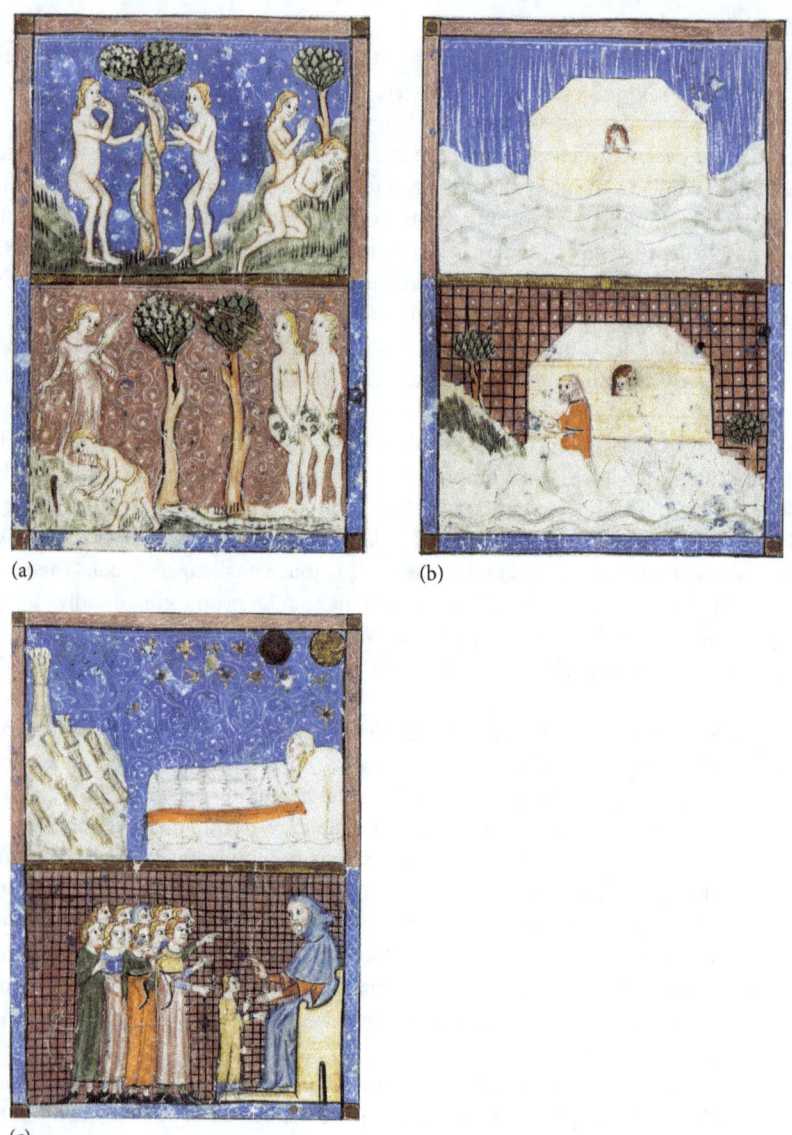

Figure 6.1a Adam and Eve eating the forbidden fruit and being expelled from the garden (Genesis 3). Miniatures from the Sarajevo Haggadah, ca. 1350 CE, courtesy of the National Museum of Bosnia and Herzegovina, Sarajevo.

Figure 6.1b Two pictures concluding the story of the flood and Noah (Genesis 6–8). Miniatures from the Sarajevo Haggadah, ca. 1350 CE, courtesy of the National Museum of Bosnia and Herzegovina, Sarajevo.

Figure 6.1c Opening the story of Joseph and his brothers; Joseph having a dream and telling it to his father (Genesis 37). Miniatures from the Sarajevo Haggadah, ca. 1350 CE, courtesy of the National Museum of Bosnia and Herzegovina, Sarajevo.

traditional Jewish way of seeing 'things always in transition, in movement, as change'.[4] The difficulty of reconciling the obvious Jewish provenance of the illuminations with their Kafka-esque unJewishness is insurmountable. The difficulty can simply be made to disappear if we jettison Kafka's modernist preconceptions and replace them with the critical framework provided by the tenth-century Islamic Brethren of Purity. In their regime of seeing, the perception of visual art is emphatically non-modern, thoroughly enchanting and altogether occult.

The charming title of the chapter containing the Brethren's discussion of images reads as follows (see Callataÿ and Halfants 2011: 87):

> On the quiddity of magic (*siḥr*); incantations; the evil eye; enticements for the training of animals; intuition; and spells; on the modalities of the actions of talismans; on what the demons of the earth, the jinn, the devils, the angels are; and on the means of their deeds and mutual influences. The objective is to clearly expound that in the world there are autonomous and imperceptible agents that are called spiritual beings.

The exposition of these topics dwells upon the ubiquitous science of astrology and its practical application in the production of talismans. The Brethren are cosmopolitan; they avoid polemics; they evince no awareness of a distinctive family of Abrahamic religions composed of Judaism, Christianity and Islam; they do not privilege monotheism over polytheism. The first subsection of the chapter treats the nexus connecting magic and visual artefacts as documented by the ancient Greek writings of Plato. Subsequent sections first address the legitimacy of magic according to the Qur'an and authentic Islamic tradition and then 'magic according to the Jews and Christians', as found in scripture, the Torah. The most detailed subsection is devoted to 'magic among the Sabi'ans, Ḥarrānians, and Ḥanifs', especially to the construction and decoration of their numerous temples, where they worship the stars and initiate new members into the esoteric mysteries of their cult.

In the subsection on 'magic according to the Jews and Christians', we are reminded of the tension between the prophet Samuel and King Saul, who in the midst of his battles with the Philistines desperately consulted a sorceress to conjure the spirit of the lately departed Samuel. We are also reminded of the episode reported in Genesis 30 where Jacob profits immensely from peeling the bark from the branches of almond and other trees and displaying the speckled branches to the breeding flocks to influence the colour of their offspring. We are told the story of 'Esau, son of Isaac, and of the son of Nimrod, son of Canaan'. The story features a description of the 'shirt (*qamīṣ*) of Adam [...] on which were to be seen images (*ṣūwar*) of every creature of God Most High: wild beasts, birds and sea animals. When Adam, God bless him and grant him salvation, wished to hunt one of the wild beasts or other creatures, he used to put his hand on its image (*ṣūratihi*) on the shirt, and that game remained bewildered, stopped and blind until [Adam] had come to it and taken it.' With the advice of his father, Isaac, Esau tricked the son of Nimrod out of ownership of Adam's shirt, so that whenever 'Esau wished to hunt some wild beast, he put his hand on its image on the shirt, and it stopped, blind, without seeing, until Esau would come and take it' (Callataÿ and

Halfants 2011: 107–9 [English]; 32–6 [Arabic]). Note that Esau and Adam did not utter a spell, but they did place a physical hand on a material image, an icon, if you will.

With the Brethren in mind, we can temporarily escape the straitjacket of modern preconceptions and take a fresh look at the medieval Hebrew illuminations. As we did with Kafka, we can draw some provisional conclusions. First: The texts do not imply that the Brethren considered their talismans capable of doing what Christians believed icons and relics were capable of doing, but the texts do allow us to catch a glimpse of the phenomenological similarity. In one tradition, material artefacts, like icons, are receptacles and agents efficaciously mediating a cosmic, Christocentric power; in the other tradition, material artefacts, like talismans, are receptacles and agents efficaciously mediating an alternative cosmic power, astrological. This too is noteworthy: The Brethren affirmed that the Jews share their belief in the potency of visual images; the Brethren also assumed that the production and use of visual images are venerable and commonplace among the Jews, as venerable and commonplace as the production and use of visual images among other ethnic and religious communities; and finally, the Brethren did not notice that Jews consider words superior to images or regard storytelling more perfect than picture-making in representing reality or in bending reality to do humanity's will. Perhaps the Brethren did not notice this hierarchy of art forms because it was non-existent in their day. Thinking with the Brethren, then, we have no reason to doubt that the artist who painted the Sarajevo Haggadah and the patrons who commissioned and used it were Jews. As for the illuminated Haggadah itself, it no longer appears to be egregiously unorthodox or anomalous, since it was native in a culture that had normalized visual images and put them gainfully to work ever since biblical times.

The Brethren of Purity have therefore brought us closer to medieval Jewish culture than Kafka was able to do. To approach even closer, one might replace the mindset of the Brethren with a critical framework built out of the raw materials supplied by the same medieval Jewish culture that produced, put to use and preserved the illuminated Hebrew manuscripts: Jewish intellectual reverberations of astrology, talismans and theurgy (Bland 2000: 130–8; 144–8). What did medieval Jews think paintings were and what work did they expect those images to do?

Medieval rabbinic law, anchored in the bedrock of Talmudic precedent, the *halakhah*, provides the most authoritative answers. Rabbi Meir of Rothenburg (1220–93) was pre-eminent among the illustrious jurists of the Rhine valley. He wrote the following responsum:

> I was asked concerning the propriety of those who illuminate their holiday prayerbooks with pictures of birds and animals. I replied: It seems to me that they certainly are not behaving properly, for while they gaze upon those pictures they are not directing their hearts exclusively to their Father in heaven. Nevertheless, in this case, there is no trespass against the biblical prohibition, 'You shall not make either a sculpture or any image' [Exod. 20.3]. [...] Furthermore, there are no grounds for even a precautionary suspicion [of idolatry] regarding the pictures, since they are merely patches of pigment lacking sufficient tangible materiality. We only suspect idolatry with regard to a protruding, engraved seal, but not with

an intaglio seal, and all the more so in this case where [the image in prayerbooks] is neither protruding nor intaglio. [The image in a prayerbook] is merely flat pigment. Moreover it seems to me that a Jew is permitted to produce images using all sorts of pigment, without thereby [encroaching] on the prohibition [against idolatry] [...] since the only forbidden image is the painted sculpture of a complete frontal view.[5]

To the question of illuminations and their ontological status, Jewish law replies: permissible 'patches of pigment'.[6] Patches of flat pigment, unlike icons, do not invite veneration; they cannot weep, shed blood if stabbed, or miraculously heal the sick, blind and crippled. To the related question of what actions paintings perform, rabbinic law replies: an undesirable, but otherwise non-sinful, innocuous distraction from devoted prayer.

Complementing Rabbi Meir's judgement that images impinge on the psyche is the opinion of another authoritative master of rabbinic law, Moses ben Maimon, physician as well as philosopher, known to the West as Maimonides (1138–1204). The distinguished art historian Joseph Leo Koerner considered him an 'iconophobe' (Koerner 2004: 209; 465, n. 36). Uncharacteristically, Koerner missed the mark. In his ethical treatise, *Eight Chapters*, Maimonides explained, writing in Judaeo-Arabic, that a person whose priorities are properly aligned

> will not trouble himself with adorning his walls with golden carving or with decorating his garments with golden embroidery, unless it be for the purpose of enlivening his soul, thus restoring it to health, or of banishing sickness from it, so that it become clear and pure, in proper condition to master the sciences. [...] It is therefore permitted to make designs and pictures on houses, utensils and garments for the soul grows weary and thought passes away as a result of constantly looking at ugly things [...] the soul must occupy itself with refreshing the senses by looking at beautiful carvings and pictures so that its weariness be removed. (Gorfinkle 1912: 72 [English]; 32–3 [Hebrew])

Almost two hundred years later, this passage was cited verbatim by Isaac ben Moses Halevi, known in Catalan as Profiat Duran, an Iberian Jewish scholar specializing in Hebrew biblical grammar, who offered pedagogic advice based on the utilitarian, hedonistic, psychotherapeutic theory of art endorsed by Maimonides:

> One should always study from the most beautiful and lovely of books, whose script is attractive and whose pages are glorious both in ornamentation and binding. One's places of study [...] ought to be beautifully decorated buildings, for by increasing one's love of learning and the pleasure one takes in it, memory is improved. Moreover the studious beholding of lovely shapes, beautiful designs and pictures, expands the soul, stimulates it, and strengthens its faculties. [...] Just as God took delight in adorning his Temple with gold, silver, precious stones and treasure, so too should it be regarding his sacred books, especially this holy book [the Bible]. [...][7]

This theory of art was equally welcome in medieval Islamic thought (Rosenthal 1992: 265-6), and it enjoyed an afterlife in early modern Jewish thought, for instance in Baruch Spinoza:

> Certainly nothing but grim and gloomy superstition forbids enjoyment [...] the more we are affected with pleasure, the more we pass to state of greater perfection; that is, the more we necessarily participate in the divine nature. [...] It is [...] the part of a wise man to refresh and invigorate himself in moderation with good food and drink, as also with perfumes, with the beauty of blossoming plants, with dress, music, sporting activities, theatres and the like [...].[8]

The persistence and popularity of this aesthetic understanding of visual art allow for the flourish of a final example. It begins with an Arabic text, *Ādāb al-filāsifa, Gnomic Aphorisms of the Philosophers*, composed by Ḥunayn ibn Isḥaq (809–73), a famous translator of Greek philosophy and science into Syriac and Arabic, a Nestorian Christian, who flourished in Baghdad, capital of the cosmopolitan Abbasid empire. The text itself deals with the practice of ancient Greek philosophers to gather in small groups in specially designated, luxuriously decorated buildings to swap wisdom.[9] Almost four-hundred years later, Ḥunayn's revised Arabic text was translated with remarkable accuracy into Hebrew by Yehudah al-Ḥarizi, under the title *Sefer musare ha-pilosofim, The Book of Gnomic Aphorisms of the Philosophers*. Ḥarizi was a gifted poet, a brilliant translator, a champion of Hebrew *belles-lettres*. Born in Toledo in 1165, capital of Castile, he travelled throughout Christian Spain, settled as an adult in Provence, and returned to the life of an itinerant, traversing Islamic North Africa, continuing eastward from Cairo into Israel, Syria and Iraq, making his living as a translator and poet. He died in Aleppo, in 1225. He was culturally ambidextrous, a linguistic amphibian, writing Hebrew prose and poetry for Jews, Arabic poetry for Jews and Muslims. He was on the lookout for wealthy and generous patrons, constantly.[10] Here is a translation of Ḥarizi's medieval Hebrew rendering of Ḥunayn's late ancient Arabic discussion of the practice of ancient Greek philosophers to gather in small groups in specially designated, luxuriously decorated buildings to swap wisdom:

> Ḥananyah said, 'the foundational reason for these gatherings was because the kings of Greece and others like them used to educate their children in wisdom and philosophy, civilizing them (*meyassrim*) with various sorts of moral and cultural refinement (*musar*). They would construct for them buildings covered in gold and decorated with all sorts of images (*tziyyurim*), indeed making these images to refresh and expand (*leharvviaḥ*) their hearts, in order that their eyes would desire to see them. So it was that the lads would diligently and studiously remain (*shoqdim*) in the halls of images to learn the lessons of moral and cultural refinement because of the images that were present there. Similarly, the Jews make ornamental designs and engravings (*pittuḥim*) in their halls (*hekhalehem*), the Christians draw images (*tziyyurim*) in their churches, while the Ishmaelites [i.e. Muslims] decorate with ornament their houses of worship. All of this is meant to refresh and expand their souls by their means and to engage their hearts with the [decorations, ornaments, and images] [...]'[11]

Once again, we encounter medieval Islamic and Jewish engagement with the role of visual art in facilitating the pleasures of *paideia* or *Bildung* and their concomitant, humanistic refusal to privilege monotheism over polytheism.

With this array of medieval Jewish legal and philosophic texts in mind, let's take one last look at the illuminations from Sarajevo. Our taxonomy is deficient. What we see cannot be classified with icons before the era of art or images during the era of art. Neither can the illuminations be classified with the disempowered, disenchanted, didactic art of the Reformation itself, analysed so elegantly and cogently by Joseph Leo Koerner. The illuminations from Sarajevo appear to enjoy a life of their own, not slavishly bound to the text they accompany. That they show rather than tell is their virtue. They are unburdened by the responsibilities of formulating verbal arguments or teaching unequivocal lessons in doctrine. They are not understood to be objects to be studied, categorically unlike sacred texts or scientific treatises to be mastered. The images are primarily charged to be fascinating, eye-catching and beautiful. We may be witnessing a medieval Jewish form of play and entertainment, a flirtation with exuberant irrationality, a counterpart to what Meyer Schapiro (1977: 1–27) expertly called the 'aesthetic attitude in Romanesque [Christian] art'. Like their Romanesque counterparts, the illuminations reveal a medieval Jewish method for tickling the fancy, refreshing the sensorium and taking delight in the surprises of visual experience. Gazing upon the images, we behold a medieval Jewish device for making Jewish history, learning and ritual practice memorable, if not enjoyable. And finally, perhaps we also encounter a medieval Jewish stratagem in Christian Europe for simultaneously performing two contradictory tasks: on the one hand, showing commonality with all the other cultures that produce and use visual art, and on the other hand, repudiating with subtle mockery the misguided visual habits and errant beliefs of their non-Jewish neighbours.

7

Real Absence: Imagining God in Turco-Persian Book Arts, 1300–1600 CE

Christiane J. Gruber[1]

O You who are Hidden in that which is hidden, You are more than all. All see themselves in You, and they see You in everything.

Farid al-Din 'Attar ('Attar 1954: 4)

Metaphysical and theological inquiries into the nature of God's divinity have been long-standing markers of the three Abrahamic faiths of Judaism, Christianity and Islam. Over the course of many centuries, thinkers, writers and artists have actively constructed various discursive models through which to describe and give shape to God and His transcendental nature. The paradigms of inquiry have fluctuated depending on time and circumstance, and thus provide us with a rich and textured picture of the diverse mechanisms, deployed through both text and image production, that have served to suggest a sense of the ineffable.

Metaphorical language and rhetorical abstractions have provided key figures of speech in conveying God's essence. Additionally, anthropomorphic descriptions have been harnessed, reflecting the generative power of the human template (Guthrie 1993: 92). Humans' general tendency to borrow from their perception and experience of the world around them has enabled them to articulate and affirm the presence of divinity, despite God's distant removal from intellectual knowledge and tactile experience.

As in other monotheistic traditions, in Islamic philosophical and speculative practices the question of God's identity or ipseity (*huwiyya shakhsiyya*) engendered fruitful discussions that sought to describe God's modality – that is, His 'whatness' or *kayfiyya* (Abrahamov 2002: 213) – and His pre-eminent status as not belonging to any genus in the natural world. Writers were particularly keen to emphasize God's capacity of summoning all of creation under the aegis of His deistic oneness (*tawhid*). Oftentimes, God is described through an epistemic process of idealization marked by imaginative verbal reconfigurations that seek to translate His transcendental properties through both anthropomorphic and paramorphic models (Schoen 1990: 137–8). In other words, God has been described in both human and supra-human terms in Islamic traditions, and these two distinct approaches reveal that, at least at the fastening of his chest cavity after it was split open and his heart purified by angels. On a more symbolic level, Muhammad's corporeal imprimatur pays tribute to his utmost status as the final, or 'seal', of all prophets within the Judeo-Christian line.

Many biographical and poetic sources also elaborate upon Muhammad's sweet-scented nature as emanating from his visit to paradise and contact with God. His body is described as smelling like the flowers of paradise, which include the rose, narcissus and anemone (Gruber 2014). He thus is thought redolent of God's presence in paradise, the latter described as His 'conserve of roses' (Nizami 1945: 110). Muhammad's contemporaries also specify that his 'seal of prophethood' was particularly ambrosial, as noted by his companion Jabir: 'The Prophet let me ride behind him, so I put my mouth on the seal of prophecy and it spread over me like musk' (al-Yahsubi 1991: 35). The Prophet's visible seal and his sensible aroma are praised by many writers because both evoke an aromatic heaven, made and inhabited by God, and also reminiscent of God's presence through the synesthetic potential of smell.

Ilkhanid painters, it appears, were keen to communicate the presence of God in Muhammad through a series of visible signs, much as artists in the medieval Christian world sought to depict Christ as a carrier of divinity by deploying choice devices like the gold halo, the mandorla and the veil (Kessler 2006: 423). In the series of paintings in the *Jami' al-Tawarikh*, for instance, Muhammad is depicted in the process of being anointed, first upon his recognition as a prophet by the Christian monk Bahira (Figure 7.1) and, later, during his battle against the Banu al-Nadir, a Jewish tribe that had been living in a fortress outside Medina (see Gruber 2009: 160, Figure 3). In both paintings, an angelic proxy emerges from or swoops down from the skies, carrying what appears to be a rose-water flask and either a scroll or a codex, both indicative of God's selection of His Messenger via anointment by scent and revelation by scripture. Through the double representation of divine smell and Holy Book, the presence of divinity becomes visually detected in the painting.

The first painting in Rashid al-Din's *Jami' al-Tawarikh* represents a well-known event from the childhood of the Prophet Muhammad (Figure 7.1). The episode is recorded in a number of early biographical texts, such as Ibn Ishaq's (d. ca. 767 CE) *Biography of the Prophet* (*Sirat al-Nabi*), and universal histories, including al-Tabari's (d. 923 CE) *The History of Messengers and Kings* (*Ta'rikh al-Rusul wa'l-Muluk*). Chroniclers tell us that, when Muhammad was sometime between nine and twelve years of age, he accompanied his uncle Abu Talib on a merchant caravan to Syria. When they and their entourage arrived in the Syrian town of Busra, they encountered in a cell a monk by the name of Bahira, who is described as particularly well versed in the so-called sacred books. It is in these Christian books that he found descriptions of Muhammad and his divinely decreed apostleship, and it is thanks to such books that he was able to recognize Muhammad as a prophet, even in his young age. Bahira thus essentially serves as a polemicized witness and guarantor of the superiority of Islam over Christianity (Abel 1986: 922).

Islamic texts highlight the fact that natural phenomena and markers on Muhammad's body helped Bahira recognize his prophetic status. First, Bahira saw a cloud taking the shape of a shield and overshadowing the Prophet (and no one else) so that he would become protected from the heat of the sun. Second, the cloud caused a tree's branches

136 *Figurations and Sensations of the Unseen in Judaism, Christianity and Islam*

Figure 7.1 Muhammad as a young boy is recognized as a prophet by the Christian monk Bahira, Rashid al-Din, *Jamiʿ al-Tawarikh* (Compendium of Chronicles), Tabriz, Iran, 1307–8 CE. Edinburgh, Edinburgh University Main Library, Ms. Arab 20, folio 45v.

to bend and droop so that they, too, would shelter Muhammad from the elements. And third, once Bahira approached Muhammad and examined him closely, he noticed on his back the seal of prophethood between his shoulders, an indexical 'trace' of God's selection that had been recorded and described in the 'sacred books' (Ibn Ishaq 2004: 80–1; and al-Tabari 2002: 412). These specific textual details stress that Muhammad's awaited arrival was foretold according to previously revealed, uncorrupted texts, and that God's favour upon him consisted in a grand cosmic umbrage as well as discernible physical marks upon his body.

The painting of Bahira recognizing the young Muhammad as the final messenger of God as included in the *Jamiʿ al-Tawarikh* provides a visual confirmation of the various themes that are particularly salient to the legitimating discourse about Muhammad's divinely decreed arrival as promised in the 'good books' (*min khayr al-kutub*, as noted in Rashid al-Din's text located immediately above the painting). In the depiction, the monk Bahira stands in his elevated cell to the right, as he holds his robe and extends his right hand to point to Muhammad, who is standing on the left. All men and even the camels turn towards the Prophet, either bowing or (as in the camels) genuflecting as they encircle him. The young Muhammad stands upright, wearing a long red tunic and a white turban. Above him, an angel has distended the blue firmament as it reaches for Muhammad's head, endowing the Prophet with heavenly scent by means of a gold rose-water flask and transmitting God's logos through the scriptural metaphor of the inscribed parchment or scroll (Rice 1976: 99).

All movements – human, animal and even cosmic – rotate around the Prophet, who serves as the centrifugal protagonist in the composition. As a result, the painting stresses Muhammad's prophetic centrality by means of compositional arrangement. It also provides a visual amplification of the text's supersessionist rhetoric, which claims that Muhammad was foretold to man and that his predestination is recognizable to a Christian witness conversant in uncorrupted scripture. Just as importantly, the composition expands upon narratives that describe Muhammad's selection by God through the protective shade of a cloud or branches. Rather than depicting God's favour through natural phenomena, the artist has stressed God's presence through the double process of uranophany (the appearance of the skies through the bend in the celestial arc) and angelophany (the appearance of an angelic being) into the world, two theographic techniques of representation found in contemporaneous European Christian paintings as well (Boespflug 1992: 15–17). The viewer of the painting is thus invited to partake not only in the visual recognition of Muhammad as prophet but, more importantly, to consider God's observable presence through His divine anointment of and scriptural revelation to His elected messenger.

Similar visual metaphors for God's symbolic propinquity to the Prophet are in operation in another painting included in Rashid al-Din's *Jami' al-Tawarikh*, which depicts Muhammad besieging the fortification of the Banu al-Nadir after the Jewish tribe had broken a treatise with him and had conspired to kill him (see Gruber 2009: 160, Figure 3). Accounts describing these sorts of military campaigns belong to the *maghazi*, or expeditions and raids, literary genre, a field of textual production that was very closely associated with works in the *sira*, or biographical, genre during the first two centuries of Islam (Hinds 1983: 63). Works in the *maghazi* genre were not just about narrating Muhammad's raids and conquests; they also were religiously inclined because military victories – and, by extension, religio-political ascendancy – are interpreted in Islamic (and other) traditions as overt signs of God's protection, intervention and election (Paret 1930: 169). Of paramount importance, *sira* and *maghazi* works make a point to stress that, for every military campaign that Muhammad and his followers undertook, Qur'anic verses were revealed to him. Such verses scripturally explain and consecrate his prophetic undertakings by literally inserting God 'into the picture'. In other words, a victory by the sword evinced the superiority of the Islamic faith by the manifest proof of God's favouritism and His presence – a presence described in the Qur'an as emerging from 'the canopies of clouds with ranks of angels' (Q 2.210 and 89.22).

Sira and *maghazi* texts inform us that it was during the expedition against the Banu al-Nadir that the entire 'Chapter of Confrontation' (*surat al-hashr*, Q 59) was revealed to the Prophet. The first verses of Q 59 describe how these Jewish 'people of the book' (*ahl al-kitab*) were pushed out of their homes and forced into exile because they 'had opposed God and His Apostle; and whosoever opposes God, then God is severe in retribution' (Q 59.4). Muhammad's biographer, Ibn Ishaq, explains these verses by stressing that it was by God's permission and decree that Muhammad and the believers were successful (Ibn Ishaq 2004, 438). Other authors point to other verses of *surat al-hashr* revealed on the occasion to highlight God's protection of the Muslim community (Q 5.11), the legitimacy of expelling traitors from their abodes, even if they are 'people of the book' (Q 59.2, 11), and the rules governing the allotment of war booty (Q 59.7) (Ibn Ishaq 2004: 438; al-Tabari 2002: 579–81; al-Waqidi 2011: 177–86).

In these texts, treason, rebellion and military resistance are not just explained as actions undertaken against the Prophet Muhammad but as against God Himself. God responds in kind by assisting His Messenger through military supremacy, itself backed by scriptural support. Such symbolic correlations between martial success and divine support are strongly reaffirmed by the Ilkhanid artists as they sought to expand the manuscript's visual programme so as to convey God's palpable presence at the side of

His Prophet. In the painting of the expedition against the Banu al-Nadir, for example, the Prophet Muhammad sits astride his mount, accompanied by his followers, as he approaches the stronghold of the Jewish tribe. Above him, an angel – most likely Gabriel – descends energetically, holding a gold rose-water flask above the Prophet's turban and a gold-brushed bound codex at the height of his waist. Above and to Muhammad's left, emerging as it were from the upper horizontal frame of the composition, appears a golden sun with shooting rays of light, towards which the members of the Banu al-Nadir perched atop their fortress raise their hands in what appear to be gestures of supplication.

Several elements in this painting are worthy of note. First and foremost, the angel Gabriel recalls Christian pictorial conventions of representing the Holy Spirit as God's hand or as a bird, both synecdochal and metaphorical representations of the divine that appear to have been known to Ilkhanid artists (Hillenbrand 2002: 145). Moreover, Muhammad's selection occurs via unguent anointment and revelation by scripture – the latter being all the more significant since the entirety of *Sura* 59 of the Qur'an is said to have been transmitted to the Prophet during his campaign against the Banu al-Nadir. The consecrated nature of the military undertaking is further expanded by visual means via the inclusion of an incandescent gold sun, here best understood as the symbol of God's immanent presence and the revelation of portions of the Qur'an – an enlightened or luminous book (*kitab munir*)[2] – to Muhammad on this particular occasion. That the besieged members of the Banu al-Nadir turn to the sun in gestures of imploration substantiates the pictorial interpretation of God as theophanous light emitted into the sensible world, a theme that pervades both speculative theology and artistic expression in Islamic traditions.

Within and beyond the clouds

When a companion of the Prophet asked Muhammad where God was located before He created the earth and heavens, Muhammad answered: 'He was in a mist with air above Him and air below Him' (Gimaret 1997: 61; al-Jawzi 2006: 84). The Arabic term used for mist – *ama* – also signifies heavy clouds or a fog. Derived from the verb 'to obscure, be blinded, render cryptic or enigmatic', '*ama*' literally means 'to not be seen' or to 'remain hidden to someone'. Within the context of this particular Hadith (Saying of the Prophet), then, God is understood as inhabiting the sky, itself an empyrean anagoge for His utmost rank (Gimaret 1997: 63, 66–9). God is associated with cosmic phenomena. Moreover, His association with aerial cumuli serves to symbolically describe Him as a spatially and intellectually nebulous entity. After all, clouds are qualitatively similar to the nature of divinity: perceptible and hence real, yet incorporeal and therefore ungraspable.

As noted previously, a number of textual accounts, such as the monk Bahira recognizing the young Muhammad as a prophet after a cloud formed above him to provide him with protective shade, stress the emergence of nebula as indexical signs for God's ineluctable presence. Such figures of speech, equating God with divine effluvium, are echoed within the pictorial arts as well. In Persian paintings dating from the thirteenth to the sixteenth century, it becomes clear that the depiction of a heavenly haze is intended to articulate a metonymy for God. In such paintings, God's miasmic co-presence with Muhammad serves to frame and thus consecrate his prophetic endeavours. In addition, the cloud motif allows for a breaching of the firmament and therefore facilitates the Prophet's levitation and eventual entry into the trans-mundane abode of divinity.

Returning to the illustrated *sira-maghazi* genre, the symbolic formula of God-as-cloud is used by Ilkhanid artists within the pictorial cycle in Rashid al-Din's *Jami' al-Tawarikh*, especially in a painting representing the Prophet embarked on his successful campaign against the Banu Qaynuqa', another Jewish tribe who also lived in a redoubt close to Medina and who also broke their agreement with Muhammad (Figure 7.2). Rather than representing the battle scene per se, the composition is framed around the Prophet as a rider, striding forward with confidence in his divinely ordained mission. Muhammad is encircled by a sky-blue mandorla framed with white clouds curling around its perimeter. Interestingly, this pictorial motif is reminiscent of the *imago clipeata*, a framing device used in medieval Christian painting to suggest Christ's presence in heaven (Kessler 2000: 128–9).

All around the billowing aperture appear legions of angels, God's mercenary angels (*ghaziyan*) sent as Muhammad's seraphic helpers during his expeditions and raids. The angels surrounding Muhammad join his ranks as he embarks on his military campaign; simultaneously, they provide a clear indication of God's intervention in an event that is once again construed as not just belonging to the realm of worldly matters but, more importantly, as a religiously consecrated enterprise.

Figure 7.2 The Prophet Muhammad, accompanied by soldiers and mercenary angels, embarks on his campaign against the Banu Qaynuqa', Rashid al-Din, *Jami' al-Tawarikh* (Compendium of Chronicles), Tabriz, Iran, 1314 CE. London, Nasser D. Khalili Collection, mss. 727, folio 67r.

At the same time as the angels serve to buttress Muhammad's mission, they also pay tribute to the revelation of scripture. For example, during the Prophet's expedition against the Banu Qaynuqa', some writers, like Muhammad's biographer Ibn Ishaq, state that the fifty-sixth verse of the 'Chapter of the Table' (*surat al-ma'ida*, Q 5.56) was revealed, stating that 'those who take God and His Prophet and the faithful as their friends are indeed men of God, who will surely be victorious'. Ibn Ishaq elaborates on this verse, clarifying for his readers that military victory is nothing more than an act of God (Ibn Ishaq 2004: 363–4).

According to the early historian al-Waqidi (d. 822 CE) – best known for his *Kitab al-Maghazi* (Book of Raids), which is entirely devoted to Muhammad's expeditions and conquests – two other verses were revealed during the campaign against the Banu Qaynuqa'. The first verse, Q 3.183 (followed by Q 3.184), speaks of Muhammad as belonging to a long line of messengers who come bearing clear signs or manifest proofs (*bayanat*) of their prophecy, as well as enlightened books (*kutub munir*).[3] The second Qur'anic revelation consists in Q 2.103, which warns that those who do not listen to God will suffer the consequences (al-Waqidi 1882, 95).

These verses are germane to an analysis of the Ilkhanid painting, which represents Muhammad framed by the opening of the sky and surrounded by God's angels as twin marks of the 'clear signs' of his prophecy. Likewise, the mention of an 'enlightened book' points to the Qur'anic verses that were gradually revealed by God to the Prophet. Such verses inscribe Muhammad's *maghazi* into a consecrated chronicle of the Islamic faith, in which God is imagined to serve as supreme activator and divine actor. By abiding to the metaphorical concept of God as existing in a brume, the Ilkhanid artists in this case use the motif of parted clouds to suggest God's immaterial substance while also forwarding the postulate that He is perceptibly Existent. Although essentially 'vaporous', the pictorial insinuations of the divine's entry into worldly affairs are clear to the picture's viewers.

In the Qur'an, it is stated that, 'it is not for any mortal that God should speak to him except by revelation (*wahyan*) or from behind a veil (*min wara hijabin*)' (Q 42.51–2). This particular Qur'anic proclamation hastened a number of exegetical exercises concerned with explaining the 'veiled' nature of God, with an interest in understanding whether it is He Himself who is veiled from humans or whether humans themselves are veiled from viewing Him because of their own intellectual and spiritual limitations (Gimaret 1997: 73). Theologians tended to concur that humans are the ones to be veiled from viewing God: ergo, they described divinity as inhabiting a zone located behind innumerable layers of veils – the term veil functioning as a semantic tool to denote God's existential removal from human visibility and comprehension.

Besides describing God as inaccessible behind such cosmic veils, authors were nevertheless keen to emphasize that God is also the Beneficent Opener (*al-Fattah*) to the door of provision and mercy as well as the spiritual Opener of human hearts and eyes by gnosis of the Truth (al-Yahsubi 1991: 128–9). In other words, God is not just shut away, jettisoned to the outer limits of the galaxy, but rather a divinity who, at times, allows for entrance into His secret mysteries. This ostensive paradox of closing versus opening was one that mystics, especially Persian Sufi authors, found useful to exploit in trying to explain God as beyond material and spatial contingencies but nonetheless present in Reality. For example, in his *Niche of Lights* al-Ghazali describes God as elevated beyond the perception of senses (*idrak al-hiss*) and imagination (*al-khiyal*). However, al-Ghazali continues, God always remains the ultimate Opener of Eyes (*fatih al-absar*), the Unveiler of Mysteries (*kashif al-asrar*) and Lifter of Coverings (*rafiʿ al-astar*) despite His removal from the sensible and notional world (al-Ghazali 1998: 1, 26).

A number of later Sufi Persian poets – most prominent among them Nizami (d. 1209 CE) and Jami (d. 1492 CE) – continued to develop the veil metaphor to describe God as stationed beyond the cosmic curvature of the firmament. By means of rhyming distiches included as encomia to God in the prefaces to their epic and romantic tales, these Persian poets also lauded God as a divine Revealer, or literally the ultimate Spreader of the Veils (*parda-gusha*) that separate heaven from earth (Nizami 1945: 89, verse 5). During the sixteenth century in Iran, during the rule of the Shiʿi-Sufi Safavids (r. 1501–1722 CE), a great number of illustrated manuscripts were produced of Nizami's and Jami's text, and it is precisely within these texts' preliminary eulogies to God, the Prophet and his ascension, that painters further developed the pictorial language of divinity. Consequently, the pictorial conventions to represent God as found in Ilkhanid illustrated histories expanded under the aegis of the Safavids' patronage of illustrated mystical texts.

The metaphorical crossovers between the pictorial language of Safavid paintings and the figures of speech used in Persian mystical poetry are easily detectable, and such links therefore necessitate an inter-arts approach to the materials. Through a text-and-image analysis, it becomes clear that Safavid painters drew upon Sufi poetic idioms to help them formulate their visual presentations of the divine, all the while diversifying the discourse over God's nature. For instance, the artist – quite possibly the famous Safavid painter Sultan Muhammad – who depicted the Prophet's *miʾraj* in the preliminary laudatio of Nizami's *Makhzan al-Asrar* (Treasury of Secrets) has experimented with new motifs (Figure 7.3).[4] The most important of these is the opening in the sky, around which angels stand, looking down upon Mecca and awaiting Muhammad's entry into the domain of the Lord.

In the preface to his *Mazkhan al-Asrar*, where the ascension painting appears, Nizami describes the Prophet's ascension as a breaching through the covering of the fixed stars (*satr-i kavakib*) and a rending of the curtain of physical creation (*parda-yi khalqat*) so that Muhammad may reach the abode of the Lord. Furthermore, in Nizami's text, Muhammad's lifting of the head towards God is described as going beyond the veil of nature (*giriban-i tabiʿat*) at the same time as the hand of union (*tawhid*, i.e., God) draws back the curtain (*parda*) or veil (*hijab*) that is the firmament. Nizami also tells us that God Himself is the door of mystery (*dar-i raz*) and that He has veiled His threshold with doorkeeper angels (Nizami 1945: 101–2; Ranjabar 1952: 27–30). These many poetic metaphors found in Nizami's text stress Muhammad's arrival in the realm of the Lord as a rending, breaking and pulling open of a covering, curtain or veil – that is, as a piercing through the skies to reach a space freed from temporal boundaries and unshackled from earthly causalities.

In the Safavid painting, the opening of the skies pays tribute to the poetic figures of speech repeatedly iterated within Nizami's text. The celestial oculus also points to a kinetic interaction between human and divine spheres, becoming in the process both

Figure 7.3 The Prophet Muhammad ascends through the heavens on the back of his human-headed flying horse, named al-Buraq, and accompanied by angelic troops as he approaches an opening in the sky, Nizami, *Makhzan al-Asrar* (The Treasury of Secrets), Tabriz, Iran, 1505 CE. Dallas, Texas, Keir Collection (on loan to the Dallas Museum of Art), III.207.

an outlet for divine effulgence and an inlet for prophetic ascent. In other words, it functions as a conduit between the profane world of mankind and the heavenly domain of God, itself the *sanctum sanctorum* that usually remains 'veiled' or shut off. Within the painting, the perforation of the veil-firmament thus serves as a visual motif that situates God in a place that is defined by its invisible illocality (*la-makan*). Through a possible unstitching of celestial seams, it also suggests God's ubiquity (*fi kulli makan*) and limitlessness (*la hadd lahu*). This harmonization of epistemic opposites within the confines of the picture plane reflects general trends found in both Islamic speculative theology (Gimaret 1997: 29) and Persian poetic works.

The motif of the parted cosmic vinculum is a hallmark of medieval Christian painting as well. Therein, the firmament acts as a kind of curtain that shields the living God from human eyes. It therefore functions all at once as celestial barrier, divine threshold and ineluctable 'cloth of blindness' (Kessler 2005: 296). In Persian paintings of the sixteenth century, similar concerns are discernible through the leitmotiv of the parted firmament, sometimes peeled open by a single angel (Figure 7.4). Within visual and textual domains, the 'cloth of blindness' that is the celestial firmament is understood as impeding a full comprehension of divinity, a nexus-cum-barrier through which only the Prophet Muhammad is allowed to travel on the night of his celestial ascension.

Divine lights and majestic colours

As can be seen from these kinds of paintings, the story of the Prophet's *mi'raj* served as the primary thematic arena in which to meditate upon God's secret nature since the ascension tale describes Muhammad's breaching through the celestial veils as he approaches the domain of the Lord (van Ess 1999). Once he arrives at the place of proximity (*maqam al-qurba*), Muhammad is allowed to enter into an intimate colloquy with and is granted a vision (*ru'ya*) of God. Questions about the nature and modality of Muhammad's beatific vision sparked a great number of speculative and exegetical texts that sought to explain how God manifests Himself through a process of epiphany (*tajalli*) and, by consequence, in what ways a human being might be able to perceive Him (Williams 2008). The combined story of the Prophet's *mi'raj-ru'ya* thus provided the archetypical narrative to explain how to approach and comprehend the numinous, and it is within illustrated manuscripts that depict Muhammad's encounter with God that further visual elaborations on the nature of divinity unfold.

Persian and Turkish paintings of the fifteenth and sixteenth centuries contributed in their own ways to the discourse on divine ipseity as luminous flux. The idea that God exists as radiant light, however, can be traced much further back in time to the beginnings of Islam. For instance, the Qur'an describes God as an illuminating, cosmic lamp, as well as a blazing heap of light upon light (*nur 'ala nur*) in the famous verse of light or *ayat al-nur* (Q 24.35). Similarly, a Hadith elaborates upon this topic, recording that the Prophet Muhammad stated that, 'God has seventy veils of light and darkness; were He to lift them, the august glories of His face would burn up everyone whose eyesight perceived Him' (cited in al-Ghazali 1998: xvii).

The Prophet's biographers, historians, exegetes, and mystical writers developed the metaphysical concept that God does not possess a form, or *sura*, per se. He nevertheless has a body, or *jism*, that consists in a purely physical sense as a mass of light without limbs (Van Ess 1989: 8). This interpretation was further strengthened by God's names and attributes that made use of light metaphors: for example, two of his names are

Figure 7.4 The Prophet Muhammad ascends through the heavens on the back of al-Buraq, as he approaches an opening in the sky pulled apart by an angel in the upper left corner, Jami, *Yusuf va Zulaykha* (Joseph and Potiphar's Wife), Qazvin, Iran, ca. 1550–1600 CE. London, British Museum, Or. 4535, folio 8v.

The Light (*al-nur*) and The Possessor of Light (*sahib al-nur*), and He is described by various authors, including Muhammad's biographer al-Yahsubi (d. 1149 CE), as The Illuminator of the heavens and earth and The One Who illuminates the hearts of believers with guidance (al-Yahsubi 1991: 127). In these many textual elaborations, God is portrayed as a detectable, albeit incorporeal, mass of light that emits rays as a means of revelation and perception (Van Ess 2000: 343).

Much as they expanded the 'veil' metaphor, Persian mystical poets also embraced and developed a metaphysics of light to describe the divine in their eulogistic encomia to God. Nizami and Jami once again emerge as leaders in the genre. For example, in his *Haft Paykar* (Seven Thrones), Nizami informs us that Muhammad ascended through the heavens, 'rending the veil of a thousand lights [until] that unveiled Brilliance reached his sight' (Nizami 1995: 9). Further describing God as the Eternal Light that is not meant for ocular perception (Nizami 1945: 192), Nizami further describes in his *Makhzan al-Asrar* Muhammad's encounter with the Lord on the night of his ascension:

> He saw the sign of that Light (*ayat nuri*) that knows no decline,
> With eyes which were beyond imagination (*khiyal*)
> The vision of Him is free from accident and matter (*bi-ard va jawhar*)
> Because He is beyond accident and matter
> He saw God as the Absolute, and this is acceptable;
> [...] Whoso was permitted to see behind that curtain,
> Went on a path which is not a road
> He exists, but is not limited to any place
> He who is bound by space is not God
> Do not deny His permanence; it is blasphemy
> Do not limit Him to space; it is ignorance
>
> (Nizami 1945: 103, 200–2)

Nizami's stanzas offer a poetic picture of God as limitless light, freed from the bonds of accident and matter. They also issue a warning against those who may attempt to limit God to spatial and temporal dimensions.

Such caveats did not go unheeded by Persian and Turkish painters, who were faced with the arduous task to depict an unrestricted, permanent and incorporeal God by means of pictorial devices. Artists who depicted Muhammad's encounter with God appear to have turned to the Persian poetic texts they illustrated, such as Nizami's *Makhzan al-Asrar* and Jami's *Yusuf va Zulaykha*, for help and guidance into what visual 'figures of speech' might be best employed to convey the ineffable qualities of the divine. As they developed their own rhetorical means to portray God, Safavid painters symbolically associated God with effulgent light.

Within the corpus of Safavid paintings, one composition that embraces this specific interpretative mode stands out because the artist overtly tackles the problem of depicting God (Figure 7.5). In this scene, the Prophet Muhammad, whose face is covered by a white facial veil and whose body is encircled by gold flames, kneels against a lapis sky. He faces a large bundle of gold flames, while light 'tentacles' reach the outer perimeter of the painting's frame. The large bundle of gold flames must be understood as a metaphorical representation of God as light, encountered by Muhammad upon his arrival at the highest horizon. That the Prophet genuflects and faces the gold blaze lends further support to this interpretation. Likewise, it recalls God's fire-like appearance to Moses on Mount Sinai as represented in European Christian manuscript illustrations of the twelfth to sixteenth centuries (Boespflug 1992: 14–15).

The painting's location within Jami's eulogy to God, Muhammad, and the *mi'raj* as included in his *Yusuf va Zulaykha* also confirms the identification of the gold bundle

Figure 7.5 The Prophet Muhammad kneels as he speaks to God, represented as a large flaming bundle, Jami, *Yusuf va Zulaykha* (Joseph and Potiphar's Wife), Qazvin or Shiraz, Iran, 1570–1 CE. Istanbul, Topkapı Palace Library, H. 1483, folio 42r.

as a stand-in for the divine. In the painting's accompanying text, the author Jami warns his readers that 'God's essence is exempt of quality, quantity and all spatial attributes. Intellect stands baffled before the essence of God: it is quite inept to pursue Him along that path' (Jami 1980: 2). Jami further informs us that God is 'free of the bonds of appearances' (Jami 1980: 4) and that He is like a bundle of blazing light: 'one spark from it flashed forth and set heaven and earth alight. Angels were dazzled by it, and sang its praises to the point of distraction' (Jami 1980: 5).

The flaming gold bundle depicted in this painting heralds God as primordial light emitted into the world as creative and igniting force. It also eulogizes God's sum total of 'light upon light', as mentioned in the Qur'an (Q 24.35). This iconographic device allows the artist to convey the notion of revelation-as-light while also reaffirming God's body as an unobservable form, a theme that is well developed within Persian encomiastic poetry. In this case, God is neither bound by the limits of space – including the picture plane, which appears ablaze with the swelling rotation of gold flames – nor is He entirely comprehensible by the faculty of ocular perception.

This conjunction of antipodal elements, positing mass against form and visibility against invisibility, is negotiated and resolved by means of a pictorial metaphor that, in a deliberate and calculated fashion, seeks to show God's epiphanic form (*mazhar*) as that of a large bundle of blazing light. To convey the radiance of God, the Safavid artist has utilized gold paint. His purposeful selection points to yet another concern that has marked Islamic painterly practices, namely how colour symbolism helped express or hint to the presence of divinity. In order to gauge how colours might have been understood, it is important to examine their use in paintings with an eye towards their various cultural and religious connotations as well as their synaesthetic qualities.

As noticeable in this and other Persian paintings of Muhammad's ascension and his encounter with God, shimmering gold and lapis blue dominate. Gold and lapis lazuli were the most expensive luxury materials essential to the production of organic and inorganic pigments used in manuscript illustrations (Porter 1992: 87). Gold was so expensive that even 'gold imitations' were devised to cut down on costs, while lapis lazuli, extracted almost exclusively from the mountains of Badakhshan, is a most rare and precious commodity (Porter 1992: 86, 94). While pigment-makers pulverized lapis and moistened it through a water solution, they frequently preferred to use gold leaf, rather than gold paint, crushed on demand in order to reduce waste to a minimum.

Beyond the economic aspects of the gold and lapis trade, both materials carried powerful symbolic connotations within Turco-Persian cultural contexts. These associations are certainly embedded within sixteenth-century manuscript illustrations of Persian poetical texts. One quick glance at the Persian words used to describe gold and lapis reveal the extent to which both luxury materials could gain new figurative meanings, especially with regards to notions of the divine.

In Persian, the word for gold is *zar*, a term that describes not only the metal itself but also money, riches and wealth. Sun metaphors also are constructed by adjectival expressions that include the word for gold; most important among these are *zarrin-sadaf* (gilt oyster or gilt mother-of-pearl), *zarrin-kasa* (gilt goblet) and *zarrin-humay* (gold phoenix). Furthermore, the Persian expression for 'profusely gilt' is *zar andar zar*, or literally 'gold upon gold' – a figure of speech that is conspicuously analogous to the Arabic metaphor of God as 'light upon light' (*nur 'ala nur*). The analogies between gold and God expand even further within Persian phraseology: for instance, the verb *dar zar giriftan*, which means 'to gild' or 'cover or overlay with gold', also figuratively signifies 'to overwhelm with benefits or favors', while the noun *zartusht* (also the name for the prophet Zoroaster) denotes supreme intelligence, divine light and first created entity (Steingass 2000: 613–17).

In Turkic cultures and languages, the term for gold (*altın*) is associated with the divine as well as royalty and luxury. Like dynastic pedigrees, including most especially the golden lineage of Chengiz Khan, gold's status reigns supreme due to its qualities as an incorruptible, pure and immaculate substance (Allsen 1997: 60, 68–9). As can be seen in these examples of Persian and Turkic terms and expressions – of which there exist many more – gold denotes wealth and blessing, the irradiant and enlightening heat of sun, divine favours and replenished blessings, and primordial being and creative intellect. These many associative connotations function as metaphors for God, echoing the Islamic theological and poetical texts that were penned over the course of centuries.

If gold provides a synesthetic proxy for spiritually sensing the presence of divinity, then blue tones best convey the metaphor of heaven. This is especially the case within a Persian literary context, in which the words for turquoise (*firuza*), lapis (*lajvard*) and azure (masc. *akhzar*; fem. *khazra*) are frequently employed to symbolize the empyrean and paradisiacal realms. The term for turquoise, or *firuza*, is linguistically linked to the words *firuz* or *firuzi*, which mean victorious, successful, happy and glorious (Steingass 200: 944). It is also used in adjectival constructs that describe heaven as a 'turquoise throne' (*firuza-takht*) or a 'turquoise vault' (*firuza-saqf*).

In their Persian eulogies describing Muhammad's approach towards God on the night of his ascension, Persian poets elaborate upon the concept of the heavenly vault as turquoise, lapis or azure in colour. For example, Nizami speaks of the sky as a 'lapis vault' (*lajvardi-saqf*) and informs us that Muhammad was 'passed on like a rose from hand to hand up this turquoise (*firuza*) carpeted stair until he reached the foot of the Throne' (Nizami 1945: 101) and that 'God creates the azure vault (*qubba-yi khadra*) without pillars' (Nizami 1945: 93). Moreover, in Turco-Mongolian cultures, God is referred to as the Sky God (*gök tanrı/tengri*), the term *gök* pointing to the celestial realms and associated with the Turkic adjectives for agreeable (*gökçe*) and beautiful (*gökçen/gökçek*) (Beffa 1978, 272). Relatedly, the Turkic term for turquoise (*firuze*) is closely aligned with *firuzi*, a word that means both victory and prosperity. These cerulean metaphors – ranging from muted azure to bright sky-blue and turquoise – are used as poetic tropes that describe the glorious celestial dwelling place of God. Just as importantly, in Persian and Turkish paintings they are deployed through blue pigments that seek to represent the locus of divinity, and hence to firmly ensconce God's presence within the picture plane.

In both Persian and Turkic cultural contexts, furthermore, the colour red has held pride of place in describing God's nature and power. Persian poets such as Nizami exploited the rhetorical potential of this particular hue, calling attention to God's luxuriousness through gem and floral analogies. For example, Nizami informs us that God adorned paradise with roses (*gul*) and narcissus (*nargis*) and mountains with rubies (*la'l*); that He created the richness of the ruby (*yaqut*) from fire and water; that He placed the blood (*khun*) of the heart in the earth; and that, upon Muhammad's arrival in the highest heaven, He prepared for the Prophet a wine (*sharab*) for him to drink. This sacramental wine, Nizami further tells us, acts as an indexical mark of God's eternal grace (*lutf-i azal*) and His mercy (*rahmat-i haqq*) upon Muhammad (Nizami 1945: 90–1, 104). In these Persian poetic descriptions, vermillion functions as a colour-based metaphor for God's precious, life-inducing, primordial and, even, Eucharistic encounter with mankind.

In Turkic cultural spheres, the colour red (*qızıl*) stands for volatility and outburst, and it can carry both positive and negative implications, revealing the extent to which certain colour values can fluctuate. In the affirmative, red is a colour for love and passion, while in the negative it stands for sedition, fury and madness, as in the Turkish expression *qızıl deli*, or 'red (raving) mad' (Beffa 1978: 250–2). The fusion of these two colour-encoded meanings – that is, ardour plus ferocity – serve as double descriptors for the passion of man's encounter with an extraordinarily powerful Deity. Thus, the colour red, along with its various connotations within Turkic cultural spheres, can help explain why the Timurid artist who painted Muhammad's encounter with God in the *Mi'rajnama* (Book of Ascension) of ca. 1436–7 CE decided to use in this particular composition – and in no other painting in the manuscript – an overwhelming amount of red, combined with billows of gold clouds, to suggest the overpowering presence of the divine (Figure 7.6).[5] Here, Muhammad genuflects in God's presence, itself made visibly real through the use of red and god. The language of colour, its synesthetic perception, and its semiotic connotations thus help broaden the spectrum of colour metaphors used in Turco-Persian painterly practices in order to suggest God's presence within the composition.

Real absence

Much as Islamic speculative and poetic texts offered word-based disquisitions on the nature of the divine, paintings produced especially in Persian and Turkish spheres from ca. 1300 to 1600 CE likewise provided working definitions or 'searching images' (Guthrie 1993: 98) that attempted to explore and provide a number of visual equivalents of mental cognitions. The image world, too, functioned as testing grounds to convey God's ineffable presence within the circumscribed boundaries of pictorial form. As a result, artistic practices in eastern Islamic lands aimed at representing God must be seen as visual speculations in metaphysics and as powerful mechanisms for persuading viewers to engage in spiritual contemplation of the divine in its multiple forms and dimensions. In other words, texts and images assisted in prompting conceptual imaginations – that is, what the theologian Fakhr al-Din al-Razi (d. 1209 CE) calls perceptions or picturations (*tasawwurat*) – for exploring God and His many attributes (Abrahamov 2002: 219).

As Muslim artists took part in the dialogue over the nature of the divine, they were successful in at least partially determining its course via the harnessing and intellectualization of the pictorial mode. By synecdoche and metaphor, they sought to strengthen the unknowability of God's essence and attributes, as well as to reaffirm His absolute difference or *mukhalafa*. This 'set-apart' quality of the sacred is one that is not particular to Islamic traditions; rather, it has been deployed in many religious contexts in order to establish both accessible and forbidden zones of interactions (Evans 2003: 35). Within Turco-Persian pictorial traditions, more specifically, artists aimed to depict God's *mukhalafa* by calling attention to the divinity's esoteric presence

Figure 7.6 The Prophet Muhammad genuflects in the highest heaven while in the gold-and-red presence of God, anonymous, *Mi'rajnama* (Book of Ascension), probably Herat, modern-day Afghanistan, ca. 1436–7 CE. Paris, Bibliothèque nationale de France, suppl. turc 190, folio 44r.

and exoteric absence, between His absence in the visible realm and His presence in the supra-formal world. It is this seeming paradox – that is, the strong affirmation of God by means of analogy combined with the visual declaration of His absolute otherness – that artists wished to underscore and promote by their own creative means.

In doing so, Turco-Persian painters used calculated devices and visual cues to convey the deistic sum (*tawhid*) of God in pictorial terms. Through such stratagems, they were successful in visually asserting that a numinous presence can be marked as much by its omnipresent reality as by its ostensible absence. As a result, images produced in premodern eastern Islamic lands developed their own sensorial regimes and domains of speculative theology in order to tackle and meet some of the most challenging questions with which man has engaged since time immemorial: namely, how God can be existentially and sensibly real, and yet so far removed from spiritual, intellectual and visual comprehension.

Part Three

Figurations and Sensations – Lives and Regimes

8

Aesthetic Sensations of Mary: The Miraculous Icon of Meryem Ana and the Dynamics of Interreligious Relations in Antakya[1]

Jens Kreinath

Introduction

Antakya – formerly Antioch – is the southernmost city of Turkey, known for its religious and ethnic diversity, with its people belonging to different Christian and Muslim denominations. It is situated with the Mediterranean to the west and borders Syria to the east and south (see Figure 8.1). In 1939, Hatay was the last province to officially become part of the Republic of Turkey (Shields 2011: 17–47, 143–75, 232–49). Now, the ethnically diverse population of about 1.5 million is primarily composed of people of Turkish and Arab descent. With its unique blend of different languages and cultures, Hatay became known for its religious tourism industry. In the early 2000s, the inception of the Meeting of Civilizations (Turk.: *Medeniyetler Buluşması*) and the interreligious Antakya Civilizations Choir (Turk.: *Antakya Medeniyetler Korosu*),[2] both initiated by the Ministry of Tourism and Culture, highlighted the city's religious coexistence. This heritage of mutual religious tolerance is evident in the celebration of annual festivals and life cycle rituals shared among members of Antakya's diverse communities (Doğruel 2009, 2013; Prager 2013; Kreinath 2016, 2017b).

Visits to ancient local sanctuaries for vowing, wishing, and celebrating saints' days have played a significant role in fostering the local culture. Although recent ethnographic research on Hatay has emphasized the continuous existence of interreligious relations and rising tensions due to the Syrian conflict (Can 2017; Dağtaş 2017), the dynamics within these communities constituting the formation of interreligious relations have not been sufficiently studied. As demonstrated in prior publications (Kreinath 2014; 2015, 2016, 2017b), saint veneration rituals at shared sanctuaries, like those dedicated to St. George, are a key factor in organizing interreligious relations. This leads to the question of how similarities in visible forms of religious practice can occur while members of various religious communities maintain different notions of the invisible in their saintly encounters.

156 *Figurations and Sensations of the Unseen in Judaism, Christianity and Islam*

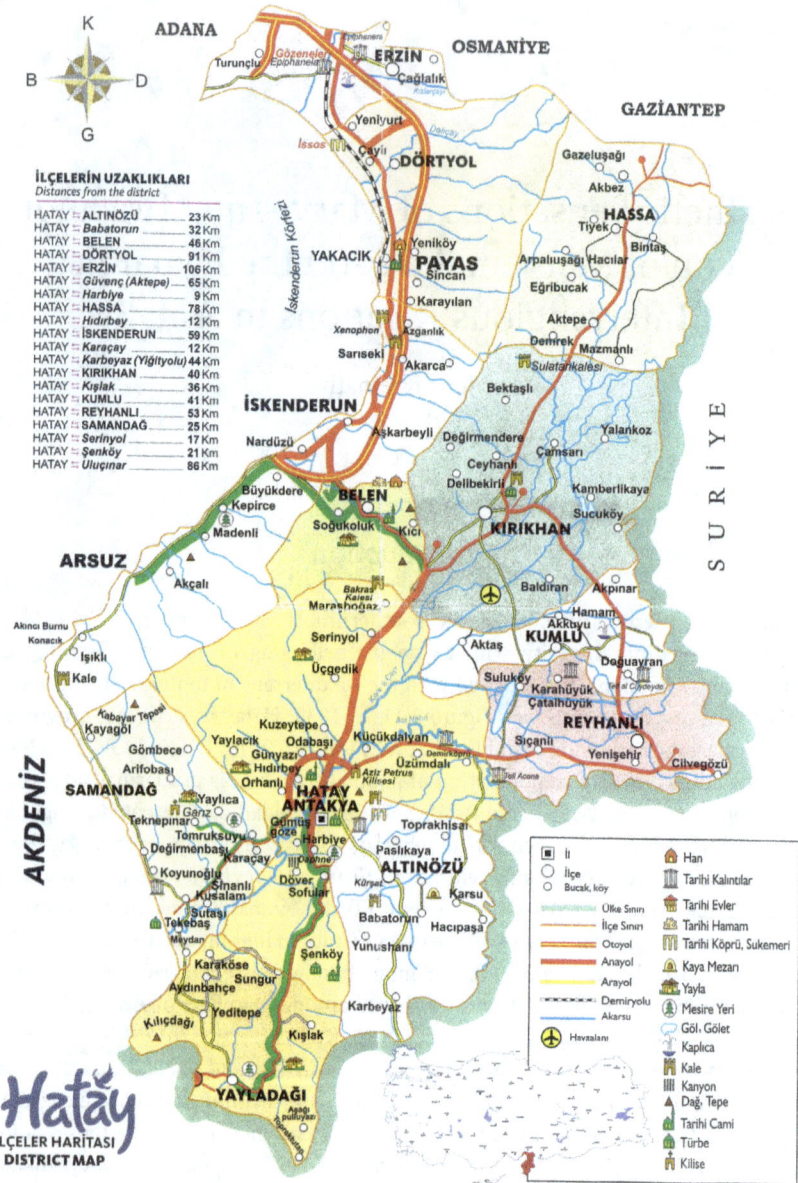

Figure 8.1 Map of Hatay. © T.C. Hatay Valiliği: Hatay governorship in Antakya.

This chapter addresses how variations in the veneration of Mary (Arab.: *Maryam*; Turk.: *Meryem*)[3] among Orthodox Christians can be explained through differences in aesthetic regimes and bodily sensations among clergy and laity, if compared with those traditions of saint veneration shared among members of the different religious communities in the context of Antakya.[4] Defined 'by their adherence to a specific regime of the sensible, which is extricated from its ordinary connection and is inhabited by a heterogeneous power' (Rancière 2004: 22-3), I refer to aesthetic regimes as a means to account for the ways in which aesthetic frameworks of perception, or in this case sensations and configurations of Mary, shape the ways in which sensational forms, such as icons of her, are perceived and experienced according to tacitly accepted perceptual standards of interpretation (Rancière 2010a: 175-6). By taking aesthetics as 'a re-configuration of sensible experience' (Rancière 2010b: 15), I aim to account for the experience of Marian apparitions by Orthodox Christian and Arab Alawite women as reflected in their accounts and take these representations of bodily sensations as empirical evidence for my case study. As Birgit Meyer succinctly put it: 'Attention to the aesthetic dimension of religion enables us above all to grasp the perspective – or should I say perceptions – of insiders' (Meyer 2009b: 719). Thus, the concept of aesthetic regime is suitable for my argument because it calls for a transformation of the sensible in 'the general distribution of bodies, voices, and capacities at work within a given community' (Tanke 2011: 72). This is precisely my argument to account for how the sensation of this interface is configured differently among members of the clergy and laity. Therefore, I employ aesthetic regime in conjunction with bodily sensations to contour the interface of the visible and invisible in the adorations and apparitions of Mary (Rancière 2010a: 138-9).

For bodily sensations, I refer to Meyer's insights in her discussion of aesthetic formations and sensational forms. To clarify my theoretical point, I specify how I utilize these concepts as follows: I agree that sensational forms like aesthetic regimes become useful by conceptualizing them as 'relatively fixed, authorized modes of invoking and organizing access to the transcendental, thereby creating and sustaining links between religious practitioners in the context of particular religious organizations' (Meyer 2009b: 707). However, this only applies to the more rigid forms of organized religious practice as instituted by the clergy, not necessarily to the less tangible forms of individual religious practice of the laity. Hence, it is also suitable to account for the laity by conceptualizing sensational forms as 'transmitted and shared; they involve religious practitioners in particular practices of worship and play a central role in forming religious subjects' (Meyer 2009b: 707). I, therefore, distinguish different aesthetic regimes and sensational forms among clergy and laity, and use bodily sensations as equivalent to aesthetic formations, namely as the part of shared experiences that helps to highlight the convergences *and* divergences of subject formation in the making of internally differentiated communities. Thus, my focus on bodily sensation may help capture 'the formative impact of a shared aesthetics through which subjects are shaped by tuning their senses, inducing experiences, molding their bodies, and making sense, and which materializes in things' (Meyer 2009a: 7).

To identify similarities and differences in these aesthetic regimes of clergy and laity, I analyse Marian veneration rituals in conjunction with official accounts of Orthodox Christian priests and personal experiences of Marian apparitions collected during my fieldwork in Hatay.[5] Starting with the veneration of Meryem Ana and her Miraculous Icon in Antakya, I argue that the aesthetic regimes and bodily sensations among Orthodox Christian clergy and laity are considerably different in relation to iconic figurations of the unseen, while saint veneration rituals among Orthodox Christian[6] and Arab Alawite[7] women share the most commonalities, including vows and wishes. To elaborate on an aesthetics of religion approach grounded in comparative research (Meyer and Verrips 2008; Grieser and Johnston 2017; Kreinath 2018), I argue that a major difference consists between the clergy and lay Christian women. The former emphasizes aesthetic regime while the latter emphasizes bodily sensation. This difference – as I submit – has implications for the organization of social relations within the Orthodox Christian community and for the dynamics of interreligious relations among Christian and Muslim women and their interactions mediated through Marian sanctuaries in Hatay.

Meryem Ana sanctuaries and places of veneration

Several places in Hatay are dedicated to Meryem Ana, most of which are the official churches and chapels of Eastern Orthodox Christian communities. For example, the Armenian Christian Church in Vakıflı and the Eastern Orthodox Church in Tokaçlı, the only Armenian and Orthodox villages in Turkey, respectively, have a documented history traceable to a remote past. By contrast, most Orthodox Christian sanctuaries in Hatay dedicated to Meryem Ana are modern constructions attributed to apparitions of Meryem Ana and known for miracles. Regardless, no interlocutor could specify the exact reasons for the sanctuaries' foundations, or their modern constructions. The Meryem Ana chapel (Arab.: *maqam*; Turk.: *makam*) at the Orthodox St. George Church in İskenderun is an example of a sanctuary allegedly built after an apparition of Meryem Ana. Although the local church authority recognizes the sanctuary, and that it is visited by members of the Christian and Muslim communities, it is unclear who or what initiated the construction of the sanctuary. The church's caretakers believe Meryem Ana appeared to the priest in a dream, and thus the chapel was built. In contrast, the priest, who affirmed that he initiated the construction, denied any association with an apparition of Meryem Ana. He maintained that he built the chapel to comply with the congregation's request for a place to venerate Meryem Ana. Regardless of the chapel's origins, its visitors attribute its existence to an apparition of Meryem.

This Meryem Ana Makamı in İskenderun is significant because of its architectural features and usages, which indicate the site's heritage and its significance for interreligious saint veneration rituals (Kreinath 2015, 2016, 2017b). Contrary to common conventions for Christian chapels, this sanctuary is oriented towards the west with the entrance facing east. Instead of an altar, there is – common to Arab Alawite sanctuaries – a rectangular cenotaph at its centre, with the upper part filled with sand wherein devotees place lit candles. Icons on the interior walls are venerated by Orthodox Christians, while the cenotaph is circled by Arab Alawites who visit the sanctuary for personal prayers (Arab.: *duʿāʾ*; Turk.: *dua*), vows (Arab.: *nadhr*; Turk.: *adak*) and wishes (Arab.: *raghba*; Turk.: *dilek*). Although the difference between vows and wishes is minimal, it is beneficial to distinguish between the two. The common feature of a vow is the promise of a sacrifice (Arab.: *kurbān*; Turk.: *kurban*), whereas a wish is an expression of desire. Vows themselves can be sealed at the presence of a wishing tree (Arab.: *nikkah*; Turk.: *dilek ağacı*), often at the sanctuaries' entrance

Figure 8.2 Wish Tree at the Meryem Ana Makamı in İskenderun. © Jens Kreinath, 2015.

(Figure 8.2). Vows are written on a piece of paper or a strip of cloth, as visible on one of the red stripes in the figure above, and if the devotee's request is fulfilled, an animal sacrifice is made in the Saint's name. According to interlocutors in İskenderun, the church authorities seem to quietly tolerate the practice of vows by turning a blind eye to them, and yet, if asked, they would certainly question the practice's legitimacy.

The Miraculous Icon in Antakya

One sanctuary in Antakya, known for a healing oil that leaks from an icon of Meryem Ana, is drawing both Orthodox Christians and Arab Alawites. The icon is in the living

160 *Figurations and Sensations of the Unseen in Judaism, Christianity and Islam*

Figure 8.3 Meryem Ana Evi in Antakya. © Jens Kreinath, 2012.

room of the caretaker's private Old Antakya house, directly accessible through the courtyard (Figure 8.3).

According to the caretaker, the icon is a modern replica from Lebanon or Syria. Locally known as the Miracle of Meryem Ana, this place is also referred to as the House of Meryem Ana (Turk.: *Meryem Ana Evi*). The icon depicts the Mother of God (Gr.: *Theotokos*; Arab.: *Walidat el-Elah*) and represents – in her body posture and hand gestures holding the Child on her left arm – a specific type of Marian icon called 'She shows the way' (Gr.: *Hodegetria*). This type of icon is named after its famous prototype, the *Panagia Hodegetria*, 'allegedly an "original" image painted by St. Luke' (Belting 1990: 115), which was venerated in the Hodegon Monastery of Constantinople, northeast of the Hagia Sophia, for its miraculous healings of the

Figure 8.4 Miraculous Icon of Meryem Ana in Antakya. © Jens Kreinath, 2012.

blind (Belting 1994: 48, 73–5). In 439 CE, the *Panagia Hodegetria* icon was brought to Constantinople as a gift of Empress Eudocia 'after its fortuitous discovery in Antioch' (Bacci 2005: 322). It was 'the most venerated image in all *Graecia*' (Belting 1994: 77), reportedly destroyed during the siege of Constantinople in 1453 CE (Tradigo 2004: 169), where it was until then considered the protector of the city and venerated for its miraculous powers (Belting 1994: 48). The *Panagia Hodegetria* is the most widely venerated icon in the Eastern Orthodox Church, evident in its multiple replicas such as the Miraculous Icon of Meryem Ana (Figure 8.4). The iconography of this figure is commonly attributed to the so-called Cretan school of iconography, with close ties to Rome and Venice during the fourteenth and fifteenth centuries (Ferrero 2001: 12–13; Eriksen 2005: 300–3). In the Eastern tradition, it is known as the Theotokos of the Passion, renowned for associations with miracles. In the Western tradition, it is known as the Virgin of the Passion, or Our Lady of the Passion, venerated 'all over the world' (Ferrero 2001: 15; Tradigo 2004: 188–9).[8]

A glass plate protects the icon, and one can see where the image absorbed a thick trace of oil. The surrounding decorations indicate its appeal to visitors from Muslim and Christian communities: to the right is a garland of three Hands of Fatima (Arab.: *khamsa*). Each of the Hands of Fatima is decorated with the same ornaments and patterns: an eye with a blue-shaded glass bead in the centre (Turk.: *nazarlık*), which serves as protection against the evil eye (Figure 8.5).[9] Both Christian and Muslim prayer beads (Turk.: *tesbih*) hang from either side of the icon. Eye-shaped and crescent-shaped metal panels are stuck into the frame along with a coin. Though these decorations indicate significant cultural and religious overlap, I did not witness Muslim women praying before the icon. Nevertheless, visitors and caretakers of the site confirmed Arab Alawite and Sunni women also come to venerate the Miracle of Meryem Ana.[10] The house is in the eastern part of the Old Town of Antakya, which was formerly inhabited by Armenians until their deportation in 1915, by Jews until their migration to Israel in 1948, and by Eastern Orthodox Christians until they moved into a neighbourhood closer to the Orthodox Church during the 1970s. Located on a cul-de-sac in a currently predominant Muslim neighbourhood, it can only be reached through a network of narrow alleys. This remote location is inaccessible to outsiders and disconnected from Antakya's traditionally Orthodox Christian neighbourhood.

The sanctuary's caretaker told me the icon became miraculous in 1979 when it began to leak oil. He remembered this miracle starting after his neighbours, whose

Figure 8.5 Miraculous Icon of Meryem Ana with the Hand of Fatima in Antakya. © Jens Kreinath, 2015.

house was also known to have a miraculous icon, moved away. The caretaker's story of the Miraculous Icon is as follows: The painting (Turk.: *resim*) – as the caretaker called the icon – was sent from Syria or Lebanon and displayed by his father. In 1979, his father saw oil all around the picture and asked his wife if she had put oil there, but she denied it. He asked her to clean it, and so she did. However, the oil returned the following day. His father got quite angry and suspicious of his wife, who denied any involvement but again cleaned the oil. On the third day, he understood the picture was the oil's source. His father, a pious man who worked for the Orthodox Church of Antakya as an Arabic instructor (Turk.: *okutman*), went to his priest to inform him of what happened. The priest came to his house, and after praying, oil immediately poured from the icon. The priest told his father: 'This is a miracle of Meryem Ana [*Bu Meryem Ana'nın bir mucizesi*]'.

After news of the icon spread, visitors were so numerous that visitation times were limited to two afternoons during the week. That same year, they were reported to the police on the suspicion that the icon was fake, and that the family was exploiting it for money. Local religious authorities (Turk.: *müftülük*) came to investigate but were unable to identify the oil's source. As a result, they took a sample of the oil and said it would be sent to a lab in Ankara for testing. After the testing was completed, they were notified that the sample had simply disappeared. Since then, Christians and Muslims from all around Turkey have come to venerate the Miraculous Icon. The caretaker and his wife have also witnessed several healings. One such miracle concerned a girl who regained her speech after visiting the Miraculous Icon. Another person was cured of stomach ulcers. The caretakers shared an example of a man, suspicious of the icon, who requested to be locked in the room with it alone. After several hours, they heard loud screaming. The man ran from the room, departing the place without taking leave. He did not return for seven years. Once he finally did, he was unable to approach the icon, as if it prevented him from coming near. The housekeeper's wife shared another miracle, stating that the Meryem Ana icon began to 'cry' on 2 August 2006, with oil streaming from Her eyes. The wife took this as Meryem Ana's response to the Israeli attack on Lebanon, which occurred in late summer that year.

Oil still leaks through the icon's surface and the wooden pillar that separates the living room from the bedroom. It is collected from a niche in the pillar with cotton balls and distributed for visitors once the cotton is saturated. I visited the site several times and attended informal prayer gatherings, usually consisting of a small group of six devotees or less. The rituals of saint veneration consisted of burning incense, lighting candles, and praying in front of the Icon of Meryem Ana. As part of the ritual, Orthodox Christians will touch the icon and rub the oil on their forehead in the shape of a cross (Figure 8.6). Commonly, devotees leave small donations and receive a piece of the oil-soaked cotton; occasionally they are invited to stay for tea or coffee and perhaps cigarettes. The high outer walls surrounding the courtyard, separating the living quarters from the kitchen and toilet, grant the gatherers some privacy. It was not until the Festival of Meryem Ana's Assumption in 2015 that the size and composition of this community of devotees became evident. Unexpectedly, I met two Orthodox Christian priests at the Miracle of Meryem Ana as they were preparing to hold a liturgical prayer service. One priest was similarly surprised to see

Figure 8.6 Orthodox Christian woman venerating the Miraculous Icon in Antakya. © Jens Kreinath, 2015.

me at the site; however, he welcomed me warmly with a handshake, as he did with other visitors. As I arrived, the courtyard was already full.

Approximately twenty devotees gathered in front of the icon. All except an elderly man were standing in the caretaker's living room – with the two priests leading a Mass. They were not wearing liturgical garments, but street clothes. At first, the caretaker attended the ritual, burning incense and lighting candles, but he soon left to prepare food to be distributed after the Mass. Other than these men and myself, only women were in attendance. None of them wore head-coverings, and some cautiously used a hand fan to relieve the heat. The space was so full, there was little room to move. The caretaker's wife was not among the attendees. After standing in the door, she left for some final preparations of food and drink.

The priests performed a regular Orthodox Mass in Arabic and followed the liturgy by taking turns reciting the special prayers selected for the day's occasion. In their liturgy, they followed standard Orthodox procedure by opening with prayers glorifying God (Arab.: *Allah*). Specific prayers recited for the day were devoted to the Virgin Mary (Arab.: *Adra Maryam*) as the Mother of God (Arab.: *Walidat el-Elah*) or called on her to be a refuge and a mediator to God. After these prayers, one priest read verses from the Bible about Mary visiting Elisabeth (Lk. 1.39-56). Invoking the liturgical formula of the Trinity, the priests recited a prayer requesting God's mercy, and the congregation recited the Lord's Prayer (Lk. 11.2-4) followed by the Sign of the Cross. In saying a prayer dedicated to Mary, the priests beseeched Adra Maryam to keep them out of harm's way. With a Hallelujah, the priests closed the ceremony with a Sign of the Cross. After the Mass's completion, one priest turned to the congregation exclaiming in Arabic, 'May your prayers be heard!' The service lasted no more than fifteen minutes.

Before leaving the living room, both priests touched the Miraculous Icon with their right hand, followed by the Sign of the Cross while joining their thumb, index and middle finger to symbolize the Trinity in a single ritual gesture. Following the priests' example, attendees formed a line to touch the icon in adoration and devotion. One attendee licked the tips of her fingers after touching the icon and made the Sign of the Cross. One younger woman had no interaction with the icon. Another woman, second to last, inspected the floor for traces of oil. Trying again, she examined the niche more closely and left the room with a suspicious gaze. A buffet of sacrificial food – mainly sweets and snacks – was displayed near the kitchen. The hosts made sure every guest received one of the treats.

Most members of the community sat on benches in the corner of the courtyard or on white plastic folding chairs. One of the priests spoke up, to be heard by all attendees, and complained about the deplorable custom of making vows. Declaring in Turkish, 'There is no need for these folkloric articles [*Bu folklorik eşyaların gereği yok*],' referring to the food served as an offering (*adak*) from a woman who was healed after a vow made at that site. One priest emphasized, 'That has no meaning [*anlamı yok*], we said this last year. Sweets, lokum, these are folkloric articles. We pray here, and then go to our Church.'

The other priest reiterated this in Arabic, citing the parable of Mary and Martha (Lk. 10.38-42), where 'Mary, sat at the Lord's feet, listening to what he taught. But Martha was distracted by the big dinner she was preparing.' He said it does not help to be busy with shallow things, referring to the preparation of the offerings. 'Mary came to listen to Gods words,' he said, and insisted that it is important to follow His will, emphasizing that all we should do is pray. Regarding this festival, he continued 'you think that Virgin Mary has only one feast, but she has four feasts, her Birth, the Annunciation, the Immaculate Conception, and the Assumption'. He criticized the Miraculous Icon's caretakers for their absence at church, even though they were fasting. The priest spoke loudly for all to hear, denouncing vows as pagan and renegade. However, most of the devotees seemed to ignore his speech, to avoid insulting the elderly Orthodox Christian woman who sponsors the meal annually. She was obviously in a bind: she promised to make these offerings after being healed to serve her community and yet her priests criticized her.

After most visitors left and the atmosphere calmed down, the sponsoring woman, who is a very devout and regular churchgoer, on the brink of tears, shared her story. Having been healed from a life-threatening illness after visiting the Miraculous Icon, she vowed to offer a sacrificial meal (Turk.: *adak*) on the Feast of Meryem Ana's Assumption. She felt torn between her vow made in a moment of despair and understanding the priests' command regarding vows. Attempting to explain her situation to me, her body moved back and forth in front of the Miraculous Icon, as if she were directly interacting with it. Later the woman, who hosted the meal, began to prepare for the church service scheduled at the Orthodox Christian Church, after a final solitary prayer at the icon. I remained for a short time before also leaving for the church service, while the caretakers stayed home. During the Mass – performed by the same two priests, now in full liturgical garment – I recognized numerous devotees sitting in the back rows who had just attended the Mass at the Icon of Meryem Ana.

Aesthetic regimes and the significance of icons in the Eastern Orthodox tradition

Although the priests held Mass at the Miraculous Icon, acknowledging the site's significance for Antakya's Orthodox Christian community, they never officially recognized this site as a sanctuary.[11] Interviews with the priests conducted prior to attending Mass provide some local theological context for the observations made at the sanctuary of the Miraculous Icon. This interview was held in their office at the Orthodox Church of Antakya. One of them started by saying that Meryem Ana is a very holy person because she is God's chosen one and gave birth to Jesus through Immaculate Conception. The other priest affirmed that the aureole around Meryem Ana's head indicates her sanctity. Pointing to a Marian icon next to him, he stressed the importance of the colours in which Meryem Ana is depicted. Though he did not specify the colour codes, I could infer his meaning – the bright blue of Meryem Ana's mantle represented the *Theotokos*, with the purple of her dress as the renowned colour of passion in the Eastern Orthodox tradition. Considering this, Meryem Ana's image on the Miraculous Icon differs only slightly, with an orange-red dress and a dark blue mantle (see Figure 8.4).

In contrast to the caretaker's words, one of the priests declared 'an icon is not a painting [*İkona resim değildir*]'. Though icons are often perceived as religious works of art (Belting 1994: 2, 9–11), the priest's statement sums up a major theological point used to justify the veneration of icons in the Eastern Orthodox Church: although icons are handmade, they are imitations of an archetypal image and originate through divine inspiration the iconographer receives in prayers (Barasch 1993: 6–7; Belting 1994: 56). An iconographer[12] I also worked with in Antakya supported this view in an interview. One must pray and meditate for hours before one can make the first stroke. Every stroke, he emphasized, must come through divine inspiration. Particularly among theologically trained Orthodox Christians, icons are interpreted as the visual equivalence of the scripture. As the iconographer insisted, icons are not painted, but written, accompanied by the recitation of a continuous prayer.[13]

One priest mentioned during our interview that the doctrine of the icon's mysterious nature is central to the Orthodox Christian faith as an expression of divine mystery. Thus, icons are objects of meditation, and liturgical prayers are recited before them (Barasch 1993: 36–9). Specific rituals related to an icon's production, or those performed for veneration, indicate that an icon is conceived as a vessel through which the respective saint communicates with the devotees (Luehrmann in this volume). In this regard, the priests perceive the icon as integral to the saint's persona. Icons are 'interactive foci of saintly presence'; they are like persons and therefore act 'as a holy person on earth would act' (Heo 2018: 92). Thus, an icon is an interface between the visible and invisible (Belting 1994: 7–9, 45–7). This view reiterates the doctrine John of Damascus articulated regarding the icon in the Eastern Orthodox tradition 'revealing the invisible is the purpose of the holy image, and therefore it is the reason for the vindication of the material, visible icon' (Barasch 1993: 206). This notion even applies to reproductions of icons and is apparent in the veneration and adoration of the Miraculous Icon.

Despite the difference in aesthetic regimes, Orthodox priests share the same traditions of icon veneration, as their spiritual orientation is geared towards the traditions of the Eastern Orthodox Church in Syria and Lebanon.[14] This became clear when asked about the *Meryem Ana Evi* in Ephesus, which was rediscovered and reinvented through the Roman Catholic Church in the late nineteenth century. For the Orthodox priests, *Meryem Ana Evi* in Ephesus is the place where St. John the Apostle brought the Virgin Mary 'to live until her Assumption' (Turk.: *göğe çıkışı* or *göğe alınışı*).[15] By contrast, the Convent of Our Lady of Saydnaya is most important to the priests, as it is the place[16] where people are healed through the oil coming from the miraculous icon – as one priest testified. According to Orthodox Christian tradition, as referred to here, this icon was painted by St. Luke and is important for the ongoing veneration of Meryem Ana, due to its association with miraculous healings.[17]

Although the priests had to recognize that both Christians and Muslims visit miraculous icons, like those in Saydnaya, they would not officially acknowledge the Miraculous Icon in Antakya due to the vows and wishes as practised by members of their own parish. Nevertheless, they noted that the Qur'an mentions Meryem Ana, with a surah of her own. However, they clarified, this is the only overlap they recognize between Christian and Muslim adorations of Meryem Ana. Theirs is an exclusively theological point of view compared to the caretakers' more apparent emphasis that Eastern Orthodox Christians and Arab Alawites all come to venerate the Miraculous Icon, with various Muslim ornaments adorning it. Differences in the perception of Meryem Ana become evident when the aesthetic regimes of sensual perception are concerned. Though the priests acknowledge healing miracles of the icons of Meryem Ana as part of the mysteries of their faith, they do not recognize apparitions of Meryem Ana in dreams; as one priest stated, 'In our culture, we do not recognize dreams [Turk.: *Kültürümüzde, rüyaları tanımıyoruz*].'[18]

Apparitions of Meryem Ana among Orthodox Christians and Arab Alawites

Apparitions of Meryem Ana, like other matters of religious belief, are not generally topics of conversation in Hatay. As one of my interlocutors once said: 'Religion in Hatay is lived, not talked about [in public].' The narrative accounts I collected among Orthodox Christian women give intimate accounts of their adorations of Meryem Ana. They are directly related to the Miraculous Icon and reveal the intimate correlation between the icon's adoration, apparitions of Meryem Ana, and experiences of vowing and healing. These accounts are contrasted with that of an Arab Alawite woman who witnessed a Marian apparition.

The icon's caretakers give the first examples of apparitions. Upon inquiring whether they had any experiences, the caretaker immediately declined. His wife, however, affirmed that Meryem Ana appeared to both her and her son. Her son shared the story of a dream from 2006, around the time the icon began to 'cry'. In his dream, he was sitting at the window when Jesus and Mary came to visit him. The three spoke and Meryem Ana told the boy, 'Your faith will exceed my faith.' I questioned him about Meryem Ana's appearance and he referred to the icon saying, 'like in the paintings [*resimlerdeki gibiydi*]' adding that she was 'like a spirit [*ruh gibiydi*]'. Meryem Ana appeared to the caretaker's wife during an evening prayer in 2010, where she witnessed 'light scattering [*ışık saçıldı*]'. As she saw the light, she began to shake and cry, understanding who had appeared to her. She was given instructions to pray for her sick aunt, who soon recovered. Sometimes during the night, she smelled burning incense. Taking it as a sign from Meryem Ana, she immediately complied and burned incense. Other than these experiences, the Miraculous Icon is more known for healings than for apparitions.

The next account is that of a middle-aged woman who experienced apparitions of Meryem Ana after visiting the Miraculous Icon. Her complex narrative is given here in full: She was concerned about infertility during her first years of marriage. An acquaintance told her about what is called *Meryem Ana Evi*, and they went there. Praying, she made a vow, 'If I would get a child, then I will visit you next year for your feast'. Upon returning home, she informed a friend of her visit, saying, 'If I get a daughter, I will name her Anna Maria.' That night she dreamed of a table full of jars resembling babies in the womb. Then a woman appeared and told her to choose her child.

Upon waking, she repeated her promise. Soon she became pregnant. During that time, Meryem Ana appeared to her in dreams (Turk.: *rüya*), telling her not to be afraid and that the pregnancy would be comfortable. In a dream just before delivery, Meryem Ana appeared to her with a rose in her hand. Meryem Ana told her, 'As I delivered Jesus I had this rose in my hand. Get this flower and put this on your belly.' That morning, her friend came to visit, bringing her a rose. She questioned her friend, who explained that an old woman gave her the rose, so she brought it to her. 'So, it was like a continuation of a dream for me. I just got this flower and put this on my belly,' she said.

After the baby's birth, her name was highly contested. Because they lived in a Muslim country, some relatives believed that a Christian name was inappropriate. This upset the woman because of her promise, and for several weeks the baby had no name. In another dream, four men noisily entered her bedroom, and shook the bed. Meryem Ana sat on a chair in a very disapproving manner, making no contact with the woman. The four men were yelling at her asking why she did not keep her promise. One of the men picked up the baby and loudly spoke her name three times in her ear, like a naming ceremony (Turk.: *isim koyma töreni*) common among Muslims. Then he told her that if she did not keep her promise, what was given would be taken away.

Finally, she named her daughter Anna Maria. In our subsequent conversation, I asked how she knew it was Meryem Ana, and she indicated that she just felt it. She did not remember the face or any specifics other than her white-cream head cover with lashes wrapped around it. Meryem Ana looked like a normal human without any light around her. She also recalled that when Meryem Ana spoke with her she was never close. Only when she was given the rose could she see Meryem Ana's hand was completely white.

As these narratives indicate, not all members of the Orthodox Christian community follow the priests' dismissal of Marian apparitions. It seems that Orthodox Christians who venerate the Miraculous Icon and see Meryem Ana in dreams also emphasize the apparitions' importance and take them very seriously. The tension between the theological command of the clergy and the lived experience of the laity also explains the difficulty of finding Orthodox Christians willing to talk about experiences of apparitions. Dreams – unlike miraculous icons – are not considered part of the authoritative tradition of saint veneration and are not supported by what priests consider divine inspiration. Thus, the aesthetics of bodily sensations as experienced by the laity stands in contrast to the aesthetic regime of saint veneration rituals instituted by the clergy.

The Marian apparitions experienced by both Orthodox Christian and Arab Alawite women share many similarities. One exemplary testimony is engraved on a marble plaque, giving a unique glimpse into the culture of saint veneration among Arab Alawites. It should be noted that this sanctuary is known by locals as Her Holiness Mary Sanctuary (Turk.: *Hz. Meryem Makamı*), while it is otherwise called Hızır Water (Turk.: *Hızır Suyu*).[19] It is located on a remote mountain dome near the Cassian Mountain range, which stretches south of Samandağ along the Orontes River valley. The Hızır Suyu sanctuary is named after the Hızır tomb at its centre – a large five-by-five cement block, about three metres high, with no apparent entrances. Next to the sanctuary is a place for guests to stay overnight for dream incubation. There is no tomb dedicated to Meryem Ana, and without the plaque supported by the iron grating, it would not be possible to identify the site.

Importantly, the site is currently recognized for the story of a woman who was healed after an apparition of Meryem Ana, even though this sanctuary was attributed to Meryem Ana long before her. The story originally in Turkish is translated here in full:

> Years ago, I got sick. I had stomach bleeding and did not leave my sick bed for seven months. One day, Hz. Meryem appeared in my dream, and she asked me to come to her Makam and said that I will be well after fifteen days. I came here and made a prayer. I vowed I would make an animal sacrifice [*kurban*] if I got better. Soon I got better but forgot to make the sacrifice. (I encountered a major financial problem.)
>
> Hz. Meryem appeared in my dream again.
>
> She said she wanted me to make the sacrifice, and that my problem would be solved if I would keep my vow [*adak*]. After a few days, I came here to fulfill it. The next day my problem was solved. I also could not get pregnant; I went to a doctor and I am told that I would not have children without treatment.
>
> I came here and wished a daughter from Hz. Meryem. I wished [*dilek*] that if I would have a daughter, I would name her Meryem. I got pregnant that month without treatment. My daughter is now six months old. I named her Meryem.
>
> MY BELIEF IN HZ. MERYEM IS ETERNAL.

The practice of engraving one's testimony on marble is not common, but the account it gives provides distinctive insights into the tradition of saint veneration among Arab

Alawites. Although its specific features are confined to the veneration of Meryem Ana, this example is worth further consideration. It exemplifies the veneration of Meryem Ana at this site, but also highlights the experience of visions and dreams among Arab Alawites more generally (Kreinath 2014, 43–9).

The testimony's narrative is atypical; various elements are omitted while others are merely alluded to. It is unclear what relation the woman had to Meryem Ana before witnessing her in a dream, or how she could be confident that it was Meryem Ana. Praying to a saint is common in preparation for dream incubations among Arab Alawites, but unmentioned here. Also, it remains unclear if she initially performed a sacrifice in Meryem Ana's name when she visited the Hz. Meryem Makamı, or the first time in response to her healing. Such a debt-based sacrifice is a significant reciprocal detail. As she appeared the second time, Meryem Ana promised to fulfil the devotee's wishes only after a sacrifice was made. The woman followed through to help resolve financial problems, which disappeared after her sacrifice.

Though not tied to her prior illness, the testimony also indicates that the woman visited the Hz. Meryem Makamı once again to make a vow because of infertility. It indicates through the indexical 'here [Turk.: *buraya*]' that this pilgrimage site was already known as the Hz. Meryem Makamı prior to her visit. Interestingly, the testimony states she only committed to naming her daughter Meryem if her wish for a daughter was fulfilled. It is quite significant, as it not only entails two apparitions of Meryem Ana but also includes the experience of healing with a clear reference to vows and sacrifices, elements common to saint veneration among Arab Alawites (Kreinath 2014, 49–53). The emphasis here is on Meryem Ana directly communicating via dreams and giving the woman instructions to overcome physical illness and financial distress. The testimony also suggests that Meryem Ana took the initiative in approaching the woman in a dream, without the woman's prayers or vows prior to her apparition. It was only after the woman was healed and had performed her sacrifice that she made the vow to name her daughter Meryem given her wish would be fulfilled. It is a common practice to name the first-born child after the saint to whom a vow was made, as the Orthodox Christian and Arab Alawite examples indicate. Despite its unique features, this testimony demonstrates that dreams, vows, healings and sacrifices are integral to rituals of saint veneration among the Arab Alawites in Hatay, and thus they share common features with apparitions of Meryem Ana experienced among Orthodox Christians, as demonstrated by the case of the Miraculous Icon.

Conclusion

This chapter argues that sensations and figurations of the unseen, exemplified by the aesthetics of Marian apparitions, are highly differentiated within religious traditions as evident in the Orthodox Christian community of Antakya. By giving primary attention to the Miraculous Icon of Meryem Ana, I explicated that the aesthetics of bodily sensations differ considerably among clergy and laity showing that their accounts are anchored in very different aesthetic regimes of Marian adorations and apparitions.

I contrasted the icon veneration practised and interpreted by Orthodox Christian clergy and laity with dreams and healings experienced among women after performing prayers and vows primarily at the Miraculous Icon. In doing so, I showed that the rituals performed in front of the icon by clergy and laity seem similar, but aesthetic regimes and bodily sensations among the Orthodox Christian clergy and the women who experienced Marian apparitions through dreams are markedly different. While the clergy emphasized the intangible presence of the invisible in the icon, the laity insisted on the tangible efficacy of the visible as represented through the icon. Addressing different aesthetic regimes of the visible and invisible, I demonstrated that clergy and laity present a different kind of evidence and speak with varying degrees of authority about Meryem Ana's presence in the Miraculous Icon. Concisely put by Hans Belting, 'It was never easy to control images with words, because, like saints, they engaged deeper levels of experiences and fulfilled desires other than the ones living church authorities were able to address' (Belting 1994: 1).

The difference in the aesthetics of the Miraculous Icon became apparent by considering bodily sensations experienced by Orthodox Christian women through their apparitions of Meryem Ana in dreams, and by contrasting their accounts with aesthetic regimes as expressed in the priests' views. Although the veneration of miraculous icons is instituted as an authoritative practice of worship in Eastern Orthodox Christianity, as the priests' interviews confirmed, the aesthetic regimes the clergy aims to institute diverge from the bodily sensations experienced by the laity, resulting in markedly different aesthetic perceptions of the icon. While the clergy understands the icon's veneration as an interface of human and divine interaction, and thus, presupposes an aesthetic regime of bodily sensation, the laity that experienced apparitions ascribes agency to the Miraculous Icon and take their bodily sensations as empirical evidence for the working of the icon in healing and for the vows sealed there. With this difference in aesthetic regimes, and the relationship between different configurations of the visible and invisible in bodily sensations and apparitions of Meryem Ana, I elaborated on how Orthodox Christian women share local Muslim traditions of saint veneration as practised among Arab Alawites.

Although the Orthodox Christian clergy and laity are unified by their belief in the icon's mystery, they differ in their aesthetic regime and bodily sensation of this mystery. The desire for healing through vows and bodily sensations made through the Miraculous Icon transcend authorized bodily practices and instituted aesthetic regimes. The difference exists in the priests' rejection of Meryem Ana's apparitions as sources of divine inspiration as well as the requests for healing mediated through the Miraculous Icon. When it comes to the appropriation of the local culture of vows, dreams and healings, the Orthodox Christian laity deviates in their bodily sensation from the aesthetics regimes of the clergy and has much more in common with local traditions of saint veneration practised among Arab Alawites. Thus, bodily sensations among the Orthodox Christian women contrast the aesthetic regime of the clergy and organize interreligious relations with Arab Alawite women, with whom they share traditions of Marian adoration manifesting in practices of praying and vowing, and experiences of apparitions, as mediated through aesthetic sensations in dreams and healings.

9

The *Ahl-i Beyt* Bodies: The Mural Paintings of Lahijan in the Tradition of Persian Shiite Figurations[1]

Pedram Khosronejad

Thy face uncovered would be all too bright,
Without a veil none could endure the sight;
What eye is strong enough to gaze upon
The dazzling splendor of the fount of light?

Abusa'id Abulkhayr (Ruba'iyat 519)

In modern Iran and throughout their entire history, the majority of Persian Shiite visual arts in which one can observe the depiction of the Prophet Muhammad, his *Ahl-i Beyt* (Imam 'Ali, Fatimah Zahra, Imam Hassan and Imam Hoseyn) and other saints are deeply connected to the folk narration (*rivayat-i 'amiyanih*) and popular literature (*adabiyat-i 'amiyanih*) of the history of the Iranian version of Twelver Shiism (*Ithna'ashari*).[2] One of the main functions of these illustrations, which appeared for the first time in royal books (Gruber 2008) during the Timurid Dynasty (1370–1506) and were seen up to the Qajar period (1785–1925), in the popular Shiite lithograph books of the period (1785–1925), was to depict visually related religious events and stories. These series of illustrations (*tasvirsazi*) are mostly decorative (*taz'ini*) and function as a bridge between the text and the reader and, as far as we know, were never used as devotional devices.

Naser al-Din Shah Qajar (b. 1831–d. 1896) should be considered the most important patron of Shiite popular rituals, performances and related material religion in modern Iran. It was during his reign (1848–96) that visual representations of the Prophet Muhammad, the *Ahl-i Beyt* and other Shiite saints were depicted in different forms (paintings, lithograph prints, photography), on different media (paper, canvas, murals, glass, tiles) and for different functions (ceremonial, devotional, decorative) in Iran. Several political, cultural, religious and artistic elements of previous centuries must have cooperated together and dissolved into each other to provide such stable ground for the flourishing of the figural depictions of these unseen Shiite holy figures (Gruber 2016).

Therefore, this period should be considered a unique time in Iranian history during which the country's supreme leader (Naser al-Din Shah), Shiite clerics ('*ulema*), artists and public adherents (*ummah*) were in an exceptional religious position and harmony. This led to the acceptance of this genre of figurative religious art in both private sectors and public spaces (temporal and permanent), such as *Hoseyniyehs*,[3] *Tekiyehs*[4] and *Imamzadehs*.[5] Here the most important function of these Shiite holy figurations is the act of religious provocation and devotion through special modes of visual communication (Ekhtiyar 2014: 2015).

After the end of the Qajar period began the Pahlavi regime (1925). The first Pahlavi king, Reza Shah Pahlavi (b. 1878–d. 1944), based on his secular and anti-Shiism ideology, severely banned Shiite public rituals and *Ta'ziyeh* performances and destroyed many *Hoseyniyehs* and *Tekiyehs*, including the most important one, *Tekiyeh Dowlat*, the royal theatre hall. This moment of history should be considered the end of the mass usage of visual representations of the Prophet Muhammad and his *Ahl-i Beyt* as Shiite devotional devices in modern Iran.

With the rapid development of print technology and the circulation of images on a massive scale, a new genre of visual depictions of Shiite holy figures came to the market during the reign (1941–79) of Muhammad Reza Shah Pahlavi (b. 1919–d. 1980). This time, visual representations of the Prophet Muhammad and other Shiite saints were used mostly in saints' shrines as votive objects (*nazri, ehdayi, taqdimi*) and in non-religious places (shops, supermarkets, taxis, etc.) as visual souvenirs only to be seen and to provoke 'the sensations of the heart' (*hes-i qalbi*) of public viewers.

Since the Iranian revolution of 1978, the establishment of the Islamic Republic and the immediate eight-year war between Iran and Iraq (1980–8), major elements and ideologies of Iranian Shiism that are nourished by the concept of Shiite martyrdom and the commemoration of holy martyred saints again became popular in Iranian society (Khosronejad 2012a). Here again we observe the mass production, circulation and usage of Shiite holy figures (the Prophet Muhammad, Imam 'Ali, Imam Hoseyn and Hazrat-i Abolfazl) in different forms (temporary banners, mural paintings, posters and flyers), but mostly as propaganda and political tools in the service of the Iranian regime (Khosronejad 2015a, b, c). One of the very new and unique innovations of the Iranian government in this regard is the production of religious fiction films about the lives of the Prophet Muhammad, Imam 'Ali and other Shiite saints in which we can observe them first as humans and then as saintly figures.

To better understand the meaning and function of visual representations of Shiite holy figures and saints in modern Iran, we need to look at them as part of the wider Iranian Shiite cultural heritage (Khosronejad 2012b), which includes the visual, textual, vocal and performative forms (rituals, ceremonies, etc.) of expression. This may help us to explain how related Persian Shiite iconographies are created and developed historically and are situated socially and culturally (Khosronejad 2012c; Suleman 2015).

In modern Iran (since the 1840s), visual depictions of the Prophet Muhammad and other Shiite saints are based on the polysemic quality of a series of visual signs and codes. These figurative iconographies appear as multilayered with signs taking on iconic, indexical and symbolic meanings. Here, viewers' interpretive strategies (including devotees, pilgrims, mourners) are inspired by their personal sentiments and reverence for saints, their knowledge of the Iranian version of Shiite history, as well as by hagiographies and the holy figures' positions in the Shiite perception (Flaskerud 2010). The popular usage of Shiite iconographies in modern Iran is deeply embedded in votive acts (*nazri*) and devotional practices (*manasik-i mazhabi*). Visual representations of the Prophet Muhammad and other Shiite saints could serve as invocational gestures to declare the faith and express the praise of a devoted community (Khosronejad 2012b).

In this context, both visualization and seeing have representative and transformative qualities. These Persian iconographies spiritually evoke the holy Shiite saints in the hearts of believers and provoke their genuine religious sensations. This is how cognitive processes transform devotees' emotions and engender their pious behaviours to facilitate making contact with the unseen Shiite holy figures. Therefore, special types of visualization and modes of seeing are necessary and significant to the dissemination of Shiite knowledge to better understand related spiritual and religious values for devotees. Within the context of the Shiite doctrine of redemption in modern Iran, both visualization and seeing function as special modes of venerating holiness and reinforcing personal piety.

The origin of Shiite mural paintings in Iran under Muslim dynasties

One of the important testimonies for the justification of the role of figurative art in the context of Twelver Shiism in Iran is the evidence of religious mural paintings. It is beyond the scope of this study to enter into the complexity of placing these paintings in a cultural, social and historical context (Khosronejad 2018). Often considered as having a status equal to that of manuscript illustration, its material remains are scarce, and it is literary evidence that in large part has fashioned current notions of the function, extent, and significance of painting programmes on interior wall surfaces (Lentz 1993: 253).

Previous studies have not only repeatedly stressed the continuity of this ancient practice from the Sasanian period (224–651 AD) into the Qajar era, but have also viewed it as a formal extension of manuscript painting (Gray 1979: 315). In this regard, Stchoukine posits:

> Iran has seen a succession of revivals of its Sasanian tradition, under Buyids [934–1062] and Samanids [819–999], under the Seljuq [1037–1194], and again under the Timurids and the Safavids [1501–1736]. When Timur [b.1336–d.1405] wished to revive the practice of celebrating his victories with mural paintings, he had to turn to artists trained in book illustration. The miniaturists were transferred to his new capital at Samarqand and put to work decorating the palaces which he was erecting in all haste. They portrayed his battles, his feasts, his court, the princes of his family, and even the ladies of his harem. (1954: 3)

Visual investigations prove that pre-Timurid mural paintings were mostly non-figurative, mostly found in western Iran on the walls of mosques and funerary constructions, often as painted stucco reliefs (Wilber 1969). Therefore, the majority of these series of mural paintings as found in surviving evidence would appear to be not only decorative, but also non-narrative in their orientation (Lentz 1993: 253). Evidence from the Timurid period proves that figurative art became part of Timurid mural painting programmes, 'but in a different guise', as Lentz suggests:

> Its genesis was obviously in the illustrative idiom, and like that idiom, was ideally suited to repetition and standardization. Its presence on walls instead apparently served a dual purpose, one evoking narrative and other non-narrative connotations. The formal visualisation in the manuscript illustration of Timurid elite life through the lens of Persian poetry and literature endowed the illustrative idiom with implications beyond the limits of the text, for it elevated and inserted Timurid royal activity into the rarified ethos of the Persian literary tradition. This visual grafting was one of a series of devices, like the dynasty's architectural programs or their relentless religious propagandizing, that encouraged an image and behavior capable of obscuring brutal political and military policies. (1993: 262)

This new genre of mural paintings was no longer strictly illustrative. In the process of moving from manuscript pages to walls, figurative paintings obviously increased in size and were engaged in some type of theatrical function. Therefore, they could be redesigned in a special visual form to express an idiomatic expression, evoking the illustrative idiom in a new and different context (Lentz and Lowry 1989). Furthermore, in the process of moving from manuscript pages to murals, these illustrative paintings were divorced from their original narrative context, but continued to exploit the linkage of the visual world and words that loaded manuscript illustration with new messages which could be cultural, political or religious. The audience of these mural paintings was probably enlarged compared to those of manuscript illustrations, but the interplay and interaction between the visual and the viewer certainly was still an exclusive experience, available only to those allowed entry into the royal complex.

During the Safavid period, Twelver Shiism became the state religion of Iran (1502), and inevitably was to have its effect on the patronage, production and usage of visual and performing arts to reflect the religious messages and sentiments of the period. Therefore, the history of the Prophet Muhammad and his *Ahl-i Beyt* were embedded in the textual and visual explanations designed to justify the Safavid claim to rule, and served in some sense as a proto-history of the new dynasty (Ruhrdanz 2000: 201). As Welch asserts:

> It was a traditional Shiite teaching [during the Safavid period] that an aspirant should strive for personal sanctity through imitation of the lives of saints and martyrs. Thus these images imply a social relationship of great importance and can be seen as statement of adherence to a religious ideal, even if it is a little vague and attenuated: they supply visual documentation that some well-dressed and well-fed Safavi aristocrats considered themselves or wished to be seen as 'Sufis at heart' who through artefacts, stigma, poetry, and pictures sought to emulate the examples set

for them by saints. Though these distant images, midway between entertainment, were not intended to be iconic or devotional or even blatantly didactic, they were consciously allegorical and could serve as oblique reminders of the ideal. (2000: 302)

One of the main vehicles which provided this new – and the fullest – expression of Shiite visual regime (figuration of the Prophet Muhammad and his *Ahl-i Beyt*) was the public performance of *Ta'ziyeh*, the popular form of Shiite ceremony in Safavid Iran (Peterson 1979: 80), whose origins are believed by many to date back to even earlier periods.[6] During these periods, the purpose of participating in or watching *Ta'ziyeh* performances was to lament the martyrdom of Imam Hoseyn, his family members and loyal companions. When little by little *Ta'ziyeh* performers included the Iranian version of Shiism into their repertoires and dramatized them for the public on stage, figural representations of Shiite holy figures and saints came to be widely accepted by adherents. However, one should not forget that *Ta'ziyeh* stories are not only about Shiite Islam, covering as they do a large corpus of Abrahamic sacred events, catastrophes, deaths of prophets and also the destiny of human society after their death on Judgement Day.

Michele Membre, a Venetian envoy to the Safavid court (1539–42), reported that 'the Sophians [Shiite Iranians] paint figures, such as the figure of [Imam]'Ali, riding on horse with a sword' (Membre 1993: 52), and Calmard's study of popular Shiite ceremonies of the Safavid period documents the usage of portable paintings of Imam 'Ali and other Shiite saints associated with the *Ta'ziyeh* performance as vehicles of state policy (Calmard 1996).

From the viewpoint of the school of large-scale religious paintings and its development during the Safavid period, we should not forget two important points which are crucial to our topic here. Firstly, the mass arrival of European paintings in the Safavid court, which was situated in the city of Isfahan; certainly these series of European oil paintings could have been good sources of inspiration for Safavid painters, encouraging them to experience new techniques and styles of painting.[7] These European oil paintings could have had two major impacts on Safavid painters and their artworks: first, the usage of full-size human figures in their paintings, and secondly, adding new topics of Christianity to their visual corpus. The second important point in this regard is the massive forced migration of Armenians from Tabriz to the city of Isfahan. While there were many important influences that the Armenian community had on the pictorial art of the Safavid period, my main interest is in their religious art, especially the mural paintings of the churches that they constructed in the city of Isfahan.[8]

Certainly, by the Safavid period, Iranian painters had inherited a good tradition of mural paintings from their predecessors. However, with the arrival of Armenians in the city of Isfahan and the construction of their churches, and additionally the decoration of their own houses in the Jolfa district, they introduced new styles and techniques of production of religious mural paintings to local painters. Those painters who decorated with murals the churches of the newly arrived Armenians of Isfahan were definitely not Iranians, but rather came to Isfahan from countries such as Armenia and Georgia. There are rumours that this group of foreign painters used the locals as their assistants and apprentices, and this is how they transferred their knowledge to the local community of Isfahani painters who trained the future generation of masters of Shiite mural paintings of saints' shrines in Qajar-era Iran. This could be confirmed by the existence of the most important and the best executed Shiite mural paintings of saints' shrines in Iran which are located today in the city of Isfahan.[9]

Therefore, the Safavid period is the key and the most important arrival point for the naissance of Persian Shiite mural paintings. But it was only during the late nineteenth century that Qajar painters depicted figures of the Prophet Muhammad, Imam 'Ali, other Shiite saints and their folk histories on a massive scale intended for the viewing of the entire public community. During the Qajar dynasty, the veneration of Shiite imams' and saints' shrines was represented by both the increasing influence of Shiite scholars of Islamic jurisprudence (*'ulema*) and, most clearly, by the fact that the public ritual of mourning for the third Shiite imam, Hoseyn ibn-'Ali, Prince of Martyrs, was conducted progressively throughout Iran.

The patronage of Qajar kings – especially Naser al-Din Shah – of Iranian Shiism, and consequently the substantial development of the physical environment of Shiite rituals and ceremonies, changed the Iranian landscape. Permanent and temporary ceremonial architecture and spaces were erected for performing public Shiite rituals and popular performances such as *Ta'ziyeh*. During the same period, for the first time *Ta'zieh* performances and their related Shiite folk stories inspired Qajar popular visual artists, including painters, to depict those sacred scenes in the form of narrative paintings (*naqashiy-i ravayi*) on large oil canvases called *pardeh* (curtain) or *shamayil* (pious icon).

This new genre of religious paintings became the focus of a type of public narrative recitation (*qisihkhaniy-i revayi*) called *pardehdari* (holding the curtain), *pardehkhani* (narrating the curtain) or *shamayilkhani* (narrating pious iconography), which was primarily for the benefit of outlying villages and poor communities in the countryside that could not participate in Muharram rituals and *Ta'zieh* performances.

Pardehkhani or *shamayilkhani* was a genre of self-employed ambulatory seasonal Shiite performing art (visual recitation). Normally the *pardehdar* (curtain holder) or *shamayilgardan* (pious icon turner) was a humble Dervish (sufi), who knew very well the stories of *Ta'zieh*. He had one or two large oil paintings (*pardeh*) of the relevant scenes in his possession and travelled from village to village all around the country. During his visits, the storyteller could install his ambulatory station in the cemetery or shrine of a holy saint to attract pilgrims, devotees and the public so that he could recite some parts of Shiite stories for them and in exchange receive some money. The main topic of the majority of these oil paintings was the scene of the Battle of Karbala, depicted in a polyscenic composition in which more than one moment of Shiite stories were depicted. This group of popular Shiite storytellers had a profound knowledge of the entire stories of *Ta'ziyeh*, and by beginning their recitation, for example, from the Battle of Karbala, could visually and mentally transfer their audiences to the scene of the Day of Judgement.

During the same period and based on Shiite popular histories, a specific genre of illustrated religious lithographic books was also published and widely circulated in Iran. These illustrated books were used particularly during *rowzihkhani* (Torab

2006), a type of Shiite ceremony which was very popular during the Qajar period and particularly concerned the dramatic stories of *Ta'ziyeh* performance. Here the main function of illustrations was to depict visually popular stories of the Iranian version of Shiism in a monoscenic composition in which only one moment of Shiite stories was depicted.

My fieldwork, long-term observations and examination of many Qajar Shiite paintings (*pardeh*, *shamayil*, lithographic books) impels me to conclude that *Ta'ziyeh* performance, ambulatory Shiite paintings and also illustrated religious lithographic books were the main vehicles for the justification and the usage of visual representations of the Prophet Muhammad and his *Ahl-i Beyt* during the Naseri period. Gradually saints' shrines became the main venues for hosting Shiite figurative mural paintings. During the same period, permanent Shiite mural paintings began to be executed and displayed on the internal and external walls of Shiite shrines and saints' mausoleums in certain cities of Iran, such as Lahijan, Isfahan, Shiraz, Kashan and Shushtar.[10]

Lahijan mural paintings

The few surviving nineteenth-century religious mural paintings of saints' shrines around the city of Lahijan in the north of Iran provide crucial information regarding the role of this religious popular art in evoking the senses and feelings of devotees by depicting the major holy figures of Twelver Shiism in different sacred scenes, such as the ascension of the Prophet Muhammad (*me'raj*) (Figure 9.1), the tragic epic of the Battle of Karbala (Figure 9.2), or the passing of the *Sirat* Bridge (*al-sirat*) on the Day of Judgement (*ruz-i qiyamat*) (Figure 9.3).

Figure 9.1 The Prophet Muhammad's Mi'raj. Qajar mural painting, Seyed Davar Kiya Shrine, Lahijan, Iran, 1997. © Pedram Khosronejad.

Figure 9.2 Imam Hoseyn holding his infant son Ali-Asghar in his arm while preparing for the final battle. Qajar mural painting, Aqa Seyed Ibrahim Shrine, Babajan Dareh, Lahijan, Iran, 1997. © Pedram Khosronejad.

Figure 9.3 Passing the *Sirat* Bridge. Qajar mural painting, Aqa Seyed Ali Shrine, Mot'alegh Mahaleh, Lahijan, Iran, 1997. © Pedram Khosronejad.

Based on my fieldwork and interviews with local devotees since 1997, I can confirm that one of the key reasons for the patronage and consequently the execution of these mural paintings on the walls of saints' shrines was to visually narrate major stories of Shiite Islam and the *Ahl-i Beyt* for devotees – local communities who were profound Shia believers and loyal to their saint's shrine, but mostly illiterate. Therefore, one of the best methods to educate them in the main topics of religion was through using such pictorial storytelling. Another reason for the execution of these Shiite visual narrations, as I discussed with the local informants, could be the absence of *Ta'ziyeh* groups, *pardehkhan* and *shamayilgardan*. The costs of performing *Ta'ziyeh* are very high, and even today not all communities can afford to bring such large performing groups to their village. Consequently, the walls of saints' shrines could be considered as one of the best supports for the visual recitation of selected Shia narratives which are the main sequences of *Ta'ziyeh*, *pardehs* and *shamayils*.

In contrast to the saints' tombs and the main doors of saints' shrines, no one touches, kisses or even approaches closely these Shiite mural paintings to receive blessings. Their sanctity is not in their materiality, but in their sacred visual reflections (*baztab-i qodsi*) in the heart (*qalb*) of devotees to evoke special feelings concerning the sacred moment depicted and to transfer mentally to those very scenes.

These mural paintings were created under the patronage of local wealthy believers (*waqif*) as an endowment act (*waqf*) and votive gesture (*nazr*) to the local saints' shrines, and executed by unknown seasonal ambulatory folk artists (*naqash-i dowrihgard-i fasli*). Not much is known about these painters, their origins, their techniques of production or even their world of aesthetics. The physical characteristics of Shiite holy figures and the composition of major scenes executed by these artists follow the illustrations of some of the previously mentioned lithographic books. My observations suggest that a majority of the artists of these saints' shrines used such pictorial samples for the creation of the main body of their artworks.

During my post-fieldwork visual analyses, I found that the visual order of most of these mural paintings rarely followed literary prototypes of Shiite histories and related events, and probably out-of-order visual sequences followed an unwritten rule rather than the exception in the majority of cases. I think artists deliberately did not follow step by step what the stories narrated. Here, artists were free to visually express their own world view with the creation of new compositions, exaggeration in the size of

Figure 9.4 Front-door mural painting. Qajar mural painting, Seyed Ali Kiya Shrine, Rankouh, Lahijan, Iran, 1997. © Pedram Khosronejad.

figures, or even the use of unusual and provocative colours. As long as they could visually convince the patron of the artwork and the viewers that this scene depicted the Battle of Karbala and these beheaded bodies belonged to the companions of Imam Hoseyn, in the rest of their work they were free (Figure 9.4).

I also found that in some cases the visual order of the stories or protagonists is closely related to the design and architectural form of the saint's shrine building, rather than the topic of painting or style of the artist. In such cases, the cycles of stories and their heroes were usually divided into neatly framed fields that corresponded directly to the basic structural parts of the shrine and not the real story. When a door or a

Figure 9.5 Lion guarding decapitated bodies, one of the episodes of the Battle of Karbala. Qajar mural painting, Aqa Seyed Muhammad Shrine, Pincha, Astaneh Ashrafiyeh, Iran, 1997. © Pedram Khosronejad.

window appeared in the middle of a work or when a wall was smaller than the painting, artists had no choice and had to employ their creativity to finish their work.

Here, the function of visual depictions of the Prophet Muhammad and his *Ahl-i Beyt* is close to the 'vision by the heart' (*al-ru'ya bi l-qalb*), a ritualistic practice performed by some Sufi brotherhoods of the Dhahabiyya in the city of Shiraz, Iran. This practice involves focusing the devotee's eye on the *shamyil* of Imam 'Ali while concentrating on one's own heart and performing the *zikr-i 'Ali* (Amir-Moezzi 2012: 28). The main point in this ritual is that without the physical aid (a painting of Imam 'Ali), new arrival devotees are incapable of visualizing the face of Imam 'Ali in their hearts. Like the above ritualistic practice, the religious mural paintings of Lahijan's saints' shrines function as physical media to strengthen the interaction between the devoted viewer and Shiite sacred stories and events. During my fieldwork in these saints' shrines, on several occasions I observed that many pilgrims and devotees were able to internalize the sacred moments of those Shia stories through lamenting for Imam Hoseyn, while at the same time looking at these mural paintings and virtually transferring to the scene of the battle. For example, the series of mural paintings which depicts the scene of the massacre of Karbala will help mentally and assist emotionally worshippers in their virtual journey to imagine themselves accompanying Imam Hoseyn. Mostly during the Muharram rituals, by lamenting in the saint's shrine which is accompanied by deep nostalgic Muharram music, devotees find themselves beside the beheaded body of Imam Hoseyn and his martyred companions.

As most of these mural paintings are depicted according to Shiite narratives, they will have their most profound emotional impacts (*ta'sir-i rouhi*) on devotees during the related ritualistic ceremonies. This does not mean that they cannot evoke the emotion (*shur*) and feelings (*hal*) of viewers outside the ceremony periods. As soon as Shiite believers see the visual representations of the beheaded body of Imam Hoseyn, they will spontaneously cry and beat their chests in memory of the sufferings of the Prince of Martyrs (*Seyid al-Shohada*) (Figure 9.5). However, as mentioned previously, such visual provocation requires a background story which is already deeply engraved in the heart of the viewer.

Concluding remarks

The theological objections to figurative visual art have been active from the early periods in Islam's history and have successfully prohibited the entrance of visual representations of human beings into any part of the religious life of the Muslim communities. Religious figurative paintings are not found in Islamic monuments outside of Iran, and orthodox religious sentiments have always been active in the prohibition of pictorial representations of human beings. Generally speaking, it has been stated that the paintings of human beings is forbidden in the Qur'an; but there is no specific mention of such prohibition in the 'Word of God'. The only verse (Q 5.90)[11] which theologians may quote in support of such condemnation of figurative visual art makes it clear that the real object of the prohibition is the avoidance of idolatry. The fact is that Shiite theologians condemned visual representations of human beings just as severely as Sunni theologians. The explanation of these facts is that the condemnation of the painting of living figures was a theological opinion common to the whole Muslim world, and the practical acceptance of it largely depended on the influence of the theologians and of course political leaders on the traditions and beliefs of a society at any one particular time. Therefore, despite the hostility of the theologians and the unsympathetic attitude of the main body of orthodox believers, there have been certain aspects of Islamic religious thought which have found expression for themselves in the form of figurative art, and the painter has been called up to depict the various scenes of Muslim religious history (Arnold 1965). As Flaskerud states (2010), aniconic attitudes prevail among Sunni theologians and Sunni popular practices, although exceptions to such positions among the Sunnis are many. Adherents to the Twelver branch of Shiism in Iran have taken a different position and can look back at a long history of producing figurative imagery, with themes from Shia hagiography to be used in the service of religion.

The stories of Shiite holy figures – the Prophet Muhammad and his *Ahl-i Beyt* – in Qajar Iran cannot be told without thoughtful consideration of the visual culture (*farhang-i tasviri*) and the culture of seeing (*farhang-i didari*) developed and practised to enhance and propagate the cult of the visual veneration of saints. In this chapter, I have endeavoured to demonstrate how the experience of seeing and visualizing Shiite holy figures could be brought to the viewer, and the viewer to the holy figures, by means of envisioning different episodes of these mural paintings. Through the power of representing the ultimate sacred figures of Shiite Islam in a great variety of visual modes and scenes, ranging from the magnificent to the most humble, believers of every class can participate in the spiritual experience of visual devotion in the proximity of the sacred locus, or from a physically distant vantage point. These series of Persian visual art allow and induce greater participation by all laity.

Visual depictions of the Prophet Muhammad and his *Ahl-i Beyt* in the form of mural paintings as described above call our attention to the existence of a figural imagery of holy figures in Persian Shiite visual culture and the importance of their sacred meanings and religious functions in the devotional life of viewers, topics which have until recently received no attention. While any type of visual representation of the Prophet Muhammad and Muslim saints is often considered non-existent by scholars of Islam, Iranian Shiite Muslims hold divergent views on the production, circulation and the usage of holy figurative imageries, particularly in the context of devotional practices.

Lahijan's mural paintings of saints help the devoted audiences to experience the unseen holy figures visually (Khosronejad 2018). Certain aspects of pilgrimage and devotional sites signalled nuances of meaning and importance to pilgrims. These Shiite mural paintings dignify and enhance the sacred spaces, thereby eliciting appropriate responses from their viewers. Taking devotees on a mental and visual excursion to Shiite sacred sites, Lahijan's mural paintings of the Qajar period bid the believer to circumambulate the shrine and follow the story in both body and soul, to look through the image itself.

In the case of Lahijan's mural paintings in saints' shrines, devotees are present with locally (*bumi*) created and culturally (*farhangi*) embedded multifaceted sensory experiences in which visualization, seeing and sensation are part of the complex Shiite visual aesthetic. To many observers, visualization and seeing are central to the recollection of holiness and saintly power; to the dissemination of religious knowledge; to the transformation of emotions; to cultic behaviour; and to the understanding of ethical values and spiritual experiences. Therefore, there are complex relationships between the visual, the unseen and Shiite aesthetical practices and sensory experiences.

The majority of the mural paintings of Lahijan are designed to create the hopes (*omid*) and shape the beliefs (*bavar*) of adherents, while at other times particular depictions help to fulfil their expectations by marking the goal of the excursion and giving physical form to spiritual aims. Indeed, anticipation colours the actual act of devotion, and visual features help to intensify the experience. These Persian mural paintings make the inaccessible accessible; they mostly illustrate the non-visible, the ethereal, and the infinite by explaining and sometimes endlessly reproducing aspects of the material and the finite.

Therefore, pilgrimage practice and devotion to the saints' shrines of Lahijan is not defined merely by the physical boundaries of travel and the shrine building, but also by the intense seeing and visualizing experience, including mural paintings, to enhance the viewers' feelings of awe (*ehtiram*) and respect (*tavaazo'*) for the Prophet Muhammad and his *Ahl-i Beyt*, while at the same time teaching them the legendary specifics regarding the history of the Iranian version of Shiism.

Through visual interpretations of Shiite events and related histories, the mural paintings of the saints' shrines of Lahijan engage the mental and emotional participation of devoted viewers. By representing the figures of the Prophet Muhammad, Imam 'Ali, Imam Hoseyn and other Shiite saints in a multitude of sacred stories within panoramic views, these mural paintings allow the Shia viewer to travel virtually and spiritually in both time and space, to participate emotionally in all related sacred events.

Just like saintly persons, these mural paintings likewise play intermediary roles in constructing knowledge and faith, in turn helping devotees conceive of and communicate with the realm of the sacred bodies and their related stories. Figurative representations of the Prophet Muhammad and his *Ahl-i Beyt* have fulfilled such roles in cultural traditions, tending to manifold devotional and pedagogical needs.

10

Photographic Practices and the 'Aesthetics of Withdrawal' among Muslims of the East African Coast

Heike Behrend

In the last years, various image theories have connected images with the specific gesture of showing and attempted to reveal their deictic potential (for example, Seitter 2002: 206; Boehm 2015: 19ff). By producing images, painters or photographers give something to see. In fact, in a picture, the gesture of showing gains its strongest expression because the transitory act of showing is fixed and materialized in the image. Yet, what is shown with visual means implies a decision to also withhold something from showing. A picture not only enables one to see but also withdraws something from visibility. It may show the front side of a person but not his or her backside, for example. The act of showing in a picture thus implicates withdrawal, effacement, concealment or veiling. Against the concept of a primary transparency of the photographic image, in the following, I will focus more on its negative and opaque qualities. As I attempt to show, at different historical times and in diverse cultural milieus, the acts of showing and concealing in photographs receive different regulations, framings and institutional connections that determine the pictures' status, power and truth.

Along the cosmopolitan East African coast, since the 1980s and in particular after 9/11,[1] reformed Muslims, followers of Wahhabism originating from Saudi Arabia,[2] have increasingly questioned figurative representations. In fact, different and opposing attitudes towards images have gained a new religious-political importance and have become intensely debated and contested, perhaps more than ever before. In addition, Muslims have actualized a gendered concept of purity ('purdah') that centres on seclusion and concealment and has been extended to prohibit the circulation of pictures of women in the public domain. In strong opposition to the West – associated with immorality and decadence – interdictions and collective moral claims on female bodies to conform to a particular aesthetics of propriety and piety have translated into new strategies of concealment and the creation of new opacities in relation to photography. Yet, as suggested by Michel Foucault, interdictions do not necessarily only function in a repressive manner; they can also become extremely productive and unleash a creative potential through finding different ways of observing as well as undermining the interdiction.

In the following I will focus on what I have called 'aesthetics of withdrawal': the various ways and techniques that process the photographic act as well as the photographic image to theatricalize the surface of the image in new ways by veiling, masking and concealing (see Behrend 2013). My argument here is that a veiled person or an opaque surface also gives something to see by creating a secondary image of defacement, thereby challenging the simple binary opposition of creation and destruction, image making and image breaking, revealing and concealing. By focusing on contradictory aspects in processes of photographic mediation, I attempt to complicate the concept of (religious) mediation more than scholars have up to now.

The 'aesthetics of withdrawal' I will explore thus centres on the process or act of becoming visible in a particular form that, however, insists on (partial) concealment of, for example, the body or face of women and thereby creates a visible screen or 'outside', hiding and protecting the 'inside' from view. This concealment or withdrawal produces a strange surplus of energy or desire that is likely to be aroused from within the defaced object itself. As Michael Taussig (1999) suggests, this visual negativity of seeing what is not given to see that is inherent in the 'aesthetics of withdrawal' lies at the very heart of a vast range of social powers and different forms of knowledge.

It is important to clarify that making the 'aesthetics of withdrawal' the subject of this contribution is not an attempt to reinstate orientalism and the old opposition, taking the West as a pursuer of visibility, truth and enlightenment and the Orient (including the East African coast) as prone to secrecy and deception. As Walter Benjamin suggested, truth is not a matter of exposure which destroys the secret but a revelation that does justice to it. Following Michael Taussig (1999) again, I prefer to dissolve the opposition between truth and secret and join both, I understand one as enveloping the other, truth being a secret and secrets holding some truth.

For centuries, and in particular after the 1980s, Muslims of the East African coast have created a complex aesthetics that shows that something is NOT shown, that something is withdrawn from visibility. In the following, I attempt to unfold this 'aesthetics of withdrawal' in relation to two different media: textiles and photography.

The coast and its media

Africa is often seen as the continent of figurative icons, of masks, sculptures, bronze castings, and 'fetishes'; yet, as Jack Goody has suggested, there are large gaps in their distribution. There were and are regions where little or no figurative art was produced or only in restricted contexts (1997: 35). Sometimes people with rich sculptural traditions and those without lived as neighbours, had access to the same resources and on various levels were in intense contact with each other. Obviously, in certain historical contexts, some people may decide against certain images, maybe in more or less conscious opposition to those who do produce these representations (Kramer 2001). Thus, it is not only monotheistic religions that have rejected and problematized figurative images and the representability of god; some polytheistic religions have also preferred the absence of figurative representations (Goody 1997: 56ff).

It seems that the East African coast was such an area where even in pre-Islamic times we have no evidence of a strong pictorial tradition. And when Islam started to spread along the coast in the eighth century, the above-mentioned (assumed) absence of figurative representations may have matched well with Islam's attitude towards images. While in other parts of Africa the process of Islamization was inimical to African artistry and material culture because Islam (like Protestant Christianity) could and would not tolerate 'idols' and other figurative representations, it seems highly probable that along the East African coast Islam established itself without iconoclastic acts and without radical rupture, this even more so because Muslims' hostility towards and refusal of figurative images seems to be a later development that may have begun when confronted with Christian (colonial) politics of images.

Ludwig Krapf, the first CMS missionary to evangelize the coastal people, mentioned the absence of 'idolatry' in his diary (15 December 1848). In fact, the material culture that archaeologists have found, such as ceramics, glass and porcelain, locally produced as well as imported from China, India, Persia and Arabia, seems to have followed the aniconic tradition. And coins, most of them probably minted on the coast, were all non-figural and, with their inscriptions in the Arabic language, can be classified as Islamic (Brown 1993).

While (probably) the production of figurative images (on material support) did not take place along the coast, there existed another tradition of visualization that centred on the production of inner images which were given expression in performances of spirit possession. Alien spirits embodied themselves as 'living images' in their mediums during possession rituals. In performative visualizations of spirit possession, 'living images' of strangers were (and still are) communicated in institutionalized forms. In fact, the absence or marginalization of visual media such as sculpture or figurative painting coincided with complex imaginative practices that centred on embodiment and in the context of spirit possession rituals were externalized so that they could be shared by other people (Kramer 2001).

Beside rituals of spirit possession, the media of scripture and textiles preceded the medium of photography and intensively shaped the visual economies of recording and processing of visibility, performance, social status and meaning in photographs (Behrend 2013).

Textiles, veils and (in)visibilities in the nineteenth century

In the nineteenth century along the cosmopolitan East African coast, a visual regime dominated that expressed origin and descent, social class and status through the quality and social value of (imported) textiles and by the amount of clothing a person used to cover his or her body. Class and status, as well as sexual difference, manifested themselves within the field of vision by withdrawing, in particular, women from visibility in the public domain. Respectable femininity demanded the veil as a kind of shield against the gaze of unrelated men in public spaces. While slaves went 'naked' and wore only the slightest of clothes usually made of the rudest and cheapest material, Omani aristocrats were distinguished by their sophisticated headdress and silk cloth. High-ranking women who were privileged to stay in seclusion would cover their whole bodies in public, including their faces, behind masks, veils and portable walls, so-called *shiraa*, carried by slaves and later forbidden by the British (Middleton 1992: 150; Figure 10.1a).

A complex technology of veiling and concealing was made available for extending women's physical seclusion outside their homes. Veils in these different forms were movable, flexible and unstable; as *shiraa*, the wall-like textiles would hide a woman completely while the other forms of veil could take the shape of what they covered, remaining suggestive of what they were hiding (Figure 10.1b).

It is important to note that men also had to cover their bodies in decent ways. The (general) dress code was inverted during times of mourning. In particular, after a chief's death, when his turban and his umbrella – both imported commodities that served as signs of chiefly authority – were buried with his body, all mourners went bareheaded, including women, and sometimes all the men would shave their heads in order to display an even more radical 'nakedness'. Again, the social hierarchy was expressed in the amount of clothing men were allowed to wear during the mourning period. While important chiefs removed only their coats and wore the *kanzu*, holders of lesser rank were not allowed to wear the *kanzu*, and untitled youths and male slaves were required to bare their chests, wearing only loincloths or *kikoi*. The social ranking was again revealed by the order in which men were allowed to resume wearing their clothes when the mourning period was over (Glassman 1995: 157). Thus, a complex dress code existed that, by the various degrees of (un)covering the head and the body, served to mark gender, inequality, liminality and differences in social status.

After the abolition of slavery, covering their heads and bodies was one of the first ways men and women of slave origin could show their 'freedom' and new status (Fair 1998: 93). When around the 1930s the *buibui*, a loose black garment that covered the entire body except for face, hands and feet, was introduced, it was quickly adopted by women of the lower classes and of slave origin to show their respectability, their adherence to Islam, and their modesty (ibid.: 82f).

It is important to note that also a veiled person gives something to see by creating a secondary image of defacement. In fact, the veil makes invisibility very visible; it makes an overt and visual point out of concealment, in the process transforming the private, individual women into her public representation of a more general kind (Dudley 2011: 65). The visual power of the veil seems to be rooted in this tension between invisibility and visibility and its intimate relationship with the body. As mentioned before, the visible screen that is provided by the veil, hiding and protecting the 'inside' from view, produces a strange surplus of desire.

Kusitiri, a Swahili term that can be translated as 'concealment', has been identified by David Parkin as a 'root metaphor', serving as an affective base for social action (Parkin 1995: 212). In fact, *kusitiri* implies not only the decent concealment of head and body of women and men with textiles, but also the control of the body, its movement, gestures and affective expression, including speech and, in particular, the art of concealing in poetry. They follow what I have called 'aesthetics of withdrawal': they give something to see (or to hear) in a specific form that insists on (partial) concealment, on withdrawal from visibility.

Figure 10.1a Women carrying *shiraa*, around 1900. © Collection Heike Behrend.

Figure 10.1b Woman with face mask. Unknown photographer, Zanzibar, 1905 (Winterton Collection).

In the 1960s and 1970s, however, the veil was disappearing in most towns along the coast when unveiling went along with aspirations for independence and modernity. Yet, as mentioned before, with the Islamic revival and its attempts to Islamize also public spaces, the veil and new Islamic clothing strongly reappeared not only to mark (female) Muslim presence but also to erase social and economic differences between wearers. The new Islamic dress imbued women with a kind of moral and religious authority that would discourage harassment and allowed them to enter public spaces confidently (cf Ahmed 2011: 87).

The introduction of photography

While the various means of veiling seem to have been able to protect, in particular, women, from being seen (and heard) by others (unrelated men), with the introduction of technical media, such as photography and video, the existing boundaries between public and private became intensely disturbed. As the proliferation of mass media has strongly foregrounded public visuality, it demanded new strategies for the protection of what should not be given to see.

Around 1860, when Indian (Christian) photographers from Goa and Christian photographers from Europe reached the coast and built up the first commercial photo studios, the above-mentioned local visual regime that shows that something is not shown, was confronted with photography, a highly inclusive medium that always gives something more to see. Before the introduction of photography there existed only a very restricted repertoire of portraiture (for example, in spirit possession rituals) and only the sultans had their portrait painted (Figure 10.2).

Common people were not celebrated in images but remembered in their names and in written or spoken poetry only. Thus, with the introduction of photographic portraiture a radical new field was opened up that had to gain acceptance against Islamic aniconism and a strongly gendered visual regime that sought to conceal (free) women's bodies and faces in the public domain. Yet, in spite of strong resistance at the beginning, Muslims too appropriated the new medium and inserted it into various domains of life, in particular rites of passage and festivities, albeit not uncontested (Behrend 2012). Indeed, portrait photography became a new technique of the self for Muslims.

Debating the medium of photography

As already mentioned, since the 1980s, within the context of a new Islamic revival, pious Muslim men and women have increasingly attempted to control and reduce the visibility of women in the public domain.[3] Since 1988 in Nairobi and since the 1990s in Mombasa, new Islamic schools called *mahad* were established especially for women to teach them what is *haram* (forbidden) and what is *halal* (allowed). In these schools, the visibility of women in photographs and other visual media was problematized and discussed. What used to be a theological debate among scholars has become increasingly popularized nowadays. In fact, interactions and oppositions between

Figure 10.2 Sultan Sayyid Said, Fort Jesus, Mombasa. © Collection Heike Behrend.

different Islamic traditions as well as interactions with the (Christian) 'West' created a more intense awareness of the ways images (of women) intruded into everyday life, opening up various debates on the 'Islamic interdiction of figurative images' in relation to visual media.

Among Muslims in Lamu the prohibition to represent human beings and animals was widely accepted; however, the reasons given varied considerably. I met some Islamic scholars who resented photographic portraits because they feared image worship – especially when the picture was hung on a wall – and saw Islamic monotheism endangered, but they accepted video because of its fleeting images that would not allow idolatry. For example, Sharif Said Hassan of Lamu, who kindly gave me an interview in October 1996, narrated the well-known story of the Prophet Muhammad, who wanted to visit a house where a picture was hanging on the wall. When he saw the picture he refused to enter. Sharif Said Hassan explained that especially photographs of dead relatives, of ancestors, encourage idol worship, which the Prophet forbade. Their representation, he said, poses a threat to monotheism.

In contrast, other Muslims claimed that photography as a picture medium should not be prohibited because it does not create what it depicts but only reproduces or represents what is already there and therefore photographers do not violate God's singular capacity of creation. Another scholar argued that only three-dimensional things can become objects of idol worship, while two-dimensional pictures of human beings or animals – because they have lost already their life-like quality – such as photographs cannot. Again, other scholars maintained that the photographic picture is already life-less; as photography freezes and immobilizes all it captures, inherent in it is an iconoclastic gesture. As vitality is already annihilated in the photographic image it cannot be considered as imitating God's creation.

In addition, in the context of the Islamic revival, *purdah* – the ideal of (gendered) modesty, purity and seclusion, that does not allow women to expose themselves in public – has been redefined to include photographs of women as well as videos, tape recordings and paintings. Pious Muslims have drawn attention to the complementary effects of unveiling and women's exposure in photographs and videos, both violating *purdah*. This is why photographs of Muslim women have disappeared completely from public spaces in Mombasa's Old Town and Lamu. In addition, in the private domain of many homes, photographs of (male and female) relatives or friends have been removed from the sitting room and either put up in the more private domain of the bedroom or stored in albums. However, I heard of only one case in which a pious woman destroyed all her photographs in order to comply with Islam's aniconism. The other women I talked to kept their photographs – more or less hidden – in albums or boxes in order to control access to them.

It is not only that photographs may reveal women's faces and bodies to unrelated men, it is also the quality of photography as a mass medium that poses special problems. When a photographer takes a picture of women dancing at a wedding, for example, he or she can produce many copies and publish them so that they may appear at a distance in time, space and context from the original event. Photographs can be displayed in contexts beyond the control of the photographed women, and this poses complex and worrying problems. In fact, since 2007, with the appropriation of digital camera phones on a mass scale, these predicaments have become ever more vexing (see Behrend 2013: 241ff).

Thus, there existed a multitude of competing voices accepting or questioning photographic portraits, covering a spectrum that at one extreme totally refused photographic portraits and at the other included more pragmatic attitudes that allowed the production of photographs in a controlled way.

Photography as unveiling

In the late 1940s, the colonial state in Kenya started to demand photographs – cropped, frontal headshots – for I.D. cards to better identify and control its subjects (Brielmaier 2003: 131). If somebody wanted to travel, open a bank account or get a driver's licence, an I.D. picture was needed. Especially in the rural areas, capturing the face for an I.D. was often the first encounter with photography as a gesture of subjection by the (colonial) state (Werner 2001).

Although identity photography is a global genre it has nevertheless accumulated resonances and nuances specific to the East African coast. Here Muslim women's veils formed an obstacle to the sight of the colonial government and its cameras. Veiled women reinforced the impression of inaccessibility. The veil discouraged the colonial photographer's scopic desire and intimated more or less clearly a refusal. Veiling and, in particular, veiling the face, was considered equivalent to resistance. And just as, for Christians and Westerners, the face marked the identity of a person, the veil was not only (mis)understood as a symbol of the oppressed status of women but also as a potentially subversive attempt to hide one's identity. Thus, the veil had to fall and faces, including those of women, had to offer themselves to the bold cameras of the photographers working for the state.

Along the Islamic East African coast, especially Muslims experienced the imposition of I.D. photography as a violent act and as humiliating. In colonial as well as postcolonial times, the central government in Kenya lay in the hands of Christians; so measures were interpreted as deliberate infringements of Islam's 'interdiction of figurative representations' and as anti-Muslim. I was told many stories about resistance to photography, particularly by pious Muslim women who wanted to go on a pilgrimage to Mecca and therefore needed a passport. I was told about Fatma, the daughter of Sheik Habib Saleh (1844–1935), the reformer and founder of the Riyadha Mosque in Lamu. She also needed a passport photograph to go to Mecca. As a woman, she was anxious about unveiling her face to the photographer, because she would thereby violate not only the interdiction of figurative representation, but also *purdah*, women's purity and modesty, that is associated with their (partial) invisibility in the public domain. This is why she burned the photograph after her pilgrimage; but fortunately, as her granddaughter Muzna Ahmed told me, the negative was saved. It was enlarged in the Bakor Studio and her descendants are happy to be able to remember her in the photograph. Photographs originally produced within the repressive colonial relationship could thus assume new purposes and meanings representing highly treasured ancestors who provided a connection between the past and the present. In this narrative, the highly ambivalent attitude towards photographic portraits produced by the state is displayed. While descendants may cherish the reworked photographs of their ancestors in new framings, they nevertheless stress in their narratives that the preservation of the pictures was not intended by the persons photographed but happened more or less accidentally.

Muslim women, in particular, associated I.D. photographs not only with foreignness, Christianity and colonization but with the act of forcefully unveiling their face and thereby violating conventions of piety and modesty. Thus, I.D. photography gained among pious (reformed) Muslims a negative connotation. The boundaries and divides such as inside/outside, private/public, female/male and inclusion/exclusion that are created by the veil were troubled and disturbed by photography. In fact, photographs were conceived as the opposite of the veil because the camera intruded into a domain conceived as private and because the camera recorded an 'excess' of visible details and surfaces that could not be controlled. The mobile medium also provoked anxieties about the easy reproduction, mobility and circulation of portraits of women among, in particular, (unrelated) men who were not supposed to see them. While veils were used to cover and conceal women's bodies and faces, photographs revealed what should have remained concealed. In the urban milieu of Mombasa and Lamu where the influence of reformed Islam (Wahhabism) is especially strong, sharp tensions arose between the global medium of photography that 'unveils' and always gives something 'more' to see, and local understandings of the appropriate use of women's visibility and led to various attempts to withdraw women from visibility and create new opacities.

Obviously, because the colonial and postcolonial government's visual politics was bent on unveiling Islamic women through photographs, it actualized and reinforced what now is seen as an essential part of local tradition, culture and religion, the veil, *purdah*, and the 'interdiction of figurative images'. When Muslim women today critically associate photography and unveiling, they refer to their experiences of forceful unveiling in front of a photographer working for the postcolonial administration and a state that insists on a visual regime of transparency.

Yet, there were also other voices. A female Islamic scholar and midwife, Asya Sunkar Salim, held in a conversation in September 2007 that, since there is no mention in the Qur'an of photographs, the Prophet did not say that photographs should not be taken. For her, photographs of women were, first and foremost, a question of modesty. As long as the photographed women cover their body according to Islamic rules, she had no objections to photographs. For her, the degree of exposure was at issue rather than the portrayal itself. She showed me her I.D. card that depicted her in passport format with her veil (*hijab*), her face not hidden. She said that nothing was wrong with photographs that enabled you to go on a *hadj* to Mecca, the pilgrimage being one of the five pillars of Islam. She saw no humiliation in being photographed and in exposing her face because in Islam, so she said, the face of women is not hidden. However, when praying in a room with photographic portraits on display, she saw the danger of distraction and usually turned the pictures to the wall to better concentrate on her prayers.

The Bakor Studio and the ornamentalization of photographs

The Bakor Studio in Lamu, situated on one of the main streets of the Old Town, was established in the 1960s (Wendl and Behrend 1998: 118ff). The founder, Omar Said Bakor, born in 1932, was a self-made man and brilliant *bricoleur*, who never went to school. His family originated in Yemen. Before opening the studio, he worked for ten years as a street photographer. He died in 1993, and his sons continued to work in his studio until recently. Bakor created a unique tradition of photo collages that I will take as examples of the 'aesthetics of withdrawal' and as an attempt to reconcile photographic portraits with local cultural and religious values, especially the 'Islamic prohibition of figurative representations' that mediated the ways through which photography has been transformed and accepted.

While rejecting figurative representations, Islamic arts have been described as favouring and concentrating on the ornament. Vegetable and geometrical ornaments are used to embellish the walls of buildings and the surfaces of objects. Highly complex mathematics, especially geometry, provided the basis for the calculations necessary for this purpose. Geometry represented not only decoration or technical skills, but also cosmological laws. And the ornament was not only decoration but – sometimes – became semantically loaded and a medium of messages (Belting 2008: 127f). In Islamic arts, many motifs and even inscriptions were ornamentalized. Ornaments were permanently transposed from one medium into another, for example, from textiles and rugs to plaster walls or wooden doors and vice versa (Grabar 1977: 236, 265). Although ornaments decorate and beautify surfaces, they also produce some sort of shutter or veil that conceals the objects and buildings they cover and thereby open up questions about the relationship between the visible and the invisible.

It was Bakor who started to ornamentalize photographic portraits. By integrating photographic portraits into floral ornaments, Bakor's collages connected to the existing local aniconic art forms of ornamental wood carvings, plasterwork in local architecture and embroidery. He transposed ornamentalization into photography, thereby giving proof of the tendency inherent in Islamic art to ornamentalize whatever comes into its realm (Figure 10.3a,b). On the East African coast, floral motifs like *waridi*, rose, or leaves of various plants like *kulabu* form well-established, named patterns, some of which are widely used in textiles, on plasterwork, wood carvings, and, of course, Bakor's photomontages.

By integrating photographic portraits in ornaments, the portraits become part of surface decoration and are combined with more general principles of Islamic aesthetics – for example, the anti-naturalistic tendency verging on abstraction, consisting in making the relationship between forms more important than the forms themselves. In this way, the surface decoration averts the viewer's risk from becoming absorbed by the photographic portrait and in this way serves as an obstacle to

Figure 10.3a, b Bakor Studio, Lamu, c. 1970. © Collection Heike Behrend.

image worship. Thus, the ornamentalization can be seen as an attempt to reduce the importance of the photographic portrait in deference to the actualized preference for aniconism along the Islamic coast. Although the artist is not allowed to imitate God's creation, through ornaments he or she gains the freedom to experiment with various parts of God's world in their abstraction and to recombine them into new ensembles. Indeed, fragmentation and recomposition of the surface conjoins decorative practice with a mediation of the photographed portrait that does not stand for itself but acts as a 'relay' or point of connection with other more abstract entities.

Iconoclastic icons

Bakor produced his collages by cutting images into pieces, especially by severing the heads of the depicted persons from their bodies and transferring them into other contexts: to montage the heads into ornaments, for example. The act of cutting, and even more so of decapitation, is deeply iconoclastic. In Islamic arts, images depicting persons or animals without heads or bodies lose the status of an image and are no longer forbidden. Artists thus make clear that they are not attempting to rival God by creating human beings.

Thus, the playful way of dealing with severed heads in Bakor's collages may be seen as an attempt to observe Islam's aniconism. By inserting an iconoclastic gesture into his collages, the portraits he produced lost their status as images. In fact, some of Bakor's

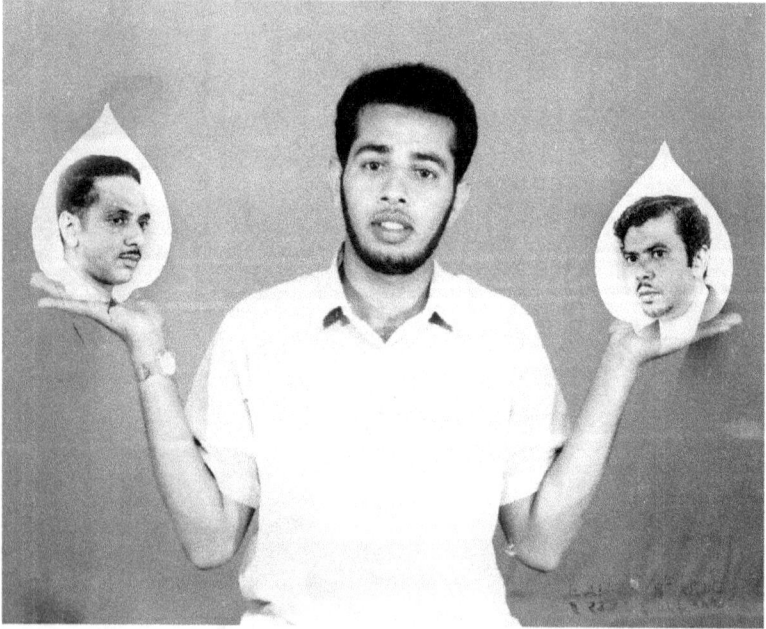

Figure 10.4 Bakor Studio, Lamu, c. 1970. © Collection Heike Behrend.

collages could be seen as 'icons as iconoclash' (Koerner 2002), icons that are made and at the same time break images. Iconoclash and icon, two mutually incompatible absolutes, become deeply engaged with each other (ibid.: 166). While on the one hand, the imposed ban on the representation of living beings seems to have inspired Bakor to evermore effective inducements to captivation by visual artifice, on the other hand, in a subversive way, he also reinstated aniconism by producing 'iconoclastic icons'. Through his collages he succeeded in acknowledging the 'interdiction of figurative images' while at the same time undermining it.

11

Moulded Imaginaries: Icons, Idols and the Sensory Environments of Eastern Orthodox Christianity

Sonja Luehrmann

If there is one descendant of the Abrahamic traditions that does not suffer from a reputation of aniconism, it is Eastern Orthodox Christianity. Nothing evokes Orthodox religiosity more than an image of worshippers (often depicted as elderly women in headscarves) lighting candles before an icon, the light reflecting from their faces and the image. And yet, even this tradition must contend with the Mosaic commandment against the making and worshipping of graven images. The resulting self-reflexive ambivalence is most famously summarized in the decrees of the Second Council of Nicaea (787), which formally ended a century of iconoclastic controversies by asking Orthodox Christians to walk a middle path between deifying and rejecting images. In the flourishing liturgical use of two-dimensional images that followed, the line between image veneration and idol worship came to be seen as a boundary between canonically rooted depiction and unrestricted mental imagery. Orthodox Christians still confront this line today, in encounters with other religious traditions as well as with changing secular image practices in a visually saturated society, where a flood of mechanically reproducible images competes for a devotee's attention. In this chapter I look at the role of authoritative tradition and sensory environments as ways to manage image-anxiety in an iconophile faith, starting from well-known histories of Byzantine struggles over the pictorial imagination and moving to more specific cases of post-Soviet image creation. In dialogue with cognitivist approaches to religion, I argue that Orthodox Christian image practices, tell us much about the relationship between religious images and the human imagination, and the role of materiality for sustaining, shaping and restraining both.

The Nicaean legacy

During a debate between Orthodox and Pentecostal clergy that took place in the provincial Russian town of Ioshkar-Ola around 2002, some enduring contrasts of Orthodox image veneration came out in a polemic against Protestant iconoclasts.

Deflecting the question of whether icons contradict the repeated Old Testament warnings against making an image of God, the Orthodox priest Father Mikhail spoke about the danger of forming images in the mind: 'Why is there such a commandment? If we are going to, one might say, make images in our heads, try to imagine God, then, of course, that would be a big mistake. A great sin that would bring quite terrible results. Quite terrible – that would be true idolatry.' Icons, by contrast, followed God's own image-making activity in the world open to human perception: 'Who was the first author, the first creator of an image of God? The Lord himself created humans in His image and likeness.'[1] In this view, the danger of idolatry lies in mentally creating a human image of God, and the answer is a canonically grounded image making that starts from seeing the divine element in human bodies.

The difficult dance between image practices and accusations of idolatry goes back to the first millennium of Christianity in the Eastern Mediterranean. The Second Council of Nicaea reinstated long-standing practices of image veneration in Hellenistic Christianity while attempting to distance Christian image veneration from 'Greek' or 'pagan' practices. While anathematizing those who refused to salute images 'as standing for the Lord and his saints', the council also condemned those who accorded them full worship (*latreia*), which was reserved for the prototypes whose grace the images mediated, but who were not identical with their images: 'Indeed, the honour paid to an image traverses it, reaching the model, and he who venerates the image, venerates the person represented in that image' (quoted in Belting 1994: 506). To accept the decisions of Nicaea meant to follow the 'middle way' that Saint John of Damascus had written about in his defence of image veneration a few decades earlier. John argued that it was 'just as bad not to offer the honor due to those who are worthy, as it is to offer inappropriate glory to the worthless' (III, 1; 2003: 81). Treated as worthy of glory in their material substance, images became idols; seen as signs of a transcendent reality, they deserved honour.

In popular practice, image and prototype were united by the emotions they evoked. As Jaroslav Pelikan argues in his magisterial treatment of the development of Orthodox Christian doctrine, the anti-iconoclastic conclusions of the Council of Nicaea were as much a defence of the legitimacy of custom and unwritten tradition in the practice of the Christian Church as a dogmatic reconciliation between the Second Commandment and Hellenistic image practices. Images of the saints, Christ and Mary were used in private and public devotions as an extension of Eastern Mediterranean practices of commemoration. Since the conversion of Constantine and the end of the persecution of Christians in 313 CE, Byzantine public space became saturated with Christian imagery. Scriptural prohibitions against image making could coexist with pious practices that seemed to flaunt these prohibitions because both were part of a common 'melody of theology' (Pelikan 1974: 133), whose basic theme was the cultivation of human reverence and love for God, be it by insisting on God's ultimate unrepresentability or by saluting and revering objects associated with divine presence. Iconophiles and iconoclasts agreed that books of scripture, crosses and the Eucharistic gifts could be objects of reverence; the former argued that painted images of divine and saintly figures should have the same status. Made present through their images, saints, angels and members of the Holy Family became 'participants in the life and service, but especially in the liturgy, of the worshiping community' (Pelikan 1974: 141), drawing on an understanding of the image as capable of making a person present that was common to the ancient Mediterranean (Belting 1994).

If representational images were more problematic than abstract symbols, this was because reverence for them had to be distinguished from adjacent image practices, such as the Roman cult of the statues of gods and emperors. The insistence on flat rather than three-dimensional images comes from this distinction, bringing with it a new set of bodily orientations to venerated objects: statues could be admired from below or carried around on pedestals; icons invited eye-level contact with the object of veneration. In the Catholic West, missionary efforts among sculpture-worshipping northern Europeans eventually led church hierarchs to abandon their condemnation of three-dimensional statues. But the preference for flat pictures was maintained in Byzantium and its mission territories, bringing with it distinct bodily stances in prayer that preceded the formal schism and continue to constitute a divide between the Orthodox East and the Catholic West today (Mahieu 2010).

In addition to the bodily stance of facing a picture rather than looking up to a statue, Orthodox art upholds distinctive limitations imposed on image creation by an authoritative tradition.[2] Since Byzantine times, icons have been organized into types that were copied from other icons or from illuminated drawings in patternbooks, such as Christ Pantocrator, Mary praying with uplifted arms as Oranta, or images representing the festival cycles of the church year (Evseeva 1998: 13). An icon's name is inscribed on it as the final act of finishing an image before it is blessed.

Following a pictorial tradition was important because critics pointed to two dangers of image veneration: either one might end up worshiping mere matter or one's own imagination. In the words of theologians at the court of Charlemagne who were critical of the Nicaean compromise, images existed only 'to commemorate past deeds and beautify the walls' (III, 16; in Bremer 2014: 199). Those who venerated them either 'pray to walls and boards' (ibid.) or may find that it is impossible to distinguish an image of Mary bearing Jesus from one of Sara holding Isaac or even that of a Greek goddess with child such as Venus (IV, 21; in Bremer 2014: 203–4). To follow W. J. T. Mitchell's terminology (1994), the problem is either that people mistake a material 'picture' (pigments on wood or canvas) for the underlying invisible reality, or that they use the 'image' evoked by the picture in their minds to make undesirable connections across religious traditions.

In the Byzantine tradition of iconography, both dangers are countered by protocols around the production of icons. Proper prayers, procedures of preparation, and blessings distance flat images from mere 'boards', while canonically sanctioned conventions prevent them from being products of an individual artist's imagination. Whereas the West increasingly allowed artists free rein in how to remind viewers of biblical stories or decorate church walls, Eastern Christianity regulated image practices by embedding their production and use in aesthetic and liturgical conventions. As iconographic motifs travelled, visual imaginaries in Slavic territories remained intimately tied to Byzantine exemplars.

In the history of Christianity in Russia, the twin dangers of deifying matter and deifying the imagination come up with varying emphasis. Peasants were often suspected of mistaking matter for divinity in their excessive attachments to relics and local shrines (Greene 2010; Levin 2003). Concern with regulating religious imaginaries arose in relation to the eschatological expectations of religious non-conformers or disputed visionary experiences (Engelstein 2003; Shevzov 2004). In nineteenth- and twentieth-century Russia, as mass-produced images multiplied, concerns about unbridled religious imaginaries were sometimes framed as critiques of Catholic spiritual practices. These debates were part of efforts to purify a vision of authentic Eastern spirituality free from Catholic doctrinal and liturgical influence (Freeze 1983). They represent a particular Orthodox identity politics that insists on an essential difference between Eastern and Western Christendom, mirroring Western discourses familiar from the Enlightenment up to Samuel Huntington's claims about the 'clash of civilizations' (Wolff 1994; Huntington 1996). But they also pose a challenge to trends in the cognitive study of religion that identify religion per se with the realm of the human imagination. To understand what is at stake in Russian Orthodox debates on right and wrong uses of visuality, it is helpful to juxtapose them to academic discussions of religion and its relationship to the material and the imagination.

Images, imaginaries, religion

At stake in the iconoclastic debates was the question whether depictions of divine and saintly beings were illegitimate creations of human minds or instances of what historians Valery Kivelson and Joan Neuberger call 'seeing into being', where 'the experience of viewing [becomes] an engine of historical or eschatological transformation' (2008: 6). This coexistence of scepticism about visual depiction with belief in the possibility of 'transcendent viewing experiences' (ibid.) speaks to a question at the heart of contemporary divisions in the study of religion: while 'lived religion' approaches privilege materiality and performance to the point of sometimes eclipsing inner worlds (Haeri 2017), the burgeoning field of cognitive studies of religion sees religion as a prime expression of the human imagination. The Nicaean 'middle way' allows us to draw on anthropologies of media and dreams to see that imaginaries and materials are not separate, but imagining the divine is intimately based in shared material practices, including those concerned with making and using religious images.

In cognitive approaches to religion, human religiosity is often equated with the exercise of individual, though genetically hardwired, imaginations. Some of the founding scholars of this field draw explicit parallels between ideas of divine agents held by modern adults and the assumed or documented mental worlds of children or prehistoric humans. Understanding religious ideas as a form of mental elaboration on perceptive clues, cognitivists trace these mental processes back to the evolutionary advantage of overdetecting agency in the environment (Guthrie 1993; Boyer 2001) or to an 'intuitive theism' which makes children attribute causes to hidden agents and form relationships with imaginary companions with unusual capacities (Kelemen 2004). Although methodologically there are big differences between the search for human evolutionary trajectories and studies of religious cognition in childhood, both fields have something in common. They treat the religious practices of modern adults as a kind of survival of forms of cognition that are functional and natural at an earlier stage of phylogenetic or ontogenetic development. If, as Kelemen suggests, 'children may be innately attuned to "godlike" nonhuman agency but need to acquire an understanding of the limitations of human minds' (2004: 297), this can mean that religious experience grows out of the unbridled development of innate imaginative potentials which non-religious adults gradually learn to suppress. Religious imagery, in this view, is of interest to researchers as an externalization of this inner world, unconstrained by what modern adults eventually learn about the laws of animate and inanimate matter.

Few students of as historically complex and variable an artistic tradition as Orthodox Christian iconography would be content to see it as nothing but an expression of universal human cognition, hardwired in the brain. Against the mentalism of cognitive approaches, where religion is first and foremost a set of ideas or cognitive habits, we might set recent calls for anthropological studies of the imagination. Sociocultural anthropologists who focus on the human capacity 'to picture in front of the inner eye something that is not necessarily present outside of it' (Meyer 2015) take this as a starting point to investigate not so much the innate workings of the human brain but rather the interplay between a particular historical situation and the plans, dreams, fears and hopes with which people look to the future or at alternative realities. As Amira Mittermaier puts it in her study of dreams in Egypt in the period leading up to the Arab Spring, dreams are agentive because they cause people to act: to travel, make amends or renew existing relationships. In her words, 'the imagination [...] is not simply a sphere of human fantasies; rather, it is an actual realm that connects dreamers to multiple Others' (Mittermaier 2011: 233). When these others include spirits of the dead, sacred texts and the Prophet, this does not detach the imagination from the human social world, but, to the contrary, opens up mental imagery to sharing with others in the same religious tradition. In Egyptian dreams and Ghanaian Pentecostal videos, religious traditions furnish shared visual idioms that can engage dreamers/creators and audiences in common interpretive efforts. At the same time, adults who practice an institutionalized religion often engage in imaginative extensions of their natural and social surroundings that contemporary Western culture associates primarily with childhood (Boyer and Walker 2000; Luhrmann 2012).

Religious traditions can vary in how much freedom to modify received imaginaries they grant contemporary practitioners. One team of psychologists was surprised to find that conservative Christian parents were more concerned about their children's imaginary companions than non-religious Americans, interpreting them as demonic (Taylor and Carlson 2000). Mittermaier's Egyptian dreamers often reported receiving visits from the Prophet Muhammad, but also scrutinized these dreams for resemblance to canonical descriptions (2011: 166).

In contemporary Russian Orthodox practice, an elaborate ritual use of images goes along with similarly restrictive attitudes towards subjecting them to fantastic modifications. For example, Orthodox responses to Mel Gibson's film 'The Passion of Christ' focused on the danger that its graphic representations of human suffering might replace the more restrained images offered by the Byzantine tradition (Dukhanin 2005: 99). In Orthodox Christology, the crucifixion is less a story of bodily suffering than one of triumph over death. Christ is shown with open rather than closed eyes and the wounds on his body are very understated, quite in contrast to the increasingly fleshly depictions in Western Christian art (Kruse, this volume).

Orthodox critics of Western imaginaries also questioned the lack of humility that went with encouraging identification between Christ and a human actor. Practising a Christmas play in a rural Russian Orthodox parish, the priest pointed out that Russian tradition required that there be no children playing Joseph, Mary and Jesus. Instead, they would be represented by a Nativity icon. 'We don't want anyone to take on too big a role,' he noted. The presence of the icon here was meant to prevent the imaginary identification between actor and role, and channel it instead towards the familiar sensory environment of a church sanctuary around Christmas time, where the Nativity icon is displayed in front of the iconostasis, and people participate in the story not by imaginary immersion, but by the bodily acts of bowing before the icon, kissing and touching it.

Orthodox image practices in the shadow of the Second Commandment thus turn our attention to the ways in which images are not just products of the imagination, but embedded in particular material traditions of depiction. The picture is not just an expression of a mental image formed by an artist, but an outcome of an authoritative tradition whose aim is to shape and constrain a 'saintly imagination' (Heo 2012) as much as to stimulate it. If we accept that most people practice religion within an established environment of artefacts, bodily practices, sounds and other sensory stimuli, then the question is no longer why people resort to supernatural explanations in the absence of sensory evidence. Rather, it is how religiously saturated environments shape human imaginaries and interactions, so that their associated 'moods and motivations' become 'uniquely realistic' (Geertz 1973) or 'intuitively counterintuitive' (Boyer and Walker 2000: 134). Some image-environments may approximate features of mental imagery, as Lambert Wiesing (2005) argues for video and 'virtual realities', where things are possible that adult viewers know are impossible in everyday life. The style of iconography that is being revived in today's Russia after the Soviet hiatus militates against some of the habits of everyday perception, but overall tends to introduce constraints on the mental worlds of devotees. This promotes a particular kind of canonically mediated realism in art, an asceticism of the imagination. There are two ways in which this ascetic realism expresses itself: in the grounding of visual imagery in tradition and collective rather than individual discernment, and in the transformation of the indexical imagery of photography through iconic resemblance and stylized conventionalization.

As we will see, the reasons for ascetic realism lie both in Orthodox Christianity's attempts to define and maintain an identity against the Christian West and in reactions against a modern media world, which mobilize older ideas about the ethical implications of seeing.

Ascetic realism as a polemical tradition

As Chris Hann (2003, 2014) has shown for liturgical music and the iconographic motif of the Sacred Heart of Jesus, attempting to inscribe civilizational divides into artistic practices is always an ideological endeavour that flares up at certain points in time and is forgotten at others. In the history of Orthodox churches, times of heightened consciousness of the ascetic correspondence of form and content in prayer and liturgy alternated with times when this was not considered as important. In eighteenth- and nineteenth-century Russia, for example, many icons were painted in the style of Western oil painting (some of them literally on canvas) using central perspective. This was also when choral music was influenced by the polyphony of Protestant chorales and Latin was an obligatory language at Russian Orthodox seminaries, because many of the texts used were Catholic catechisms and manuals (Chakovskaya 2014; Freeze 1983). In the second half of the nineteenth century, a search for more distinctively Orthodox ways of worshipping and exercising piety began, with effects that are still influential in Russia today, in part because for the first time the reform efforts extended to laypeople as well as to monastics. Influential clergy such as Feofan the Recluse (Govorov, 1815–91) and Ignatii (Brianchanninov, 1807–61) popularized a set of writings from the Hellenistic and Byzantine period known in Greek as the *Philokalia* (love of goodness), in Russian as *Dobrotoliubie*. A Church Slavonic translation, aimed mainly at members of the clerical estate, appeared in 1793, but the modern Russian translation of 1877 signalled the growing attention to the piety of lay people. Both Feofan and Ignatii combined counsels for their lay spiritual children with critiques of Catholic spirituality. Ignatii's critique focused especially on what he termed daydreaming (*mechtatel'nost'*), a vice he found represented by his near-namesake, Ignatius of Loyola, and Teresa of Avila. In Ignatian spiritual exercises, the Russian bishop criticized the wilful mental visualization of the Holy Trinity and events from Christ's life:

> [Ignatius of Loyola] had such a heated and sensitized imagination that, as he affirmed, he only needed to wish for it and put in a bit of effort, and before his eyes appeared, by his choice, hell or paradise. [...] It is well known that the real saints of God receive visions only by the grace of God and through God's action, and not by human will and their own efforts; they [the visions] come unexpected and are rare. (quoted in Osipov 2001: 123, ellipses in that publication)

For these nineteenth-century critics, restricting one's imagination in prayer was an Orthodox way that signalled a return to teachings of the early church fathers and contradicted post-schismatic Catholic practice. This interest in distinctively 'Eastern' forms of prayer was also linked to a turn away from Western-style oil paintings to a desire to learn from the classical icons of Byzantium and fifteenth-century Russia (Yazykova 2010). For post-Soviet Russian Orthodox Christians living in a world of dramatically multiplied religious imagery, this ascesis of the imagination takes on a new meaning. Aleksei Osipov, a professor of the Moscow Spiritual Academy speaking to students in 1992, quotes Saint Nile of Sinai (fifth century) and Saint Simeon the New Theologian (eleventh century) both warning against the desire to see angels or Christ with one's eyes, lest one see demons instead or fall into the vice of self-delusion (*prelest'*) (2001: 121). The warning against making up images during prayer, though by no means shared by all Eastern church fathers (Noble 2005), was well known among Orthodox laypeople in early twenty-first-century Russia. I repeatedly heard it referred to by Russian Orthodox friends when I told them about fieldwork among Russian

Pentecostals, who, like the Californian evangelicals studied by anthropologist Tanya Luhrmann (2012), were very free in their imagination of the divine.

In a world saturated by competing visual imaginaries, originating both from other confessions and from the secular world, Orthodox Christians mobilized older concerns about vision as an entry point for sinful ideas that had developed in constant interchange with Catholic ideas on the topic (Rolland 2017). A new, post-Soviet generation of literate and often self-educated Orthodox believers were suspicious of what they saw as a widespread use of visual media to promote human vanity or self-interested messages. They turned to Byzantine and classical Russian visual canons for a safer alternative, representing the spiritual merits of past generations and a different way of looking at the world.

Spiritualizing the contemporary: New icons

In contemporary Russian iconography, ascetic realism manifests in two ways: anchoring new iconographic motives to older visual styles through copying and collective discernment, and using modern media such as photography to restrain the imaginative components of icons and indexically link them back to material reality. New motives emerge when new saints are canonized – for example, the almost 2,000 new martyrs and confessors who have been canonized for persisting in their faith during the period of Soviet anti-religious repressions. They also come up with new ritual occasions as the Church responds to changing political and social concerns.

An example of anchoring a new motive to traditional visual styles is the creation of the icon of the Holy Innocent Infants of Bethlehem, used since the 1990s by a new kind of religious actor: family values activists looking for symbols of aborted foetuses. Prior to the 1990s, the scene of Herod's slaughter of Bethlehem's children in search of the new messiah existed as a *kleimo*, a small square image in a frame around an icon of the Nativity of Christ. In an interview, the iconographer Nataliia Maslova explained that the idea to use the Infants of Bethlehem came from one of the priests in the movement, who asked her to work with her teacher, the well-known iconographer Irina Vatagina, to turn the *kleimo* into a prayer icon.[3] This meant changing the composition so that the central figures faced outward towards the viewer, inviting a bodily pose of eye-level contemplation that had been the Eastern Christian preference since Byzantine times (Luehrmann 2016). It also involved moving the depictions of slaughter to the background, foregrounding a group of children clad in white, whose only sign of suffering is that some of them appear to be weeping, drying their eyes with their robes. As Nataliia pointed out, the red background remains a sign of martyrdom:

> When I was looking for materials on how they were killed, especially in later icons there are simply terrible scenes – they hack them, they pierce them, terrible. We chose a calm scene. Although the fact that it is on a red background – I certainly like the cinnabar background. I like cinnabar colour just by itself, but cinnabar

background in iconography is reserved for either prophets or martyrs. So as martyrs we decided to give them a red background.

Instead of the graphic depiction of suffering that would have been characteristic of eighteenth- and nineteenth-century Russian icons and even more so of contemporary Western representations of abortion (Luehrmann 2018b), Nataliia's icon offers a constraint that is achieved through convention. It hints at suffering through colour and posture, while aiming for an overall effect she described as 'calm' (*spokoino*) and 'respectable' (*blagorodno*). In recalling the collaborative endeavour that led to the new icon, Nataliia minimized her own creative or emotional input in favour of the effort to be faithful to the past through learning from books and theological consultation:

> Irina Vasil'evna [Vatagina] said supply yourself with books, nothing should come from your head, look and compose. And I probably made not quite fifty, but thirty sketches, small fragments with the composition of the icon. And Father [Dimitrii] looked at them all carefully and chose one. And said now work out this fragment for a large format, in consultation with Irina Vasil'evna. This means, in our Orthodox, how do you call it, denomination, there is such a rule: that a newly created icon has to be created collectively. A member of the clergy has to participate and an artist and, of course, a consultant, so it has to be a collective creation.

The term I translate here as 'collectively', *soborno*, can also be understood as 'conciliar'. It invokes the idea of dogmatic authority in the Orthodox Church as flowing from the council of clergy and believers, but also nineteenth-century Slavophile notions of the contrast between Russian collectivism and Western individualism. In reflecting on this practice in an interview with a Western visitor, Nataliia seemed to find it important to stress the denominational characteristics of the Orthodox Church, as if searching for a specifically 'Orthodox' way of creating something new. Whereas artistic originality is downplayed, the scope of the problem of abortion is magnified by evoking a biblical story that, at various times in Church history, has stood for the persecution of Christians or the eternal battle between good and evil.

The twentieth century not only created new ritual causes, but also new saints, priests and laypeople who were martyred under Soviet rule. In many regions of Russia, Orthodox clergy and laypeople research local faithful who died or were imprisoned under Lenin and Stalin, and present their records to a central canonization commission in the Moscow Patriarchate. If archival evidence shows that a person was arrested for reasons of Orthodox faith and did not name or accuse others during interrogations, that person can be included among the new martyrs and confessors (Christensen 2018). In creating icons of these new saints, directly copying older models is not possible. Instead, ascetic realism becomes a matter of ensuring physical resemblance through archival research and photographic evidence, and then transforming the portrait into an icon by following rules of stylization.

For iconographers engaged in the task of creating such new icons, maintaining the distinctive features a saint had during life was very important, and thought to confront the devotee with an image of what a saint actually looked like in a spiritual sense.

Figure 11.1 Icon of the Hieromartyr Nikolai Riurikov. Tsarevokokshaisk workshop, 2007. Courtesy of Stanislav Popov.

In the icon workshop of the diocese of Ioshkar-Ola and Marii El, the first step for creating new icons of recently canonized saints was to locate photographs. Once found, iconographers did not copy them exactly, but tried to find an image of the spiritual state of the person as a saint. This usually meant depicting the person as neither very old nor very young (occasionally at around the age of death), and without any signs of torture or suffering – only the cross in the hands of martyrs references their violent death. Although they provided the name for Charles Saunders Peirce's idea of iconicity, icons in the neoclassical style are a mix of 'icon' and 'symbol' in a similar way as is a topographic map: they have strongly iconic features in that they aim to reproduce the proportions and physical characteristics of a prototype. But they also use conventional symbolism of dress, attributes and colour to produce the effect of an encounter with a person's spiritual essence. Just as modern mapmakers often work from satellite imagery and GPS measurements, iconographers of contemporary saints work from the indexical medium of a photograph (cf. Hanganu 2010).

Its grounding in historical research notwithstanding, there is a mystical side to ascetic realism. Elena, who paints icons in the workshop, recalled Father Nikolai Riurikov (1884–1943), a canonized priest of whom there was only an early photograph

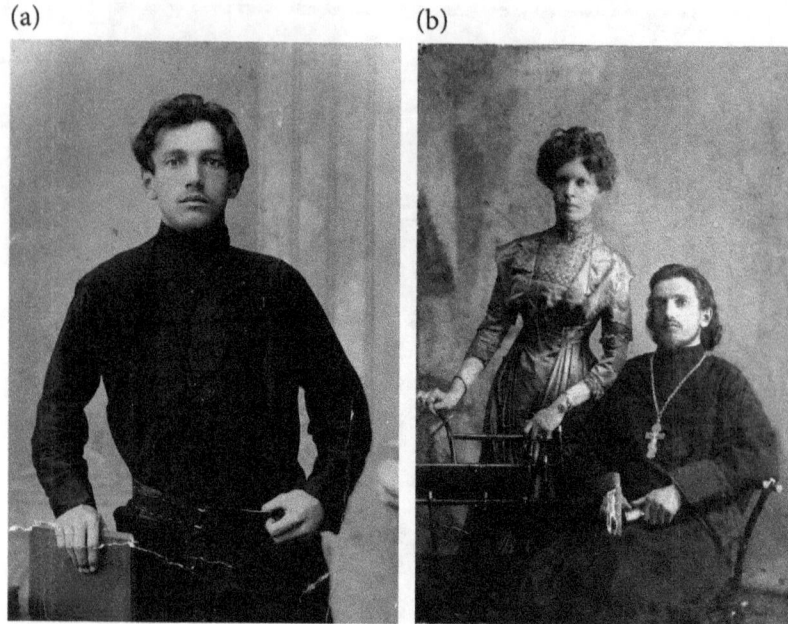

Figure 11.2a, b Father Riurikov, early (a) and late (b) photo. Courtesy of the archive of the canonization commission of the diocese of Ioshkar-Ola, Russian Orthodox Church.

of a still beardless youth before ordination, although he died at almost sixty years of age. She painted the icon depicting him as a more mature priest, using her imagination to alter the youth's appearance. Later, a relative brought another photograph, and it turned out that she had been very close to what he looked like. Elena related this story without special commentary, but, together with others like it, it seemed to confirm the reality of the Orthodox faith by showing how God guided the imaginations of the faithful. These new icons were neither just paint on wood nor figments of an individual imagination, but images whose truth was grounded in their ability to bring together visible reality and invisible essences.

Media of restraint

While outsiders may see iconography as the height of Orthodox imagination, for its contemporary creators and defenders these images are emphatically non-imaginary. Iconography in its neoclassical understanding attempts to bind mental images to constraints of a similar strength as those that govern perception of the natural world, in order to save worshippers from the idolatry of worshipping their own imagination, or from being taken over by imaginaries produced by the media and by other religious denominations. To safeguard its role as arbiter of Orthodox visual heritage, the Russian Orthodox Church has even gone to court against contemporary artists, as in the much-publicized 'Caution, Religion' trial against a Moscow art exhibition held in 2003. The exhibit at the Sakharov Center included what many considered to be caricatures of traditional icons, and a group of Orthodox activists sued it for 'inciting religious hatred' (Bernstein 2014). Controlling the development of Orthodox visual imaginaries is a way in which the Church affirms its identity vis-à-vis the plethora of other confessions and world views vying for followers in contemporary Russia, while offering its own mediascape as an alternative to secular viewing practices.

How do laypeople take up these messages of restraint? From conversations with engaged Orthodox laypeople in various Russian cities, my impression is that people do use Orthodox media as inspiration for imaginary encounters with divine forces – they recognize saints from icons in the faces of unknown passers-by and see Jesus or Mary in their dreams. While thus disregarding some of the warnings against individualized imaginaries, what these interlocutors valued about Orthodox media in contrast to secular and religious alternatives was the aesthetic restraint in taking over their imaginations. 'Not overwhelming', 'not forcing itself on you' and 'not distracting' were phrases I often heard about Orthodox iconography, music and liturgy (see also Engelhardt 2018). This contrasted both to the violence and pace of television and the louder and more in-your-face forms of Protestant worship and proselytizing. Paradoxically, these same interlocutors often expressed surprise how I could spend so much time in Orthodox services and not become Orthodox: they expected the sensorium of Orthodox worship to respect the inner boundaries of believers, but overwhelm the defences of a visitor.

Imageless prayer may be difficult to achieve, but by pointing to the persuasiveness of Orthodox aesthetics, my interlocutors showed awareness of something cognitivist scholars on religion often forget: people come to religious practice not just with the evolutionarily conditioned affordances of the human mind and its developmental stages, but through the experience of a sensory environment that is both outcome and congelation of centuries of debate over right doctrine and right ways of doing things. These environments are no more imaginary than the cityscapes people live in. Rather than seeing religious imagery as flowing from a uniquely imagination-rich sphere of human life, the contemporary pathways of Orthodox iconography help us understand how religious media provide both stimulation and guidance for imaginative elaboration.

Conclusion: Icons and idols

As the Eastern Orthodox tradition shows, use of devotional images can coexist with, and indeed encourage, restrictive ideas and doubts about what makes an image fit for sacred use. Where idolatry is associated with unauthorized flights of fancy rather with image use per se, material images can function to restrict the religious imagination as well as encourage it.

Many ethnographies of modern religious life seem to suggest an opposite dynamic, where being involved in a religion means transgressing the limits to normal sensory experience. Tanya Luhrmann (2012) tells us about evangelical Christians in the United States who are encouraged to literally treat God as an imaginary companion: pour 'him' a cup of coffee and sit down for a chat. Charles Hirschkind (2006) transcribes Egyptian sermons in which Muslims are invited to picture the tortures of hell in 'television style'. Birgit Meyer's Ghanaian Pentecostal film-makers eagerly use the capacity of video to make visible forms of action that beings can perform in the imagination, but not in everyday perception – disappear, pass through walls and windows, and so on (2015). The followers of a Sufi shaykh in Amira Mittermaier's ethnography expect to see him in their dreams and receive messages from him after his death (2011).

However, when reading these ethnographies carefully, none of these groups simply encourages believers to follow all imaginative inclinations. US evangelicals parse their thoughts for those that are 'from God' and those that are not; collective interpretive sessions in Egypt distinguish dreams that process personal experiences from externally inspired 'dream visions'; vivid reminders of the torments of hell distract listeners from more sinful flights of fancy; and Ghanaian video, while depicting actions that contradict the laws of Newtonian physics, draws on African and European demonologies that already predetermine how evil may be depicted and what evil entities do. Like Orthodox iconographers, these groups draw boundaries between permissible and impermissible imaginaries, but the importance and relative permeability of such boundaries may vary between different contexts.

For a comparative study of the legacies of the Second Commandment in the Abrahamic traditions, the Orthodox Christian case reminds us to distinguish the meanings attached to 'idols' from those of 'images': depending on what perceived dangers they are set against, idols may be bad (or badly used) pictures or not pictures at all, but imaginary creations of the human mind. As Ann Taves points out in her study of religious innovation that seeks to bring together cognitivist and historical methodologies, collective discernment in small groups is often where followers of a particular spiritual path differentiate between divine revelation and human flights of fancy. What will enable a group to 'tune in' (Taves 2016: 230) on an emerging consensus is often the resonance of new creations with prior religious media in which divinity is known to manifest. For example, the stone plates seen by Joseph Smith, the founder of Mormonism, were reminiscent of the plates on which the biblical Moses received the Ten Commandments (Taves 2016: 38). By contrast, accusations of idolatry may adhere to ways of picturing the divine that lie outside of or deviate from the mediatic canon of a religious tradition.

In the secularized and religiously diverse environment of post-Soviet Russia, the charge of 'idolatry' serves to draw a boundary between the sensory environment created by the traditional media of the Church and a visually saturated modern mediascape. By associating the former with emotional restraint and the latter with boundless excess, contemporary iconographers both affirm the possibility of picturing divine persons and the impossibility of doing so through the medium of an individual mind.

Part Four

Desires for the Unseen: Art and Religion

12

From Ponte Sant'Angelo to Basilica di San Pietro: Figuration and Sensation in Bernini's Pilgrimage Route in Rome

Øyvind Norderval

According to the medievalist Niklaus Largier, one important hermeneutical key to understanding Christian mysticism in the Middle Ages is the combination of spiritual sensation and emotion linked to the passion of Christ:

> [...] the emotional engagement of the soul with God and Christ implies not only a transformation of the passions but in most cases sensual experience as well, [...] a perception of the divine in terms of a highly emotional experience of taste and touch. (Largier 2009: 1, 6–10)

According to Largier, this combination of spiritual sensation and emotion was the basis for the spiritual programme that Ignatius of Loyola (1491–1556) later drew up in his *Exercitia Spiritualia*, written 1522–4 (Largier 2009: 13). The goal of his 'Spiritual Exercises' is reached when one experiences being in spiritual contemporaneity with the *locus* where everything happened in the story of Jesus. In what follows, I shall argue that Gian Lorenzo Bernini (1598–1690), in his layout for the approach to the Vatican, followed a holistic schema inspired by Jesuit spirituality. It was elaborated with its starting point in the idea that Saint Peter's, with the tomb of Peter, was the goal of the pilgrims' visit to Rome. The path starts at the bridgehead of the Ponte Sant'Angelo and ends in the high choir with the *Cathedra Petri*.

Jesuit theology played a central role in the development of the Roman baroque, in which Bernini was a very important actor. Can one argue for the probability of a close link between Jesuit mysticism and Bernini's art? Was his project a visualization of revelation through the emotional dimension, with the emphasis on the 'here and now' – the encounter between the individual and the divine? This question is hotly debated in Bernini scholarship. Some see a link (Kuhn 1970: 297–9; Bukdahl 1999: 53), but few have attempted to analyse in depth the connection between Ignatius's text and the forms of artistic expression in Bernini's individual projects. Others maintain that there is no clear link and that Bernini's views and his artistic profile were determined eclectically (Mormando 2011: 241). In this chapter, I shall attempt to interpret Ignatius's

Latin edition (1548) and Bernini's art alongside each other in order to see whether the *Exercitia* could have inspired Bernini to create sculpture and architecture that open the door to spiritual sensation and emotion as one walks from the Ponte Sant'Angelo to Saint Peter's. It goes without saying that such a link cannot be positively demonstrated, since Bernini himself said nothing on this subject. Still, the relationship between text and monument is interesting, in the form of a hermeneutical reflection on the interpretation of texts and monuments. In fact, H. G. Gadamer opens the door to such an interpretation through the emphasis he places on 'the classical' in philosophical hermeneutics. This category embraces everything from art and literature to theology, jurisprudence and philosophy (Gadamer 1990: 107–75). This is a demanding task, but with the gain of shedding new light on the history of the impact (in the broad sense) made by both the monuments and the texts.

Gian Lorenzo Bernini (1598–1680) was one of the most important artists in the Italian high baroque, and his activity as architect and sculptor enjoyed canonical status for a long time in Italian Counter-Reformation art. One central portion of his work was his long-lasting involvement as the chief architect for Saint Peter's Church and the Vatican area, which covered roughly fifty years. He worked during the reigns of eight popes, three of whom – Urban VIII, Alexander VII and Clement IX – were his most important patrons. After Carlo Maderno died in 1629, Bernini was appointed chief architect for Saint Peter's, at the age of thirty-one. The first commissions he received in this project were inside the church itself: the baldachin over the papal altar was his first major task (1623–34), together with the *Cathedra Petri* (1647–53). Saint Peter's Square (1656–67) and the decoration of the Ponte Sant'Angelo (1667–9) were among his last commissions.

There is much to indicate that Bernini must already at a rather early date have had a complete plan of construction, which was developed and expanded over time. Several historians of art and architecture have made this affirmation, without undertaking a complete iconographic analysis or investigating the sources of inspiration that underlie a holistic interpretation of this kind. It is simply presupposed, without any great effort to demonstrate the connections. In his standard work on architectural history, Spiro Kostof points out that Bernini had a complete plan for the Vatican area from the entrance at the Ponte Sant'Angelo up to Saint Peter's Square and Saint Peter's Church itself, but he does not discuss the ideological aspects of this gigantic baroque site (Kostof 1995: 506–7; Cf. Sedlmayr 1985: vol. II, 23 ff.; Wittkower 1955: 17ff; Hibbard 1965: 205; Kuhn 1970: 297; Weibel 1909). But what constitutes the conceptual framework for this holistic project?

The baroque and the Jesuits

There is a clear link between baroque art and architecture and the Jesuit order with regard to theology and philosophy. In its origins, the Roman baroque was an expression of the Catholic Counter-Reformation, in which the Jesuit order supplied the ideological presuppositions for the decisions that were taken at the Council of Trent. This was where the Catholic Church drew up its strategy for responding to the

Protestant Reformation. This strategy included uniform modes of artistic expression as it is programmatically stated in the twenty-fifth session (Waterworth 1848: 232). Jesuit churches in Rome such as Il Gesù and S. Ignazio mark a fundamental epochal transition with their clear ideological forms of expression in order to awake emotions in the believers.

The baroque marks a new orientation with regard to the harmonious and balanced ideals of the Renaissance. The Catholic baroque had its foundation in the ideals of the Counter-Reformation, which found it important, in a changing word, to underline Catholicism's victory and its awareness of its power (Bukdahl 1999: 43–68). The goal was to exercise influence and to awaken people to a religious decision and consciousness. We find here exaggerated movement and dynamic rhythms of motion, and a prominent place is given to the imposing expressions. We see this clearly in sculpture and architecture, which were to be Bernini's chief occupation. In church architecture, the programme of the Counter-Reformation often finds expression in buildings with colossal elements, and magnificent façades that employ dramatic, contrary or strongly contrasting forms of expression – such as the interplay between convex and concave forms, a frequent use of colonnades and cupolas, the interplay between light and darkness, and between the building and empty space. Sculpture is characterized by a modelling of the human body that vibrates with life, and with a dramatic language of gestures that expresses movement and energy. A sculpture may be concentrated around its own centre, or it can be given a spatial expansion (Gardner 2001: 721). It was also essential that the sculpture could be looked at from several sides, thereby giving dynamic various optic facets to the message it was meant to express. In this way, the religious truths could be made visible with a strong emotional and sensational impact, and the church could appear in the eyes of the beholder as the victor in the contemporary battle for minds. There was a conscious play on feelings. Baroque inspired by Jesuits is religious propaganda; visual propaganda was a means of carrying conviction to the believers (Levy 2004: 110). Heinrich Wölfflin describes the difference between Renaissance and baroque in this way:

> [T]he pathos of the post-classical period is in the desire to be sublimated in the infinite, in the feeling of overwhelmingness and unfathomableness. The comprehensible is refused, the imagination demands to be overpowered. It is a kind of intoxication with which the Baroque architecture fills us, particularly the huge church interiors. We are consumed by an all-embracing sensation of heaviness, helpless to grasp anything, wishing to yield totally to the infinite. The new religious fervor kindled by the Jesuits finds a perfect outlet in the contemplation of the infinite heavens and countless angels and choirs. It revels in the imagining the unimaginable, it plunged with ecstasy into the abyss of infinity. (Wölfflin 1966: 86; cf. 137–43)

This clearly was a development of Ignatius's ideas about the human person's encounter with the holy through meditation, as found in his *Exercitia Spiritualia*, a text meant as a guide in meditation techniques, to be followed over the space of four weeks (Woodrow 1995: 31–63; O'Malley 1993: 37–50). It reviews the life, death and resurrection of

Jesus, with the aim of testing oneself. The emphasis lies on the human person's insight into himself through religious empathy, the recognition of one's sins, discipleship and obedience to God and the Church, which is represented by the hierarchy: 'We shall understand this [...] as any method of examining our own conscience, and also of meditating, contemplating, praying mentally and orally, and finally of dealing with any other spiritual activities' (ES §1).[1] Ignatius appeals to the believers' co-creative activity, and inspires them to experience the gospels' stories about Jesus. The believer is present in what happens; this strengthens the life of faith and creates an intense space for meditation and interior visualization. This emotional contemporaneity is expressed through the importance of 'a certain mental recreation of the place [...], during any meditation [...] for example of Christ, we shall see with a sort of imaginary vision a physical place representing what we are contemplating' (ES §47; cf. Bukdahl 2017: 68–9).[2]

The goal of this insight is the interaction between what Christ has done for the human person through his suffering and the return that the human person makes to Christ. One is to imagine 'Jesus Christ in front of me, attached to the cross. Then I should look within myself for the reason why the infinite Creator Himself became a creature, and deemed it worthy to come from life eternal to a temporal death for my sins' (ES §53).[3]

The Italian art philosopher Mario Perniola describes the Jesuit aesthetics as a position between the traditional opposition between iconophilia and iconoclastia. The Jesuit aesthetics represents a simulacrum – a likeness – not a copy of the real, that becomes truth in the contemplation of the viewer (Perniola 2001: 164–70; cf. Bukdahl 2017: 67–9).

The biography published by Gian Lorenzo Bernini's son Domenico in 1713 makes it clear that Gian Lorenzo had a close relationship to the Jesuit order from the age of forty onwards. The Jesuit church Il Gesù in Rome became his spiritual home. Every Friday for forty years, he attended devotional services there on the theme of how to attain a blessed death. He received Communion in this church at least once a week. He visited the church every day after his work was finished, and took part in the adoration of the Blessed Sacrament. He recited the rosary of the Blessed Virgin and prayed her Office on his knees, as also the seven penitential Psalms. And he did this regularly until his death (Bernini 2011: 229). One of his closest friends and spiritual guides was Giovanni Paolo Oliva, the general of the Jesuit Order at the time, and the successor of Ignatius Loyola. Oliva used to say that, in discussing spiritual matters with the Cavaliere, he felt obliged to prepare himself carefully, just as if he were going to a doctoral thesis defence (Bernini 2011: 229). Oliva was also in charge during the construction of the Jesuit church S. Andrea al Quirinale that Bernini had been commissioned to design (Marder 1998: 196; Bernini 2011: 370 n. 35).

Ponte Sant'Angelo

At the bridgehead of the Ponte Sant'Angelo, the magnificent and elegant transition to the Borgo area, with its many sculptures the visitor walks into the realm of the Vatican

(Weil 1974; Avery 2006: 162–73). As so often in Rome, artists and architects were obliged to take account of what had survived from the past; this was true not least of Bernini's many commissions in the Vatican area. The Ponte Sant'Angelo and the surrounding area had a number of important symbolic features. This applied first of all to the bridge itself, which is one of the oldest in Rome, the Pons Aelius that was built by Emperor Hadrian, in addition to Hadrian's mausoleum on the Borgo bank of the river. The Pons Aelius was the chief artery linking the city centre and the Vatican area for fifteen centuries. The fact that this was the entrance to the Vatican area is also made strongly visible by the huge loggia looking onto the bridge that Julius II erected in 1505. When the pilgrims reached the Vatican area from the centre, they met the imposing bridge with the mausoleum, while the pope could welcome them and greet them from the loggia.

The bridge as we see it today is Bernini's work. Clement IX gave him the commission to renew the bridge as soon as he became pope in 1667, and the work was completed in 1669. The bridge's importance as a transition to the pope's own territory was highlighted and given a completely new programmatic orientation through Bernini's linkage to the triumphalism of the Counter-Reformation and to the contemporary ideals of piety. Earlier decorations had messages that were partly unclear, but here, Bernini created an entire programme that includes both the bridge and Hadrian's mausoleum. It also contains references to the goal of the pilgrimage, Saint Peter's Church. The theme that binds everything together is based on the motif of angels, a motif that had been connected to this place since the early Middle Ages (*Legenda Aurea* XLVI, 4; Maggioni 1998).

Bernini retained the statues of Peter and Paul that Clement VII had set up at the bridgehead in 1534. In this way, Peter and Paul appeared as the guardians of the bridge and of the Vatican area for travellers reaching the point of entry from either of

Figure 12.1 Ponte Sant'Angelo and Hadrian's mausoleum, Rome (Wikimedia Commons). Author: Jean-Pol Grandmont.

the three medieval roadways that converged here at the Zampa d'oca (goose foot), the Via Papalis, Via Recta and Via Peregrinorum/Mercatoria (Nykjær 2004: 21–2). The statues thus stand guard over the entrance to the Vatican area and have programmatic inscriptions: Peter has *Hinc humilibus venia* (Here there is pardon for the humble) and Paul *Hinc retributio superbis* (Here there is punishment for the proud). Both texts allude to 1 Pet. 5.5. Peter and Paul have their well-known attributes, Peter the keys to bind and loose (Mt. 16.18-19) and Paul the sword of the Spirit (Eph. 6.17).

Here, at the end of the pilgrimage routes, therefore, the visitors are made aware from the very outset that they have reached the point of transition to the Vatican area, the gate to penitence and salvation. The bridge collects all believers and sets them on a path caught in the tension between pardon and punishment. The path over the bridge is meant to kindle a religious recognition of one's own shortcomings and to make visible Christ's suffering and Christ's grace (Kuhn 1970: 299; Sedlmayr 1985: 23ff). Bernini develops this further in his design for the ten angels that stand on the bridge's balustrades. In this way, he exploits the legendary history and name of the citadel and of the bridge for this penitential program. But as Ignatius said at that same time, the angels are first and foremost bringers of the message of the divine truth. He writes:

Figure 12.2 The angel with the superscription I.N.R.I., Ponte Sant'Angelo, Rome (Wikimedia Commons). Author: Marie-Lan Nguyen.

It is proper to God and to his good angel to fill up the soul, which they move, with true spiritual gladness after taking away all sadness and trouble (ES §329). The good spirit does it gently, peacefully, and delightfully, like a drop of water falling on a sponge. (ES §335). [4]

[…] the angels, carrying the sword of divine justice, have supported me without quivering, have protected me and even helped me with their intercessions. (ES §60) [5]

Bernini himself carved only two of the statues, but the draft for the entire series is his; he gave younger pupils the task of carving the other sculptures. All the figures are angels bearing symbols linked to the story of Jesus's passion – the so-called *arma Christi* – with inscriptions drawn primarily from the Vulgate. The angels face inwards to the path over the bridge, so that they meet the believers' gaze and awaken gravity and repentance in them. The angels were mounted on plinths like those of Peter and Paul at the bridgehead. This means that the beholder is required to lift up his eyes in order to get a view of God's messengers. Besides this, each angel is placed on a little cloud that emphasizes the angels' heavenly origin, while their garments ruffle in the wind.

But Bernini's intention here is not only to refer to Jesus's passion as a historical event: in the spirit of Ignatius, the angels are messengers as they stand on their little clouds, and they are meant to make Christ's passion a present reality that bears witness to the believers' redemption. In this way, the beholder who looks at the instruments of torture will look into himself and experience a religious awakening through the recognition of his sin and through the gift that he makes of himself to God (Kuhn 1970: 299). When we compare this with Ignatius, we find that he argues for self-examination as follows: '[…] according to our goal, [I shall] ask for sorrow, tears, anguish and other similar interior pains, so that I suffer with Christ suffering for me' (ES §203).[6]

When one begins to walk from the bridgehead, the angels show the way by means of the story of Jesus's passion, and create sensation and emotion through what one sees: a pillar ('My throne was in a pillar of cloud': Sir. 24.4), a scourge ('I am ready for the scourge,' Ps. 37.18; see Mk 15.15), a crown of thorns (Mk 15.17), Veronica's veil, the cross with the inscription 'INRI', nails (Zech. 12; Jn 19.37), clothes and dice ('They cast lots for my garments'; Ps. 22. 18; see Mk 15.24), a sponge on a rod, and a lance (Jn 19.34-5).

There are many medieval texts that meditate on the passion of Christ – on the *arma Christi* (Venatus Fortunatus/web) – as well as pictorial and sculptural representations of the symbols of this suffering. The number of symbols could vary from eight to twenty-one (Cooper and Denny-Brown 2013). A comparison with §§292–7 in Ignatius's *Exercitia* displays a striking correspondence to Bernini's sculptural interpretation of those instruments of Jesus's torture that are the starting point when one sets out on the pilgrimage route:

He remained bound all that night. [Here, the pillar too is included.] The guards around Him ridiculed and maltreated Him. (ES §292) [7]

Pilate ordered that Jesus be scourged; the soldiers crowned Him with thorns and clothed Him with a purple garment, and then laughed at Him, saying: 'Hail, King of the Jews!' and hit his face. (ES §295,2) [8]

Christ carried his cross. (ES §296,2) [9]

He was crucified between two brigands; the sign said: 'Jesus the Nazarene, King of the Jews'. (ES 296,3) [10]

And his garments were divided. [11]

He shouted 'I'm thirsty' when they gave him vinegar. (ES §297,2) [12]

His side, perforated by the lance, put forth water and blood. (ES 297,3) [13]

Taken on its own, this is not a clear indication of influence from Ignatius or the Jesuits, but there is an obvious agreement in the motifs and in the underlying spirituality, whether we read the *Spiritual Exercises* or look at Bernini's sculptures. The only motif we do not find in Ignatius is Veronica's veil. Here, Bernini probably chose to draw a line from the bridge to the relic of the veil in the cupola area in Saint Peter's.

The concentration on Jesus's sacrificial death is also a clear allusion to the Counter-Reformation understanding of the Eucharist as a sacrificial action – a re-presentation of Jesus's sacrifice that is meant to give the beholder insight into his own sinfulness in the light of death and judgement, and of the redemption in which one can receive a share. This perspective is central in Ignatius: Christ 'instituted the holy sacrament of the Eucharist, as a sign of the supreme love' (ES §289; cf. O'Malley 1993: 152–5).[14] Participation in the Mass, and thereby in the sacrifice of Christ's body and blood, is seen here as necessary for the human person's salvation (Weil 1974: 158–9; Nykjær 1999: 296–7). Christ's death was *sacrificium*, and the sacrifice of the Mass is *sacrificium*. Ignatius puts this as follows: '[...] tears are shed, provoking that love, either because they come from sorrow with regard to sins, or from the meditation of Christ's passion' (ES §316).[15]

In this way, as Mogens Nykjær emphasizes, the bridge becomes not only a Via Crucis, but also a Via Triumphalis, that is to say, the path to salvation (Nykjær 1999: 294). It is the beginning of the penitential path that leads to Saint Peter's. The human person can thus achieve clarity in his existential choices and attain perfection through concentration on the sacrifice of Christ.

Saint Peter's Square

Bernini had envisaged a new access to Saint Peter's Square by means of a restructuring of the Borgo area down towards the Tiber, since that was the only point from which one could see Michelangelo's cupola in its totality (Avrey 2011: 211–5; Kostof 1995: 506ff; Lees-Milne 1967: 270–8; Nykjær 1999: 243–73; Hibbard 1965: 151–6). But although work on this project was stopped, it is an impressive sight when one enters the colossal oval square that opens to embrace and include the visitor. There can be no doubt that one is entering here the centre of the Roman Catholic Church.

In his work on the Square itself, Bernini had to take account of a number of factors that limited his options. The Vatican palace to the north with its entrance was an obvious limitation, as was the wall that led to the Borgo. It was also necessary for the

Figure 12.3 Overview from St. Peter's basilica towards Ponte Sant'Angelo and Hadrian's mausoleum, Rome. Statues of the saints of the church are placed on the top of the colonnades (Wikimedia Commons). Author: David Iliff.

Square to accommodate as many people as possible with a free visual opening both onto Saint Peter's Church with its loggia and onto the papal palace. To the east, Bernini had to take account of existing buildings. And the construction of the Square had to attempt to provide a visual framework for Carlo Maderno's broad façade.

The Square, which had not been given an architectonic form at that time, contained two other elements that Bernini had to take account of. The obelisk had originally been placed in the central spina of Caligula's stadium, but it was moved by Pope Sixtus V in 1586 from its location on the south side of Old Saint Peter's to its present position in the Square. There was also a fountain on the square, which had been erected by Carlo Maderno in 1614. The fountain could be moved, but not the obelisk, which therefore had to form the centre in the new Square.

There was already an ideological programme connected to the obelisk, and it was easy for Bernini to develop this further. The obelisk had a long history of tradition, since it came from Heliopolis in Egypt, where it was erected by Pharaoh Mencares in 1835 BCE. It was brought from Egypt to Alexandria by Augustus. Caligula brought it to Rome in 37 CE and set it up in his stadium. When Pope Sixtus V moved the obelisk from the south side of the church, he consecrated it in a comprehensive ritual of exorcism, in order to place it in its new context (cf. Cole 2009: 57–76). The ball on top, which according to tradition contained Caesar's ashes, was replaced by a bronze cross. The exorcism that was performed marked a rejection of the obelisk's Egyptian and Roman pagan background; but in the contemporary context, this was also a demarcation against the Protestant Reformation, as we can see in the inscriptions that Sixtus V had carved into the new base for the obelisk. These express a very clear Counter-Reformation programme. To the east, he had the following inscription carved: 'Behold the cross of the Lord. Flee, o adversaries. The lion from the tribe of Judah has conquered.'[16] On the west side of the obelisk, which faces the façade of Saint Peter's, the message is addressed to those who leave the church: 'Christ conquers. Christ reigns. Christ rules. May Christ defend his people against all evil.'[17] This applies to the true believers: it is for them that Christ has conquered everything, and he protects them. At the same time, the inscription declares that the pope is the universal ruler in both the religious and the political spheres. This was the ideological framework on which Bernini had to build further.

How did Bernini resolve the extremely complicated task of uniting existing buildings and monuments with a new structuring of the Square? The centre became the obelisk with its programmatic inscriptions. He rebuilt Maderno's fountain and moved it. He also set up an identical fountain, so that the two now flank the obelisk. Bernini conceived of the Square as a construction that would embrace the believers and usher them into the Holy of Holies, as the final point of the pilgrim journey.

The Square is divided into two. First of all, one enters a broad oval space garlanded by two semicircular arms with four rows of columns in depth, placed in such a way that if one stands in the south or north centre of the oval, the columns will cover each other, and one will see only those in the front row. In the continuation of the oval space up towards the church, Bernini constructed two corridor wings that create a separate space in front of the façade of the basilica. This part of the Square is formed as a trapezoid, so that the wings incline outwards towards the façade, the so-called *piazza retta*. This makes possible an entrance to the papal palace to the north through the colonnades, while the trapezoidal form makes Maderno's façade look narrower than it really is. Most of this space consists of a colossal staircase construction with steps that have the form of an arc in the middle and are straight on each side. This marks the final ascent to the Holy of Holies before one enters the colossal vestibule.

The entire Square thus appears as a unified whole, since the half-circular porticoes have the same height as the lateral wings of the upper Square. Bernini's theological message is clear: the one hundred and forty statues of the church's martyrs that Bernini set up on the two sides of the Square lead up to the façade of the church. On the top of the façade are statues of Christ and the apostles, except for Peter, since he is inside, in the sacred room. It is Christ and his saints who meet the visitors and embrace them and lead them into the sanctuary (Kuhn 1970: 300).

On this point, there are no obvious references to the programmes of Ignatius or the Jesuits, but it is nevertheless interesting to see how Ignatius in the *Exercitia* affirms that the imagination, the ability to picture things, is decisive for the spiritual exercises. With the aid of the imagination, one can find oneself in the presence of God and the saints already in this life: '[...] a sort of imaginary re-creation of the place, where I see myself standing before God and all the saints with the desire, and persevering in it, of finding out the manner by which I could best please God Himself' (ES §151);[18] '[...] the saints have interceded for me' (ES §60).[19]

Bernini has gone one step further, from an abstract idea to concrete art that *recreates* such a scene in the heart of the urban space. It is tempting, therefore, to read the programme of the square as an architectural implementation of the spiritual exercise prescribed by Ignatius. Saint Peter's Square can be regarded as a heavenly tribunal where the saints appear, and can be petitioned to intercede for the believer making his way into the Holy of Holies. In Bernini's version, the oval Square, with the colonnades on each side crowned by the statues of the saints and the staircase leading up to the vestibule, embraces all the believers from the surrounding world 'in order to give a maternal welcome to the Catholics to confirm them in the faith, to the heretics in order to reunite them to the Church, and to the infidels in order to open their eyes to the true faith' – as he himself put it (Lees-Milne 1967: 272).

Saint Peter's Church

When Bernini began working in the Vatican, Saint Peter's was almost finished; it had been consecrated in 1626. A succession of architects had been involved, including Bramante, Rafael, Michelangelo, della Porta, Vignola, Fontana and finally Carlo Maderno, who erected the nave and the façade, which was completed in 1614. In the vestibule with the entrance to the papal palace, Bernini set up his equestrian statue of Emperor Constantine, the first Christian emperor, who built Old Saint Peter's. In the eighteenth century, an equestrian statue of Charlemagne was placed at the other end of the narthex. While this demonstrates the church's collaboration with the imperial power, these monuments also mark a boundary, since they stand outside the sacred room.

Leaving the vestibule, one goes in and encounters a harmonious room that draws one up towards the Holy of Holies. The original Renaissance interior was transformed by Bernini's plans into a baroque interior. In this connection I intend to shed light on his decorations in the central axis of the church – the nave and the choir. Sculpture and architectonic elements gave the interior serenity, with its balanced proportions, elements that express precisely the baroque ideal: it appeals intensely to both the intellect and the senses, and can therefore move the visitor and promote a religious emotion. Bernini's colossal baldachin, over the papal altar directly under the cupola, and Peter's alleged tomb are the central visual focus in the interior. At the same time, the baldachin also marks the point where one descends to Maderno's *confessio*. The altar is placed directly above Peter's supposed tomb, where the pallia, the honorific vestment worn by the archbishops who are the apostles' successors, are kept in a chest. It is here that power and tradition are handed on to others. Through the baldachin, Bernini's oval stained-glass window, depicting the Holy Spirit in the form of a dove, shines above Peter's empty throne, the so-called *cathedra*. The visitor who enters the church is struck to see that the interior is constructed in such a way that, as one draws nearer to the central cultic point (the papal altar), the papal power is visualized more and more strongly through an escalation of the effects. As one makes one's way along Maderno's nave, one passes Bernini's reliefs of selected popes from earlier ages. These are executed in multicoloured marble and set in medallions on the columns. The ground plan is based on a strong artistic and ideological dramaturgy.

Bernini's project in the cupola area and in the choir behind it has a fundamental unified programme that should not leave the believer in any doubt: here one is at the foundations of the Catholic Church, here the truth and the unity of the Church are made visible, and here lies the basis of the claim to power that is made by the Church and the pope. Bernini's entire project in this part of the church interior stands for the

Figure 12.4 The baldachin and the papal altar, St. Peter's basilica, Rome (Wikimedia Commons). Author: Jean-Pol Grandmont.

self-consciousness that the church had regained after the setback it had suffered as a consequence of the Reformation.

It is only when one moves up through Maderno's nave that one gets an impression of the colossal dimensions of the church. When one enters the cupola space in the transept, one inevitably looks up at Michelangelo's and Domenico Fontana's cupola; at the same time, thanks to Bernini's design, the interior itself abolishes some of the loftiness. The baldachin is a colossal construction with deep foundations, which took ten years to build. The papal altar stands on an elevated base with stairs leading up to it from all sides. This makes the altar functional as a cultic site that is visible from every point, while the height of the base both allows everyone in the huge interior to see it and demonstrates that this is the central point for the Petrine tradition. The baldachin frames the base of the altar, and four columns hold up the canopy of the baldachin. It is strikingly high in relation to its quadratic base; the construction is 28.5 metres in height.

In the cupola drum, in a flood of light, we read the celebrated words spoken by Jesus to Peter, which are the very axiom of the Catholic understanding of the papacy: 'Tu es Petrus, et super hanc petram aedificabo Ecclesiam meam.' This is the caption for what Bernini has carried out in the space below: 'You are Peter, and on this rock I will build my Church' (Mt. 16.18). This represents the authoritative interpretation of the papal altar and of the baldachin above it. This is in opposition to the Greek Orthodox piety where the mystery is veiled behind the iconostasis and curtains. In St. Peter's you experience the holy through the elevations of the visible elements.

The baldachin stands in an unbroken tradition that goes back to the early church, but the final product is entirely Bernini's own, a combination of an altar ciborium and a processional baldachin (Lees-Milne 1967: 250–3; Nykjær 1999: 163–75; Francia 1975: 80; Hibbard 1965: 75–80). The baldachin is full of symbols. The four helical columns with their décor of grape branches and bees – the latter a motif from Urban VIII's coat of arms – have their point of departure in the four pairs of columns from the grave complex in Constantine's Old Saint Peter's. These are still present in the church, in the small loggias on the four supporting pillars. The symbolic function is clear. The baldachin states in a compact manner what is involved here: this is the tomb of Peter, the prince of the apostles. Over this tomb is the altar on which only the pope celebrates Mass. The baldachin rises up in its enormous height and culminates in a globe supported by four volutes and adorned with a cross. Angels stand on the edge of the volutes. Two angels float on the draperies and hold the papal tiara between them. Under the canopy of the baldachin floats a dove, the symbol of the Holy Spirit. Everything beneath this – the sacramental element, and ultimately the church's organization and power structure – is a result of Christ's victory and institution, which is administered by each pope in his pontificate.

This is intensified by Bernini's decoration of the cupola room. He has placed sculptures in niches on each of the four pillars that support the cupola, depicting Veronica with the veil, Empress Helena with the cross of Jesus, Longinus with the lance, and the apostle Andrew with his x-shaped cross. Bernini planned everything, but it is only the statue of Longinus that is the work of his hands. He gave friends and pupils the task of making the other sculptures according to his instructions, as was also the case with the sculptures on the Ponte Sant'Angelo: Francesco Mochi – Veronica; Andrea Bolgi – Helena; Francesco Duquesnoy – Andrew. Above each niche is a small logia. According to tradition, the sacred relics to which the statues allude are kept in the room behind the loggia. Likewise, according to tradition, the helical Constantinian columns mentioned above are said to come from Solomon's Temple. Historically speaking, this is an impossibility, but the reuse of the pillars demonstrates Bernini's ability to reshape tradition and create it anew through renewal in his own days.

The sculptures in the cupola room look either towards the altar or towards heaven. The saints are important enough, but they point to the most important relic, namely, the tomb of the one who was appointed by Christ himself as the leader of the church, and whose successors are mediators between heaven and earth. This takes place through Christ's presence in the Eucharist. In this way, what Ponte Sant'Angelo hinted at is brought to its fulfilment: here, the believer stands at the ultimate vision of Christ's sacrifice and of its consequences for the believer and for the church. Bernini has created a cupola room that points to the essentials in the tridentine Catholic self-understanding: the sacrifice of the mass celebrated by the pope as the successor of Peter. In the Eucharist the Catholic believers are invited to have the experience of the true belief through emotion and sensation. Ignatius describes this with an allusion to Lk. 24.13ff: the story of the disciples on the road to Emmaus. Jesus doesn't just break bread for them, he gives them Communion, and they recognized him (ES §303).[20]

When one goes behind the high altar, one discovers that the stained-glass window with the dove, which one sees between the pillars of the baldachin when one enters the church, is part of a large bronze sculpture over the altar at the back wall of the choir, the so-called *Cathedra Petri* (Lees-Milne 1967: 278–81; Francia 1975: 87–90; Nykjær 1999: 191–201; Hibbard 1965: 159–62). The oval alabaster stained-glass window is part of this

Figure 12.5 The Cathedra, St. Peter's basilica, Rome (Wikimedia Commons). Author: Sergey Smirnov.

composition, and the rays of light from the dove – the symbol of the Holy Spirit – are materialized out from the window in bronze and radiate over Peter's empty throne, which truly hangs between heaven and earth. It is surrounded by a host of angels, two of whom hold the papal tiara above the chair. The throne is carried by four church fathers, two from the West (Ambrose and Augustine) and two from the East (Athanasius and John Chrysostom). The message is arranged in a very subtle manner: there had been a schism between the Western and the Eastern Churches since 1054, and Bernini has presented the papal power here as universal – one of the great points of contention that had led to the schism in earlier times. Here, the universal papacy is presented as inspired by the Holy Spirit, as if the schism had never occurred. Lees-Milne quite correctly points out that the depiction of the church fathers from East and West is meant to symbolize the Church's unity, by means of a reminder that the Eastern Church was subordinate to the universal rule of papal power. The Eastern Church has never accepted such an understanding; on the contrary, the pope's demand for supremacy was one of the most important causes of the breach. The group of sculptures thus constitutes a remarkable visualization of papal triumphalism. A further message is also given: Peter's chair is empty, but at the same time Peter is present thanks to his burial place under the high altar, and the reigning pope is Peter's vicar as the leader of the universal church *Summus Pontifex Ecclesiae Universalis*, 'High priest of the entire Church'.

The demand for power and the demand for truth merge here. But does the spirituality of that age offer any critical rejoinder to this demonstration of power? Is not that spirituality rather oriented towards the obedience and humility of the individual? There can be no doubt that the individual is called to obedience and humility in Ignatius's *Exercise*. But it also sheds light on this aspect of Bernini's work by means of Ignatius's Counter-Reformation view of the Church and of authority. What is the ultimate goal for the one who carries out the *Exercitia Spiritualia* as a penitential exercise? It is to recognize in one's sentiment that Catholic Christianity is the only true and correct Christianity. One is ultimately confronted with the *Ecclesia triumphans*, the power of the Church, and the final chapter in the *Exercitia Spiritualia* is a framework for the entire text:[21] it concerns the true views one ought to hold in order to belong to the Church.

Here we are told, inter alia, that one must relinquish one's own judgement and obey the Church and its hierarchy (ES §353). One must go to confession, take part in the Mass, and receive Communion in accordance with the Church's regulations (ES §354). One must admonish other Christians to do the same (ES §355). One must praise saints, relics, and all that the veneration of the saints involves (ES §358). One must praise the laws about fasting and abstinence, and the days and times linked to these laws (ES §359). The particularly interesting point is that Ignatius links all this to honouring the church building and religious images because of what they represent (ES §360). For Ignatius, this is connected to the obligation to observe all the commandments of the Church. One must not oppose them, but should rather defend them and show respect for the church's teaching (ES §§361; 363). This culminates in a description of what agreement with the Church means: 'if the Church defines as black something that appears white to our eyes, we must in like manner declare it black' (ES §365).[22] Human beings are thus meant to lead their lives within the boundaries set by the Church, in order thereby to discover how one can serve God and obtain salvation for one's soul (see ES §§55–6). Faith is linked to the individual sphere through sensational and emotional experience with the sacred topography. The church complex designed by Bernini, therefore, was envisaged as playing a specific role in communicating and generating the spirituality and ideological programme of that age.

Conclusion

Bernini's great projects in the Vatican area, from the Ponte Sant'Angelo via Saint Peter's Square up to the *cathedra* in Saint Peter's, demonstrates his ability to combine architecture and sculpture. His greatest gift as an architect was the ability to work on existing architecture and urban space in a comprehensive transformation and new creation. He was first and foremost a sculptor. I believe that his architectonic interventions, for example in the case of Saint Peter's Square, support this claim, since even Saint Peter's Square, the only architectonic element in his work on the pilgrimage route, presents in many ways the appearance of a work of sculpture.

In light of the coherence of the complex detailed above, across installations that had decades in the making, it seems likely that there was a comprehensive plan guiding Bernini's throughout the decades in which he was the chief architect at Saint Peter's. His entire project with the pilgrimage route, Saint Peter's Square, and Saint Peter's Church is marked by a profound empathy with the Catholic Church's dogmas, praxis and organization, as this is expressed in the type of spirituality and the kind of metaphysical thinking characteristic of the Jesuit order (Lees-Milne 1967: 280–1). When we interpret the sculpture and architecture in the light of Ignatius's *Exercitia*, we catch sight of a spiritual vision that they shared, although there is no basis for asserting that Bernini simply wanted to translate Ignatius's text into a work of art. Indeed, the work of art seems to break open the parameters of the subjective inwardness in Ignatius's text, and to establish a visual and spatial vision for the whole of society, understood as the fellowship of believers. Nevertheless, Ignatius and Bernini arguably share a common vision for their work: namely, to go out beyond the rational and to awaken the inner religious sentiment in the beholders that will move them to recognize themselves as sinners in the encounter with the Church as the authoritative mediator of the Christian faith. In this way, one can say that Bernini was both an artist and a theologian (Kuhn 1970: 317). His art and architecture were thus a result of the spirit of the Council of Trent, but mediated through his own artistic talent, which came to set a decisive imprint on the baroque as an epoch (Lees-Milne 1967: 280–1).

13

Figuration and 'Aesthetics of the Sublime': Aspects of Their Interplay in Christian Art

Else Marie Bukdahl

In the Western world, artworks have often been regarded as visualizations of pre-established ideas and concepts, so it is understandable that church art has frequently been interpreted as a precise artistic representation of the biblical texts and other texts relating to ecclesiastical history (cf. Banning 1980: 124–34). However, artists from Leonardo da Vinci to Wassily Kandinsky have always been aware that the language of form can communicate experiences and knowledge that the written and spoken word are either unable to express adequately or simply cannot capture. The word never coincides with the artistic expression. The French philosopher Maurice Merleau-Ponty outlines in an original and clear manner how artists are able to visualize perspectives and reveal traces and significances that philosophers and scientists cannot grasp with their tools alone. He quotes Leonardo da Vinci, who maintained that there is a special knowledge expressed in what he called a 'pictorial science', which does not speak with words (and still less with numbers) but with *oeuvres*, which exist in the visible just as natural things do and which nevertheless communicate through those things 'to all the generations of the universe' (Merleau-Ponty 1964: 186).

Merleau-Ponty adds that Rainer Maria Rilke calls the 'pictorial science' of Leonardo 'a silent science' which 'brings into oeuvre the forms of things whose seal has not been broken' – it comes from the eye and addresses itself to the eye. We must regard the eye as the 'window of the soul' (1964: 186). Furthermore, artists and aestheticians have often emphasized that visual art has a greater openness than the so-called logocentric disciplines in which concepts and categories have a prominent place. Visual art as idiom opens up a field that concepts must necessarily restrict. And visual art may also contain a more open view than even its 'sister genre', poetry, can communicate. Finally, visual art also has a particular, expressive power because it engages all the senses, the imagination, reason and often the entire body in a very direct way.

Since the earliest development of Christian art[1], prominent artists have tried to find an answer to a fundamental artistic and theological question: How can one represent the unrepresentable, that is, the holy, the paradox of faith, the Trinity, the resurrection of the flesh, or the coming of the Holy Ghost? The biblical Hebrew legislation against idolatry has been regarded by most artists, not as a ban, but as a challenge and an expression of the acknowledgement that attempts to depict the sacred by means of a human figure, or a representation of scenes from the everyday world, renders the unrepresentable to become limited, indeed often completely determined by mundane ideas and concepts. It is therefore difficult for the beholder to understand that the sacred, or the divine, is supposed to be different, lies beyond the human sphere of power, reason and imaginative abilities, to give the world new meaning and open up new perspectives.

The violent conflict that arose during the eighth and ninth centuries between iconoclasts and iconolaters may be regarded as sharply delineated interpretations of the biblical law against idolatry. The iconoclasts wanted to banish visual art from the interiors of churches. They feared it might tempt churchgoers to worship images and lead to a profanation of the sacred. The iconolaters emerged victorious, but the debate provoked by this conflict continued over the centuries that followed – although in less dramatic form – and continues to this day. This debate has always created new orientations in the aesthetic debate and in visual art. It constitutes a recurrent theme of past as evidenced in artworks like Caspar David Friedrich's landscape paintings from the period of German romanticism, Gianfranco Baruchello's paintings from the 1960s and in Jean-François Lyotard's philosophy from the 1980s (Bukdahl 2005: 11–13; Bukdahl 2016: 128–30, Figure 1).

The image ban and medieval, Renaissance and baroque art

The great artists who left their imprint on the churches of the Middle Ages, the Renaissance and the baroque were well aware that there was a major difference between the preaching of the gospel and their own visual interpretations of scripture. They saw clearly, for example, that a human figure modelled by a visual artist could engender fixed ideas to a far greater degree than interpretations of human beings and gods conveyed in language. This is because language is capable of suggesting an idea, for example, of God's power of creation and love, without describing God as a person from the everyday reality.

With the aim of avoiding the restrictive bonds of the image – and the pitfalls of recognizability – the artists have often captured or indicated the divine by means of abstract or non-figurative artistic effects, which produce openings in fixed patterns of ideas and interpretation. They have used sculptural devices, like a veil, for example, to reduce the similarity to the human body, or painterly idioms that created planes of colour and transitions, which achieved their effect mainly by means of their own fullness of expression. The most important factor has, however, always been light, with its rapidly changing modulations that continually create new contexts and new perspectives – both in works of art and in their interplay with architecture. Light is ubiquitous; it sweeps darkness aside. Light comes to everyday environments and penetrates everything, but humans cannot seize it, nor can they control it. Similarly, God's love is thought to permeate the common world; it is omnipresent, but it is beyond the human sphere of power.

In the stained-glass windows of Gothic churches the beholder is confronted with scenes from scripture and from legends of the saints. But artists have placed them so high up on the walls that the intensely bright blue, red and golden areas often blur the narrative elements and create an abundance of light, which both unites and radiates an aura of transfiguration over church architecture and its visual art. It is precisely this wealth of light that becomes a symbolic expression of God's omnipresent love or 'the city [that] had no need of the sun, neither of the moon, to shine in it; for the glory of God did lighten it' (Rev. 21.23).

The monk Theophilus was one of the few artists in the Middle Ages to describe the view of the art of his time.[2] The central element in it was – as in Byzantine art – the creation of an expressive language of form capable of visualizing the spiritual dimension, especially the paradox of faith. He emphasized that God's Paradise, God Himself and the risen Christ can best be visualized through an almost celestial play of light and colour, what Theophilus called 'the radiant splendor of the pieces of glass and the manifold qualities of the priceless craftsmanship', along with various abstract elements of ornamentation. And if 'the eye of man [...] marks the abundance of light from the windows, it admires the inestimable beauty of the glass and the variety of the costliest work' (Holt 1957: 8), which provides a sense of the presence of God.

This medieval theory of light, which originated in a metaphysical world view, is visualized in works like the North Rose of Chartres Cathedral (about 1235) and in the North Rose of Notre Dame in Paris (1250–60). The light streaming through these glass windows is so powerful that it volatilizes the small figures in small squares and circles with the Virgin Mary and the infant Jesus in the centre of both rosettes. It is thus the light that is the central signifying power. In the western bays on the south side of the nave in the Chartres Cathedral, featuring the top of the arcade, the *triforum* and the clerestory glass windows, one can clearly see how much the colourful light dominates the biblical scenes and figures.

The glass windows, which glow like jewels, pouring vivid colours onto the floor of the cathedral, create an impression of a curtain of light, symbolic of Christ's love for his followers. In these two Gothic cathedrals, it is first and foremost the light entering the church space from the stained-glass paintings that unifies the architecture and sculpture in a visionary unity. The light represents the newly resurrected Christ, seen not as a judge, but as the light of the world and its saviour. The intense light space of the church is to give the eye, the thoughts and the mind an impression of this in a way that the written or spoken word is unable to express with the same strength, and which can also not be conveyed through images from the world. This is to evoke the divine creative power and the love of God, which is shown to cast a transfigurative light over the lives of the audiences.

The great Renaissance master Leonardo da Vinci also saw this perspective. He called God 'the light of all things', and appointed the visual artist as 'the explorer of light'. Throughout his life Leonardo tried to find the order, or the whole, that was the fundamental structure 'in the splendid book that lies open before our eyes: the cosmos' (Monty 1953: 42). But his last series of biblical drawings, for example *The Deluge* or *Visions of the End of the World* (1514–15) (Figure 13.1), which contains a labyrinthine network of local orders and perspectives leading into an infinite space, reveals that his search remained fruitless. Dynamic, spiralling movements reminiscent of powerful waves throw stone fragments around in the open pictorial space. Trees are crushed and

Figure 13.1 *The Deluge. Visions of the End of the World*, Leonardo da Vinci. 1514–15. Drawing on paper. Pen and black ink with wash. 162 × 203 mm. Royal Collection, Great Britain. Leonardo da Vinci (Public domain), via Wikimedia Commons.

appear to be moving out of the lower half of the pictorial space. This is undoubtedly a visualization of the idea that the world will end in a massive flood, which will blot out all life on earth. But these drawings also reveal that in his final years Leonardo became convinced that neither the divine nor the end of the world could be summed up in a single concept, expressed by a single image or visualized in a clear figurative language. The non-figurative pictorial language may be interpreted as the bearing element in the drawing, communicating a powerful impression that the spectators are facing the end of the world.

A similar experience often pervaded the period that followed, the baroque, giving rise to the creation of images that were conceived independently of natural forms or the ideals of antiquity and were therefore able to reveal new aspects of scripture and highlight the divine by means of bold architectural and artistic devices. This characteristic emerges particularly in Michelangelo Merisi da Caravaggio's paintings and Giovanni Lorenzo Bernini's sculptures. In baroque art, light is used to render God's power and Christ's love visible. It often comes from a source that is difficult to identify and moves in dramatic circles and spirals, pushing aside the deep darkness. This powerful light is highly visible in *The Conversion of Saint Paul* (1601) by Caravaggio. He dramatizes the precise moment when Saul falls off his horse and lies on the ground, blinded by the light emanating from Christ, who is not present as a figure, but who appears as a voice, talking to him. The intense waves of light reveal the result of Christ's activity – the conversion of Saul, who later became Paul the Apostle.

An astonishing number of artworks contain multiple layers of meaning. For example, Caravaggio's *The Conversion of Saint Paul* requires special knowledge, of the Bible and ecclesiastical history. This knowledge occupied an increasingly diminished role in cultural life during the Age of Enlightenment and in the ensuing centuries. Today it features almost exclusively in ecclesiastical contexts. Unlike words, however, images have a dimension that is immediately accessible. Both figurative and non-figurative art is imbued with presence and intensity and can, in principle, be experienced by all, irrespective of individual or cultural background.

The Conversion of Saint Paul – which has moved and inspired thousands of churchgoers and other visitors from all layers of society – may arouse in those without knowledge of its biblical background an experience of a strange event, which enters into their daily lives, arouses their imaginations and opens new perspectives. A level of figurative experience like this can be found, but only in a weaker version, also in writing, for example, in Arabic or Chinese poetry and the typographical experiments of 'concrete poetry', such as the works of Guillaume Apollinaire. The encounter with texts of this kind can – even if one is unable to read them – create an experience of beauty, but they still lack the presence and intensity of visual art.

In the *Ecstasy of Saint Teresa* (1614–52) by Bernini, Teresa and the angel are also illuminated by an intense light, which filters through a hidden window in the dome of the surrounding aedicule, and is underscored by gilded stucco rays: 'The supernatural event of Teresa's vision is raised to a sphere of its own, removed from that of the beholder, mainly by virtue of the isolating canopy and the heavenly light' (Whittkower 1980: 160). Teresa's passionate experience of religious ecstasy is visualized in the highly complex, almost abstract network of folds in the drapery, which renders her body almost invisible. Christ is only represented by the powerful light.

However, the art of the Middle Ages, the Renaissance and the baroque also reveals that both sculptors and painters were convinced that the evangelical accounts of Christ's life on earth could be rendered visible by artistic representations of scenes from the ordinary human world. For these artists, it was a fundamental idea in Christendom that Christ became a human being unto his death – wholly and completely – and was familiar with the many facets of human life, including despair and suffering. However, the depictions of the surrounding world created by artists like Titian, Leonardo, Bernini and Caravaggio were never conventional or traditional. This is because they embraced artistic interpretations of their own era's latest advances in natural science, which they had often created or developed themselves – for example, studies of anatomical dissections, breakthroughs in the science of colour, the development of linear perspective in the Renaissance and the baroque's concept of infinite space. The artists wanted no doubt to show that the gospels address a world undergoing constant transformation determined by continuous conflicts between chaos and order. The beholder was therefore enabled to understand that the Christian message was not confined within traditional limits, but was always able to withstand the penetrating light and challenges of contemporaneity. This applies to works like Titian's dramatic painting, *Crowning with Thorns* (1542), in which the viewer's involvement is inescapable. Viewers are confronted with a very dramatic and brutal scene in which two soldiers violently twist the crown onto Jesus's head using canes. By employing vivid, luminous tints of colour, vibrant, loose brushwork, subtle tones and the forceful modelling of the figures, Titian sought to demonstrate that Jesus was a human being right up to his death and who, for the sake of humankind, suffered the pains and mortality that belong to the world. Titian also interpreted the old biblical story in his own intense Renaissance idiom. His contemporary audiences could thus experience the story as having currency and relevance for themselves.

Artists such as Caravaggio produced interpretations of the gospels, which shattered the familiar concepts of the world and Christianity held by priests and believers, who were sometimes offended and demanded that the works be removed. Mostly, however, this was not the case. Caravaggio's monumental painting, *Madonna of the Pilgrims* (1603–4), was placed in Sant'Agostino in Rome. The elite of Rome were shocked when they saw that the dirty soles of the man's feet were so close to the spectator that they could not avoid looking at them, but the painting remained in place. Caravaggio wanted to highlight the fact that this pilgrim and his wife were very common and contemporary people, with whom the viewers could identify. Madonna and the little Jesus look like they could be a Roman mother and her child. But their elevated position and the mysterious *clair obscur* remove them slightly from the human world, discreetly revealing that they are holy persons who love and take care of humankind.

Burke's and Kant's concept of 'the sublime'

During the eighteenth century, the age of the Enlightenment, the ideal of the clear light of reason and empirical, scientific method occupied a prominent position. As a result, conventional Christian mythology and morals were ousted from their previously dominant position. Christianity nevertheless managed to retain a quite dominant position, but only through its being 'modernized'. Cultural and political life became increasingly independent from ecclesiastical life, gradually emerging as autonomous social fields. The many connecting strands between Christian art and advances in the fields of philosophy and art that had left their mark on the earlier periods became less pronounced.

In the mid-1800s, however, Edmund Burke, in his book *A Philosophical Enquiry into the Origin of Our Ideas of the Sublime and Beautiful* (1757), questioned the optimistic belief of his contemporaries that humans, by applying reason, could acquire an exhaustive understanding of the world and gain control of it. It was especially his portrayal of 'the sublime' as a 'sentiment or a passion' and a boundary-transgressing experience that was in focus. Burke pointed out that everything the imagination cannot sum up in a single impression – the darkness of night, the wide-open space and the 'infinity' – arouses a sensation or 'a feeling of the sublime'. The very fact that these attempts to synthesize fail abysmally evokes 'horror' and 'terror'. But this 'terror' is mingled with a sensation of 'delight' because 'the terror-causing threat becomes suspended', and because it reveals new experiences and ways of looking at our world, that have so many uncovered perspectives. Through an interpretation of what he called 'the sublime', Burke found that humans are incapable, either through their imagination or through their reason, of understanding and controlling the world.[3]

At the end of the century, Immanuel Kant, in his *Critique of the Power of Judgment* (1790), was the first to connect the determination of 'the sublime' with the biblical law against picturing God. He was convinced that 'the sublime' could best be exemplified by biblical ideas of non-figurative representation. Because, by forbidding ancient believers to create images of their God, their imagination, or *Einbildungskraft*, was not limited. They had a clear understanding that the sacred, or God, could not be contained or visualized by a human figure from our world. Kant argues that there is therefore 'no more sublime passage in Judaic law than the prohibition of idolatry insofar as one is called, in the name of the tradition, to inventively rupture the tradition' (Keenan 2005: 175).[4]

An encounter, for example, with the vast firmament, the wind-swept sea, the absolutely great or divine, everything the imagination cannot conceive within a single image, arouses an experience of 'the sublime'. For Kant, one's inability to grasp the grandeur of 'the sublime', like experiencing an earthquake, thus demonstrates the inadequacy of one's sensibility and imagination. Or in his own words: 'The sublime is that, the mere capacity of thinking which evidences a faculty of mind transcending every standard of sense' (Kant 1986: 98).

According to the interpretation of Løgstrup, what awakens a sense of 'the sublime' around us and within us is thus what threatens us, what we cannot measure and what we cannot surmount, but which frees our abilities – our reason and will – within us. It is these abilities, in particular, which elevate humans above nature:

> It is, in some sense, a power struggle that takes place. In nature we suffer defeats, physical and sensual, where power is crushed, our imaginative ability fails, but reason and ethics prevail. The duality of the feeling of 'the sublime' is defeat and victory, aversion and desire. (Løgstrup 1965: 103)

Reason is thus able to perceive the crisis of imagination and conceive an idea of the activity of 'the sublime'.

The challenge for the visual artist is thus how to depict the infinite, the absolute, the sacred, or other phenomena that produce an experience of 'the sublime', or of grandeur. Kant posited his aesthetic of 'the sublime' mostly on the experience of nature (Meredith 1986: 109–11). But he may also have had in mind that artistic effects, which have no association with existing figurative concepts, can indicate what is impossible to summarize in a single impression or in an image – the absolute or the divine. Exposing 'the sublime' allows an opening or a fractured surface to emerge, which can never be sealed or healed, thus registering the fact that here was something humans could not grasp, that limits have been established for their imagination and senses, but that human abilities like reason and will have been liberated.

The Italian philosopher Mario Perniola stressed that Kant's definition of 'the sublime' is the core in what he calls 'a theological aesthetics':

> However theological aesthetics takes its roots in Kant's *Critique of the Power of Judgement* just where he distinguishes the sublime from the beautiful: whereas the beautiful implies a sensitive form which is adequate for human faculties, so that it seems to be predisposed to our judgement, the sublime cannot be held in any sensitive form, so that it is enjoyed not for its correspondence to the interest

of senses, but for its opposition. Therefore, we can find in the sublime an aesthetic experience which implies a sort of transcendence regarding the world. The sublime is conceived differently by Kant and by Hegel: according to the former only nature allows us to experience the sublime, whereas according to the latter it is linked with the form of symbolic art. (Perniola 1955: 22)

Perniola believes that Kant's concept of 'the sublime' should be the core of a theological aesthetic, because 'the sublime' – in contrast to 'beauty' – is not expressed through a 'sensitive form' and is also not experienced via the senses. 'The sublime' refers to the infinite, 'that is why it is reason that is set into motion, because it casts out its ideas of what lies beyond the reach of our senses' (Løgstrup 1965: 104). The experience of 'the sublime' therefore opens up encounters with the divine, the holy and the various metaphysical dimensions. And experiences arising from the encounter with 'the sublime' liberate the artist from any dependence on traditional art forms. And in attempting to present the unpresentable, he or she achieves new artistic experience and creates new visual principles, which also provide possibilities for interpreting Christian themes in a new way.

The concept of 'the sublime' and new breakthroughs in modern church art

During the nineteenth and twentieth centuries new departures in the visual arts took place to a marked degree in non-religious art – this is above all the area in which interpretations of innovations arose in cultural and social life and in the natural sciences. But striking exceptions do exist, for example, in the Christian art by Eugène Delacroix, Henri Matisse and Emil Nolde.

Various interpretations of Burke's and Kant's definitions of 'the sublime' also appeared in the nineteenth and twentieth centuries and the new millennium every time philosophical systems, political ideologies or dogmatic aesthetic outlooks blocked the possibility of innovation in the art world and particularly new interpretations of Christian art. In the field of philosophy it was positivism, among others, which blocked advancements of this kind. Positivism is a theory that confines itself to the data of experience and excludes metaphysical systems and religion. And in the field of aesthetics, notions like art for art's sake hindered the emergence of advancements in the exploration of the metaphysical and religious aspects of art. This art theory required art to avoid social, political, moral and religious themes and concentrate instead on the creation of beauty.

It is precisely because 'the sublime' is associated with biblical aniconism and involves the religious dimension of the artistic and cultural environment that figurative art's ability to visualize the divine was subjected to renewed scrutiny. The emergence of non-figurative art in the second decade of the twentieth century provided new opportunities for interpreting the divine. These possibilities were further developed in the decades that followed. In addition, the encounter with 'the sublime' directed the gaze out towards the infinite space, made old rules disappear and provided space for new breakthroughs in both art and culture. Finally, the encounter with 'the sublime' also creates a new understanding of the fact that we cannot control our world, and thus contains an indirect criticism of things like the new theories of the 'control society', which were advanced at the end of the twentieth century and beginning of the new millennium (Deleuze 1990: 240–7).

Of course, the artists of the nineteenth, twentieth and twenty-first centuries working with interpretation of biblical and ecclesiastical themes occupy a varied, partly Protestant, partly Catholic foundation and with different artistic approaches. And this theological and artistic foundation departs quite significantly from the previously described conditions in the theological and artistic fields that the artists worked under prior to the Age of Enlightenment. But it was in the Renaissance in particular and in the following centuries that artists all shared their pursuit of answers to the question of which demands could be made of the Christian art of their time to avoid it being completely upstaged by images belonging to a bygone era. These artists, who created new artistic departures, aspired to make art that would be seen to have currency and relevance for a contemporary audience, one only has to think of Titian's *Crowning with Thorns* (1542), *The Conversion of Saint Paul* by Caravaggio, Caspar David Friedrich's romantic *Cross in the Mountains* (Tetschen Altar) (1808), Emil Nolde's expressionist *Life of Christ* (1911–12) and Gerhard Richter's non-figurative stained-glass window in Cologne cathedral (2007), for example.

An artist who became very involved in this discussion about 'the sublime' was Barnett Newman, a Jewish American painter who, together with Marc Rothko, created a striking new departure in the 1950s, which has had far-reaching consequences. In his paintings and writing he presented an original interpretation of 'the sublime' and its roots in the Hebrew Bible. In 1948, in an article entitled 'The Sublime Is Now', he wrote that, because

> the Greek dream prevails in our time, the European artist is nostalgic for the ancient forms, hoping to achieve tragedy by depicting his self-pity over the loss of the elegant column and the beautiful profile. [...] Instead of making *cathedrals* out of Christ, man, or 'life', we are making [them] out of ourselves, out of our own feelings. The image we produce is the self-evident one of revelation, real and concrete, that can be understood by anyone who will look at it without nostalgic glasses of history. (O'Neill 1990: 170, 173)

Between 1958 and 1966 Newman created his monumental work *Stations of the Cross*, inspired by the words uttered by Christ on the cross: 'My God, my God, why hast thou forsaken me?' The work consists of a cycle of fourteen pictures (Figure 13.2). But 'Why fourteen? Why not one painting?' asks Barnett Newman. To this he answers:

> The Passion is not a protest but a declaration. I had to explore its emotional complexity. That is, each painting is total and complete by itself, yet only the fourteen together make clear the wholeness of the single event. [...] I wished no monuments, no cathedrals. I wanted human scale for the human cry. [...] The cry, the unanswerable cry, is world without end. But a painting has to hold it, world without end, in its limits. (O'Neill 1990: 190)

Figure 13.2 The 14 pictures from *The Stations of the Cross*, Barnett Newman, 1958–66. Magna or oil on canvas. About 198 × 153 each. National Gallery of Art, Washington DC. Courtesy of the National Gallery of Art.

The Stations of the Cross reveals the artistic strategies that formed the core of Barnett Newman's departure from modernism. The beholder is confronted by none of the familiar figurative and abstract pictorial elements. The effect of the work is achieved solely by the open space, the powerful but simple composition and the large, extremely luminous expanses of colour. His palette consists only of black, raw canvas and white, because he wanted the canvas to become colour and to possess a sense of light (O'Neill 1990: 190).

The fourteen paintings are very intense and luminous, but also simple and sombre, because they visualize the stations of the cross. The French philosopher Christine Buci-Glucksmann rightly observes that the fourteen *Stations of the Cross* express very clearly and convincingly the experience and insight that the abstract expression of spirituality can awaken. She describes this effect as follows: 'Because', as she says 'here, it is from the empty, from the scanning rhythms of an active and dynamic emptiness that an idea of the "spiritual" is born which permeates the entire twentieth century.'[5] However, as Menachem Wecker points out, there are examples in *The First Station of the Cross* of fragments of figuration (Figure 13.3). These are small, barely visible crucifix figures:

> The portrait-oriented, black-and-white paintings and their bold stripes initially appear to be fully vertical in their thrusts, like crosses without horizontal shafts. But upon closer inspection, the vertical stripes, or 'zips,' as Newman called them, which he created with the help of masking tape, bleed colour from side to side, as a cross would if it were vibrating like a plucked guitar string. Each stripe, in a sense, consists of multiple miniature crosses, and subtle stains throughout the paintings could stand in as blood, sweat or tears. (Wecker 2012: 1)

Barnett Newman wrote that *The Stations of the Cross, Lema Sabachtani* were not just about the agony of Jesus, but also addressed the human condition. In his catalogue statement, he writes:

> *Lema Sabachtani* – why? Why did you forsake me? Why forsake me? To what purpose? Why? This is the Passion. This outcry of Jesus. Not the terrible walk

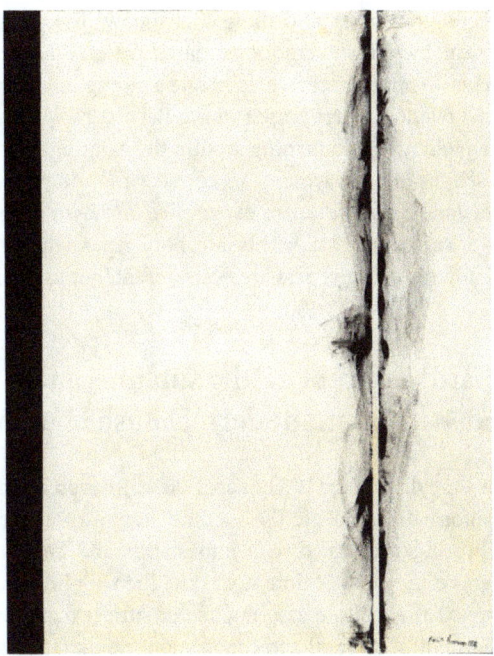

Figure 13.3 *The First Station of the Cross*, Barnett Newman. Magna on canvas. 197.8 × 153.7 cm. National Gallery of Art, Washington DC. Courtesy of the National Gallery of Art.

up the Via Dolorosa, but the question that has no answer. This overwhelming question that does not complain, makes today's talk of alienation, as if alienation were a modern invention, an embarrassment. This question that has no answer has been with us so long – since Jesus – since Abraham – since Adam – the original question. (O'Neill 1990: 180)

It is not just the agony of Jesus that one is confronted with in *The Stations of the Cross*, but as Newman explained, 'each man's agony: the agony that is single, constant, unrelenting, willed – world without end' (O'Neill 1990: 180).

In conversation with David Sylvester, Newman remarked, 'I hope that my painting has the impact of giving someone, as it did me, the feeling of his own totality, of his separateness, of his own individuality, and at the same time, of his connection to others who are also separate' (O'Neill 1990: 257–8). Barnett Newman's intention is not just intended as a reminder of the biblical story of the *Fourteen Stations*, and he does not want to show it in static pictures. For him it is not enough for believers to follow a priest in a procession around the church stopping at each station. He is convinced that the *Stations* demand action from the participants: recitation of prayers, reflection and walking from one to the next. This active engagement is fundamental to Newman's understanding of his painted series. The viewer contemplates the subject and proceeds – along with other viewers – to experience each of the paintings singly and in sequence, considering their bodily relation to individual paintings but also turning their heads to look at the preceding canvases and those that follow. The paintings demand the viewer's active physical, mental and emotional participation (Hellstein 2014).

The paintings have an open space, which create a strong interaction between them and the viewers. This relation is very important to Barnett Newman, because walking, looking, reflecting, meditating and turning around the paintings can establish physical and metaphysical self-awareness, which can connect the individual to other people and create an understanding and even an experience of shared suffering and ultimate mortality. Humans are all connected by this fate, both separately and together, but the prospect of Christ's love and forgiveness are ever present, but in a very discreet way.

J. F. Lyotard's concept of 'the sublime' and a radical new departure in modern Danish church art

In the 1980s, which were dominated by the rapid dissemination of knowledge, symbols and images in the information society, 'the sublime' reappears and creates perspectives and openings in a world so saturated with information and images that any form of immersion in it seems difficult. This time it was the French philosopher Jean-François Lyotard who interpreted 'the sublime' as a fragmented surface that cannot be restored by ideological and philosophical attempts at reconciliation. He characterized 'the sublime' as follows: 'Kant's reflections on "the sublime" appear as a rupture, occurring like the crash of a meteorite onto the surface of the book. [...] This is the ontological earthquake that modernity is all about' (Juhl 1988: 133, 135). Lyotard's analysis of 'the sublime sentiment' or 'the sentiment of the sublime' incorporates Kant's interpretation, but has lost its metaphysical connotations. In Lyotard's own words: 'We can conceive the infinitely great, the infinitely powerful, but every presentation of an object destined to "make visible" this absolute greatness or power appears to us painfully inadequate' (Lyotard 1986: 77).

But pain is replaced by the pleasure of gaining an experience and discovering hitherto unknown, intense forces. For the artist, the experience of 'the sublime' generated by the encounter with 'the formless' or 'the raw natural mass' means liberation from age-old rules and pre-established models. In the attempt to grasp absolute greatness, the unlimited and the immeasurable – that which cannot be visualized – new principles for artistic creation are discovered. Experience gained from this encounter with 'the sublime' is concentrated in the work of art that creates new dense units of meanings in the infinite space. Lyotard is convinced that the essence of the impact of 'the sublime' in visual art 'consists in the experience that the absolute leaves its mark in the work, whatever form it may take' (Lyotard 1992: 21). Or as the Danish aesthetician Carsten Juhl remarks: 'By interfering with the raw mass of nature [...] form is created. Faced with the formlessness of the absolute great, the work starts to set boundaries' (Juhl 1986: 77).

'The sublime' in a work of art is not only its exposure of the unlimited, that which cannot be represented but only suggested, but also that the work of art is what Lyotard calls 'an event' and Heidegger called *ein Ereignis*, which makes it apparent that something new is coming into view (Lyotard 1984: 43). The artwork becomes the event, the mark in reality, which makes spectators realize that concepts, categories and words do not suffice to comprehend reality.

Lyotard lectured frequently at the Royal Danish Academy of Fine Arts in Copenhagen, which is why he has influenced Danish artists like Hein Heinsen and his church art. Hein Heinsen has represented extreme positions in Danish art since the 1960s. He has always been engaged in visualizing or pointing to new images of the world and creating perspectives and unexpected correlations previously characterized by well-trodden paths. He has, for example, independently created parallels to the path first initiated by Newman and later taken up in minimal art and the new departures in the visual arts that followed in its wake. His church art in particular has also been inspired to a striking extent by 'the aesthetic of the sublime' (especially in Lyotard's version) and the view of a world in a constant process of transformation. His encounter with 'the aesthetic of the sublime' has confirmed his view that the sacred can never be contained within a figure or within general philosophical interpretations.

The depiction of figures has thus almost never appeared in any of his large church projects, such as those in St. James's Church in Roskilde (1974), Fyllingsdalen Church near Bergen, Norway (1980), St. John's Church in Vorup (together with Stig Brøgger) (1993) and Holte Church, Trørød (2012). But this does not mean that Heinsen rejects figures in church art. The absence is because the empty sepulchre, and the significance of the event associated with it, is for him the central feature of Christianity and thus incapable of being depicted adequately in a figurative language.

Various mostly non-figurative interpretations of Christ's death on the cross, the empty sepulchre and the resurrection are basic elements of Heinsen's large artistic elements in his church art. Most of them are altarpieces.

When creating the monumental altarpiece in Fyllingsdalen Church near Bergen in Norway (Figure 13.4), Heinsen incorporated the interior of the church in the surroundings. He demarcated the place that permitted the greatest possible degree of rigour in the categories of form that were to express what he regards as central to the Christian faith: the empty sepulchre and the resurrection. He exploits the intense play of light, which the architect Helge Hjertholm, created by means of the glass constructions that are a distinctive feature of the architecture of the church. Heinsen placed his decoration behind the altar. The large, sombre stone – 4.5 metres high – is fastened to the wall and cut into four parts. It is made of reddish-brown slate, speckled with mica. It appears mysterious and indeterminate and therefore refers not only to nature but also to an unknown location. This heavy, monumental stone, which weighs over a ton, forms a striking contrast to the slender cross, which divides it into four parts. The cross is composed of small pieces of glass in various thicknesses, which constantly catch the light. The rear wall of the church consists of ordinary industrial slabs, the linear pattern of their joints forming an interplay with the lines of the cross. The cross, whose lines are interrupted at several points, is therefore constantly related to our own reality. Seven shafts of chromium-plated steel that reflect the light intensify the luminous power of the work. Heinsen's decoration is a symbol without determined significances. In an interview about his project in the church, he stressed that this interior should be characterized by two fundamental concepts: distance and nearness. Theologically speaking, the words that are parallels to distance and nearness are sacredness (in the sense of *tremendum et fascinosum*) and love (in the sense of brotherhood) (Andersen 1989: 61–2). The altarpiece in Fyllingsdalen Church is very

Figure 13.4 Hein Heinsen. Altarpiece, Fyllingsdalen Church near Bergen, Norway, 1980. Photo: Hein Heinsen, courtesy of the photographer.

much determined by these two poles. The heavy, black stone is a reference to one of the most mysterious events: the empty sepulchre, which expresses an anticipation of what is to come – the resurrection. The idea of the empty tomb cannot be rendered visible by images from the ordinary world, because it expresses the incomprehensible, the absolutely great, which engenders an experience of 'the sublime', or of the limits to the human grasp of the world. The slender cross refers to Christ's love. Its luminosity shatters the darkness and fills the interior with light. Christ's love appears in this church project not only as the sacred, or 'the sublime', which lies beyond the human sphere of power, but also as that which is close at hand, which discloses a new dimension in everyday lives and emerges as an undeserved gift.

In Holte Church in Trørød (2102), Heinsen modelled the three sides of the altar table. They resemble a ploughed field. Only the plough furrows are visible. They are so vividly depicted that the viewer almost gets the feeling that the furrows are in the process of being turned. They seem to visualize an act of creation – something new in the process of coming into being. On the altar, there is a dynamic, abstract figure, which gives an impression of the coming of the Holy Spirit, its power and unpredictability (Figure 13.5). In a sense, the Creation is linked to unprecedented change created by the coming of the Holy Spirit.

Biblical aniconism and its inclusion by Kant in the category of 'the sublime' has always been a prominent element in Heinsen's interpretation of church art and his own artistic production. He sums up his concept of 'the sublime' as follows:

> The law against images of the divine is a way of acknowledging that imitative images determine reality, confine the world and convert it into a permanent, manageable form. The image thus becomes a substitute for the world while at the same time eliminating the individual. [...] The best works of art in history always have fissures

Figure 13.5 Hein Heinsen, Altarpiece, Old Holte Church, Denmark, 2012. Photo by Poul Heinsen, courtesy of the photographer.

that provide space for the beholder. In other words, the law against idolatry is an attempt to maintain that the world is greater than our purposes with it: the world retracts from our grasp. But, one might ask, should we not as a consequence refrain from creating images? No, images are necessary, for without them we would cling to the old images that cover up reality. New images are necessary in order to break down set views; they point to the transgression of borderlines, the infinite, the divine. Images devoid of 'the sublime' are petty, provincial and conservative. (Andersen 1989: 61–2)

A number of prominent artists working with Christian themes dating as far back as the Byzantine era have considered the limitations of the possibilities of expression in the language of figurative art. Artists are often forced to acknowledge that non-figurative tools can convey aspects of Christianity, which the vocabulary of figurative form can only achieve in a very limited way. This is first and foremost the case with the holy, the paradox of faith, the Trinity, the resurrection of the flesh and the coming of the Holy Ghost. This insight is often inspired by artists' particular understanding of biblical aniconism, which later became one of the fundamental elements in the concept of 'the sublime passion'. It was precisely this encounter that artists – and artists working with Christian themes in particular – had with 'the sublime', which became a fruitful source of inspiration and a liberating force in periods where unilateral cults of reason, antiquated rules and entrenched models dominated the art world. This was a frequent occurrence in the eighteenth century, the Age of Enlightenment and the century that followed. But in the twentieth and twenty-first centuries the experience of 'the sublime' has also meant a liberation from rules, models and fashionable trends. In attempting to present the unpresentable – the divine or the infinitely great – artists gained new artistic experience and acquired a new space for their creative activity. For them, the experience of 'the sublime' was also the discovery of a fracture that can never be healed, revealing that it – whether understood as the divine or as an unrepresentable 'beyond' in excess of understanding and depiction – is forever beyond the human sphere of power.

14

Seeing, Hearing and Narrating Salome: Modernist Sensual Aesthetics and the Role of Narrative Blanks

Ulrike Brunotte

Introduction and guiding questions

Since fin de siècle paintings, Oscar Wilde's play and Richard Strauss's opera, the figure of Salome has been embedded in modern visual regimes so centrally that she can be defined as 'a sign of the visual as such' (Bucknell 1993: 503–26). Yet the name 'Salome' is not mentioned in the biblical stories of the death of John the Baptist; her dance is without narrative description and is as yet unembellished by the 'seven veils'. The name of the young woman, however, the stepdaughter of Herod Antipas, is found in *Antiquities of the Jews* (Greek 93–4 CE), a work by the Jewish historian Flavius Josephus (born 37 CE in Jerusalem, died after 100 in Rome). His Salome had nothing to do with the dance and never demanded the Baptist's head. It is precisely these kind of narrative 'blanks' and uncertainties in the canonical biblical stories and in ancient historical documents that have been filled in by the imagination, first by religious commentators in the patristic literature and then by the arts (see Inowlocki 2016: 356–67). The figure of Salome became a religious and artistic icon of luxuriant interpretations in the nominally authoritative commentaries of early Christianity and later in Renaissance and baroque art. In the nineteenth century her revival was increasingly effected through narrative media, folk stories and literature; around the fin de siècle, dance, paintings and opera made her an intermedia popular icon. Only Wilde's play, and then Richard Strauss's opera, however, aestheticizes visual desire, producing an aesthetic spectacle of symbolist and biblical metaphors. In the opening scene of Strauss's opera, Salome's visual–physical attraction is contrasted with the fascination of the disembodied 'holy' voice of the prophet, proclaiming God's message from the depths of the cistern.

This chapter proposes the hypothesis that it is from the 'absence' – the 'blank space' within the biblical narratives – that modern, multimedia aesthetics draws its formula of self-reflection as 'purely aesthetic' and a sacralization of the aesthetic. The guiding questions will be: How have narrative gaps and specific narrative strategies opened a virtual space of imagination in the process of aesthetic response? How have they helped to transfer the imaginary of this response into a picture, image and iconic body? And how, if at all, has this synergetic transmission between different media and art forms been 'reflected upon'? Building on Becker-Leckrone's research, the chapter further asks if Salome's fetishized body has silenced her biblical and family story and rendered 'its intertextuality virtually invisible' (1995: 242). The case study at the end of the chapter refers to Strauss's opera as the Salome figure's most powerful and resilient global medium of presentation. The discussion focuses on the 'work on myth' (Blumenberg 1985) done by Claus Guth in his production of *Salome*, performed at the Deutsche Oper in Berlin in January 2016. Guth uses empty spaces without singing and 'gaps' in the libretto to insinuate an interpretation that radically reverses the traditional one and triggers confusion, new 'mental images' and critical thoughts in the viewer (see also Høgasen-Hallesby 2014: 195). By stepping into the blind spots and revitalizing storytelling on stage, Guth's production makes it possible to break with a stereotypically repeated orientalist opera plot and to retrieve Salome's hidden story.

Fragmented storytelling and the pathos formula

The story of Herodias, her daughter, and their part in the Gospel narrative of the death of John the Baptist in Matthew and Mark, ranks among the most influential of 'fascination stories' in the Bible, to use Klaus Heinrich's (1995) term. From the very start, its narrative constitution is based on narrative gaps, parallel narratives and intertextuality, the last particularly with references to the biblical canon and Josephus's version of the story, which supplied the name of 'Salome'. Its longue durée and the transformation of the gospel story into the Salome myth are a consequence partly of the polysemy of the mythical and early patristic narrations, and partly of the affective impact of the figure of Salome as a *pathos formula*. In Aby Warburg's *Mnemosyne Atlas*, Salome plays a significant role as an emotionally charged figure of cultural memory (for further information see Brunotte 2013).

Megan Becker-Leckrone (1995) has analysed 'the intertextual and "fetishist" obsessions with the fin de siècle Salome figure' (Dierkes-Thrun 2011: 15). She asks how 'a narrative has become a woman, how the gospel story has become the Salome myth, has become Salome?' (Becker-Leckrone 1995: 242). 'The dancer got the name Salome for the first time from Isidore of Pelusium, who combined the story of the canonical gospels with the Josephus' report' (Rohde 2000: 267). Certainly, as Barbara Baert (2014) has demonstrated, the influence of the early patristic commentaries on the imputations of Salome's moral corruption and the idea of her 'evil' dance should not be underestimated. In these narratives Salome was already an icon of the perennial interconnection between death, dance and (female) attraction. It was first Wilde, however, and after him Strauss, who gave the 'girl' Salome a voice of her own and let her say that she wants the head of John to satisfy her own desire. Against this background, the question of how the many Salome narratives have become the story of a modern femme fatale and a fetishist body gains even more importance (Baert 2014: 251).

The name 'Salome' is not mentioned in the Bible; her dance is not described until the patristic interpretations; nor is there any biblical reference to the 'seven veils'. It is precisely these kinds of narrative 'blanks' or 'gaps' in the biblical stories, to use a central term of Wolfgang Iser's (1978) theory of aesthetic response, that have been supplied by the imagination – first by religious commentators and then, mainly in the nineteenth century, by literature, opera and the other arts. As Helmut Pfeiffer has emphasized: 'It is precisely out of the biblical "blank" of the nameless narrative function that modern aestheticism acquires its formula of self-reflection that is the "purely aesthetic". And it is the "void" of this "purely aesthetic" which, around 1900, is filled by an epochal imaginary.'[1] At the peak of its fascination, 'Salome's body was decidedly the obsession of late nineteenth-century European, especially French culture' (Hutcheon and Hutcheon 1998). Referring to Friedrich Nietzsche's aesthetic theory, encapsulated in his dictum, 'It is only as an aesthetic phenomenon that existence and the world are eternally justified' (1993: 32), Dierkes-Thrun notes that 'Wilde realized the potency of vivid literary representations of eroticism couched in terms of metaphysical longing, creating imagery that fused sexual lust with a desire for the divine and vice versa' (2011: 25). Thus, what occurred was an aestheticization of the sacred or a sacralization of the aesthetic – a process of reversal in which the figure of Salome became the icon of decadence and in which aestheticism played an essential role. Dierkes-Thrun even goes a step further and claims: 'In Oscar Wilde's *Salome*, it is religion for aesthetics' sake, not the other way round' (ibid.: 30).

Biblical intertextuality

The following brief analysis of the style, intertextual relations and narrative function of the story of Salome/Herodias and the death of John the Baptist in the Bible focuses on the Gospel of Mark, because, compared with its parallel in Mathew, Mark reported the story in an extensive, highly vivid and detailed fashion. In contrast to Matthew, who clearly integrates his much shorter version of the story into his narrative of Jesus activities, Mark, by referring to this past event, even interrupts the Gospel's linear narrative flow, with its focus on Jesus's passion. I use the NRSV (1998), Mk 4.17-29:

> For Herod himself had sent men who arrested John, bound him, and put him in prison on account of Herodias, his brother Philip's wife, because Herod had married her. For John had been telling Herod, 'It is not lawful for you to have your brother's wife'. And Herodias had a grudge against him, and wanted to kill him. But she could not, for Herod feared John, knowing that he was a righteous and holy man, and he protected him. When he heard him, he was greatly perplexed; and yet he liked to listen to him. But an opportunity came when Herod on his birthday gave a banquet for his courtiers and officers and for the leaders of Galilee. When Herodias's daughter came in and danced, she pleased Herod and his guests; and the king said to the girl, 'Ask me for whatever you wish, and I will give it'. And he solemnly swore to her, 'Whatever you ask me, I will give you, even half of my kingdom.' She went out and said to her mother, 'What should I ask for?' She replied, 'The head of John the baptizer'. Immediately she rushed back to the king and requested, 'I want you to give me at once the head of John the Baptist on a platter'. The king was deeply grieved; yet out of regard for his oaths and for the

guests, he did not want to refuse her. Immediately the king sent a soldier of the guard with orders to bring John's head. He went and beheaded him in the prison, brought his head on a platter, and gave it to the girl. Then the girl gave it to her mother. When his disciples heard about it, they came and took his body, and laid it in a tomb.

The story is clear enough: the nameless daughter of Herodias, the 'girl' in the Greek text, is a mere 'instrument' in the hands of her hating and power-hungry mother. She and her dance are still undescribed. It is obvious that for the narrator the dance, which is only mentioned in passing, is not of great importance. He focuses his narrative skills on the description of the wily mother and the misuse of her daughter. Moreover, the biblical commentaries are unanimous that this narrative is not a historical report of John the Baptist's death. The Jewish historian Flavius Josephus, who gave Herod's daughter the Hebrew name 'Salome' (Ant. 18.135-6), omits mentioning her in connection with the beheading of John the Baptist (Ant. 18.116-19). Of particular relevance to the narrative style of the story is its reduced but finely developed language. The narration is economical in the extreme, refrains from taking sides and yet describes the key emotions – Herodias's hatred and Herod's ambivalence. Nevertheless, the story not only relates the events but depicts the whole atmosphere of the scene and, in the second half, even constructs a quasi-dramatic pace hastening to the beheading.

Following the commentators, the detached and impartial narrative perspective resembles the concise style of a Hellenistic novella, a literary genre that uses fragments of folklore poetry (see Wellhausen [1923] 2010: 121; Pesch 1976: 337–44, 339; for more recent research on the Hellenistic novella and the Salome story, see also Baert 2014). These ancient novellas can be described, as Tolbert has observed, as 'literature composed in such a way as to be accessible to a wide spectrum of society, both literate and illiterate' (1978: 70; see also Hägg 2012 and Neginsky 2013: 15). In Mark's introduction, however, the Christological message and function of John's death as the advance notice of Jesus's death are clearly mentioned. Moreover, there are some obvious intertextual relations to the Hebrew Bible: Herodias resembles Queen Jezebel, who tried to kill the prophet Elia, and Herod resembles King Ahab. The display of Herodias's own daughter, however, a Judaic princess, before a male audience, and her misuse for political reasons, are without precedent. As many commentators have pointed out, even in Greco-Roman culture only prostitutes could attend the second part of a banquet, with its various notorious entertainments (Neginsky 2013: 12). Further, the spare and impartial narrative style stresses the cruelty of the events. The action reaches its dramatic peak in the scene where the girl presents the head of the prophet to her mother, like a precious gift on a platter.

In the biblical stories, Herodias's daughter is innocent. She has no independent relationship to, let alone, desire for, the prophet. She is a young virgin and there is nothing about a desire for the Baptist's death. In the long visual tradition of Salome paintings, it was the Italian baroque painter Caravaggio who most intensely expressed her deep sadness in a painting of 1607/10 entitled: *Salome with the Head of John Baptist*.

The first hint of the girl's independent significance in the early story can be seen in Herod's oath: 'Whatsoever you shall ask of me, I will give you, even the half of my kingdom.' Here an intertextual approach, using the biblical concordance, uncovers an interesting layer of meaning. Some commentators have remarked that, by Herod's time, the expression 'you can have even half of my kingdom' had become a 'proverbial saying' without real meaning (Neginsky 2013: 21). Yet it is worth mentioning that the oath is a quotation from the book of Esther (Est. 5.3-6; 7.2) of the Hebrew Bible, referring to the time of the Persian Diaspora.

Admittedly, the constellation of figures in the two stories is very different: on the one hand we have Salome, upon whom a name is first conferred by Josephus, the stepdaughter of the Tetrarch of Galilee and a pawn in the hands of Herodias, her mother; on the other hand, the young Jewess Esther, who resolutely represents and saves her people, in spite of being – and because she is – in the position of the Persian queen. In the first story a Jewish prophet and holy herald of Christ is killed by Herod; in the second, the head of a group conspiring against the Jews is executed by the Persian king. Yet by quoting the Persian king's oath in Mark's gospel story, the narrator creates an intertextual relationship between the two narratives: even though Mark's denomination of Herod as 'king' is not without irony: both 'kings' are willing to give the power over half a kingdom [...] to a young and beautiful Jewish woman. Moreover, both stories are characterized by an Orientalized or, in Herod's case, Hellenized, setting, a banquet or a feast. Last but not least, the beauty of a young Jewess, woman or girl, becomes the decisive turning point of the narration.

Liminal figures and transgression

Taking into account the longue durée of the story up to modernity, these biblical narratives might be interpreted as already foreshadowing the figure of what has become known as the 'beautiful Jewess'. The Orientalization of female Jews even in the nineteenth century often refers to biblical figures. Anna Dorothea Ludewig has emphasized the biblical precedent of the ambivalent figure of the beautiful Jewess:

> Eve, first woman and therefore first Jewish woman, is both the mother of humanity and the mother of sin. [...] The story of Abraham's wife, Sara, taken to the Pharaoh's harem on their journey to Egypt, can be viewed as representative. [...] Although he has already gathered a number of beautiful women in his harem, it is the Jewish woman, a 'stranger', who most captivates him. [...] Also Ester, as many other Jewish women beside her, acts as a bridge, as an intermediary between the Jewish and the non-Jewish world. (Ludewig 2014: 222–3)

Nevertheless, in nineteenth-century literature and opera, the beautiful Jewess was a *liminal figure*, which marked and crossed borders of gender norms, religion and culture (Valman 2007: 2). Whereas Esther is an unambiguous positive example, it was the Jewish heroine Judith whose ambivalent fascination best represents the possible ambivalence within the figure of the beautiful Jewess. In an extremely threatening situation for her people, Judith uses her beauty to seduce and then behead the Assyrian military commander, Holofernes, thus saving her village and her people from the aggressor. Even Judith, as a heroine of her people, could be interpreted within the traditional canon of patriotic and moral conduct. Salome's deed, however, transgresses against the religious core and, at least in Wilde's and Strauss's versions, could no longer be 'saved' by inclusion in a religious universe. Dierkes-Thrun writes: 'In Wilde's hands, the legend of Salome hence becomes a thought experiment of taking the pursuit of beauty to its utmost extreme, following it literally into murder and death, while distorting the moral and religious dimensions into aesthetic surfaces, divesting them of their guiding and regulating functions' (2011: 29).

The depiction of Herodias and Salome as 'archetypical, corrupting women and relatives of Eve', in the words of Rosina Neginsky (2013: 3, 18), started very early. Christian commentators used the Salome story as a cautionary tale for educational purposes and to shape the view of woman in society. They creatively filled in the 'narrative gaps' and unsaid dimension of the biblical stories by producing the vivid picture of the self-assured and evil daughter in league with the wily mother. The central narrative blank within the biblical stories, as Barbara Baert (2014) maintains, was the dance. Focusing their imagination on Salome's dance, early commentators already employed graphic terms to describe and simultaneously demonize it. For John Chrysostom, writing in the fourth century, Herodias and Salome are pure evil: 'The feast is a satanic performance [...] with a dance that, in its shamelessness, overshadows even the performances of prostitutes'[2] (see also Levine 2008). Chrysostom concludes his denunciation thus: 'Where there is dance, there too is the devil' (Rohde 2000: 70). A Christian commentator of the twelfth century places Salome's dance in the pagan, Dionysian sphere and depicts it as an expression of wild bacchantic frenzy: 'she was dancing "shamelessly" and in the way of the maenads and Corybants, jerking her hair through the air and exposing her body bit by bit to the audience' (Ceramaeus n.d.: 70–2). These early descriptions already demonized, paganized and so transformed Salome's dance into a scandalous image. In nineteenth-century Salomania, the pagan, mainly Dionysian subcode of the dance will remain, but now somewhat extended into the 'Oriental'. Because orientalism has been closely connected to visual culture, it was likely that opera, the monumental Gesamtkunstwerk, would become the most successful medium for presenting Salome. Here performance approaches image and the exotic is most strongly highlighted (Høgasen-Hallesby 2014: 187). Especially in Arnold Schönberg's opera *Moses und Aaron* (composed 1930–2; premiered 1952), it is the 'Dance around the Golden Calf' that presents not only the 'almost overwhelming power of the graven image (*pessel–temunah*) [...], but [...] also central "exotic" features of pagan rites and their bodily-sensual character [...]' (Assman n.d.: 19, cf. further Sherwood, this volume).

Transfigurations: The visual and the spiritual

The second part of this chapter focuses on the historical peak of European Salomania, the fin de siècle. During this time, the figure of Salome stepped out of the religious story about John the Baptist. The nineteenth century, a century in which women tried to re-enter the workforce and fought for political rights, 'produced some 2,789 works of art and literature in which Salome was the central figure. This image played a crucial role in creating the myth of women in the period' (Neginsky 2013: 74). During this phase of European art and popular culture Salome became iconic. At the same historical moment, when first literature seemed to assume the lead in her representation, the story was also transfigured (see Largier on Auerbach, in Meyer 2015a: 155–6) into a highly popularized image and, finally, the fetishized and commercialized body of the dancing Salome.

> She is first of all an icon in western visual culture, in the many depictions of her holding or kissing the Baptist's severed head in various positions, as represented either in the vivid pictures of Gustave Moreau or in the refined black and white lines of Audrey Beardsley. [...] Salome has [also] come to demonstrate what western culture anxiously has to control: women, children, bodies, sexuality and the orient. (Høgasen-Hallesby 2014: 179)

In Wilde's play *Salome* (1891), the act of looking, gazing and seeing is fundamental in two ways: as the dominant activity of the main characters, as well as the audience, and as a recurring theme of reflection and desire. Salome's story 'is embedded in our visual imagination so effectively that, in a way, she [...] can be thought of as a sign of the visual as such' (Bucknell 1993: 503–26). The play explores the desire to 'unveil' the body, and it places this desire in a series of visual metaphors and visions that connects the sensual with the aesthetic and the sacred. Wilde's presentation of the Judean princess as desiring Jokanaan's ideal body and as searching for 'spiritual rebirth' (see also Koritz 1994: 62) connects her with the tradition of the Carthaginian priestess Salammbô in Flaubert's eponymous novel, and also with that of Salome's dance in Flaubert's 'Hérodias'. In this highly sensualized story, published in 1877, 'the young dancer mimics the searching, yearning movements of a lost soul for God' (Dierkes-Thrun 2011: 26). In a letter Wilde himself compared his Salome to the virgin priestess and the mystic Santa Teresa of Avila: 'My Salome is a mystic, the sister of Salammbô, a Sainte Thérèse who worships the moon' (quoted in Ellmann 1988: 376). During the second half of the play, however, her yearning becomes purely sensual. After Jokanaan's death, Salome at last kisses the lips of the severed head.

As is not unusual in symbolism, the realm of aestheticized beauty and 'ideal art' abounds in spiritual and mythical references. Moreover, the play 'thematizes a stark contrast between the verbal and the visual' (Wallen 1992: 124). The visual is connected with the ambivalent status of Salome as an 'acting icon': she is the one who is 'looked upon', worshipped and desired, and who desires to see the body of Jokanaan. For her, 'seeing' is a bodily and sensual act. Holding the severed head of John the Baptist in her hands at the end of the play, she exclaims: 'If you had looked at me you would have loved me.' Jokanaan, on the other hand, represents the new (Christian) religion in a very 'puritan' fashion: he refuses to look upon Salome, whom he condemns as 'daughter of Babylon', and covers his eyes at the seductive beauty of her body. In an invisible, disembodied voice, rising out of the cistern, he praises the new religion and desires to hear only the words of his God. The modernist artistic 'work on myth' (Blumenberg 1985) reinvents and retells the biblical story, unearthing and elaborating the myth within its own cultural and historical context. In Wilde's 'remaking of the iconic myth, a story about the death of John the Baptist [is] turned into the story of the dancing girl' (Høgasen-Hallesby 2014). It should be noted, however, that in the gospel stories of Matthew and Mark, the narrative flow is also interrupted as the 'girl' stages her body in dance.

In Western culture the dominance of the visual sense has been connected with the idea of a distancing, powerful gaze. This, often gendered, idea of the 'gaze' (see Mulvey 1975/1999) is considered superior to the other senses, in part because it was defined as being detached from what it observes' (Hutcheon and Hutcheon 1998: 15). When in 1905 Richard Strauss turned Wilde's play into an opera, Salome was given a singing voice, cast as a dramatic soprano, and merged with the figure of the diva. Opera as such is an embodied art form in which the voice cannot be imagined as disembodied. 'Indeed', as Hutcheon and Hutcheon point out, 'opera owes its undeniable affective power to the overdetermination of the verbal, the visual and the aural – not to the aural alone' (Hutcheon and Hutcheon 2000: 206). In Strauss's *Salome*, the body on stage gains even greater importance because, for nearly ten minutes, the singer does not sing at all, but only fills visual space with her dance.

Considering the late-nineteenth-century self-reflective versions of the Salome story, it is possible to develop a more general theory about the relation between narration and imagination, the visible and the invisible, the body and the disembodied voice. All these opposites are connected to the question of how the biblical story, which in itself is already intertextually constituted, can be mediated and figured in modern artworks and how artistic 'work on the myth' has elaborated and developed new facets of sense in retelling and re-enacting myth. This chapter works with the hypothesis that the 'blank spaces' within the biblical narratives, in interplay with an increasingly colourful presentation of Salome and her dance in the authorized patristic commentaries and her mnemonic role as a *pathos formula*, have helped to create her fascination and the flourishing line of reinventions and variations. It is out of these traumatic, unsaid and overdetermined tensions that modern aesthetics draws 'its formula of self-expression as the – often sacralised – "purely aesthetic"' (Pfeiffer 2006: 310).

Aesthetic response theory and mental images

Wolfgang Iser's groundbreaking and influential theory of aesthetic response describes the interactive dynamics between text and reader. It asks how the 'negations' or 'gaps' in a narrative leave a virtual space for the imagination of the reader to produce (new) meaning. In the preface to his book *The Act of Reading* of 1978 (German edition: 1976, *Der Akt des Lesens*), Iser wrote: 'Effects and the responses are properties neither of the text nor of the reader; the text represents a potential effect that is realized in the reading process' (Iser 1978: ix). The act of reading becomes, not unlike the performative speech act in Austin's theory, a creative and transformative process. The reader-driven concretization and fictional actualization of the artwork is described as an 'affective' and 'aesthetic effect' that 'marks a gap in defining qualities of language. [...] Thus, the meaning of a literary text is not a definable entity but, if anything, a dynamic happening' (22). This theory of 'creative blanks' was influenced by Roman Ingarden's theory of literary indeterminacy. It also originated in collaboration and discussion with the philosopher Hans Blumenberg in the debates of the Constance group 'Poetics and Hermeneutics'. The theory of aesthetic response and Iser's later work on *Literary Anthropology* (1993) are closely connected with Blumenberg's considerations on the polysemy of mythical narration, as may be seen in Blumenberg's famous book *Work on Myth* (1985). There he maintains that mythical narrations circulate continuously and are constantly being retold and reinvented in folk traditions, in artworks and even in their academic interpretations. As Ben de Bruyn has observed: 'The importance of Blumenberg's work for Iser's thinking on topics such as montage, metaphor, myth, reality, productivity and modernity cannot be stressed enough' (2012: 47). Iser focuses on the unsaid, invisible, undetermined or only implied meanings in literary narration, which, in the process of reading, trigger our imagination and can sometimes even induce the effect of shock (131). As a kind of productive 'negativity' (225), these 'blanks can function as a dynamic factor to bring forth – at least potentially – infinite possibilities' of remembrance, imagination and actualization. Narrative gaps or 'empty spaces' allow the reader to reconsider their expectations and produce mental images: 'it stimulates communicative [...] activities within us by showing us that something is being withheld and by challenging us to discover what it is with the help of "processes of imagination"' (Iser 1989: 140–1). 'Blanks' are for Iser phenomena of tilting or tipping, in which a sudden shift of perspective occurs (1978: 212).

Since the 1980s, Iser's theory of aesthetic response has been applied to other media such as film (as he himself had already done), artworks, visual culture and opera (see de Bruyn 2012). In his book *An Anthropology of Images*, Hans Belting (2014) demonstrates that Iser's anthropological reflections also apply to the analysis of visual culture. The art historian Christiane Kruse has also begun to develop Iser's theory of 'narrative blanks' into a general theory of media (Kruse 2003: 291).

As pointed out previously in this chapter, there are already narrative gaps in the biblical story. In his book *Intertextuality and the Reading of Midrash*, Daniel Boyarin connects a narratological approach and ideas of narrative gaps to the interpretative retelling and rewriting of the Midrash: 'The gaps are those silences in the text which call for interpretation if the reader is to "make sense" of what happened, to fill out the plot and the characters in a meaningful way' (1990: 41). The Midrash is very different from modern exegesis, but perhaps it can be connected to what we find in patristic literature and to artistic and narrative 'work on myth' in Blumenberg's sense. The striking intertextuality of the Salome corpus in the gospel story, let alone its retelling and reinvention up to modernity, is already a good example of the 'imaginative effect' of its narrative 'blanks'. But the theory of the 'imaginative effect' of narrative 'blanks' can also help understand the transformation and transfiguration of the textual corpus, first into an image and then into a dancing body.

Sensuality and religion

The church fathers' narrative inventions of Salome and her dance were already full of visual, graphic and sexual imaginations. Thus it is not surprising that, at least since 1000 CE, Salome, as a *pathos formula* (Brunotte 2013:), has been an icon of the visual arts and depicted first and foremost as a beautiful woman and a dancing body. The nineteenth century revived the sexualizing and demonizing patristic commentaries and transformed them, producing modern Salomania. The figure of Salome was popularized as the embodiment of the femme fatale and became the icon of the symbolist movement, which sought to attain the 'divine' through art. At the peak of its cultural impact in Europe, Salomania embraced painting, photography and, in addition to the opera, various performances of the 'Dance of the Seven Veils' by female burlesque and barefoot dancers. It was above all the Canadian dancer Maud Allan who embodied Salome in Europe (see Brunotte 2012). Even when Allan, in her *Vision of Salomé*, impersonated the Oriental princess wearing only a daringly scanty costume, she meant to present Salome as an innocent girl fascinated by John the Baptist's religious message. As Amy Koritz notes, quoting Allan's autobiography, Allan tried 'to express the "ecstasy mingled with dread" that signalled [Salome's] impending spiritual awakening' (1996: 67).

Wilde's presentation of the Judean princess as desiring Jokanaan's ideal body, *and* as searching for spirituality, introduces her as an icon of aestheticism. However, even when Salome's yearning for the Baptist's body becomes purely sensual, Wilde has her use variations of the erotic-spiritual language of Salomon's *Song of Songs*. After Jokanaan's death, Salome at last kisses the lips of the severed head. In the novel *À Rebours* (*Against Nature*), published in 1884, in which one of Gustave Moreau's famous pictures of Salome functions as a symbol of decadence, Joris-Karl Huysman humanizes the 'essential modernist crisis of faith [...] and inscribes empathy for the human condition into Moreau's Salome figures as well as into Des Esseintes's character' (Dierkes-Thrun 2011: 40). As in Flaubert's and Huysman's narrations, it was Salome's dance which became central in the multimedia reinventions of Salome. It was also the nineteenth century in which narrative media entered into direct cooperation with the visual arts to retell Salome's story. In this connection it should be emphasized again that the famous 'Dance of the Seven Veils', which even scholars have often projected onto the biblical story, was Wilde's invention. Wilde, however, created a 'dramatic blank' and left the mental imagination of the dance to the reader and the theatre director. In his play there was no specific stage direction as to how the dance should be envisioned. On the other hand, Wilde's French version of the play, published in 1891, was inspired by Gustave Moreau's painting *Salome Dancing before Herod* (1876). Wilde was also inspired by the description of the painting that he encountered as an enthusiastic reader of the fifth chapter of Huysmans's novel. Midway through a description of the picture, the narrator Des Esseintes changes tense, steps out of the narrative past and creates the impression of the 'absolute presence' of Salome's 'apparition': 'She is almost naked! In the heat of the dance her veils have become loosened, the brocaded robes have fallen away, and only the jewels protect her naked body' (Huysmans [1884] 2008: 103–4 quoted in Neginsky 2013: 168).

Pictorial narrativity and the creation of an 'apparition'

As this example demonstrates, in Huysmans's novel there is already a tension between the narration and the visual, the said and the seen, narrative temporality and the 'frozen image' of Salome. This tension becomes even more relevant in Wilde's play, where it functions as a medium to reflect on the relation between Salome and Jokanaan. Wilde's play is

> [...] built around a series of visual metaphors and explores the obsessive desire to gaze upon the body [...], the central tension of the play, between Iokanaan and Salome, revolves around his refusal to look at Salome and his desire to 'listen but to the voice of the Lord God', whereas she demands to see and to touch Iokanaan. The play aligns the field of vision with the body and with sexual desire, in contrast to the verbal field, which is aligned with the immaterial and the suprasensual. (Wallen 1992: 124)

In this context, metaphors and processes of veiling and unveiling, secrecy and truth gain momentum. Here Iser's idea of 'mental image' and Belting's use of this concept in his 'anthropology of images' can be rendered productive. What is important for the analysis is that Iser's aesthetics of narrative 'blanks' is itself full of visual metaphors. Iser even emphasizes 'the picture character of the imagination [*Bildcharakter der Vorstellung*], which emerges in the reader out of the unsaid' (1994: 220). A few lines later he even goes so far as to say that '"[i]maging" depends upon the absence of that which appears in the image' (1978: 137). In fact, though it was Wilde's play that gave Salome's dance the famous name of the *Dance of the Seven Veils*, it 'leaves the dance undescribed' (Hutcheon and Hutcheon 1998: 215). Thus Marjorie Garber rightly argues that '[i]n its non-description, in its indescribability, lies its power, and its availability for cultural inscription and appropriation' (1993: 341).

In modern literary tradition, it was Gustave Flaubert who first filled in this central 'blank' of the biblical story. In his narrative 'Herodias' (1877) he invented a highly sensual, Orientalized description of Salome's dance. Neginsky maintains that this 'description arouses the senses of all spectators present at the banquet [...]' and was also meant to 'overwhelm the reader' (2013: 162). Drawing on iconographic traditions, Flaubert's narrative is a literary example of writing the visual, in which 'the ways of plastic and literary expressions mutually enhance each other' (150, 164). According to James Heffernan, the modern use of *ekphrasis* focuses not on a simple description, but on a 'verbal representation of a visual representation' (1993: 3–4); picturalism 'is the generation in language of effects similar to those created by pictures' (Neginsky 2013: 150; see also Heffernan 1993 and Tooke 2000: 3). To increase the affective intensity of the scene, the chronological narration of events ceases. The 'mode of representing temporal events as action stopped at its climatic moment. [...] It gave rise to the literary topos of *ekphrasis*, in which a poem aspires to the atemporal "eternity" of the stopped-acting [...]' (Steiner 2004: 150). As in Huysmans's famous description of Salome's dance through the mouth of his protagonist Des Esseintes, a transfer of tense from past to present reinforces the impression of 'eternity' and a nearly epiphanic immediacy. This creates the impression of 'frozen time'. Especially, the break in narrative flow produces an instantaneous experience of 'the instant', which takes on the form of a mental image and a 'living picture'. In an article entitled 'The Fetishization of a Textural Corpus', Becker-Leckrone (1995) argues that it is precisely through modern literature's use of theses narrative tools that the story of Salome has been transformed into an icon, body and fetish. 'Des Esseintes' "Salome," she writes, 'is, obviously, the woman rather than the story, a body rather than a text. "She" is the object of his fascination, [...] his fetish' (240).

In sum, this section started with the idea that it is from the 'the unsaid', the 'blanks' within the biblical narratives, that modern aestheticism, in interplay with the imaginative patristic commentaries, draws its formula of self-reflection as the 'purely aesthetic' (Pfeiffer 2006: 310). And it is exactly the epoch of fin de siècle aestheticism that used this biblical episode and its 'blank' female figure to focus its reflection on the sensual and transgressive impact of aesthetic media. It was Wilde who invented the *Dance of the Seven Veils*, but who, at the same time, played with the imaginary power of the 'blanks' by leaving Salome's dance undescribed in his drama. Not without connections to the modern crisis of faith in the way it is represented in Wilde's play and in Huysmans's novel, the figure and the dance of Salome became an icon of symbolism and of decadence (Brunotte 2012). Petra Dierkes-Thrun argues that Wilde's modern Salome embodied a 'transformation of the religious aspect into a tool of seduction – and hence the fusion of the spiritual and the sexual' (2011: 31). The symbolists also believed that art was a '"theurgical activity" [...], a vehicle for bringing the divine on earth through the soul' (Nezhinskaia 2010: 11). The creation of the femme fatale within symbolist art and literature had therefore an ambivalent structure. Majorie Garber also maintains that 'the Salome myth provides a much more equivocal narrative than the essentializing exaltation of "the exotic, feminized Eastern Other"' (Garber 1993: 340).

Strauss's opera, narrative blanks and the fetishizing of a body

It was Richard Strauss's opera of 1905, the first modernist music drama, which completed and fixed the modern transformation of the Salome story in the Orientalized fetish of the dancing femme fatale. The opera filled in the narrative blanks of the *Dance of the Seven Veils*, and by shortening Wilde's text in the libretto, silenced crucial parts of Salome's story. As Strauss confided to his diary in 1942, he wanted to write an Oriental opera and a 'Jewish opera' (Judenoper): 'I've long found fault with Oriental and Jewish operas because they lack an Eastern atmosphere and blazing sun. This lack inspired in me (for my own opera) really exotic harmonies, which shimmered in strange cadences, like shot silk' (Strauss 1949: 224).[3] In her groundbreaking interpretation of 2008, Karla Hoven-Buchholz asks the following question: 'What veiled the unveiling of Salome?' Comparing Strauss's libretto and Oscar Wilde's play, which was used by Strauss in its German translation, she searches for the suppressed history and the untold narratives that were concealed and made invisible behind the dance of the femme fatale. Her conclusion is that Strauss invented not only the Orientalized *Dance of the Seven Veils* in his nearly ten minutes of dance-music, but also that, by cutting out important narrative parts of the play, he himself created narrative blanks which trigger a specific affective imagination in the audience (363–5). Hoven-Buchholz claims that it was these blanks together with Strauss's creation of an Orientalized *Dance of the Seven Veils* that powerfully influenced the cultural imagination of the ancient and modern Orientalized Jewish 'Other' and cast the figure of Salome as the sexualized, murderous femme fatale (see Seshadri 2006 and Brunotte 2015).

In contrast to the opera, Wilde's play does not omit Salome's story from the scene. It is at the same time an example of stylized symbolist language and a reflection upon and parody of it. The author performs and presents the *habitus* of aestheticism. As we have seen, Wilde refuses to focus on the dance. For him Salome is a mystic and even tragic heroine. The opera, by contrast, focuses on the dance and Salome's final monologue addressed to the severed head. As Helmut Pfeiffer has stressed:

> Approximately a quarter of the entire opera of one hundred minutes is filled with the Dance of the Seven Veils [...] and the final monologue. This is a very great difference and shift in comparison with the text of Wilde's play, which was in any case a play to be read. [...] Especially the monologue with the head, which uses Wagnerian lyrical time extension, focuses on the exhibition of a woman whose [...]

Figure 14.1a,b Interpretation of Richard Strauss's opera 'Salome' by Claus Guth, Deutsche Oper Berlin, January 2016. Photo: Monika Ritterhaus, courtesy of the photographer.

body has become a voyeuristic object: '[…] what the audience encounters is less a character singing than a woman, *as* woman, acting out a multiple debasement: scopic, erotic, artistic, linguistic'. (Pfeiffer 2006: 334–5, Kramer in Pfeiffer 1990: 281)

For Hoven-Buchholz, by cutting out important parts of her story, Strauss did even more to intensify the creation of Salome as the body-icon of the femme fatale. Even in recent opera productions, these narrative blanks still have an affective impact on the audience by rendering her story unheard. For example, Strauss omits all narrative information about Salome's tragic and even incestuous position within the Herod-Herodias family. Wilde's play, Hoven-Buchholz emphasizes, informs the reader that Salome knows how and where her father was murdered. Herod's brother, Herodias's former husband, was killed by Herod in exactly the same cistern in which John the Baptist is later imprisoned. Against this backdrop, her interest and 'love' for Jokanaan, his voice and message, acquires a different, a more childlike and spiritual meaning beyond the purely sensual one. Wilde invented a Salome in the image of a tragic heroine, a young girl torn between murderous and unresolved family dynamics, very much like Orestes or Hamlet (2008: 365, 366–70). In Strauss's opera *Elektra*, which was premiered two years after *Salome*, one has the strong impression that Hofmannsthal and Strauss were creating a continuation of Salome's story.

A very recent interpretation of Strauss's *Salome* (premiered January 2016) by Claus Guth, at the Deutsche Oper in Berlin, confirms Hoven-Buchholz's analysis. Guth liberates the opera from all its Oriental and sexualized readings and places Salome again in the thick of the fatal dynamics of family relations, especially the struggle between her mother and Herod. In his interpretation, Salome's behaviour is the result

Figure 14.2 Interpretation of Richard Strauss's opera 'Salome' by Claus Guth, Deutsche Oper. Berlin, January 2016. Photo: Monika Ritterhaus, courtesy of the photographer.

of trauma, abuse and failed communication. The audience must relinquish what generations of opera directors have made them believe about Salome the femme fatale. Guth used silent stretches within the singing and 'gaps' in the libretto for a radically reversed critical interpretation, which triggers new 'mental images' and thoughts in the audience. In particular, Guth's interpretation avails itself of the ten minutes of music normally reserved for the dance to narrate Salome's long history of abuse and suffering at the hands of her stepfather Herod.

He tells these stories by having them performed as in a puppet show by six children who are Salome's doubles. Dressed in the same costume as Salome, they range from a little girl of six to a young girl of approximately eighteen. They all have to 'dance' with Herod, and this dance immediately loses its seductive, 'erotic' meaning. Here the narrative is heard again behind and through the formerly fetishized body. In the retrieval of the suppressed story of a family and the untold narrative of Salome's abuse, the audience can discover even in Strauss's *Salome* a tragic heroine reminiscent of Orestes and Hamlet. Salome suddenly becomes a *pathos formula* not only of violence, perversity and passion, but also of trauma, suffering and the search for spiritual healing.

The Art of Incarnation: Loss and Return of Religion in Houellebecq's *Submission*

Christiane Kruse

Embodiment and pretence

The publication of Michel Houellebecq's novel *Soumission* (*Submission*) in France – as well as in Germany and Italy in translation – sparked a torrent of controversy in Europe with its plotline. In the year 2022, a French coalition government is led by a charismatic Muslim named Muhammad Ben Abbes. Reality eclipsed this provocative fiction only hours after the novel's release on 7 January 2015: Islamic State militants launched their deadly terror attack on the editorial offices of the *Charlie Hebdo* satirical magazine in Paris.

In Houellebecq's novel, Ben Abbes, as the new president of France, pursues humanitarian ideals and a measured, culturally conservative Islamism that permits polygamy and suppresses women's emancipation. He staffs every educational institution in the country with Muslim converts. One of them, Robert Rediger, becomes president of the Sorbonne, now financed by one of the royals of a Gulf state. The protagonist and narrator, François, loses his tenure as a professor of literature. The Islamist government, while appearing tolerant towards the laity and people of other faiths, still pursues a restructuring of society according to Islamic moral values. This triggers a fictitious internal conflict that nevertheless compels the reader to contemplate the real consequences of the Enlightenment, the history of the Western world, and the loss of metaphysics and humanist ideals.

Submission can be categorized as a classic *Entwicklungsroman*, or coming-of-age novel. Since his youth, François has stumbled from one crisis to another in a futile search for cultural identity, the central theme of the book. For his sole subject of literary research, he has chosen the writer Joris-Karl Huysmans, whose works of the Decadent movement provide a historical backdrop to address the concept that the loss of metaphysics, represented by Christendom, is to blame for the decline of the Western world in modern times.

In a conversation towards the end of the novel, not long after the Sorbonne has changed hands, Robert Rediger, the new head of the institution, tries to persuade François to resume teaching as a Muslim convert. He asserts atheism has no solid basis in the West. Strictly speaking, Rediger says, there are very few 'true atheists'; rather, there are those who, like Dostoyevsky's Kirilov, pass themselves off as atheists and humanists and '[...] reject God because they wanted to put man in his place. They were humanists, with lofty ideas about human liberty, human dignity' (Houellebecq 2015: 209). Considering the unfathomable creation and beauty of the universe, Rediger concludes there is no reason to doubt the existence of God. Not a single scientist from Newton to Einstein could have been an atheist, he goes on, because 'the universe obviously bears the hallmarks of intelligent design, that it's clearly the manifestation of some gigantic mind'. Sooner or later, these assertions would be reintroduced, since the intellectual debate of the twentieth century could be summed up as a battle between communism – that is, 'hard humanism – and liberal democracy, the soft version'. Thus 'the return of religion' should be inevitable (Houellebecq 2015: 212). And yet, in the novel, no return to Christendom is in the offing because it has done little more in the past century than deal with its own downfall and that of its once-rich culture. *Submission*'s premise is that the era of the Decadent Movement in the late nineteenth century comes to an end in the twenty-first and thus that only a conversion to Islam can deliver redemption. Upon reading Rediger's book, *Ten Questions Concerning Islam*, which is full of photographs of Islamic art, François quickly finds convincing reasons to convert, which, until then, had been missing for him. François then becomes a Muslim, but whether France can forge a new cultural identity in moderate Islam is a question left open.

In the course of their conversation, the narrator comes to the realization that he can't really justify his own atheism. To claim there is no God would be 'pretentious', which Rediger affirms with conviction. 'That's the word. At the end of the day, there's something incredibly proud and arrogant about atheist humanism. Even the Christian idea of incarnation is laughably pretentious. God turned Himself into a man [...]' (Houellebecq 2015: 211). This is the theme explored in my chapter. In the following pages, I will summarize the art theory and practice of depicting skin in painting to explain how the dystopia of *Submission* could arise and to highlight the role of art in this process.

Embodiment and the depiction of flesh in painting

During Italy's early humanism period around 1400, *incarnazione* became a strong metaphor in painting (Kruse 2003: 175-224). Cennino Cennini introduced the central chapter of his *Il Libro dell'arte* with 'the method and system for working on the wall, that is, in fresco; and painting and doing the flesh [*incarnare*] for a youthful face' (Cennini 2015: 100). Cennini described a painting technique he called incarnation (*incarnazione*) as a successor to hand positions required for painting a human face on a wall in the fresco technique (Figure 15.1).

In the end, the reader – in those days, the student of painting – would be capable of applying this method. The English term incarnate for the painting of flesh in art arose from Cennini's *incarnazione* technique. 'And do a sensible amount of it,' he wrote, 'because you have to complete one head of a young female or male saint like

Figure 15.1 Giotto: *Adoration of the Magi*, detail: head of the Virgin Mary, fresco, 1304–6, Padova, Scrovegni Chapel. Giuseppe Basile (ed.), *Gli affreschi della Capella degli Scrovegni a Padova*, Milan: Skira, 2002, p. 185.

Our Most Divine Lady in one day' (Cennini 2015: 101). He then explained how to mix pigments and how to sketch. In conclusion, he wrote: 'And go sensitively over the whole face and the hands where there has to be flesh colour [*dove ha a essere incarnazione*] in the same way' (Cennini 2015: 101). Cennini referred to the process of painting skin as *incarnazione*, which requires three different jars of pale pink pigment. The purpose of the colour gradation is the three-dimensional appearance of the human face, to which Cennini applied the term relief (*rilievo*). Cennini wanted to use the human face as an example to explain how to treat the surface of a picture with a specific technique of colour application to render a human face on a wall surface.

Cennini assigned a central concept of theology to his art theory. It is commonly conceived that the history of the dogma of embodiment started in the Prologus of the Gospel according to St. John (1.14), where it is stated 'that the logos (Christ) became flesh'. Presumably, it was Irenaeus, the Greek Catholic theologian, who first coined this Theologoumenon into a single noun: *sarkosis* (flesh-becoming), declaring that salvation in the sense of participation in divine immortality is only possible through the incarnation of God (Michel 1923: 1446–85; Lanczkowski 1982: 368–82). The new terminology quickly gained importance in the liturgy of the celebration of the Eucharist and was used in the formulation of faith ever since the Council of Nicaea. In the same vein, the Roman Catholic Church adopted the term *incarnatio* und *incarnari* (become flesh) through the translation of Irenaeus's commentary in the Eucharist liturgy.

The incarnation of the Word of God in the Gospel According to St. John designates the humanization of God in the person of Jesus. According to classical Christian theology, what had been the Word of God in the Old Testament became flesh and blood in the New Testament, namely Christ. The 'verb-ization' of *incarnari* designates incarnation as a process of transformation – that of words into flesh – which also signifies a change in substance with the material difference between word and flesh. Incarnation also means the invisible presence of God made visible through the person of Jesus. Theologians throughout time have agreed that incarnation is a mystery, something supernatural that no human mind can truly comprehend, hence the incarnation of God in the form of Christ as one of the great foundations of Christian teachings.

Incarnazione as a medial process

The synthesis revealed in the above-mentioned theological contexts, formulated from *incarnazione* as a meta-pictorial metaphor, is one of the building blocks of Western art. Cennini used the term in multiple meanings as a way of redefining the process of painting icons on a wall. The first part of the medial process described in the procedure of fresco painting is the transfer of liquid, amorphous colour substance in solid form from icons of significance that are only readable once they are fixed to a surface. This ushered in the successive emergence of icons on walls that were once blank. The artistic creation (*creatio*) complements the divine in that it recreates what God was said to have set in motion. This is why *Il Libro dell'arte* begins with the creation story of Genesis. We can also speak of an epiphany of iconic signs, which illuminates their intended analogy to the incarnation of logos and their emergence in the world.

The process of drawing Cennini described as a painting technique could be learned because it's an *arte* – a craft – that anyone could undertake with enough practice and skill. Cennini interpreted *incarnazione* as a modern painting technique that joins the traditional understanding of theological incarnation as one of the great mysteries of Christian faith to a concept of art. In this sense, Cennini's meaning of *incarnazione* is personification; that is, the coming-into-being of a bodily image on a surface that has the appearance of a natural human figure. He referred to the illusion of three-dimensionality adopted by the viewer as *rilievo* (relief). Painting, he wrote, was *imitatio naturae* (imitation of nature, or *mimesis* in Greek), which, as he repeatedly explained, had been practised in painting since Giotto. Cennini designates *incarnazione*, or personification in the sense of the likeness of a human body in an image, as *ritrarre del naturale* (to take out of nature). Because the painting technique lends the images in icons a similarity relation to the living things and objects they depict, they have a mimetic, illusionistic quality. The significance of *incarnazione*, therefore, lies in the iconicity of the pictorial representation. That is what differentiates them from the non-representational characters theologians use to convey the mystery of faith; they bear no apparent resemblance to what they depict.

By the beginning of the fifteenth century, the mimetic–illusionistic image concept whose technique Cennini spelt out in his treatise permeated all European painting. Numerous Renaissance painters displayed embodiment in their work

(Kruse 2003: 225–68), among them the legendary Lukas, the first Christian painter, who produced – that is, embodied – a picture of the Madonna (Figure 15.2). In the following pages I will outline the further development of the theory and practice of *incarnazione*, along with the ensuing expulsion of Christian theology from matters of art in the modern period.

In the mid-sixteenth century, Giorgio Vasari wrote this description of Leonardo da Vinci's Mona Lisa: 'The mouth with its opening, and with its ends united by the red of the lips to the flesh tints of the face [*l'incarnazione del viso*], appeared, indeed, to be not colours but flesh' (Vasari 1903, 35; Bohde 2007: 56). The theology-tinged term is not used in the context of a religious painting, but in a description of the iconic image of Lisa del Giacondo, a Florentine entrepreneur whose portrait Vasari probably never saw with his own eyes. *L'incarnazione del viso* characterizes the life-like sheen of the painting materials that have the effect of human flesh. Vasari's artist biographies

Figure 15.2 Raphael (workshop): *Saint Luke painting the Madonna and Child*, oil on wood, Rome, Academy of Saint Luke. Andreas Henning (ed.), *Die Sixtinische Madonna. Raffaels Kultbild wird 500*, Munich, London and New York: Prestel, 2012, p. 167.

mention this term only eleven more times. In the seventeenth century, Gian Pietro Bellori refers to the unique nature of the painting as *incarnazione*. In this sense, Caravaggio freed paints from their effects of make-up and vanity and returned their 'blood and flesh' tones (*il sangue, e l'incarnazione*) for which the vitality and genuine nature in figural depiction is intended (Koos 2007: 66). Art theory of the early modern period thus combined incarnation theology, painting techniques and materials, vitality and the creation of works in a new constellation that metaphorically redefined art.

Flesh and the soul

French art theory of the seventeenth century marked the first break in the history of embodiment in art. Allusion to theological dogma was avoided; in the painting of flesh, the emphasis was on *carnation* and *chair* (flesh), such as in the work of Roger de Piles (Fend 2007: 87-8). The *Dictionnaire de l'Académie française* of 1694 defines incarnation exclusively as the theological embodiment of Jesus, while *incarnat*, according to Cennini, refers to any colour that resembles human skin: 'A type of the colour red that is similar to living flesh' (*Espèce de couleur rouge, qui ressemble à celle de la chair vivre*) (Fend 2007: 100, note 1). There's a reason for this differentiation: the painting of flesh and the colour of flesh were now considered modern among art scholars who debated the supremacy of the antiquities over the modernism in the *Querelle des Anciens et des Modernes*. Roger de Piles considered Rubens the painter who was masterful at seducing and deceiving the viewer: the more convincing the visual deception, the greater the artist (Fend 2007: 89). This amounted to a sharp demarcation between reality and image, between real and iconic presence – in which art comprised a pretence of reality.

Now the focus turned to the emotions whose intimations are visible in the skin. In the early seventeenth century, the discovery of the principle of blood circulation spurred painters' interest in medical research that would explain the correlation between physiology and emotions. In his observation of Rubens's *Andromeda*, Roger de Piles noted the presence of fear when blood has appeared to drain away from the extremities, turning the skin pale. Rubens adopted a depiction of skin that would render the passions of the soul visible. Complexion became a metaphor for the 'soul of painting' because 'the soul is the final consummation of the living, and that which gives one life' (*L'âme de la peinture est le coloris. L'âme est la dernière perfection du vivant, & ce qui lui donne la vie*) (De Piles 1677: 138). This signalled a defeat of the argument against proponents of *dessin* (drawing) and the antiquities. On the other hand stood the notion that human beings possess something divine, the eternal soul – thus the advent of depicting flesh in painting. The basic issue was – as with Cennini – deriving a painting technique for iconic presence. A metaphysical concept of the art of painting nevertheless grew out of a purely physical-technical concept of depicting flesh in pictures. Through the use of colour, painting, if only in appearance, rendered the invisible visible – namely, the soul that animates the flesh. As de Piles comments on Rubens's *Drunk Silenus*, the appearance of the living compels the viewer to easily imagine they could feel the warmth of blood if they put out their hand (*qu'on s'imagine facilement que si l'on y portait la main on sentirait la chaleur du sang*) (De Piles 1677: 89). In this sense, the art of painting became an intermediary between physiology and metaphysics.

Around the mid-sixteenth century, Counter-Reformation theologians decried the portrayal of naked flesh in painting because of its potential to arouse lust in anyone who viewed it (Hecht 2012: 336–43). Despite the movement's strict morals, a theory of art promoting the depiction of flesh in paintings helped to legitimize it during the seventeenth century.

Diderot and the 'Nervous Canvas'

In the eighteenth century, interest in art theory shifted to the sensitive subject of skin. In the *Encyclopédie* by Jean le Rond d'Alembert and Denis Diderot, physicians such as Henri Fouquet referred to *sensibilité* in his definition of skin as a sensitive organ, a nervous canvas (*toile nerveuse*) (Fend 2007: 93; Benthien 2002: 120–1). In his *Notes on Painting*, Diderot defended his 'truth of nature' against the Academy's scholarly 'study of the écorché' whose 'gestures, postures, and figures are false, forced, ridiculous, and cold' (Diderot 1995: 194). Instead of a pilgrimage to the Louvre, artists were instructed to observe everyday life in narrow streets and alleys to 'get the right ideas' about what to paint. As a result, study at the Academy patterned after Diderot had another concept. 'Children, adults, mature men, old men, subjects of all ages, of both sexes, [should be] drawn from all walks of life. [...] After the drawing sessions a trained anatomist would explain the écorché to my student, with constant references to the living, animated nude body' (Diderot 1995: 196). Then comes the paint itself: 'Someone with a vivid sense of colour fixes his eyes on the canvas; his mouth hangs open, he paints; his palette is the very image of chaos. It's into this chaos that he dips his brush, pulling from it the stuff of creation [...]' (Diderot 1995: 197).

A report followed to list everything the painter had captured: birds, flowers, trees and animals. Finally, 'he sits down again, and you see him give birth to flesh [...]' (Diderot 1995: 197). That is Diderot's own creation story. A godlike genius was at work, incarnated, as well as a bold character allowed to display his every mood. And the most difficult for him to grapple with was flesh:

> It's an interaction of red and blue which is all but imperceptible; it's blood, life, the very despair of the colorist. He who developed a feeling for the flesh has taken a great step forward; the rest is nothing in comparison. Thousands of painters have died without acquiring a feeling for flesh, and there will be thousands more who'll die without acquiring it. (Diderot 1995: 199)

The range of emotions unleashed despair among the colourists: as the models posed during sittings, their rush of different thoughts brought about changing feelings that manifested in their skin tone:

> Because I picture Grimm or my Sophie, and my heart beats fast, tenderness and serenity becoming visible on my features; joy is released through my every pore, my heart dilates, my small sanguinary reservoirs are set vibrating and the barely perceptible color of the fluid thus activated augments the bloom and life of my

flesh. [...] what a torment for them, then, is the human visage, this canvas that becomes excited, animated, flushed, or pale, that expands or contracts in tandem with the infinite multitude of alternatives sustained by this light, fleet expiration we call the soul? (Diderot 1995: 201)

The importance of theology waned as the Enlightenment took the science of physiology to embodiment. The soul materialized in a double sense – both physiologically and in painting.

Flesh without soul

In the first half of the eighteenth century, the French royalty's renunciation of religious painting, which resulted from the desacralization and demystification of King Louis XV's absolute monarchy, had a fundamental impact on French art criticism. The Catholic Church's crackdown on Jansenist theology had resulted in the spread of Jansenism across all levels of society, while the Jesuit order had been banned by royal edict in 1764. These two developments brought about a collapse of the alliance between the Church and the crown and are seen as the causes of the waning significance of the Catholic religion as well as the ungodliness of the Enlightenment (Schieder 1997). From then on, there was a decline in art commissions with religious content, not least because of a lack of funds in religious institutions. Religion-themed paintings found favour predominantly among private collectors, if at all, because of their artistic value. When the Marquis de Véri ordered a pendant as a companion piece to *The Adoration of the Kings*, a painting by Fragonard, it was '[to prove] his genius with a peculiar contrast, an exuberant, passionate painting known as *Le Verrou*' (Schieder 1997: 201). *The Lock*, which depicts a lover trapping his paramour in a bedroom, as well as *The Adoration of the Kings*, corresponded to the advanced assessment of art that followed the 'downfall of the sacred genre hierarchies' called for by the French Art Academy director, Jean-François de Troy, who said a genre painting should hang next to a history-themed painting (Schieder 1997: 201–3). Jean-François Marmontel, in his *Memoires*, noted a secularized approach to religious painting regarding the work of François Boucher (Figure 15.3): 'He did not see the Graces in a good place; he painted Venuses and the Madonna like the nymphs of the coulisses; and both his language and his pictures bore the stamp of his models' manners and the tone of his studio' (Schieder 2006: 61).

Diderot complained about Boucher's portrayal of the Virgin Mary, who, like the prostitutes and angels in his paintings, resembled indecent satyrs. The painting motifs that provoked offence in the Counter-Reformation movement were adored by Salon visitors and detested by the clergy, especially renderings of Maria Magdalena, with their voluptuous curves and abundant display of flesh.

The Madonna with make-up

The portrayal of skin played a significant role in painting and was a prominent artistic criterion (Koos 2014: 195–214). Diderot found fault with Boucher's embodiment of

Figure 15.3 François Boucher: *Rest on the Flight to Egypt*, 1737, oil on canvas, St. Petersburg, The Hermitage Museum. Alastair Laing (ed.), *François Boucher 1703–70*, Paris: Réunion des Musées Nationaux, 1986, p. 279. cat. no. 68.

make-up, which the artist painted both on the faces and on the derrières of his nude models, and recommended the observation of nature as a remedy (Démoris 2006: 201–2). If the painter were to follow his fantasies nonetheless, that would be *faux* (false) and *manière* (manner). As to the arousal of sexual desires inspired by paintings of unclothed women, art critics sometimes adopted the moral stance of the clergy as though it were their own. Given the naked feet, hips, breasts and derrières depicted in Carle van Loo's *Bathers*, Diderot commented in the Salon of 1759 that people would sooner be drawn to their own vices than to the painter's talent. Étienne La Font de Saint-Yenne, the founder of the publication on art critique, similarly remarked that paintings should touch the soul and not the senses (Démoris 2006: 203). For critics, art during the reign of Louis XIV showed the scale – with Boucher's work the pinnacle – of the modern period's decadence, in which the extensive use of pale pink (*rosé*) for the colour of (white) skin demonstrated the main symptom of the period's demise (Figure 15.3): 'That is now the general complexion of almost everything we produce in literature and in painting: everything is rose-coloured and lasts no longer than the rose' (Démoris 2006: 203). Make-up became a synonym for the court with its wealthy upstarts, especially for the king's mistresses. In 1759, before the Salon's publication of the painting *Madonna and Child with the Young St. John the Baptist*, which Madame de Pompadour had commissioned from Boucher, an anonymous art critic made this comment:

[...] the demeanour of the Madonna is neither modest nor decent, but coy and sensual. I wonder what is the difference between this figure and dancers; with the exception of make-up, which is not applied in a hideously thick layer on her face, I see no difference at all; and yet, the rest of the painting is not spared of this colour. (Wine 2002: 25)

Whoever read this probably knew that Madame de Pompadour was an amateur singer and dancer prior to her rise to the aristocracy, and thus took a closer look at the picture. The art criticism of the Enlightenment around 1750 was considerably distanced from the once religiously motivated, theologically legitimated embodiment paintings.

Banishing the soul

Following the Enlightenment, the technique of depicting skin and flesh in painting was based on the latest discoveries in the field of medicine. Flesh was now understood to be a tissue composed of muscle, fat, lymphatic and blood vessels, skin and the epidermis. As modern histology heralded the beginning of tissue differentiation, artists expanded their knowledge of the skin and underlying flesh with treatises such as *The Anatomy of the External Forms of the Human Body* (*Anatomie des formes extérieures du corps humain*) (Paris 1829). The publication provided artists with a deeper understanding of the skin as a membrane between outer appearance and internal physiology.

At the same time, the influence of positivism, with its scientific regard of the human body, advanced the concept of portraying skin in paintings in accordance with French art theory and practice in the nineteenth century. As such, what transpired was not merely the expulsion of incarnation theology from the depiction of flesh in painting, for which positivism and its founder Auguste Comte had paved the way. In his earlier work, *The Course in Positive Philosophy* (1830–42), Comte formulated his 'law of three stages' based on the intellectual and social development of the individual and of humanity according to laws and processes spanning three stages: the theological or fictitious stage of childhood, the metaphysical or abstract stage of youth, and the scientific or positive stage of adulthood (Kruse 2008: 28–39; Lepenies 2010). Together they comprise the path of the human spirit to its perfection.

The first theological or fictitious stage was marked by an inquiry into the nature of existence, whereby humankind created otherworldly deities in hopes of attaining a certainty of faith not found on earth. Next, in the metaphysical or abstract stage, humankind tried to make sense of the world without drawing on otherworldly entities. But still present was the question: 'Why are we here?' Only when this question is relinquished [...] can humanity finally be explored to the fullest – the positive nature functional relationships – without looking for ultimate causes (Lepenies 2010: 22).

By combining empirical observation with logical thinking, humanity is able to infer the constancy of relationships among phenomena according to natural laws. Going by this evolutionary history of humanity, Comte followed a ranking of the sciences, which he formulated in his *Encyclopedic Law*. This brought the natural sciences to a sequence according to their increasing complexity: mathematics, astronomy, physics, chemistry, biology and finally sociology as a science of the highest complexity.

In Comte's perception, theology was incompatible with progress, while metaphysics was incapable of contributing to societal stabilization. Instead, he asserted, positivism could accommodate both progress and order. Wolf Lepenies considered 1844, when Clotilde de Vaux, Comte's 'great, albeit unfulfilled love' died, a turning point in the philosopher's thinking: 'In Positivism, feelings now have their place; art assumed an equal role alongside science, and the positivist movement became a religion with strict dogmas, precise rituals and a strong drive for conversion, which the religion's founder hopes to impart to his disciples' (Lepenies 2010: 23–4). From 1851 on, positivism became a 'religion of humanity' a 'religion without God, in which humanity took the place of a supreme being'. According to Comte, 'While the Protestants and Deists always attacked religion in the name of God, we, on the contrary, must ultimately abolish God in the name of religion' (Lepenies 2010: 25). This brings to mind a famous quotation supposedly by the pathologist Rudolf Virchow: 'I have dissected thousands of corpses, but nowhere have I have found a soul.'

The depiction of skin in painting as social criticism according to Zola

Émile Zola's literature and art criticism, which is categorized under the canon of naturalism, associated the depiction of skin and flesh in painting with the sociopolitical and scientific discourses of positivism. Matthias Krüger explains how Zola's anti-aristocratic, anti-bourgeois stance was reflected in the embodiment painting of his time and attests to his 'basic anti-metaphysical premise' that corresponds to the positivist world view of Auguste Comte (Krüger 2007: 175). In Zola's art critique, the smooth, silky skin of ladies of the aristocracy is mirrored in the smooth surfaces of the pictures, which he scorned as a symbol of a decadent academic Salon painting. Parisian society was in fact divided over the choice of paintbrush with which to portray it. Instead of a fine badger hairbrush (*blaireau*) that lent a glossy, powder puff-like surface to anaemic-looking ladies' portraits in the style of Alexandre Cabanel, Zola asked painters to use the rough bristle brush (*brosse*), which leaves traces in the colour substance and emphasizes the painting materials to achieve 'a brutal tableau, treated with an ingenious harshness' (*un tableau brutal, traité avec les rudesses du genie*) that reveals 'the flesh and blood of the painter' (*la chair et le sang du peintres*) (Zola 1959: 173 and 97).

By contrast, the painting style of the Salon painter, criticized as sleekly anaemic, reduced a subject to a 'pomaded and putrid carcass' (*cadavres pommadé et fleuri*). Cabanel's famous painting *La Naissance de Vénus* (Figure 15.4) is for Zola '*une lorette*' (a floozy), but not one of flesh and bones – that would be indecent – rather of a sort of pinkish-white marzipan' (Zola 1959: 111). Art critics, among them Joris-Karl Huysmans, came up with absurd metaphors to vilify academic painting: 'take Venus, just a badly blown-up *baudruche* [a type of rubber balloon sold at fairgrounds] from head to toe. No muscles, no nerves, no blood' (*Prenez la Vénus de la tête aux pieds, c'est une baudruche mal gonflée. Ni muscles, ni nerfs, ni sang*) (Huysmans 1969: 19).

The Art of Incarnation 271

Figure 15.4 Alexandre Cabanel: *The Birth of Venus*, 1863, oil on canvas, Paris, Musée d'Orsay. Michel Laclotte (ed.), *La peinture à Orsay*, Paris: Edition Scala, 1986, p. 25.

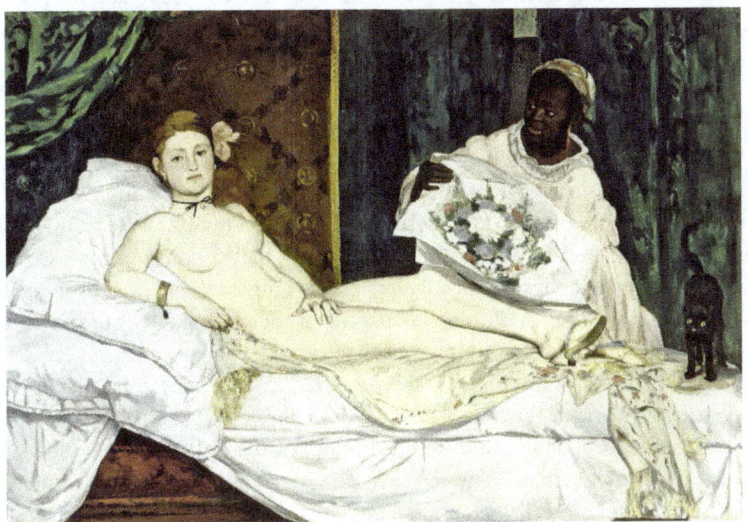

Figure 15.5 Edouard Manet: *Olympia*, 1863, oil on canvas, Paris, Musée d'Orsay. Françoise Cachin (ed.), *Manet 1832–63*, Paris: Réunion des Musées Nationaux, 1883, p. 177.

As Zola explained in the example of Manet's *Olympia*, which caused a scandal in his Salon of 1865 (Figure 15.5), the portrayal of skin in painting was in demand. For a true depiction of life, literati and artists alike had to 'penetrate the flesh' (*pénétrer dans les chairs*), because 'the view from the operating theatre is revolting for anyone who has no love for the austere truth' (*la vue d'une sale amphithéâtre est au contraire écœurants pour ceux qui n'ont pas l'amour austère de la vérité*) (Zola 1979a: 326). The painter had roughened the originally smooth surface of the picture with a bristle brush so the strokes were visible and the skin attained a consistently grooved appearance. For Zola, the truth resided not in the brain, but in the flesh. In his novel, *Thérèse Raquin*, he explored a 'curious case of physiology' the way a surgeon would dismember living human beings.

Zola pursues the subjects of his research, like Manet, with 'brutal and ingenious coarseness'. They are 'supremely controlled by their nerves and blood' (*souverainements dominés par leurs nerfs et leur sang*), 'devoid of free will' (*dépourvus de libre arbitre*); they 'are human brutes, nothing more' (*sont des brutes humains, rien de plus*) (Zola 1979: 24). They are subject to 'dull passions, instinctive urges, and the confusion of the brain as a result of a mental breakdown' (*le travail sourd de passions, les poussées de l'instinct, les détraquements cérébraux survenus à la suite d'une crise nerveuse*) (Zola 1979: 24). Zola's characters who commit murder out of lovers' passion have no 'higher existence […] there is no presence of a soul whatsoever: […] I wanted it that way' (Zola 1979: 24). Whoever wants to discover the 'mechanism of life' (*mécanisme de la vie*) should not be beguiled with the superficiality of beautiful skin, but rather embrace the crude facts of human nature with scientific ethos. Part of the physical constitution of a human being is a 'temperament' (*tempérament*), governed by blood and nerves, which is responsible for one's moral thinking and behaviour.

The loss and revival of religion

This brings us back to the opening premise of Michel Houellebecq's novel, *Submission*, which presents the loss of metaphysics as the loss of Christianity. The character François is researching Joris-Karl Huysmans, who, like Émile Zola, Huysmans's older contemporary, adhered to positivism, a philosophy that promised progress through science by pitting metaphysical speculation against empirical, logical reasoning. Émile Littré, a follower of August Comte, predicted that the physiology of the brain would ultimately subjugate a metaphysical world view and thus vanquish every religion. Understanding the workings of the brain meant reducing theology and metaphysics to their physiological principles. According to Zola's physiological art theory, an artwork is not an expression of the mind, but a product of the body: 'like all things, art is a product of human beings, a human secretion; our bodies sweat the beauty of our works' (*Comme tout chose, l'art est un produit humain, une sécrétion humaine; c'est notre corps qui sue la beauté de nos œuvres*) (Zola 1959: 83). Hence his reaction to Manet's Olympia: 'I affirm that this canvas is truly the flesh and blood of the painter and that he will never produce such a work again' (*Je prétends que cette toile est véritablement la chair et le sang du peintre, et que jamais il ne la référa*) (Zola 1959: 97).

But the human spirit cannot be expelled from matters of art that easily. On the contrary, art has been raised to the level of a god that demands everything from its disciples. In Zola's novel *The Masterpiece* (*L'Œuvre*), the painter, Claude, consumes his artwork, unable to bring it to completion. He grows insane and hangs himself in front of the painting for which his wife had posed as a model for months of agonizing sittings, observing '[…] how he made her legs the gilded columns of a temple and her body a blaze of red and yellow, a star, magnificent, unearthly. Nudity thus enshrined and set in precious stones, demanding to be worshipped, was more than Christine could tolerate' (Zola 1993: 342). The painting that Claude produced in the spirit of modernism leaves him in a state of social isolation and poverty. But art is still his only true religion. He sacrifices his son, his wife and himself to godly art in the devout belief that his works will not only outlive him; they will achieve eternity.

Back to François, Houellebecq's protagonist, and Huysmans, his real-life research subject, whose body of work was also influenced by the naturalism of his era. *Against Nature* (*A Rebours*), Huysmans's novel published in 1884 and a theme of *Submission*, was supposed to be a naturalistic work styled after Zola. Today it's considered the 'Bible of Decadence'. Huysmans's main character, Jean Floressas Des Esseintes, is a neurotic aristocrat who flees from reality into rural exile, where he creates an artificial, mystical world filled with intoxicating sensory stimulation that drives him to the edge of mental derangement. In the end, he believes only faith in the kingdom of God will redeem him. The book concludes with a short prayer: 'O Lord, pity the Christian who doubts, the sceptic who would believe, the convict of life embarking alone in the night, under a sky no longer illumined by the consoling beacons of ancient faith' (Huysmans 2008: 181). The hereafter becomes his salvation from a godless reality.

Submission as defence against decadence

In Houellebecq's novel, François traces Huysmans's path through the Decadence movement and his conversion to Catholicism. He enters the monastery where Huysmans had looked for meaning in his life but couldn't find it. François then makes his way to Rocamadour, one of the most important places of Christian pilgrimage in France. In the chapel of Notre-Dame, he thinks 'again of Huysmans, of the sufferings and doubts of his conversion, and of his desperate desire to be part of a religion' (Houellebecq 2015, 138–9). In Rocamadour, he gazes at the cult statue of the Black Madonna:

> It was something mysterious, priestly and royal that surpassed Péguy's understanding, to say nothing of Huysmans. [...] She had sovereignty, she had power, but little by little, I felt myself losing touch, I felt her moving away from me in space and across the centuries while I sat there in my pew, shrivelled and puny. After half an hour, I got up, fully deserted by the Spirit, reduced to my damaged, perishable body, and sadly descended the stairs that led to the car park. (Houellebecq 2015: 139)

In *Submission*, François, as an intellectual, appears almost victimized by the Enlightenment in a secularized, Western world, where ritual objects that once bore religious significance were now merely valued for their aesthetics. His search for God is fruitless, even in the church, which now stands as a mere remnant of a fallen culture – at least to those who came of age with the teachings of the Enlightenment.

The moderate Islam now embraced by the members of the Sorbonne in the novel fills them with the spirit of a new godliness that holds a realm of physical pleasure in store. Unwilling to relinquish their Western-liberal mindset, they devote themselves to overindulgence of Middle Eastern delicacies, exquisite French wine and – following Islamic tradition – polygamy. *Submission* serves up a swan song of Western civilization as an elegy and laments what remains of its sensual beauty, which François has pursued in the course of his literary research and now exists only in his memory. His very identity is steeped in his knowledge of civilization as far back as the Middle Ages. The melancholy engulfing François over this sense of loss corresponds with his lack of personal relationships and the emptiness of sexual escapades which the author describes in pornographic terms. Nadia, a Muslim, escort and Diderot student, 'was sexually conscientious'. Instead of the intimacy of human touch, François experiences merely an array of orifices.

As science advances further into the cosmos to discover the origins of the universe, it provides proof of God without searching for it. In a conversation with François, Robert Rediger, the president of the Sorbonne in Houellebecq's novel, justifies a return to religion in the twentieth century by quoting Einstein, who said, 'God doesn't play dice.' Humanism, communism, fascism and liberalism are all self-convinced expressions of atheism, he says, that have left European nations 'bodies without souls'. Rediger concludes: 'That Europe, which was the summit of human civilization, committed suicide in a matter of decades' (Houellebecq 2015: 214). Only a few characters in *Submission* advance this root cause analysis and see it reflected in globalization and the country's national and colonial legacies, as well as in the political apathy of a population that does not feel represented by its leaders but perceives only the abstract power machinations of political parties. France's leadership by an Islamic government is presented as an almost logical consequence and collateral damage of this development, because the author continually introduces cunning new arguments to suggest how this could happen.

In conclusion, Houellebecq delivers a pronouncement whose words are uttered by the president of the university. Robert Rediger has fulfilled his dream to inhabit the house where Dominique Aury wrote *Story of O*, which he finds a 'fascinating book' because of its grandiose yet simple premise: 'that the summit of human happiness resides in the most absolute submission. [...] For me there's a connection between woman's submission to man, as it's described in the *Story of O*, and the Islamic idea of man's submission to God' (Houellebecq 2015: 217). As for the Koran: 'What is the Koran, really, but one long mystical poem of praise? [...] for the Creator, and of submission to His laws' (Houellebecq 2015: 217–18). The author's anthropological humanism discovers the self in the other and reveals the inherent and structural equality of religions and cultures. The question of which culture dominates the other depends on political power and its agents.

And yet the novel's message for adherents to advanced Western civilization, with its achievements in art, literature, music and science, is not a cynical one: even in the face of decline, 'Judeo-Christian' culture still thrives amid diversity, beauty and abundance. It is reflected above all in its effect on people who both staked their faith in it and forged their identity in its past treasures. Only literature – and this is the self-referencing message of *Submission* – is still capable of giving voice to human and divine spirit in the very face of its loss.

Afterword: The Visual Culture of Revelation

David Morgan

The chapters comprising this book have productively explored a host of interrelated themes – imagination, sensation, figuration, images, the destruction or banning of images, and the aesthetics of perception and feeling that organize this range of experience. Attentive readers will not have missed that a golden thread running through the fabric of work is embodiment as a fundamental feature of the three religions that occupy the authors: Judaism, Christianity and Islam. To be sure, the traditions differ from one another in important ways on the treatment of the body as a culturally conditioned and historically constructed set of sensibilities and affordances. But in every case, the dynamics of sensation and representation, the use of and anxiety about imagery, and the forms of perception and imagination produce the matrix in which the sacred takes shape, in particular, how both transcendence and revelation are understood to operate.

In each of the religious traditions examined by the authors, transcendence and revelation characterize the interface of divine and human at every turn. The deity in each case transcends human control, comprehension and physical limitation. And any claim to knowledge about or access to the deity rides on the deity's self-revelation to humankind. Each of these deeply interlinked ideas clearly shows that these religions are obsessed with the enforcement and negotiation of boundaries. Durkheim considered one of the elementary features of religion to be the construction of sacrality and we find that fully at work in the maintenance as well as the crossing of boundaries – both the separation of divine from human and the separation of objects, words, rites, spaces, food, animals and people that are able in turn, by virtue of consecration, to approach the divine.

The deity in each tradition is inconceivable without the concepts of transcendence and revelation: an unseen, incomprehensible and all-powerful deity manifests itself in a distinctly determinative way – as the one who covenants with a particular people, as the one who takes on flesh in the person of the messiah, and as the one who makes known to his prophet his will for the true path. Each act becomes the authoritative basis for knowing what the deity expects of followers. Yet as soon as we say that, it is necessary to recognize that the function of revelation and transcendence is more than a matter of producing knowledge. They are forms of imagination no less than categories for properly understanding particular deities.

It is certainly true that for each of these religious traditions, but especially for Christianity and Islam, the product of divine revelation is correct knowledge or teaching – the etymological origin of *orthodoxy*. But the study of religion in the past several decades has come to stress that religions are more than cognitive claims and normative formulae. A religion, in other words, is more than a creed or doctrine and the institutional authorities that endorse it. Certainly, this is one important aspect, especially in the book-driven traditions of Judaism, Christianity and Islam. But the contributors to this volume have urged in various ways, with broadly ranging forms of evidence – from art, architecture and sensation to aesthetic experience in addition to a careful study of textual traditions – that images and other forms of figuration not only register religious values, but shape and generate them. In chapter after chapter, the authors point us to embodiment and imagination as characteristic features of these three religions.

Transcendence and revelation are forms of imagination inasmuch as they figure the unfigurable, making it accessible in some manner, as least something one can talk about and act towards. I would like to argue that everything people imagine is grounded on something embodied and actual. God is like a king – vaunted, remote, majestic, powerful, glorious. These are forms of transcendence that promise the possibility of the other feature of religion – revelation. That which is hidden can come to light, the remote can come near, the concealed can be unveiled. The invisible can become visible. Of course, it is not a complete identification of the deity with its figuration, although opponents of imagery such as the eleventh-century Muslim scholar al-Juwayni (see Gruber in this volume) or sixteenth-century Protestant John Calvin insisted that any formulation of God in the imagination is a creation of something other than the deity, and is therefore idolatrous. Likewise, Calvin and the thirteenth-century Shafi scholar, al-Nawawi, regarded the act of imagination as a presumption on God's majesty and sovereignty (see Shaw in this volume). Calvin referred to the human mind as a 'perpetual forge of idols' because the imagination produced an image of the biblical God that was not the deity, and therefore a lie, or an idol.[1] Al-Nawawi indicated that making a picture of any living thing 'imitates the creative activity of God' and will result in 'grievous punishment' (see Shaw).

Yet every tradition compares the deity to something, a sensation, a king, a maker (potter, architect, artist). The divine essence may be hidden and incomprehensible, but it remains possible to speak of the deity and to characterize his attitude or disposition towards human beings and the created world. The divine is figurable, yet not reducible to a figure. The body's coordinates remain the framework for thought and feeling and therefore are indispensable as the means of configuring a relationship between human and divine. Terje Stordalen (this volume) considers the role of darkness and emptiness as fitting evocations for the divine in the Temple of Jerusalem. And Else Marie Bukdahl (this volume) explores the philosophical tradition of the sublime as a vital resource for theological aesthetics and modern Christian artists from Caspar David Friedrich to Gerhard Richter. The comparable task for Jews, Christians, and Muslims, in spite of their many differences, is not to capture the hidden nature of the deity, but rather to prepare the body to respond via imagination to the divine. Kalman Bland in this volume quotes a thirteenth-century Aramaic rendition of a ninth-century Arabic text by a Nestorian Christian, Ḥunayn ibn Isḥaq, living in Baghdad. Ḥunayn noted that the architectural spaces of Jews, Christians, and Muslims all exhibit ornamental designs or images: 'All of this is meant to refresh and expand their souls by their means and to engage their hearts with the [decorations, ornaments, and images]' (see Bland in this volume, p. 130.). The function of art, in other words, may be said to shape the sensory and imaginative conditions for worship. Anxieties about the presumption of this practice, the menace of overextending it, persists in all three religious traditions. But the propriety of theological constraint is not the concern of scholars. Instead, the evidence – textual and material – points us to develop a recognition of aesthetic sensibilities as a fundamental aspect of religious experience and to complexify our understanding of the categories of revelation and transcendence as grounded in figuration and sensation, in embodiment.

To non-believers, revelation undermines natural order as an extraordinary event. But for those who believe, for those immersed in an ongoing relatedness to their deities, revelation is how the gods make themselves known, how they warn, punish, assist, encourage, reward and nurture their followers. A divinity's act of revelation may be unusually special or daily events, but in every case, the revelation answers to a perceived need or problem, a body of lore, ritual practices, a community's situation, and a history of invocation and valuation. This means that signs or omens are not simply arbitrary or invented. Their structure is motivated – by tradition, by exigence, by the power that produces them, and by the consequences of their occurrence since every sign, if it is to persist as a sign, must be couched within an interpretive narrative after it occurs. Thus, signs are both arbitrary and motivated. They are the product of a system, a grammar and syntax that organizes signs into intelligible patterns; but they are also the manifestation or expression of unseen forces. This double life of the sign is critical for any engaging account of revelation because the two characteristics of signs often function to conceal one another in the service of the religious enterprise of supernaturalizing revelation, or, for that matter, the scholarly project of reducing revelation to historical construction or ideological artifice.

An example will make these general characteristics clear. According to the four Gospel narratives of the New Testament, following his execution, Jesus was buried. A few days later something happened that the early community debated and eventually experienced as a powerful sign: when some of his followers visited the grave to anoint his body, Jesus was gone. The tomb was empty. Contemporary Jewish authorities had feared that Jesus's followers would secret the body away (Matt. 27.64-6). But for the devotees who believed or soon came to believe that Jesus was not dead, the empty tomb became a sign of his resurrection, more specifically, his triumph over death and the power of sin. God had not abandoned Jesus on the cross, as Jesus himself had feared in the grip of despair.

What precisely happened, a moment-by-moment narration of what took place after he expired on the cross and was laid to rest, is not represented in the New Testament account, written within sixty or seventy years of Jesus's death. But Paul's letters, produced before the Gospels, make it clear that a basic teaching of his included Christ's bodily resurrection three days after his death (see 1 Cor. 15.3-7). Only one brief biblical text, 1 Pet. 3.19-20, states that Jesus, having been 'made alive again', descended to hell to preach to those who had died in the days of Noah's flood. This bare passage became the canonical warrant for the 'harrowing of hell', and was expanded to include the early biblical patriarchs including Adam and Eve. The idea was asserted as early as the second century and narrated in detail in the fourth-century Gospel of Nicodemus. The belief had become so established by the fourth century that the phrase '*descendit ad inferos*' was included in the Apostles Creed. The Gospel of Nicodemus describes the 'Lord of Glory' bursting the doors of hell asunder and startling the power of darkness while Jesus reclaims Adam. It is a triumphant account worthy of a victorious saviour, the sort of narration that would have appealed to fourth-century Christians who had witnessed the vindication of their religion in imperial Rome. It was not the story of a humble Palestinian carpenter put to death by Rome, but a paean to a glorious ruler who descends to the dark vaults of hell to reorganize cosmic history en route to enthronement at the right hand of the monarch of the universe.

For nearly one thousand years, the standard iconographical practice in Byzantine and Western Christian art was to depict the resurrection, or *anastasis*, of Jesus by showing him in the act of harrowing hell. By the thirteenth century, however, that began to change. A remarkable set of images published in 1511 by the German artist Albrecht Dürer (1471–1528) portrayed the image of the harrowing in a woodcut cycle, *The Passion of Our Lord Jesus*. But on the following page, Dürer also presented a more recent depiction of the subject of the resurrection, the version that became the iconic motif of Christ's resurrection in European art during the fourteenth and fifteenth centuries (Figure 16.1). Dürer's inclusion of both images in his Passion narrative is a remarkable redundancy: the revelation of the essential salvific event in the life of Jesus is shown *twice* – once as a trip to hell and a second time as a bodily appearance at his tomb. Why? What do we learn about the nature of revelation and its signification in visual culture in this doppelgänger? It had become critical since the twelfth century, when a series of condemnations of the Cathar reform movement in southern France rejected as heresy what amounted to a neo-Gnostic view of matter as inherently evil among the Cathars. The view included a rejection of the incarnation and of the sacraments. The Cathars likewise dismissed the physical resurrection of Jesus as a corrupt teaching.[2] The conflict culminated in long and bloody violence during the thirteenth-century Albigensian Crusade. The mainstream Church responded by stressing the orthodoxy of Christian teaching and the Dominicans were deployed in the inauguration of the Inquisition to ferret out the heresy and endorse orthodox views. Such views were ubiquitously propagandized by thirteenth- and fourteenth-century devotional art that portrayed the physical body of Jesus resurrected at graveside in iconography that directly informed Dürer's *Passion*.

In Dürer's *Resurrection of Christ* (see Figure 16.1), Jesus stands atop the still-closed tomb, which bears the seal and is surrounded by a Roman guard as proof of the miraculous nature of the event in contrast to detractors who insisted his corpse had been stolen from the grave (Matt. 27.64-6). In a silent nocturnal scene, the risen Christ appears in a smoky burst of light that unfurls from the point at which his feet touch the obdurate stone lid. If we take the biblical accounts recorded in three Gospels (Matthew, Luke and John) as ancient sources that serve to motivate visual representation of the resurrection of Jesus as a physical event, it is striking that Dürer's woodcut portrays a moment that is not narrated by the New Testament at all. Elements of the picture draw

Figure 16.1 Albrecht Dürer, *The Resurrection of Christ*, in the woodcut cycle *The Passion of Our Lord Jesus*, 1511. Public domain.

from the Gospel of Matthew such as the detail of soldiers gathered about the tomb are described as dispatched by Pilate at the request of the Pharisees (Matt. 27.62-3). But in fact, it was not until the later Middle Ages that the representation of the resurrection of Jesus showed him at the tomb.

This meant inventing new iconography that filled in the gaps of the Gospel accounts (see Brunotte's discussion in this volume of the 'blanks' of texts). In effect, the revelation of the biblical text was extended by the visual programmes such as Figure 16.1. A scene that did not appear in any of the Gospels was created as the precise moment of the physical resurrection of Jesus. Revelation, in effect, is an event portrayed in tandem with the contextual need for it. And details in Dürer's woodcut show how the event itself adjusts the written accounts to provide a visual bulwark against which orthodoxy could find a secure footing from which to endorse its view of matter and spirit and their relationship to one another. But by 1511, the Cathar heresy had faded from memory. Indeed, Dürer and most of his viewers may have been quite unaware of it. This forgetting of the origin of the motif at work in Figure 16.1, however, is part of the power of the image: it replaces that origin with the pervasive notion of portraying the event itself.

Why doesn't the disjuncture of visual portrayal and historical narrative disrupt the credibility of the image? The image only scantly conforms to what the New Testament records. In Matt. 28.2-4 we read that on Easter morning 'an angel of the Lord descended from heaven and came and rolled back the stone, and sat upon it. His appearance was like lightning, and his raiment white as snow. And for fear of him the guards trembled and became like dead men.' This is as close as anything in the Gospel narratives of the resurrection comes to Dürer's image and those of countless others since the fourteenth century. Evidently, visual tradition compensates for the shortcomings of the textual record. A Northern European tradition of two centuries of portraying the event motivated Dürer's image more than the biblical texts. His woodcut looked like the resurrection because it looked like scores of images that viewers had seen before. Revelation is recognizable when it conforms to a standard of seeing what people understand to be the truth. Like many artists before him, Dürer showed the soldiers in the foreground as sleeping, though in the dimly lit middle distance we note that a few are awake and witnessing the event that flashes before them. As solid as Jesus appears to be, he stands entirely within the fulminating aura that surrounds him. His triumphal banner billows in what must be a sudden rush of air at his corporeal appearance and the outward press of smoke and light seem to suggest that the very fabric of reality has opened up, unpeeling to reveal the physical man who will step forth into the three-dimensional realm of the created world, where he will take up the rather furtive series of post-Easter appearances unevenly narrated in the Gospels of Luke and John. His resurrection appears as an eruption along the very axis of death marked by the staff he holds. And the momentary character of it is marked by the gestures of recognition evident in one or two soldiers even as those nearest us continue to snore.

The purpose of the spreading cloud about Jesus is to convey his miraculous return, to perform his epiphany as a form of ontological unveiling. The laws of matter and energy are being controverted in a theatrical moment of great drama. A momentous event is in the making, something profound unfolds before viewers, who behold a stage effect. They watch a presentation that meets those of faith when it reaches beyond the stage to touch them. In order to connect with viewers and enact revelation, Dürer's image needs to break out of the scene, a time frame, or a register that separates the event from the time and space of those looking at it, listening to it and expecting something from it. In Figure 16.1, the body of Jesus must cross from death to life and from the past to the present. Put differently, three different registers must coincide in a single, scintillating moment of presence to one another: the afterworld from which Jesus steps, the world of the narrated present into which he steps, and the world of the viewer to which he presents himself. This third register often eludes our notice. Images readily cloak the very situated act of being seen, as if they unveiled their content without the apprehension of those looking on. This is certainly the magic that Dürer deploys in his narrative cycle of the Passion of Jesus. It is an effect that is very familiar to modern viewers of cinema and photographic essays: viewers may regard themselves as a passive presence who do nothing more than watch. But the aspect of seeing that I want to draw attention to is be-*holding*, taking a grip on what is seen in the sense of imposing one's bodily, cultural, temporal conditions in the act of seeing. Revelation does not happen without this dimension since these conditions structure the act of reception.

This arc of movement from past to present, from unseen to seen, from transcendent to immanent is the *point* of images like Dürer's. I mean by 'point' what Roland Barthes called the 'punctum' of photographs: the pricking or wounding that an image exerts on viewers independently, acting as something in itself and not as a representation of something else (Barthes 1993: 26–7, 45). This point becomes clear in the title page of Dürer's *Passion* (Figure 16.2), in which the scourged Jesus, taunted by a soldier, is nestled within a cloudy border and from which he peers piercingly into the eyes of viewers. The scene draws from a brief description in the Gospels, but goes far beyond it. Matthew 27 indicates that Pilate's soldiers placed a crown of thorns on Jesus's head, a reed in his hand, and mocked him. What is *striking* about this image is the way in which Jesus gazes outward, beyond the scene, seeking out the eye of the viewer. We also note the similar use of an unfurling cloud in which the scene is nested. Why is it there? Perhaps it frames the humiliation of Jesus and his address to viewers as an act of revelation, a reaching out from the past to the viewers' present. It shows Christ's

Figure 16.2 Albrecht Dürer, *The Mocking of Christ*, in the woodcut cycle *The Passion of Our Lord Jesus*, 1511. Public domain.

suffering as ongoing and for the viewers, motivated by them as well as benefitting them. The abusive soldier stands in for latter-day viewers, whom a Latin verse below the image addresses directly as mirroring the soldier who mocks Jesus: 'You are guilty of striking me often.'

> These cruel wounds I have borne for you, man,
> And paid for your sickness with my blood.
> God cancels your wounds with my wounds and your death with mine:
> For you I was made a creature,
> Yet you are ungrateful to me, and you prick my wounds
> Again and again, you are guilty of striking me often.
> Is it not enough that I once suffered so many torments under the Jews?
> Now, my friend, you may rest.[3]

The same image was sometimes used to illustrate the cover of Luther's 1519 sermon, 'Meditation on the Passion of Christ', where we read the same indictment of the sinner: 'when you see nails piercing Christ's hands, you can be certain that it is your work. When you behold his crown of thorns, you may rest assured that these are your evil thoughts' (Luther 1969: 9). In the visual culture of revelation, the image serves to link the historical with the existential, the past with the present, the metaphysical with the bodily in an act of imagination that unfolds in an embodied experience. Revelation is the claim an event makes on viewers as an event that exerts a fundamental change, breaking into the viewer's world by two orders of reality drawing near to one another. Dürer used the smoky clouds to set off such moments of encounter (see, for instance, his title page of the Apocalypse, the Birth of Mary and the Coronation of the Virgin). His woodcut cycles were full of miraculous moments from scripture and the life of Mary, but the unfurling clouds are only used to highlight events that negotiate the proximity of the two domains before viewers.

Certainly the configuration of past and present or transcendent and immanent will take the form that particular cultural circumstances enable, which means within the terms of the sensory regime that prevails, grounds a particular visual culture, or what Meyer in this volume refers to as the 'specific, socially situated visual regimes, including those offered by religious traditions across time and space' (Meyer 85).[4] In the case of Dürer's sixteenth-century work, unfolding on the cusp of late medieval European Roman Catholic visual piety and early modern pictorial narrative, revelation is not only represented, but is visually evoked as a visceral empathy that wounds the viewer with shame for being complicit in Christ's suffering. The image mediates in the sense of acting on viewers as an agent of the unseen and being acted upon by viewers. Those who gaze upon the image join the soldier in mocking Christ, evoking a shame that motivates viewer empathy with him. It is a membrane that joins viewers with the biblical subject in an intimate give-and-take that makes human and divine present to one another, bringing them nearer by linking the viewer's body to the body of Jesus. Imagery like Dürer's performs a mimesis between the bodies they portray and the bodies of those who look upon them, thereby enabling beholders to imagine in corporeal immediacy the deity who suffers for and with them.

Notes

Introduction

1. In this respect our volume differs from the volume *Das Bild Gottes in Judentum, Christentum und Islam* (2009), whose editors Hesslinger and Leuschner frame the question of the representability of God in a normative, theological manner (2009: 10–11).
2. See also the notable work of art historians working on Christian images and Christian stances towards images, as Gottfried Boehm, Hans Belting, David Freedberg, Joseph Körner and Christiane Kruse (all featuring in the chapter by Meyer), and the important engagement on the part of scholars in religious studies with art history in the volume by Luiselli, Mohn and Gripentrog (2013).

Chapter 1

1. Experts now agree that ancient Israel certainly did not avoid all use of images; see Uehlinger in this volume and also the useful overview in Mathys (2013). Still, many biblical texts (which are not necessarily representative of all 'ancient Israel') do convey a concern about iconic representations of the deity.
2. For further information about different ways of counting and recognizing this command in different Jewish and Biblical traditions, see Yvonne Sherwood in this volume, p. 64. Unless explicitly noted, biblical citations are taken from the New Revised Standard Version of the English Bible.
3. This distinction between a de facto, tolerant aniconism and a later intolerant and programmatic iconoclasm is made for instance by Mettinger 2006: 273–6, 289–91. Mettinger was one of the leading voices in a recent exploration of aniconic religion in ancient Western Asia, cf. Mettinger 1995.
4. Adding to the passages from Deuteronomy 4 and 5 cited above, see for instance Deut. 5.8; 7.5, 25; 9.12, 16; 12.3; 27.15; 29.17; 32.21.
5. For example, Deut. 10.8; 12.12; 16.11, 16; 18.7; 19.17; 26.5-13; 27.7; 29.10-14; 31.11.
6. Scholarship concerning the sources is deeply divided, as illustrated in these two examples: DeVries (2003) speaks without hesitation about the sources of the story and implies that these may be old. (The Greek text has more references to sources available for the redactor, and DeVries takes the Greek as the older text.) Van Seters (1997) argues that all text is contemporary with the deuteronomists, which to him means just before the fall of Jerusalem in 586 BCE. I tend to date the DtrH later than Van Seters does, and so I am inclined to believe there were, in fact, sources documenting details of the Temple that fell to the Babylonians. I do agree with Van Seters, though, that these sources probably dated to the period, just before the fall of the Temple. However, all this is very complex and need not be definitively decided for the current purpose.
7. See Exod. 24.16; 40.35; Num. 9.17-18.22; 10.12; 14.14, 2 Sam. 22.12; Ps. 31.20; Isa. 4.6, and so on.

8   The Greek of v. 13 makes a point out of the contrast between light and darkness: 'A sun hath Yahweh established in the heavens, but he hath purposed to dwell in thick darkness' (cf. DeVries 2003: 114; Sweeney 2007: 132).
9   As the reader will realize, this is a rendition only of the most basic insights in Rancière, whose main interest lies in how aesthetics in a wide sense is bound up with politics. His 'aesthetic regime of art' denotes one specific configuration of art and politics: the (Western) ways of conceiving, understanding and seeing art. This regime emerged in the nineteenth century and '[…] simultaneously establishes the autonomy of art and the identity of its forms with the forms that life uses to shape itself' (Rancière 2004: 23). In the world of the Bible, art had not established its own domain, so much of this reflection would be anachronistic for our purpose. However, one insight in Rancière's reasoning still applies, namely that societies establish certain distributions of the sensible, and these contribute to (and reflect) given social orders (cf. Rancière 2004: 18–19, etc.). This is the point I rely on here.

Chapter 2

1   Both '*taswir*' and '*surat*' can correspond to the English designation 'picture', but may have differing connotations in different times and places. '*Taswir*' can refer to a picture or representation in general, and thus also to explication, as in the hermeneutical interpretation of the Qur'an, also called *taswir*. '*Surat*' means 'chapter' in Arabic (as in, a section of the Qur'an), but can also mean an impression or image.
2   Although often translated as religion, '*al-din*' might be better conveyed as way of life (Ahmed 2015: 187–8).

Chapter 3

1   In his excellent chapter in this volume, Terje Stordalen asks how the deuteronomists could have lived out their aniconic convictions 'in real life', given that they did not live in a cultural vacuum. The same question applies to God.
2   An allusion to Gotthold Lessing's taxation metaphor distinguishing between the 'gross' of scripture (gross, sometimes, in both senses) and the 'net'. In Lessing's view, the pure, net, meaning of the Bible was what should be kept. See Lessing 2005: 123.
3   To nuance this a little further, I should add that, depending on the geographical location, Protestantism or Catholicism also became a mirror of Judaism and Islam.
4   'To moloch' has been variously interpreted as the proper name of a god, as the term for a particular kind of fire sacrifice, and as the reference to a king. See for example Smelik 1995. Even if Moloch were finally to be exposed as an accident of misreading, it is way too late in the day to demystify and eradicate the old divinity. Like the golden calf, Moloch has a vibrant modern life well beyond the reach of the Bible and the protests of biblical scholars (for example in the work of Karl Marx, Allen Ginsburg and Friedrich Nietzsche). Biblical scholars do not have the power to kill.
5   According to traditional Christian dramas of supersession, the Old Testament is the shadow cast by the sun of Jesus, who comes first (even though historically he comes later). Similarly, here, the M-God is the shadow who came first, who was buried, and who rose and became stronger than the body, precisely because he had no fleshy form.

Chapter 4

1 Thanks to Ulrike Brunotte, Pooyan Tamimi Arab, Jeroen Beets, Christiane Kruse, Wendy Shaw, Terje Stordalen, Christoph Uehlinger and, as always, Jojada Verrips for their critical and constructive comments and superb suggestions. The work on this project is situated in the research programme Religious Matters in an Entangled World (www.religiousmatters.nl), generously sponsored by the Netherlands Foundation for Scientific Research (NWO) and the Royal Netherlands Academy for Arts and Sciences.

2 Through my anthropological research on local appropriations of missionary Protestantism in Ghana, I encountered the limits of what I took to be characteristic of this strand of Christianity as well as of my scholarly approach to religion at large. This prompted me to deploy an alternative, material approach which takes the body, sensations, objects, images and rituals seriously as authorized harbingers that convey to believers a sense of divine presence, making God real for them (e.g. Meyer 2012). Actually, my inclination to opt for a material approach to religion was grounded in a deep puzzlement about how to find a conceptual space to accommodate the explicit and deliberate human engagement in 'doing' religion and effecting a genesis of divine presence, which I encountered in my research among Protestants and Pentecostals in Ghana.

3 Notwithstanding notable exceptions, conceptually ambitious approaches to visual culture in the field of religious studies are still scarce. In resonance with emergent alternative approaches to the making and use of images and their aesthetic effects (Morgan 2007, 2012, 2015; Pinney 2004; Promey 2014; see also Dubuisson 2015; Luiselli, Mohn and Gripentrog 2013), over the past years I have sought to contribute to breaking conceptual ground for studying images as particular, embodied religious media (Meyer 2012, 2015a).

4 What is known as the Second Commandment in the Reformed and Greek Orthodox traditions (Exod. 20.4-6, see also Deut. 5.8-10) is included in the First Commandment for Catholics, Lutherans and Jews. The divergent Christian traditions of numbering only come together again at the end, with Reformed Christianity having the tenth commandment 'Thou shall not covet', and Catholics and Lutherans differentiating it into two commands.

5 Kant: 'Vielleicht giebt es keine erhabenere Stelle im Gesetzbuche der Juden, als das Gebot: du sollst dir kein Bildniß machen, noch irgend ein Gleichniß, weder dessen, was im Himmel, noch auf der Erden, noch unter der Erden ist u.s.w. Dieses Gebot allein kann den Enthusiasm erklären, den das jüdische Volk in seiner gesitteten Epoche für seine Religion fühlte, wenn es sich mit andern Völkern verglich, oder denjenigen Stolz, den der Mohammedanism einflößt' (1960 (orig. 1790): 274).

Translation: 'Perhaps in the code of the Jews there is no passage more sublime than the commandment: Thou shall not make onto thee any graven image, or any likeness of a thing that is in heaven above, or that is in the earth beneath, or that is in the water under the earth etc. This commandment alone can explain the enthusiasm that the Jewish people felt for its religion in its civilized epoch when comparing itself to other peoples, or the pride which Mohammedanism instills' (translation mine).

6 Latour has a wide definition of the image: 'any sign, work of art, inscription, or picture that acts as a mediation to access something else' (2002: 16).

7 German original: 'ein ungreifbares und fernes Sein zu vergegenwärtigen, ihm eine derartige Präsenz zu leihen, die den Raum der menschlichen Aufmerksamkeit völlig

zu erfüllen vermag. Das Bild besitzt seine Kraft in einer Verähnlichung, es erzeugt eine Gleichheit mit dem Dargestellten'.

8 He does not take into account that images of God – famously as an old man with a beard – have been made and reproduced over and over again, for instance via illustrated Bibles (see Kruse 2003: chapter 3, and below).

9 Particularly instructive is the attention Kruse pays to differences in evoking a sense of the unseen between artists' stance towards images and theologians' stance towards text. For instance, discussing miniature depictions of the creation of the world in the medieval Lambeth Bible, she demonstrates that the images fill descriptive blanks in the text with concrete visual information (see also Brunotte in this volume) and, in so doing, guide – or even 'occupy' – the imagination of their beholders (2003: 137–55). Analysing the specificity of the visual exegesis undertaken by medieval painters, she identifies an image–text syntax that suggests a priority for images over the text not only on the level of the illustrated Bible, but also in a semantic sense, according to which the things and their names and images were created before the biblical text could narrate the creation of the world.

10 Of course, as an art historian Belting focuses on images. But I do not take this statement to imply that pictures are the only media through which deities become present. In this sense, 'iconic presence' is one mediated presence of the transcendent next to others.

11 In her recent long essay 'After Debrosses: Fetishism, Translation, Comparativism, Critique' (2017), Rosalind Morris insists that fetishism and idolatry were separate discourses, and criticizes Böhme for eliding the difference between them (2017: 165). I take her point that it is important to not project an assumed congruence of fetish and idol on historical texts and to remain alert to the fact that fetish and idol refer to different things. At the same time, however, these two terms were used interchangeably by mission societies such as the NMG (see below). The point here is to trace the actual use of these two terms in encounters between missionaries and Africans, and the repercussions of this use for the ways in which indigenous cult objects are spoken about.

12 With thanks to Angelantonio Grossi for alerting me to the media channel of this pastor and to Azizaa (see below).

13 Original: 'Daher fürchte ich mich, einen Ölgötzen zu verbrennen. Ich habe Angst davor, der Teufelsnarr würde mir etwas antun, obwohl ich (einerseits) die Schrift habe, und weiß, dass Bilder nichts vermögen und weder Leben, Blut noch Geist haben, und doch hält andererseits mich die Furcht [gefangen] und macht, dass ich mich vor einem gemalten Teufel, vor einem Schatten, vor einem Geräusch eines leichten Blattes fürchte und ich gehe aus dem Weg, was ich mannhaft suchen sollte [sc. Bilder zu verbrennen]'.

Chapter 5

1 'Aniconism' is a problematic concept for several reasons. First, scholars have deployed 'aniconic' and 'aniconism' 'as key terms, yet with meanings and values that can vary dramatically' (Gaifman 2017: 343). Secondly, through its via negationis it implies an understanding (and often rejection) of its opposite (see Huntington 2015 with reference to early Buddhism). Thirdly, as an '-ism' it has a propensity to reification and tends to be used in overgeneralizing ways. In my view, there is a long way to go from aniconic ritual practices (de facto aniconicity) to 'aniconism', let alone 'anti-iconism'.

My own use of the term in this chapter is, as a rule, restricted to ritual/cultic contexts where the non-figurative representation of one or several deities and focused communication with a deity is at stake. In such contexts, a non-figural object may function as a representation, a medium of presence and a focus of attention in much the same way as a figurative icon or an image (Schipper 2013).
2. Gaifman discusses definitions, examples and comparative perspectives; Aktor, working on data from Hindu traditions, suggests that 'aniconism' be conceptualized as a spectrum rather than dichotomically contrasted to 'iconism'. One article in the collection (Jensen 2017) offers an interesting discussion of biblical data, but the linkage of 'aniconic propaganda' to 'religious seriousness' betrays the author's own, strongly normative, interest. See van Asselt 2007 on the epistemic bind between the prohibition of images and Protestant identity.
3. Space does not permit to elaborate here on the roughly contemporaneous temple on Mount Garizim, which seems to have reflected a very similar aesthetic regime (Hensel 2016).
4. Nadav Na'aman (2017) has offered one of the first attempts to make sense of the new discoveries within established knowledge. As he rightly states, 'The proximity of the Moẓa temple to Jerusalem is remarkable, since the Jerusalemite authorities must have considered it a legitimate temple and the cult held therein acceptable' (Ibid.: 4). To Na'aman, however, anthropomorphic and zoomorphic figurines suggest a 'non-Judahite connection' (Ibid.: 10). He therefore suggests that this temple might be a place mentioned in the biblical 'ark narrative' (1 Sam. 4.1b-7.1 and 2 Sam. 6.1-20a), namely the 'House of Obed-Edom the Gittite', that is, a Philistine. This is not the place to discuss the hypothesis in detail. Whether or not the temple was run by Judahites, it will have offered an opportunity structure to local Judahites. What I find remarkable in terms of epistemic regime is that Na'aman has brought in the argument of ethnic and religious distinctiveness only a few months after the preliminary publication of the finds, to the effect that the finds could be conceptually separated from Judahite religion – a typical process of 'othering' as it were, by a highly respected secular historian.

Chapter 6

1. I have discussed the historical and conceptual ground against which Kafka's opinions are expressed in Bland 2000: 13–58 and Bland 2008: 155–76.
2. The pictures from the Sarajevo Haggadah chosen for display were selected from memory of the oral presentation in Oslo in 2015, as the late professor Bland did not specify the selection in his manuscript (the editors).
3. For more recent scholarship, focused on iconography, see Kogman-Appel 2006: 16, 99–110 and Epstein 2011 (passim).
4. For the conventional, tendentious wisdom asserting Jewish preference for the word and rejection of the image, see Belting 1994: 7, 42, 144.
5. For a translation of the entire responsum and supporting documentation, see Bland 2001.
6. For a discussion of the affinity between Talmudic law and Byzantine practice regarding two-dimensional images, see Bland 2004.
7. For a more complete English translation of the original Hebrew and supporting documentation, see Bland 2001: 284–5; 294–6.

8   From the Scholium to Part IV: Proposition 45 in *The Ethics* in Spinoza 1994.
9   For the Arabic original, see Badawi 1985: 51. Compelling doubts about the reliability of Badawi's edition and cogent arguments for the Persian provenance of elements of the text are presented by Zakeri 2004: 173–90. For fuller background on Ḥunayn and this text, see Griffith 2008.
10 For biographical background and a full offering of his poetry, see Alḥarizi 2003.
11 For the Hebrew original, see Loewenthal 1896: 7.

Chapter 7

1   A longer version of this article, containing further illustrations, was originally published in German; see Gruber 2009.
2   For a discussion of the term '*kitab munir*' as denoting the Qur'an, see Ayoub 1984: 396.
3   The expression '*kitab munir*' is also used to describe other holy scriptures known as 'sacred scrolls' (*zubur*), including the Torah and Gospel.
4   For the painting's history, date (910 AH/1505 CE), and attribution to Sultan Muhammad, see Robinson 1976: 178–9; and for a historical and religious contextualization of its salient visual motifs, see Gruber 2011.
5   On this Timurid illustrated manuscript of the 'Book of Ascension', see in particular Gruber 2008; Séguy 1977.

Chapter 8

1   I would like to thank Terje Stordalen and Birgit Meyer for helping shape the initial idea and the final product through their invitation to the initial conference at the Zentrum Moderner Orient (ZMO) in Berlin, and for their continuous support as part of the project at the Center for Advanced Studies (CAS) in Oslo. I would also like to acknowledge student research assistants Brent Kennedy, Jeffrey Leddy and Briana Winter for copyediting and proofreading the text. I further extend my appreciation to Sirana Jamkartanian for her generous help with the Arabic sections. Finally, I am most grateful to Refika Sarıönder for her uncompromising and persistent criticism of my work. All remaining errors are undeniably mine.
2   The Turkish term '*medeniyetler*', properly translated as 'civilizations', might be irritating and requires further contextualization. Here, locals demarcate historical epochs of major empires that once ruled. Besides, *medeniyetler* has a distinct connotation with religion and the religious foundations of a 'civilization' that *Medeniyetler Buluşması* could be translated as the 'Meeting of Religions', and *Antakya Medeniyetler Korosu* as 'Antakya Interreligious Choir'. In recent usage, *medeniyetler* refers to monotheistic religions that are commonly considered religions of the book.
3   I follow the Turkish convention of using the proper name of Meryem in conjunction with the honorary title of Mother (Turk.: *Ana*), as used for female saints. Meryem Ana is common among Turkish Christians and Muslims, along with other honorary titles – like that of Saint Mary (Turk.: *Hazreti Meryem* or Hz. *Meryem*). Nevertheless, these terms do not translate easily into a language with an established convention of Virgin Mary. Although Mary is perceived as a virgin in various interpretations of Christianity and Islam, there is no equivalent Turkish convention that would capture the notion

of the Virgin (Turk.: *Bakire*), and I have not encountered that usage in Hatay. This, however, does not exclude the existence of such a concept, as it becomes apparent in the Arabic liturgical language used among Orthodox Christians in Antakya, where theological notions are pronounced in formula like Virgin Mary (Gr.: *Panagia Maria*; Arab.: *Adra Maryam*) or Mother of God (Gr.: *Theotokos*; Arab.: *Walidat el-Elah*).

4 Bodily sensations in Marian veneration and the impact different aesthetic regimes of bodily sensation among Orthodox Christians have on interreligious relations with Muslims have received little attention. Examples of adorations and apparitions of Meryem Ana suggest that in the aesthetic regime the frame shapes the focus, but in bodily sensation the focus shapes the frame. The clergy emphasize aesthetic regimes and laity emphasize bodily sensations.

5 I conducted ethnographic fieldwork on interreligious relations in Hatay during the summers between 2010 and 2015; my interview partners included Eastern Orthodox Christians and Arab Alawite Muslims. My findings are based on participant observation and semi-structured interviews.

6 Orthodox Christians in Antakya traditionally speak Arabic as their mother tongue and the Greek Orthodox Church of Antakya (Turk.: *Antakya Rum Ortodoks Kilisesi*) follows the Greek Orthodox liturgy in the local Arabic dialect (Usluoğlu 2012, 122).

7 Arab Alawites, also Alaouites, Alawis, or formerly Nusayri, a branch of Twelver Shia Islam, venerate Ali ibn-Talib, the cousin and son-in-law of Prophet Muhammad. Alawites, who originated in the ninth century, identify themselves as Muslims. Due to their unique form of Islam that has elements of Christianity in it (Friedman 2010: 67–173), many Sunnites consider Alawites to be heterodox. While their saint veneration at pilgrimage sites remains open for women and children and are commonly visited by members of other religious groups, prayer rituals, essential to their beliefs, are reserved for initiated male members. Most Arab Alawites live in the coastal mountain ranges at the Mediterranean Sea stretching from Lebanon and Syria to Southern regions of Turkey (Procházka-Eisl and Procházka 2010: 49–110; Winter 2016: 141–6, 220–8).

8 The *Theotokos* is usually depicted in a bright blue shirt and a dark red mantle with the Child in a white shirt and a golden cord. The Miraculous Icon in Antakya follows an iconographic tradition of the 'Virgin of the Passion' type also named as 'Our Lady of Perpetual Help' as represented in a Byzantine icon of the Cretan school (Ferrero 2001: 12; Nes 2005: 58–9).

9 Following the Muslim tradition, the *khamsa* serves apotropaic purposes and aims to bring fertility to the beholder (Apostolos-Cappadona 2005: 355). The *nazarlık* is believed to protect against misfortunate caused by the evil eye (Turk.: *nazar*), consisting of an eye-shaped amulet as a blue glass bead with an 'eye' made from circles of white and light blue with a dark blue dot in the middle. Particularly in modern Turkey, the blue glass bead gained popularity as part of Turkish folk and tourist culture (Breu and Marchese 2005: 204). The 'eye in hand charm combines the *hamsa* hand with the blue glass beads of Turkey and Greece and is popular in the Christian world' (Scranton 2012: 90).

10 It is not unknown for Arab Alawites to venerate icons even those of Meryem Ana (Procházka-Eisl and Procházka 2010: 176, 263, 267).

11 The only exception for a recent recognition of a miraculous icon is the sanctuary of Our Lady of Soufanieh, which became a site for Marian apparitions, where weekly prayers are held in front of an icon which is of a similar Hodegetria type as the Miraculous Icon in Antakya (Bandak 2013: 129–30; Aubin-Boltanski 2014: 512, 515–20).

12　This iconographer lived and worked with Father Paolo Dall'Oglio until 2012 in the renowned Al-Khalil community at the Deir Mar Musa al-Habashi, a monastery of the Syriac Catholic Church located some 60 miles (97 kilometres) north of Damascus, where Muslims and Christians prayed and fasted jointly (Loosley 2004; Pénicaud 2016).

13　It is a widely held assumption among Eastern Orthodox Christians, that icons are equivalent to the Holy Scripture: 'Icons are words in painting' (Scouteris 1984: 11; see also Pentcheva 2006: 635).

14　It should be noted that the Orthodox Church of Antakya is historically ascribed to the diocese of Aleppo and the Orthodox patriarchate in Damascus, not to the patriarchate in Istanbul as one might assume. Furthermore, it is important to emphasize that the divine liturgy is recited and celebrated in Arabic and not in Greek. This is due to historical circumstances which cannot further be developed here.

15　Roman Catholic Christians are the primary worshippers in Ephesus with an increase of pilgrimage groups in the twentieth century (Pülz 2010: 252).

16　Located some twenty miles (or thirty-two kilometres) north of Damascus, 'deep in Muslim territory' (Kedar 2001: 63), the Saydnaya convent is one of the oldest Christian monasteries hosting a most miraculous Marian icon, as it began in 1168 to dispatch liquid and subsequently 'grow flesh from breasts to navel, emitting from the breasts an oil-like liquid that would heal the sick' (Kedar 2001: 63). This icon 'covered with human flesh, instead of paint' and yielding 'prodigious sweat' (Bacci 2004: 2), is believed to be an icon painted by St. Luke the Evangelist himself (Immerzeel 2007: 16), called 'The Celebrated' (Arab.: *Chaghoura*). Since the Crusades, the *Chaghoura* icon is venerated by Muslims and Christians 'during the feasts of the Assumption (15 August) and Nativity (8 September)' (Immerzeel 2007: 15). Since the crusaders, who 'played an important role in promoting the worship of the 'incarnated icon' […] and in disseminating the relic of the holy oil' (Bacci 2004: 2), the tradition of shared veneration continued until the twenty-first century (Dalrymple 1998: 186–91).

17　Considering that Antakya is home to Christianity's oldest church, and that St. Luke the Evangelist is thought to have written his gospel there (Glover 2009), the Miraculous Icon might hold great significance for Orthodox Christian devotees.

18　Arab Alawites recognize dreams and visions as integral to their culture (Kreinath 2014).

19　The sanctuaries of local pilgrimage sites are commonly called station (*makam*) or visit (*ziyaret*), indicating the apparition of the saint at that site.

Chapter 9

1　This chapter is the result of my fieldwork since 1997 in the city of Lahijan and in its neighbouring villages in the north of Iran. The first initiative to run this project came from the Centre for Anthropological Studies of the Iran Cultural Heritage Organisation, at that time directed by my master's thesis supervisor, Mohamad Mirshokrayi, to whom I am deeply grateful for his kind support and academic advice. My observations on Lahijan's shrines follow from intensive participation observation of Shiite rituals in the shrines and then my interviews with the keepers (khaadem) of these shrines and with pilgrims. To make comparisons I then studied the mural paintings of saints' shrines in Isfahan, Shiraz and Dezful. I am deeply grateful to A. Montazerolghaem, F. Mahmoudi and W. Floor for their kind support during my research on this topic. I am also grateful to Birgit Meyer and Terje Stordalen, the editors of this volume, for their comments and feedback on an earlier version of this work.

2 The term Twelver refers to its adherents' belief in twelve divinely ordained leaders, known as the Twelve Imams, and their belief that the last imam, Muhammad al-Mahdi, lives in occultation and will reappear as the promised Mahdi. For more information on this topic, see: Amir-Moezzi 2015.
3 Hoseyniyeh is a congregation hall for Shiite commemoration of rituals, ceremonies and festivities, especially those associated with the commemoration of the martyrdom of Imam Hoseyn.
4 Tekiyeh is a congregation hall for the performance of Ta'ziyeh, which are held during the month of Muharram on the occasion of Imam Hoseyn's martyrdom.
5 Saints' shrines and mausoleums.
6 According to the Iranian version of Shiism, in 680 AD a battle took place in the desert of Karbala, situated in present-day Iraq. There originated the ritual and myth of Imam Hoseyn, which persist in all Shiite communities. Imam Hoseyn, the champion of the Shiites, the son of 'Ali and Fatemeh and the grandson of the Prophet Muhammad, was, according to tradition, on his way to join the community in Kufa when he, his seventy-two loyal followers, and his entire family were overtaken by the hordes of the Sunni caliph Yazid (b. 647–d. 683 AD) and killed in a bloody battle in that arid desert on the day of Ashura, the tenth of the month of Muharram. All Shiites, but particularly Iranians, congregate each Muharram and the following month, Safar, in a passionate re-enactment of the scene of Karbala.
7 For more information on this topic see Landau 2012.
8 For more information on this topic see Landau and Van Lint 2015.
9 Based on my own fieldwork, 2011.
10 For more detailed information on Shiite mural paintings of Iran during the Qajar period, see: Akhaviyan 1996; Calmard 1996: 179; Kamali 2006; Khosronejad 2018; Mahmoudinejad 2009; Mahmoudi and Tawossi 2011; Massé 1938: 297, 305, 38; Mirzaee Mehr 2007; Shad Qazvini 2010.
11 'O believers, wine and games of chance and statues and (divining) arrows are an abomination of Satan's handiwork; then avoid it.'

Chapter 10

1 9/11 has not only reinforced the ancient opposition between the Christian West and Islam, but has also inscribed itself into existing conflicts in Kenya on a national, regional and local level. In Kenya in 1998, thousands of men and women had already experienced the 'Embassy Bombing' of Nairobi and since then have suffered a whole series of terrorist attacks. Under the conditions of heightened vulnerability and aggression, a spiralling process of progressive alienation took place between Muslims and Christians.
2 Since the 1980s, a number of Muslim-led welfare organizations, mosques, schools and societies have been founded, most of which were funded by Arab countries, in particular, Saudi Arabia, to provide education, religious training and medical care. They promote a reformed Islam, 'Wahhabism', named after the Muslim scholar Muhammad Ibn Abd al Wahhab (1703–92) that is highly text-oriented and denounces 'un-Islamic' practices such as spirit possession and the celebration of Maulidi.
3 When, in 2011, I visited the town of Kwale that has a strong Muslim presence and lies to the south of Mombasa, I realized the impact of reformed Islam centres on big cities such as Mombasa (and Nairobi). Thus, it seems that the gendered withdrawal from (photographic) visibility is mainly an urban phenomenon and has not (yet) reached the rural areas.

Chapter 11

1 Transcript provided by the Missionary Department, Archdiocese of Ioshkar-Ola and Marii El, Russian Orthodox Church.
2 My understanding of authoritative tradition is based on the work of Talal Asad, who took the term from the philosopher Alasdair McIntyre and introduced it to the anthropology of Islam. For Asad, a tradition is a living, developing conversation where people weigh a variety of past sources to set standards for present behaviour and future trajectories (Asad 2009 [1986]). For applications of the concept to Orthodox Christianity, see Bandak and Boylston 2014; Luehrmann 2018a.
3 Irina Vatagina was a student of Mariia Sokolova (monastic name Mother Iuliana, 1899–1981), an iconographer whose life's work connected the Soviet period to the early twentieth-century searches for a renewal of iconography in the classical spirit. Sokolova taught iconography at the Moscow Spiritual Academy from 1958 until the 1970s, and trained many icon painters who were active in the late Soviet and early post-Soviet period, including Vatagina (Yazykova 2010: 125).

Chapter 12

1 [...] intelligitur modus quilibet examinandi propriam conscientiam; item meditandi, contemplandi, orandi secundum mentem et vocem; ac postremo alias quascunque spirituales operationes tractandi.
   All citations are taken from the Ignatius Jesuit Center edition by E. Jensen (n.d.).
2 [...] ratio quaedam componendi loci; pro qua notandum est [...] ut puta de Christo, effingendus erit nobis secundum visionem quandam imagariam locus corporeus, id quod contemplamur repraesentans.
3 [...] imaginando Iesum Christum coram me adesse in cruce fixum. Itaque exquiram mecum rationem, qua Creator ipse infinitus fieri creatura, et ab aeterna vita ad temporariam mortem venire pro peccatis meis dignatus sit.
4 quod proprium est Dei et angeli cuiusque boni, veram infundere spiritualem laetitiam animae, quam movent, sublata tristitia et perturbatione omni. [...] bonus quidem leniter, placide ac suaviter, sicut aquae stilla in spongiam illabens.
5 [...] angeli, divinae iustitiae gladium ferentes, aequo me animo tulerint, custodierint, suisque etiam iuverint suffragiis.
6 [...] pro voti consecutione, poscere maerorem, planctum, anxietatem, et caeteras id genus paenas interiores, ut Christo patienti pro me compatiar.
7 Permansit ligatus tota illa nocte. Circumstantes eum satellites illudebant, vexabant [...]
8 Iesum flagellis caedi iussit Pilatus; milites eundem spinis coronarunt, atque purpura induerunt.
9 Baiulavit Christus crucem suam.
10 Inter duos latrones crucifixus fuit, adscripto titulo: Iesus nazarenus rex iudeorum.
11 Et divisa sunt vestimenta eius.
12 Exclamans (sitio) quando eum aceto potaverunt.
13 [...] et latus lancea confossum aquam et sanguinem effudit.
14 Sanctissimum eucharistiae sacramentum instituit in signum summae dilectionis.
15 Quando etiam lachrimae funduntur, amorem illum provocantes, sive ex dolore de peccatis profluant sive ex meditatione passionis Christi.

16 ECCE CRVX DOMINI FUGITE PARTES ADVERSAE VICIT LEO DE TRIBU IUDA
17 CHRISTVS VINCIT CHRISTVS REGNAT CHRISTVS IMPERAT CHRISTUS AB OMNI MALO PLEBEM SUAM DEFENDAT
18 est loci cuiusdam imaginaria constructio, in quo videam meipsum coram Deo sanctisque omnibus, cum desiderio adstantem atque perscrutantem, quonam pacto ipsi Deo placere queam potissimum.
19 pro me intercesserint sancti.
20 Rogatus, cum eis mansit, fractoque ipsis pane disparuit; qui subito in Hierusalem reverse, nuntiaverunt apostolis quomodo vidissent eum, et in fractione panis agnovissent.
21 The title of the concluding section is: Regulae aliquot servandae, ut cum orthodoxa ecclesia vere sentiamus: 'Some rules to be observed in order to truly feel with the orthodox Church'.
22 Si quid, quod oculis nostris apparet album, nigrum illa esse definierit, debemus itidem quod nigrum sit pronuntiare. – See also § 56.

Chapter 13

1 The word 'art' was used for the first time in reference to the visual arts like painting and sculpture in the early seventeenth century and the term only came into wider use in the period that followed (*Oxford English Dictionary*: 120). Artistic expertise was previously called 'skill' or 'craft' with the associated word, 'artisan'. Or they were called 'painters' or 'sculptors'. They were members of a particular occupation and were not normally characterized as people with a vision and a calling in the same way that they are today. But with the emergence of Egyptian art from about 3000 BC, we do encounter in certain instances a recognition of the special creative power of visual art and its ability to communicate experience and knowledge in an intense and vivid way, in both secular and religious contexts. Several artists, including Phidias and Leonardo, wanted to share a place at the muses' table with the poets, who were believed to be endowed with a creative imagination and a high degree of learning. The artists of the Renaissance were the first to achieve this distinction. They were elevated to the status of 'twin brothers of the poets' (Lee 1967: 41, 67). The meaning of the word 'art' thus started to make inroads into the art and cultural life of the Renaissance, but not into the meaning of the word itself.
2 Theophilus was possibly a Benedictine monk. It has been suggested (particularly by Eckhard Freise) that he is the artisan monk Roger of Helmarshausen. He worked as an artist and author between 1100 and 1107 in St. Pantaleon's Church in Cologne, and he moved to Helmarshausen Abbey in 1107. His main work is called Diversarum Artium Schedula (1100–20). See Freise (1981).
3 Burke 1967, see particularly the chapters 'Of the Passion caused by the Sublime' and 'Vastness' and 'Infinity': 57–8 and 72–4.
4 The original German passage does not use the concept idolatry though: 'Vielleicht gibt es keine erhabenere Stelle im Gesetzbuche der Juden, als das Gebot: Du sollst dir kein Bildnis machen' (Kant 1979: 201). ET, Kant 2000: 156: 'Perhaps there is no more sublime passage in the Jewish Book of Law than the commandment: Thou shalt not make unto thyself any graven image.'
5 Buci-Glucksmann 1996: 15. See also Bukdahl 2017: 103.

Chapter 14

1 'Gerade aus der biblischen Leerstelle der namenlosen narrativen Funktion gewinnt der Ästhetizismus die Selbstreflexionsformel des "rein Ästhetischen", um in dessen Leere ein epochales Imaginäres einströmen zu lassen' (Pfeiffer 2006: 310).
2 John Chrysostom: '"Wo eben ein Tanz ist [...]" [...] O welch ein teuflisches Gastmahl! Welch ein satanisches Schauspiel! Welch sündhafter Tanz und noch sündhafterer Tanzlohn! [...] Wo eben ein Tanz ist, da ist auch der Teufel dabei' ([350 -407] (Rohde 2000: 68, 70).
3 Richard Strauss (1949: 224): 'Ich hatte schon lange an den Orient- und Judenopern auszusetzen, daß ihnen wirklich östliches Kolorit und glühende Sonne fehlt. Das Bedürfnis gab mir (für meine eigene Oper) wirklich exotische Harmonik ein, die besonders in fremdartigen Kadenzen schillerte, wie Changeant-Seide'.

Afterword

1 Calvin 1989: 97. For further discussion, see Morgan 2015: 1–2.
2 For discussion of the history of the understanding and portrayal of the resurrection of Jesus, see Bynum 1995: 197–9; on the Cathar heresy, 214–20.
3 From Kurth 1963: 214, my translation:

> *Has ego crudeles homo pro te perfero plagas*
> *Atque meo morbos sanguine curo tuos.*
> *Vulneribusque meis tua vulnera, mortesque mortem*
> *tollo deus: pro te plasmate factus homo.*
> *Tucque ingrata mihi: pungis mea stigmata culpis*
> *Saepe tuis, noxa vapulo saepe tua.*
> *Sat fuerit, me tanta olim tormenta sub hoste*
> *Iudaeo passum: nunc sit amice quies.*

4 Meyer (2006: 20–3) has referred to this as 'sensational form'. I have examined the embodied nature of seeing in religion, Morgan 2012.

References

Introduction

Behrend, H. (2013), *Contesting Visibility: Photographic Practices on the East African Coast*, Bielefeld: Transcript.

Behrend, H., A. Dreschke and M. Zillinger, eds (2014), *Trance Mediums & New Media: Spirit Possession in the Age of Technical Reproduction*, New York: Fordham.

Belting, H. (2001), *Bild-Anthropologie: Entwürfe für eine Bildwissenschaft*, Munich: Fink Verlag.

Belting, H. (2016), 'Iconic Presence: Images in Religious Traditions', *Material Religion*, 12 (2): 235–7.

Boehm, G. (1997), 'Die Lehre des Bilderverbots', in B. Recki and L. Wiesing (eds), *Bild und Reflexion: Paradigmen und Perspektiven gegenwärtiger Ästhetik*, 294–306, Munich: Fink Verlag.

Eckhart, Meister (1936), *Expositio sancti Evangelii secundum Iohannem, Lateinische Werke*, eds. K. Christ et al., Band 3, Stuttgart: Kohlhammer.

Flood, F. B. (2013), 'Inciting Modernity? Images, Alterities and the Contexts of "Cartoon Wars"', in P. Spyer and M. M. Steedly (eds), *Images That Move*, 41–72, Santa Fe: SAR Press.

Foucault, M. (1969), *L'Archéologie du Savoir*, Paris: Editions Galimard.

Gaifman, M. (2017), 'Aniconism: Definitions, Examples and Comparative Perspectives', *Religion*, 47 (3): 335–52.

Geimer, P. (2018), *Inadvertent Images: A History of Photographic Apparitions*, trans. G. Jackson, Chicago: The University of Chicago Press.

Grieser, A. and J. Johnston, eds (2017), *Aesthetics of Religion: A Connective Concept*, Berlin and Boston: de Gruyter.

Hesslinger, M. R. and E. Leschner (2009), 'Einleitung', in E. Leuschner and M. R. Hesslinger (eds), *Das Bild Gottes in Judentum, Christentum und Islam*, 8–14, Petersberg: Michael Imhof Verlag.

James, W. (1917), *The Varieties of Religious Experience: A Study in Human Nature*, New York: Longmans, Green and Co. Available online: http://www.gutenberg.org/files/621/621-h/621-h.html#toc7 (accessed 19 June 2018).

Kruse, C. (2003), *Wozu Menschen malen: Historische Begründungen eines Bildmediums*, Munich: Fink Verlag.

Largier, N. (2012), 'Allegorie und Figuration: Figuraler Realismus bei Heinrich Seuse und Erich Auerbach', *Paragrana*, 21 (2): 36–46.

Largier, N. (2017), 'The Media of Sensation', in K. Norget, V. Napolitano and M. Mayblin (eds), *The Anthropology of Catholicism: A Reader*, 316–26, Oakland: The University of California Press.

Largier, N. (2018), *Spekulative Sinnlichkeit: Kontemplation und Spekulation im Mittelalter*, Zürich: Chronos.

Luiselli, M. M., J. Mohn and S. Gripentrog, eds (2013), *Kult und Bild: Die bildliche Dimension des Kultes im Alten Orient, in der Antike und in der Neuzeit*, Würzburg: Ergon.
Meyer, B. (2012), 'Mediation and the Genesis of Presence: Towards a Material Approach to Religion', Inaugural Lecture, Utrecht University.
Meyer, B. (2013), 'Material Mediations and Religious Practices of World-Making', in K. Lundby (ed.), *Religion Across Media: From Early Antiquity to Late Modernity*, 1–19, New York: Peter Lang.
Meyer, B. (2015), *Sensational Movies: Video, Vision, and Christianity in Ghana*, Oakland: University of California Press.
Mitchell, W. J. T. (2008), 'Four Fundamental Concepts of Image Science', in J. Elkins (ed.), *Visual Literacy*, 14–30, New York: Routledge.
Morgan, D. (1998), *Visual Piety: A History and Theory of Popular Religious Images*, Berkeley: University of California Press.
Morgan, D. (2012), *The Embodied Eye: Religious Visual Culture and the Social Life of Feeling*, Berkeley: University of California Press.
Morgan, D. (2015), *The Forge of Vision: A Visual History of Modern Christianity*, Oakland: University of California Press.
Morgan, D. (2018), *Images at Work: The Material Culture of Enchantment*, Oxford: Oxford University Press.
Orsi, R. (2012), 'Material Children: Making God's Presence Real through Catholic Boys and Girls', in G. Lynch, J. P. Mitchell and A. Strhan (eds), *Religion, Media and Culture: A Reader*, 147–58, London: Routledge.
Orsi, R. (2016), *History and Presence*, Cambridge, MA: Harvard University Press.
Plate, B., ed. (2015), *Key Terms in Material Religion*, Oxford: Bloomsbury.
Port, M. van de (2010), Inaugural Lecture, Vrije Universiteit Amsterdam.
Promey, S. M., ed. (2014), *Sensational Religion: Sensory Cultures in Material Practice*, New Haven: Yale University Press.
Stolow, J. (2005), 'Religion and/as Media', *Theory, Culture & Society*, 22 (4): 119–45.
Stolow, J. (2012), 'Introduction: Religion, Technology and the Things in Between', in J. Stolow (ed.), *Deus in Machina: Religion, Technology, and the Things in Between*, 1–22, New York: Fordham University Press.
Stordalen, T. (2013), 'Media of Ancient Hebrew Religion', in K. Lundby (ed.), *Religion across Media: From Early Antiquity to Late Modernity*, 20–36, New York: Peter Lang.
Vásquez, M. A. (2011), *More Than Belief: A Materialist Theory of Religion*, Oxford and New York: Oxford University Press.
Vries, H. de (2001), 'In Media Res: Global Religion, Public Spheres, and the Task of Contemporary Religious Studies', in H. de Vries and S. Weber (eds), *Religion and Media*, 4–42, Stanford: Stanford University Press.
Weigel, S. (2015), *Grammatologie der Bilder*, Frankfurt am Main: Suhrkamp.

Chapter 1

Aichele, G. (2001), *The Control of Biblical Meaning: Canon as Semiotic Mechanism*, Harrisburg, PA: Trinity Press International.
Bland, K. (2000), *The Artless Jew: Medieval and Modern Affirmations of the Denial of the Visual*, Princeton, NJ: Princeton University Press.

Bloch-Smith, E. (1992), 'The Cult of the Dead in Judah: Interpreting the Material Remains', *Journal of Biblical Literature*, 111: 213–24.

Bloch-Smith, E. (1994), '"Who Is the King of Glory?" Solomon's Temple and Its Symbolism', in M. D. Coogan, J. C. Exum and L. E. Stager (eds), *Scripture and Other Artifacts: Essays on the Bible and Archaeology in Honor of Philip J. King*, 18–31, Louisville, KY: Westminster John Knox Press.

Boehm, B. D. and M. Holcomb (2008), 'Jewish Art in Late Antiquity and Early Byzantium', in *Heilbrunn Timeline of Art History*, New York: The Metropolitan Museum of Art. Available online: http://www.metmuseum.org/toah/hd/jewa/hd_jewa.htm (accessed 8 February 2018).

Busink, T. A. (1970), *Der Tempel von Jerusalem: Von Salomo bis Herodes, eine archäologisch-historische Studie unter Berücksichtigung des westsemitischen Tempelbaus, Band I: Der Tempel Salomos*, Studia Francisci Scholten Memoriae Dicata 3, Leiden: Brill.

Christensen, D. L. (2001), *Deuteronomy, Vol. I: 1 – 21:9*, Nashville, TN: Thomas Nelson.

Cogan, M. (2000), *1 Kings: A New Translation with Introduction and Commentary*, New York: Doubleday.

Derrida, J. (1976), *Of Grammatology*, trans. G. C. Spivak, Baltimore: Johns Hopkins University Press. (Originally published in French in 1967.)

DeVries, S. J. (2003), *1 Kings*, Nashville, TN: Thomas Nelson.

Freedman, D. N. and P. O'Connor (1995), 'כרוב - Kerub', in G. J. Botterweck and H. Ringgren (eds), *Theological Dictionary of the Old Testament*, vol. 7, 307–19, Grand Rapids, MI: Eerdmans.

Gäde, G. (2010), 'Menschwerdung oder Buchwerdung des Wortes Gottes? Zur Logozentrik von Christentum und Islam', *Zeitschrift für Theologie und Kirche* 132: 131–52.

Gaifman, M. (2017), 'Aniconism: Definitions, Examples and Comparative Perspectives', *Religion*, 47 (3): 335–52.

Hartley, J. E. (1992), *Leviticus*, Dallas, TX: Word Books.

Holter, K. (2003), *Deuteronomy 4 and the Second Commandment*, New York: Peter Lang.

Hurowitz, V. A. (1992), *I Have Built You an Exalted House: Temple Building in the Bible in Light of Mesopotamian and Northwest Semitic Writings*, Sheffield: JSOT Press.

Hurowitz, V. A. (2005), 'YHWH's Exalted House: Aspects of the Design and Symbolism of Solomon's Temple', in J. Day (ed.), *Temple and Worship in Biblical Israel*, 63–110, London: T. & T. Clark International.

Jenson, P. P. (1992), *Graded Holiness: A Key to the Priestly Conception of the World*, Sheffield: JSOT Press.

Kasdorff, H. (1969), *Ludwig Klages Werk und Wirkung: Einführung und kommentierte Bibliographie*, 1–2 vols, Bonn: H. Bouvier.

Keel, O. (1972), *Die Welt der altorientalischen Bildsymbolik und das Alte Testament: Am Beispiel der Psalmen*, Zürich: Benziger Verlag.

Keel, O. and C. Uehlinger (1992), *Göttinnen, Götter und Gottessymbole: Neue Erkentnisse zur Religionsgeschichte Kanaans und Israels aufgrund bislang unerschlossener ikonographischer Quellen*, Freiburg: Herder.

Kletter, R. (1996), *The Judean Pillar-Figurines and the Archaeology of Asherah*, Oxford: Tempus Reparatum.

Knohl, I. (2006), *The Sanctuary of Silence: The Priestly Torah and the Holiness School*, Winona Lake, IN: Eisenbrauns.

Knoppers, G. (1995), 'Prayer and Propaganda: Solomon's Dedication of the Temple and the Deuteronomist's Program', *Catholic Biblical Quarterly*, 57: 229–54.

Köckert, M. (2009), 'Vom Kultbild Jahwes zum Bildverbot. Oder: Vom Nutzen der Religionsgeschichte für die Theologie', *Zeitschrift für Theologie und Kirche*, 106: 371–406.
Labuschagne, C. L. (1966), *The Incomparability of Yahweh in the Old Testament*, Leiden: Brill.
Lang, B. (1995), 'כפר – Kipper, כפרת – Kapporet, כפר – Koper, כפרים – Kippurim', in G. J. Botterweck et al. (eds), *Theological Dictionary of the Old Testament*, vol. 7, 288–303, Grand Rapids, MI: Eerdmans.
Larsen, M. T., ed. (1979), *Power and Propaganda: A Symposium on Ancient Empires*, Copenhagen: Akademisk forlag.
Levine, L. I. (2012), *Visual Judaism in Late Antiquity: Historical Contexts of Jewish Art*, New Haven, CT: Yale University Press.
Mathys, H.-P. (2013), 'Bilder und Bildverbot in Israel – Der Mensch als Bild Gottes', in M. M. Luiselli, J. Mohn and S. Gripentrog (eds), *Kult Und Bild: Die Bildliche Dimension des Kultes im Alten Orient, in der Antike und in Der Neuzeit*, 111–62, Würzburg: Ergon.
Meshel, Z. (2012), *Kuntillet 'Ajrud (Horvat Teman): An Iron Age II Religious Site on the Judah-Sinai Border*, Jerusalem: Israel Exploration Society.
Mettinger, T. N. D. (1995), *No Graven Image? Israelite Aniconism in Its Ancient Near Eastern Context*, Stockholm: Almqvist & Wiksell International.
Mettinger, T. N. D. (2006), 'A Conversation with My Critics: Cultic Image or Aniconism in the First Temple?' in Y. Amit, E. Ben Zvi, I. Finkelstein and O. Lipschits (eds), *Essays on Ancient Israel in Its Near Eastern Context: A Tribute to Nadav Na'aman*, 273–96, Winona Lake, IN: Eisenbrauns.
Otten, W. (2007), 'The Tension between Word and Image in Christianity', in W. van Asselt, P. van Geest, D. Müller and T. Salemink (eds), *Iconoclasm and Iconoclash: Struggle for Religious Identity*, 33–48, Leiden: Brill.
Pietsch, M. (2007), 'Von Königen und Königtümern: Eine Untersuchung zur Textgeschichte der Königsbücher', *Zeitschrift für die alttestamentliche Wissenschaft*, 119: 39–58.
Ranciere, J. (2004), *The Politics of Aesthetics: The Distribution of the Sensible*, London: Continuum.
Reade, J. (1979), 'Ideology and Propaganda in Assyrian Art', in M. T. Larsen (ed.), *Power and Propaganda: A Symposium on Ancient Empires*, Copenhagen: Akademisk forlag.
Schenker, A. (2004), *Die Älteste Textgeschichte der Königsbücher: Die hebräische Vorlage der ursprünglichen Septuaginta als älteste Textform der Königsbücher*, Fribourg: Academic Press.
Schenker, A. (2006), 'The Ark as Sign of God's Absent Presence in Solomon's Temple: 1 Kings 8.6–8 in the Hebrew and Greek Bibles', in P. McCosker (ed.), *What Is It That the Scripture Says? Essays in Biblical Interpretation, Translation and Reception in Honour of Henry Wansbrough OSB*, 1–9, London: T&T Clark.
Schweitzer, S. J. (2011), 'The Temple in Samuel–Kings and Chronicles', in J. Corley and H. van Grol (eds), *Rewriting Biblical History: Essays on Chronicles and Ben Sira in Honor of Pancratius Beentjes*, 123–35, Berlin: de Gruyter.
Stordalen, T. (2012), 'Locating the Textual Gaze – Then and Now', *Material Religion*, 8 (4): 521–4.
Stordalen, T. (2013), 'Media of Ancient Hebrew Religion', in K. Lundby (ed.), *Religion across Media: From Early Antiquity to Late Modernity*, 20–36, New York: Peter Lang.
Stordalen, T. (2014), 'Imagined and Forgotten Communities: Othering in the Story of Josiah's Reform (2 Kings 23)', in E. Ben Zvi and D. Edelman (eds), *Imagining the Other and Constructing Israelite Identity in the Early Second Temple Period*, 182–200, London: Bloomsbury.
Sweeney, M. A. (2007), *I & II Kings: A Commentary*, Old Testament Library, Philadelphia, PA: Westminster John Knox Press.

Uehlinger, C. (1997), 'Anthropomorphic Cult Statuary in Iron Age Palestine and the Search for Yahweh's Cult Images', in K. van der Toorn (ed.), *Anthropomorphic Cult Statuary*, 97–155, Leuven: Peeters.
Uehlinger, C. (2005), 'Was There a Cult Reform Under King Josiah? The Case for a Well-Grounded Minimum', in L. L. Grabbe (ed.), *Good Kings and Bad Kings*, 278–316, London: T&T Clark.
Van Seters, J. (1997), 'Solomon's Temple: Fact and Ideology in Biblical and Near Eastern Historiography', *CBQ*, 59: 45–57.
Vogt, P. T. (2006), *Deuteronomic Theology and the Significance of the Torah: A Reappraisal*, Winona Lake, IN: Eisenbrauns.
Weinfeld, M. (1972), *Deuteronomy and the Deuteronomic School*, Oxford: Oxford University Press.
Wilson, I. (1995), *Out of the Midst of Fire: Divine Presence in Deuteronomy*, Atlanta, GA: Scholars Press.
Wilson, I. (2005), *Merely a Container? The Ark in Deuteronomy*, London: T&T Clark.
Wilson, I. D. (2012), 'Judean Pillar Figurines and Ethnic Identity in the Shadow of Assyria', *JSOT*, 36 (3): 259–78.
Zobel, H.-J. (1974), 'ארון – "arôn"', in G. J. Botterweck and H. Ringgren (eds), *Theological Dictionary of the Old Testament*, vol. 1, 363–74, Grand Rapids: Eerdmans.
Zwickel, W. (2013), 'Der Tempel Salomos im Kontext der Ikonographie und der archäologischen Funde', in J. Verheyden (ed.), *The Figure of Solomon in Jewish, Christian and Islamic Tradition: King, Sage and Architect*, 57–84, Leiden: Brill.

Chapter 2

Abou el Fadl, K. (2007), *The Great Theft: Wrestling Islam from the Extremists*, New York: HarperOne Publishing.
Ahmad, M. I. and H. W. Glidden (1968), 'Muslims and Taswir: Translated from the Journal of Al-Azhar', in E. Gräf (ed.), *Festschrift Werner Caskel*, 250–68, Leiden: Brill.
Ahmed, S. (2015), *What is Islam: The Importance of Being Islamic*, Princeton: Princeton University Press.
Arnold, T. (1928), *Painting in Islam, A Study of the Place of Pictorial Art in Muslim Culture*, Oxford: Clarendon Press.
Brisson, L. (2004), *How Philosophers Saved Myths: Allegorical Interpretation and Classical Mythology*, trans. C. Tihanyi, Chicago: University of Chicago Press.
Creswell, K. A. C. (1946), 'The Lawfulness of Painting in Early Islam', *Ars Islamica*, 11/12: 159–66.
De Saussure, F. (1976), *Course in General Linguistics*, Oxford: Duckworth.
Dunyā-al, I. A. and A. A. I. Muhammed (1938), *Tracts on Listening to Music: Being Dhamm al-malahi and Bawariq al-ilma'*, trans. J. Robson, London: Royal Asiatic Society.
El-Rouayheb, K. (2010), 'From Ibn Hajar al-Hatami (d.1566) to Khayr al-Din al-Alusi (d. 1899): Changing Views of Ibn Taymiyya among Non-Hanbali Sunni Scholars', in Y. Rapoport and S. Ahmed (eds), *Ibn Taymiyya and His Times*, 269–318, Oxford: Oxford University Press.
Flood, F. B. (2002), 'Between Cult and Culture: Bamiyan, Islamic Iconoclasm, and the Museum – Afghanistan', *The Art Bulletin*, 84 (4): 641–59.
Flood, F. B. (2009), *Objects of Translation: Material Culture and Medieval 'Hindu-Muslim Encounter*, Princeton: Princeton University Press.

Fudge, B. (2006), 'Qur'anic Exegesis in Medieval Islam and Modern Orientalism', *Die Welt des Islams*, New Series, 46 (2): 115–47.
Gruber, C. (2009), 'Between Logos (Kalima) and Light (Nur): Representations of Muhammad in Islamic Painting', *Muqarnas*, XXVI: 229–62.
Gruber, C. and A. Shalem, eds (2014), *The Image of the Prophet between Ideal and Ideology: A Scholarly Investigation*, Berlin and Boston: de Gruyter.
Guytas, D. (1999), 'Farabi', *Iranica*, Vol. 9, Fasc. 2: 208–13. Available online: http://www.iranicaonline.org/articles/farabi-i (accessed 16 September 2016).
Halliwell, S. (2002), *The Aesthetics of Mimesis: Ancient Texts and Modern Problems*, Princeton, NJ: Princeton University Press.
Harris, R. and M. Stokes, eds (2017), *Theory and Practice in the Music of the Islamic World: Essays in Honour of Owen Wright*, London: SOAS Musicology Series.
Ibn Taymiyya, *Majmu al-Fataawaa*. Available online: https://islamqa.info/en/7222 (accessed 27 September 2016).
Ibric, A. (2006), *Islamisches Bilderverbot vom Mittel- bis ins Digital Zeitalter*, Vienna: LIT Verlag GmbH.
Kabbani, M. H. S. (1995), *The Naqshibandi Sufi Way: History and Guidebook of the Saints of the Golden Chain*, Chicago: Kazi Publications.
King, G. R. D. (1985), 'Islam, Iconoclasm, and the Declaration of Doctrine', *Bulletin of the School of Oriental and African Studies*, 48 (2): 267–77.
Koch, E. (2010), 'The Mughal Emperor as Solomon, Majnun, and Orpheus, or the Album as a Think Tank for Allegory', *Muqarnas*, 27: 277–311.
Lavoix, H. (1859), 'La Peinture Musulmane', in Paris Socïete Orientale de France, *Revue de l'Orient, de l'Algerie, et des colonies*, IX.
Levinas, E. (1969), *Totality and Infinity*, trans. A. Lingis, Pittsburgh: Duquesne University Press.
Naef, S. (2003), *Y a-t-il une 'question de l'image' en Islam?*, Paris: Téraèdre.
Necipoğlu, G. (1995), *The Topkapi Scroll: Geometry and Ornament in Islamic Architecture, Topkapi Palace Museum Library MS H. 1956*, Santa Monica, CA: Getty Center for the History of Art and Humanities.
Netton, I. R. (1992), *Al-Farabi and His School*, London: Routledge.
Neuwirth, A. (2003), 'Qur'an and History – A Disputed Relationship', *Journal of Qur'anic Studies*, 5 (1): 1–18.
Nizami, G. (1991), *Das Alexanderbuch / Iskandarname*, trans. J. C. Bürgel, Zürich: Manesse Verlag.
Northwood, H. (2015), 'Making Music with Aesop's Fables', in J. Bell and M. Nass (eds), *Plato's Animals*, 13–27, Bloomington: Indiana University Press.
Paret, R. (1976/7), 'Die Entstehungszeit des Islamischen Bilderverbot', *Kunst des Orients*, 11 (1–2): 158–81.
Plotinus (1991), *The Enneads*, trans. S. Mackenna, London: Penguin Classics.
Rifai, K. (2011), 'Listen: Commentary on the Spiritual Couplets of Mevlana Rumi', trans. V. Holbrook, Louisville, KY: Fons Vitae.
Robson, James, trans. (1938), *Tracts on Listening to Music by 'Abd Allāh b Muḥammad Ibn Abī al-Dunyā; Aḥmad b Muḥammad al- Ġazālī*, London: Royal Asiatic Society.
Shaw, W. M. K. (forthcoming), *What Is 'Islamic' Art: Between Religion and Perception*, Cambridge: Cambridge University Press.
Shehadi, F. (1995), *Philosophies of Music in Medieval Islam*, Leiden: Brill.
Subrahmanyam, S. (2010), 'Globalising Cultures: Art and Mobility in the Eighteenth Century', *Ars Orientalis*, 39: 39–83.

Wade, B. (1998), *Imagining Sound: An Ethnomusicological Study of Music, Art, and Culture in Mughal India*, Chicago: University of Chicago Press.
Walker, A. T. (1928), *Painting in Islam, A Study of the Place of Pictorial Art in Muslim Culture*, London: Clarendon Press.
Watt, K. (2002), 'Thomas Walker Arnold and the Re-Evaluation of Islam 1864–1930', *Modern Asian Studies*, 36 (1): 1–98.
Wright, O. (2010), *Epistles of the Brethren of Purity: On Music, An Arabic Critical Edition and English Translation of Epistle 5*, Oxford: Oxford University Press.

Chapter 3

Anidjar, G. (2006), 'Secularism', *Critical Inquiry*, 33 (1): 52–77.
Asad, T. (2008), 'Historical Notes on the Idea of Secular Criticism', The Immanent Frame: Secularism, Religion, and the Public Sphere. Available online: https://tif.ssrc.org/2008/01/25/historical-notes-on-the-idea-of-secular-criticism/ (accessed January 2016).
Belting, H. (1994), *Likeness and Presence: A History of the Image before the Era of Art*, Chicago: University of Chicago Press.
Bori, P. C. (1990), *The Golden Calf and the Origins of the Anti-Jewish Controversy*, trans. D. Ward, Atlanta: Scholars Press.
Cohen, H. (1995), *Religion of Reason Out of the Sources of Judaism*, trans. S. Kaplan, Atlanta: Scholars Press.
Freud, S. ([1939] 2001), *Moses and Monotheism: An Outline of Psychoanalysis and Other Works*, trans. J. Strachey, Standard Edition of the Complete Psychological Works of Sigmund Freud, vol. 23, London: Vintage.
Halbertal, M. and A. Margolit (1988), *Idolatry*, trans. N. Goldblum, Cambridge, MA: Harvard University Press.
James, W. (2002), *Varieties of Religious Experience: A Study in Human Nature*, London: Routledge.
Kant, I. ([1790] 1951), *Critique of Judgment*, trans. J. H. Bernard, New York: Hafner Press.
Kant, I. ([1797] 1964), *The Metaphysical Principles of Virtue*, trans. J. Ellington, Indianapolis: Bobbs-Merill.
Keane, W. (2007), *Christian Moderns: Freedom and Fetish in the Mission Encounter*, Oakland: University of California Press.
Latour, B. and P. Weibel, eds (2002), *Iconoclash: Beyond the Image Wars in Science, Religion and Art*, Cambridge, MA and London: MIT Press.
Latour, B. (2011), *On the Modern Cult of the Factish Gods*, Durham, NC: Duke University Press.
Lessing, G. E. (2005), *Philosophical and Theological Writings*, ed. H. B. Nisbet, Cambridge: Cambridge University Press.
Masuzawa, T. (2008), 'Troubles with Materiality: The Ghost of Fetishism in the Nineteenth Century', in H. de Vries (ed.), *Religion: Beyond a Concept*, 647–67, New York: Fordham University Press.
Mitchell, W. J. T. (1994), *Picture Theory: Essays on Verbal and Visual Representation*, London and Chicago: University of Chicago Press.
Mitchell, W. J. T. (2005), *What Do Pictures Want? The Lives and Loves of Images*, Chicago and London: University of Chicago Press.
Morgan, D. (2015), 'Thing', in S. B. Plate (ed.), *Key Terms in Material Religion*, 253–61, London and New York: Bloomsbury.

Plate, S. B. (2015), 'Words', in S. B. Plate (ed.), *Key Terms in Material Religion*, 275–80, London and New York: Bloomsbury.
Rancière, J. (2007), *The Future of the Image*, trans. G. Elliott, London: Verso.
Sawyer, D. (2002), *God, Gender and the Bible*, London: Routledge.
Scarry, E. (1985), *The Body in Pain: The Making and Unmaking of the World*, Oxford: Oxford University Press.
Schmidt, L. E. (2000), *Hearing Things: Religion, Illusion and the American Enlightenment*, Cambridge, MA: Harvard University Press.
Smelik, K. A. D. (1995), 'Moloch, Molekh, or Molk-Sacrifice? A Reassessment of the Evidence Concerning the Hebrew Term Molekh', *Scandinavian Journal of the Old Testament*, 9 (1): 133–42.
Smith, M. S. (2016), *Where the Gods Are: Spatial Dimensions of Anthropomorphism in the Biblical World*, New Haven: Yale University Press.
Toorn, K. van der (2007), *Scribal Culture and the Making of the Hebrew Bible*, Cambridge, MA: Harvard University Press.
Trenchard, J. (1709), *Natural History of Superstition*, London.
Vasari, G. (1550), *Lives of the Most Excellent Painters, Sculptors and Architects*, First Preface, Florence.
Vial, T. M. and M. A. Hadley, eds (2001), *Ethical Monotheism, Past and Present: Essays in Honor of Wendell S. Dietrich*, Providence: Brown Judaic Studies.
Waters, F. (2011), 'Poussin Vandalism Sparks Museum Fee Debate', *The Telegraph*, 19 July. Available online: https://www.telegraph.co.uk/culture/art/art-news/8647250/Poussin-vandalism-sparks-museum-fee-debate.html (accessed 28 June 2018).

Chapter 4

Asad, T. (1993), *Genealogies of Religion: Discipline and Reasons of Power in Christianity and Islam*, Baltimore: Johns Hopkins University Press.
Belting, H. (1990), *Bild und Kult: Eine Geschichte des Bildes vor dem Zeitalter der Kunst*, Munich: C.H. Beck.
Belting, H. (2001), *Bild-Anthropologie: Entwürfe für eine Bildwissenschaft*, Munich: Fink Verlag.
Belting, H. (2016), 'Iconic Presence: Images in Religious Traditions', *Material Religion*, 12 (2): 235–7.
Boehm, G. (1994), 'Die Bilderfrage', in G. Boehm (ed.), *Was ist ein Bild?*, 325–43, Munich: Fink Verlag.
Boehm, G. (1997), 'Die Lehre des Bilderverbots', in B. Recki and L. Wiesing (eds), *Bild und Reflexion: Paradigmen und Perspektiven gegenwärtiger Ästhetik*, 294–306, Munich: Fink Verlag.
Böhme, H. (2006), *Fetischismus und Kultur: Eine andere Theorie der Moderne*, Reinbek bei Hamburg: Rowohlt Taschenbuch Verlag.
Brunotte, U. (2013), 'Bilderkult und Ikonoklasmus: Die Lehre von der Inkarnation und das reformatorische Problem der Verkörperung', in M. M. Luiselli, J. Mohn and S. Gripentrog (eds), *Kult und Bild: Die bildliche Dimension des Kultes im Alten Orient, in der Antike und in der Neuzeit*, 181–202, Würzburg: Ergon.
Dubuisson, D. (2015), 'Visual Culture and Religious Studies: A New Paradigm', *Method & Theory in the Study of Religion*, 27 (4–5): 299–311.

Freedberg, D. (1989), *The Power of Images: Studies in the History and Theory of Response*, Chicago: The University of Chicago Press.

Hecht, C. (2016), *Katholische Bildertheologie der frühen Neuzeit. Studien zu Traktaten von Johannes Molanus, Gabriele Paleotti und anderen Autoren*, 3rd edition, Berlin: Gebr. Mann Verlag.

Jakiša, M. and M. Treml (2007), 'Bilderordnungen als Gegenstand kultureller Verhandlungen: Bemerkungen zum Bilderverbot in Literatur und Religion', *Trajekte*, 15 (8): 42–6.

Kant, I. ([1790] 1960), *Akademieausgabe von Immanuel Kants Gesammelten Werken Band 5. Kritik der Urteilskraft*. Available online: https://korpora.zim.uni-duisburg-essen.de/kant/aa05/274.html (accessed 31 May 2018).

Keane, W. (2007), *Christian Moderns: Freedom and Fetish in the Mission Encounter*, Oakland: University of California Press.

Keane, W. (2018), 'On Semiotic Ideology', *Signs and Society*, 6 (1): 64–87.

Koerner, J. L. (2004), *The Reformation of the Image*, Chicago: The University of Chicago Press.

Kohl, K.-H. (2003), *Die Macht der Dinge: Geschichte und Theorie sakraler Objekte*, Munich: C.H. Beck.

Kruse, C. (2003), *Wozu Menschen malen: Historische Begründungen eines Bildmediums*, Munich: Fink Verlag.

Latour, B. (2002), 'Whats is Iconoclash? Or is there a World beyond the Image Wars?' in B. Latour and P. Weibel (eds), *Iconoclash: Beyond the Image Wars in Science, Religion and Art*, 14–37, Cambridge, MA and London: MIT Press.

Leyten, H. M. (2015), *From Idol to Art: African 'Objects-with-Power': A Challenge for Missionaries, Anthropologists and Museum Curators*, Leiden: African Studies Centre.

Luiselli, M. M., J. Mohn and S. Gripentrog (2013), *Kult und Bild: Die bildliche Dimension des Kultes im Alten Orient, in der Antike und in der Neuzeit*, Würzburg: Ergon.

Meyer, B. (2012), 'Mediation and the Genesis of Presence: Towards a Material Approach to Religion', Inaugural Lecture, Utrecht University.

Meyer, B. (1999), *Translating the Devil: Religion and Modernity among the Ewe in Ghana*, IAL-Series, Edinburgh: Edinburgh University Press; Trenton, NJ: Africa World Press.

Meyer, B. (2010), '"There Is a Spirit in That Image." Mass Produced Jesus Pictures and Protestant Pentecostal Animation in Ghana', *Comparative Studies in Society and History*, 52 (1): 100–30.

Meyer, B. (2015a), *Sensational Movies: Video, Vision, and Christianity in Ghana*, Oakland: University of California Press.

Meyer, B. (2015b), 'Picturing the Invisible: Visual Culture and the Study of Religion', *Method and Theory in the Study of Religion*, 27 (4–5): 333–60.

Mitchell, W. J. T. (2005). *What Do Pictures Want? The Lives and Loves of Images*, Chicago: University of Chicago Press.

Mohn, J. (2013), 'Von den Kult-Bildern zum Bilder-Kult "romantischer" Kunstreligion: Religionsgeschichtliche Interpretationen zu Philipp Otto Runges Zeiten-Zyklus in religionsaisthetischer Perspektive', in M. M. Luiselli, J. Mohn and S. Gripentrog (eds), *Kult und Bild: Die bildliche Dimension des Kultes im Alten Orient, in der Antike und in der Neuzeit*, 203–42, Würzburg: Ergon.

Morgan, D. (1998), *Visual Piety: A History and Theory of Popular Religious Images*, Oakland: University of California Press.

Morgan, D. (2007), *The Lure of Images: A History of Religion and Visual Media in America*, New York: Routledge.

Morgan, D. (2015), *The Forge of Vision: A Visual History of Modern Christianity*, Oakland: University of California Press.
Morris, R. C. (2017), 'After de Brosses: Fetishism, Translation, Comparativism, Critique', in R. C. Morris and D. H. Leonard (eds), *The Returns of Fetishism: Charles de Brosses and the Afterlives of an Idea*, 133–319, 362–89, Chicago: The University of Chicago Press.
Olukoya, D. K. (2009), *100 Facts about Idolatry*, Lagos: The Battle Cry Christian Ministries.
Pels, P. (1998), 'The Spirit of Matter: On Fetish, Rarity, Fact and Fancy', in P. Spyer (ed.), *Border Fetishisms: Material Objects in Unstable Spaces*, 91–120, New York: Routledge.
Pinney, C. (2004), *Photos of the Gods: The Printed Image and Political Struggle in India*, London: Reaktion.
Promey, S. M., ed. (2014), *Sensational Religion: Sensory Cultures in Material Practice*, New Haven: Yale University Press.
Ross, D. H. (2014), 'The Art of Almighty God: In His Own Words', *African Arts*, 47 (2): 8–27.
Sherwood, Y. (2014), *Biblical Blaspheming: Trials of the Sacred for a Secular Age*, New York: Cambridge University Press.
Spieth, J. (1911), *Die Religion der Eweer in Süd-Togo*, Göttingen: Vandenhoeck and Ruprecht.
Van Asselt, W. J. (2007), 'The Prohibition of Images and Protestant Identity', in W. J. van Asselt, P. van Geest, D. Müller and T. Salemink (eds), *Iconoclasm and Iconoclash: Struggle for Religious Identity*, 299–311, Leiden: Brill.
Von Bodenstein-Karlstadt, A. (1522), *Abthunung der Bilder*. Available online: https://www.uni-due.de/collcart/es/sem/s12/material/index.htm (accessed 29 May 2018).
Wendl, T. (1991), *Mami Wata: Oder ein Kult zwischen den Kulturen*. Münster: Lit.
Westermann, D. H. (1906), *Wörterbuch der Ewe-Sprache. II. Teil Deutsch-Ewe Wörterbuch*, Berlin: Dietrich Reimer.

Chapter 5

As usual in interdisciplinary settings, this chapter can only refer to a very limited selection of a vast secondary literature from different fields (Levantine archaeology, biblical studies, history of religion\s).

Ahlström, G. W. (1970/71), 'An Israelite God Figurine from Hazor', *Orientalia Suecana*, 19/20: 54–62.
Aktor, M. (2017), 'The Hindu *pañcāyatanapūjā* in the Aniconism Spectrum', *Religion*, 47 (3): 503–19.
Allen, S. (2014), *The Splintered Divine: A Study of Ištar, Baal, and Yahweh Divine Names and Divine Multiplicity in the Ancient Near East*, Berlin: De Gruyter.
Anthonioz, S. (2015), 'La destruction de la statue de Yhwh', *Cahiers du Cercle Ernest Renan*, 269: 1–15.
Assmann, J. (1996), 'The Mosaic Distinction: Israel, Egypt, and the Invention of Paganism', *Representations*, 56: 48–67.
Becking, B. (2013), 'Silent Witness: The Symbolic Presence of God in the Temple Vessels in Ezra-Nehemiah', in N. MacDonald and I. de Hulster (eds), *Divine Presence and Absence in Exilic and Post-Exilic Judaism*, 267–82, Tübingen: Mohr Siebeck.

Berlejung, A. (2009), 'Twisting Traditions: Programmatic Absence-Theology for the Northern Kingdom in 1 Kgs 12:26–33* (the "Sin of Jeroboam")', *Journal of Northwest Semitic Languages*, 35: 1–42.

Berlejung, A. (2017), 'The Origins and Beginnings of the Worship of YHWH: The Iconographic Evidence', in J. von Oorschot and M. Witte (eds), *The Origins of Yahwism*, 67–92, Berlin: De Gruyter.

Biran, A. (1999), 'Two Bronze Plaques and the ḥuṣṣot of Dan', *Israel Exploration Journal*, 49 (1/2): 43–54.

Bloch-Smith, E. (2015), 'Massebot Standing for Yhwh: The Fall of a Yhwistic Cult Symbol', in J. J. Collins, T. M. Lemos and S. M. Olyan (eds), *Worship, Women, and War: Essays in Honor of Susan Niditch*, 99–115, Providence, RI: Brown University.

Dalman, G. (1906), 'Ein neugefundenes Javebild', *Palästina-Jahrbuch*, 2: 44–50.

Doak, B. R. (2015), *Phoenician Aniconism in Its Mediterranean and Ancient Near Eastern Context*, Atlanta, GA: SBL Press.

Gaifman, M. (2012), *Aniconism in Greek Antiquity*, New York: Oxford University Press.

Gaifman, M. (2017), 'Aniconism: Definitions, Examples and Comparative Perspectives', *Religion*, 47 (3): 335–52.

Gaifman, M. and M. Aktor, eds (2017), *Exploring Aniconism*. Thematic Issue of *Religion*, 47 (3): 335–519.

Garfinkel, Y. and M. Mumcuoglu (2016), *Solomon's Temple and Palace: New Archaeological Discoveries*, Jerusalem: Bible Lands Museum Jerusalem and Washington DC: Biblical Archaeology Society.

Gilmour, G. (2009), 'An Iron Age II Pictorial Inscription from Jerusalem Illustrating Yahweh and Asherah', *Palestine Exploration Quarterly*, 141 (2): 87–103.

Gilula, M. (1979), 'To Yahweh Shomron and His Asherah', *Shnaton la-Miqra*, 2: 129–37 (Hebrew). XV–XVI (English abstract.)

Gitler, H. and O. Tal (2006), *The Coinage of Philistia of the Fifth and Fourth Centuries BC: A Study of the Earliest Coins of Palestine*, Milano: Ennerre and New York: Amphora Books/B. & H. Kreindler.

Grieser, A. and J. Johnston, eds (2017), *Aesthetics of Religion: A Connective Concept*, Berlin: De Gruyter.

Hensel, B. (2016), *Juda und Samaria: Zum Verhältnis zweier nach-exilischer Jahwismen*, Tübingen: Mohr Siebeck.

Houtman, D. and B. Meyer, eds (2012), *Things: Religion and the Question of Materiality*, Bronx, NY: Fordham University Press.

Hulster, I. J. de (2013), '(Ohn)Macht der Bilder? (Ohn)Macht der Menschen? TC242.5 in ihrem Entstehungs- und Forschungskontext', in A. Lykke (ed.), *Macht des Geldes – Macht der Bilder*, 45–68, Wiesbaden: Harrassowitz.

Huntington, S. L. (2015), 'Shifting the Paradigm: The Aniconic Theory and Its Terminology', *South Asian Studies*, 31 (2): 163–86.

Jensen, H. J. L. (2017), 'Aniconic Propaganda in the Hebrew Bible, or: The Possible Birth of Religious Seriousness', *Religion*, 47 (3): 399–407.

Jeremias, J. (1993), 'Thron oder Wagen? Eine aussergewöhnliche Terrakotte aus der späten Eisenzeit in Juda', in W. Zwickel (ed.), *Biblische Welten: Festschrift für Martin Metzger zu seinem 65. Geburtstag*, 41–60, Fribourg: Universitätsverlag and Göttingen: Vandenhoeck & Ruprecht.

Keel, O. (2001), 'Warum im Jerusalemer Tempel kein anthropomorphes Kultbild gestanden haben dürfte', in G. Boehm (ed.), *Homo Pictor*, 244–82, Munich and Leipzig: K. G. Saur.

Keel, O. (2007), *Die Geschichte Jerusalems und die Entstehung des Monotheismus*, Göttingen: Vandenhoeck & Ruprecht.

Keel, O. and C. Uehlinger (1998), *Gods, Goddesses, and Images of God in Ancient Israel*, Minneapolis: Fortress Press and Edinburgh: T&T Clark.

Kisilevitz, Sh. (2015), 'The Iron IIA Judahite Temple at Tel Moẓa', *Tel Aviv*, 42 (2): 147–64.

Köckert, M. (2007), 'Die Entstehung des Bilderverbots', in B. Groneberg and H. Spieckermann (eds), *Die Welt der Götterbilder*, 272–90, Berlin and New York: De Gruyter.

Köckert, M. (2009), 'Vom Kultbild Jahwes zum Bilderverbot. Oder: Vom Nutzen der Religionsgeschichte für die Theologie', *Zeitschrift für Theologie und Kirche*, 106: 371–406.

Levenson, A. T. (2011), *The Making of the Modern Jewish Bible: How Scholars in Germany, Israel, and America Transformed an Ancient Text*, Lanham: Rowman & Littlefield.

Levenson, J. D. (2012), *Inheriting Abraham: The Legacy of the Patriarch in Judaism, Christianity, and Islam*, Princeton: Princeton University Press.

Levine, L. I. (2013), *Visual Judaism in Late Antiquity: Historical Contexts of Jewish Art*, New Haven, CT: Yale University Press.

Lowin, Sh. L. (2011), 'Abraham in Islamic and Jewish Exegesis', *Religion Compass*, 5 (6): 224–35.

Mazar, A. and N. Panitz-Cohen (2008), 'To What God? Altars and a House Shrine from Tel Rehov Puzzle Archaeologists', *Biblical Archaeology Review*, 34 (4): 40–7, 76.

Meshel, Z. (2012), *Kuntillet 'Ajrud (Ḥorvat Teman): An Iron Age II Religious Site on the Judah-Sinai Border*, Jerusalem: Israel Exploration Society.

Meshorer, Y. and Sh. Qedar (1999), *Samarian Coinage*, Jerusalem: Israel Numismatic Society.

Mettinger, T. N. D. (1995), *No Graven Image? Israelite Aniconism in Its Ancient Near Eastern Context*, Stockholm: Almqvist & Wiksell International.

Mettinger, T. N. D. (2006), 'A Conversation with My Critics: Cultic Image or Aniconism in the First Temple?' in Y. Amit et al. (eds), *Essays on Ancient Israel in Its Near Eastern Context: A Tribute to Nadav Na'aman*, 273–97, Winona Lake, IN: Eisenbrauns. *Reports from a Scholar's Life: Select Papers on the Hebrew Bible*, 153–77, Winona Lake, IN: Eisenbrauns, 2015.

Meyer, B., ed. (2009), *Aesthetic Formations: Media, Religion, and the Senses*, New York: Palgrave Macmillan.

Mohan, U. and J.-P. Warnier (2017), 'Marching the Devotional Subject: The Bodily-and-Material Cultures of Religion', *Journal of Material Culture*, 22 (4): 369–84.

Morgan, D., ed. (2010), *Religion and Material Culture: The Matter of Belief*, London: Routledge.

Na'aman, N. (1999), 'No Anthropomorphic Graven Image: Notes on the Assumed Anthropomorphic Cult Statues in the Temples of YHWH in the Pre-Exilic Period', *Ugarit-Forschungen*, 31: 391–415 = *Ancient Israel's History and Historiography: The First Temple Period* (Collected Essays, vol. 3), 311–38, Winona Lake, IN: Eisenbrauns, 2006.

Na'aman, N. (2017), 'The Judahite Temple at Tel Moẓa near Jerusalem: The House of Obed-Edom?' *Tel Aviv*, 44 (1): 3–13.

Niehr, H. (1997), 'In Search of YHWH's Cult Image in the First Temple', in K. van der Toorn (ed.), *The Image and the Book: Iconic Cults, Aniconism, and the Veneration of the Holy Book in Israel and the Ancient Near East*, 73–95, Leuven: Peeters.

Niehr, H. (2003), 'Götterbilder und Bilderverbot', in M. Oeming and K. Schmid (eds), *Der eine Gott und die Götter: Polytheismus und Monotheismus im antiken Israel*, 227-48, Zürich: TVZ.

Ornan, T. (2006), 'The Lady and the Bull: Remarks on the Bronze Plaque from Tel Dan', in Y. Amit et al. (eds), *Essays on Ancient Israel in Its Near Eastern Context: A Tribute to Nadav Na'aman*, 297-312, Winona Lake, IN: Eisenbrauns.

Otten, W. (2007), 'The Tension between Word and Image in Christianity', in W. van Asselt et al. (eds), *Iconoclasm and Iconoclash: Struggle for Religious Identity*, 33-48, Leiden: Brill.

Promey, S., ed. (2014), *Sensational Religion: Sensory Cultures in Material Practices*, New Haven, CT: Yale University Press.

Römer, T. (2015), *The Invention of God*, Cambridge, MA: Harvard University Press.

Schipper, B. U. (2013), 'Kultbilder im antiken Israel: Das Verhältnis von Kult und Bild am Beispiel der anikonischen Kultobjekte', in M. M. Luiselli, J. Mohn and S. Gripentrog (eds), *Kult und Bild: Die bildliche Dimension des Kultes im Alten Orient, in der Antike und in der Neuzeit*, 163-80, Würzburg: Ergon.

Stavrakopoulou, F. and J. Barton, eds (2010), *Religious Diversity in Ancient Israel and Judah*, London: T&T Clark.

Tatum, W. B. (1986), 'The LXX Version of the Second Commandment (Ex. 20,3-6 = Deut. 5,7-10): A Polemic against Idols, Not Images', *Journal for the Study of Judaism*, 17: 177-95.

Thomas, R. (2016), 'The Identity of the Standing Figures on Pithos a from Kuntillet 'Ajrud: A Reassessment', *Journal of Ancient Near Eastern Religions*, 16 (2): 121-91.

Uehlinger, C. (1996), 'Israelite Aniconism in Context' [review of Mettinger 1995], *Biblica*, 77: 540-9.

Uehlinger, C. (1997), 'Anthropomorphic Cult Statuary in Iron Age Palestine and the Search for Yahweh's Cult Images', in K. van der Toorn (ed.), *The Image and the Book: Iconic Cults, Aniconism, and the Veneration of the Holy Book in Israel and the Ancient Near East*, 97-156, Leuven: Peeters.

Uehlinger, C. (2003), 'Exodus, Stierbild und biblisches Kultbildverbot: Religionsgeschichtliche Voraussetzungen eines biblisch-theologischen Spezifikums', in C. Hardmeier, R. Kessler and A. Ruwe (eds), *Freiheit und Recht*, 42-77, Gütersloh: Gütersloher Verlagshaus.

Uehlinger, C. (2006), 'Arad, Qiṭmit – Judahite Aniconism vs. Edomite Iconic Cult? Questioning the Evidence', in G. Beckman and T. J. Lewis (eds), *Texts, Artifacts and Images: Revealing Ancient Israelite Religion*, 80-112, Atlanta, GA: Scholars Press.

Uehlinger, C. (2015), 'Distinctive or Diverse? Conceptualizing Ancient Israelite Religion in Its Southern Levantine Setting', *Hebrew Bible and Ancient Israel*, 4 (1): 1-24.

Van Asselt, W. (2007), 'The Prohibition of Images and Protestant Identity', in W. van Asselt et al. (eds), *Iconoclasm and Iconoclash: Struggle for Religious Identity*, 299-311, Leiden: Brill.

Wyssmann, P. (2013), 'König oder Gott? Der Thronende auf den Münzen des perserzeitlichen Samaria', in A. Lykke (ed.), *Macht des Geldes – Macht der Bilder*, 1-19, Wiesbaden: Harrassowitz.

Zevit, Z. (2001), *The Religions of Ancient Israel: A Synthesis of Parallactic Approaches*, London and New York: Continuum.

Chapter 6

Alḥarizi, J. (2003), *The Book of Taḥkemoni: Jewish Tales from Medieval Spain*, trans. D. S. Segal, Portland: Littman Library of Jewish Civilization.
Badawi, A., ed. (1985), *Hunain ibn Ishaq: Adab al-Falasifa*, Kuwait: Éditions de l'Institut des Manuscrits Arabes.
Belting, H. (1994), *Likeness and Presence: A History of the Image before the Era of Art*, trans. E. Jephcott, Chicago: University of Chicago Press.
El-Bizri, N., ed. (2008), *The Ikhwān al-Ṣafā and Their Rasā'il: An Introduction*, New York: Oxford University Press.
Bland, K. (2000), *The Artless Jew: Medieval and Modern Affirmations and Denials of the Visual*, Princeton: Princeton University Press.
Bland, K. (2001), 'Defending, Enjoying, and Regulating the Visual', in L. Fine (ed.), *Judaism in Practice*, 281–97, Princeton: Princeton University Press.
Bland, K. (2004), 'Icons vs. Sculptures in Christian Practice and Jewish Law', *Jewish Studies Quarterly*, 11: 201–14.
Bland, K. (2008), 'Idols of the Cave and Theater: A Verbal or Visual Judaism', in A. Norich and Y. Z. Eliav (eds), *Jewish Literatures and Cultures: Context and Intertext*, 155–76, Providence: Brown Judaic Studies, 2008.
Callataÿ, G. de (2005), *Ikhwan al-Safa': A Brotherhood of Idealists on the Fringe of Orthodox Islam*, Oxford: One World.
Callataÿ, G. de and B. Halfants, eds and trans. (2011), *Epistles of the Brethren of Purity: On Magic I – An Arabic Critical Edition and English Translation of Epistle 52a*, New York: Oxford University Press.
Epstein, M. M. (2011), *The Medieval Haggadah: Art, Narrative, and Religious Imagination*, New Haven: Yale University Press.
Goodman, L. E. and R. McGregor, eds and trans. (2009), *Epistles of the Brethren of Purity: The Case of the Animals versus Man before the King of the Jinn*, New York: Oxford University Press.
Gorfinkle, J. E., ed. and trans. (1912), *The Eight Chapters of Maimonides on Ethics* (Shemonah Perakim), New York: Columbia University Press.
Griffith, S. H. (2008), 'Ḥunain ibn Isḥāq and the *Kitāb Ādāb al-Falāsifah*: The Pursuit of Wisdom and a Humane Polity in Early Abbasid Baghdad', in G. A. Kiraz (ed.), *Malphono w-Rabo d-Malphone: Studies in Honor of Sebastian P. Brock*, 135–60, Piscataway, NJ: Gorgias Press.
Hamdani, A. (2007), 'Religious Tolerance in the Rasā'il Ikhwān al-Ṣafā', in Y. T. Langerman and J. Stern (eds), *Adaptations and Innovations: Studies on the Interaction between Jewish and Islamic Thought and Literature*, 137–42, Louvain: Peeters.
Janouch, G. (1953), *Conversations with Kafka*, trans. G. Rees, New York: Frederick A. Praeger.
Koerner, J. L. (2004), *The Reformation of the Image*, Chicago: University of Chicago Press.
Kogman-Appel, K. (2006), *Illuminated Haggadot from Medieval Spain: Biblical Imagery and the Passover Holiday*, University Park, PA: Pennsylvania State University Press.
Loewenthal, A., ed. (1896), *Sefer Musre Haphilosophim* ('Sinnsprüche der Philosophen'), Frankfurt a. Main: J. Kauffmann.
Rosenthal, F. (1992), *The Classical Heritage in Islam*, trans. E. and J. Marmorstein, New York: Routledge.
Roth, C. (1962), *The Sarajevo Haggadah*, New York: Harcourt, Brace & World.
Schapiro, M. (1977), *Romanesque Art: Selected Papers*, New York: George Braziller.

Spinoza, B. (1994), *A Spinoza Reader: The Ethics and Other Works*, ed. and trans. E. Curley, Princeton: Princeton University Press.

Zakeri, M. (2004), 'Ādāb al-filāsifa: The Persian Content of an Arabic Collection of Aphorisms', in E. Gannagé et al. (eds), *The Greek Strand in Islamic Political Thought: Proceedings of the Conference Held at the Institute for Advanced Study*, Princeton, 16–27 June 2003. Beirut: Imprimerie catholique.

Chapter 7

Abel, A. (1986), 'Bahira', in H. A. R. Gibb et al. (eds), *The Encyclopaedia of Islam*, 2nd edn, 922–3, Leiden: Brill. Available online: http://dx.doi.org/10.1163/1573-3912_islam_SIM_1050 (accessed 6 November 2017).

Abrahamov, B. (2002), 'Fakhr al-Din al-Razi on the Knowability of God's Essence and Attributes', *Arabica*, 49 (2): 204–30.

Allsen, T. (1997), *Commodity and Exchange in the Mongol Empire: A Cultural History of Textiles*, Cambridge: Cambridge University Press.

'Attar (1954), *The Conference of the Birds, Mantiq ut-Tahir: A Philosophical Religious Poem in Prose*, trans. C. S. Nott, London: Jonus Press.

Beffa, M.-L. (1978), 'Référence directe et connotation: Remarques sur les noms des couleurs en turc et en chinois', in S. Tornay (ed.), *Voir et nommer les couleurs*, 249–57, Nanterre: Université de Paris X.

Blair, S. (1993), 'The Development of the Illustrated Book in Iran', *Muqarnas*, 10: 266–74.

Blair, S. (1995), *A Compendium of Chronicles: Rashid al-Din's Illustrated History of the World*, London: Nour Foundation in Association with Azimuth Editions and Oxford University Press.

Boespflug, F. (1992), 'Un étrange spectacle: Le buisson ardent comme théophanie dans l'art occidental', *Revue de l'Art*, 97 (1): 11–31.

Evans, M. (2003), 'The Sacred: Differentiating, Clarifying, and Extending Concepts', *Review of Religious Research*, 45 (1): 32–47.

Al-Ghazali (1998), *The Niche of Lights/Mishkat al-anwar*, trans. D. Buchman, Provo: Brigham Young University Press.

Gimaret, D. (1997), *Dieu à l'image de l'homme: Les anthropomorphismes de la sunna et leur interprétation par les théologiens*, Paris: Cerf.

Gruber, C. (2008), *The Timurid Book of Ascension (Mi'rajnama): A Study of Text and Image in a Pan-Asian Context*, Valencia: Patrimonio Ediciones.

Gruber, C. (2009), 'Realabsenz: Gottesbilder in der islamischen Kunst zwischen 1300 und 1600', in E. Leuschner and M. Hesslinger (eds), *Das Bild Gottes in Judentum, Christentum und Islam*, 153–79, Petersberg: Michael Imhof Verlag.

Gruber, C. (2011), 'When *Nubuvvat* Encounters *Valayat*: Safavid Paintings of the Prophet Muhammad's *Mi'raj*, ca. 1500–1550', in P. Khosronejad (ed.), *Shi'ite Art and Material Culture: Iconography and Religious Devotion in Shi'i Islam*, 46–73, London: I.B. Tauris.

Gruber, C. (2014), 'The Rose of the Prophet: Floral Metaphors in Late Ottoman Devotional Art', in D. Roxburgh (ed.), *Envisioning Islamic Art and Architecture: Essays in Honor of Renata Holod*, 227–54, Leiden: Brill.

Guthrie, S. (1993), *Faces in the Clouds: A New Theory of Religion*, New York and Oxford: Oxford University Press.

Hillenbrand, R. (2002), 'The Arts of the Book in Ilkhanid Iran', in S. Carboni and
L. Komaroff (eds), *The Legacy of Genghis Khan: Courtly Art and Culture in Western Asia, 1256–1353*, 135–67, New York and New Haven: Yale University Press.

Hillenbrand, R. (2014), 'Muhammad as Warrior Prophet: Images from the World History of Rashid al-Din', in C. Gruber and A. Shalem (eds), *The Image of the Prophet between Ideal and Ideology: A Scholarly Investigation*, 65–75, Berlin: de Gruyter.

Hinds, M. (1983), '"Maghazi" and "sira" in Early Islamic Scholarship', in T. Fahd (ed.), *La vie du prophète Mahomet: Colloque de Strasbourg (octobre 1980)*, 57–66, Paris: P.U.F.

Ibn Ishaq (2004), *The Life of Muhammad: A Translation of Ishaq's Sirat Rasul Allah*, trans. A. Guillaume, Karachi and New York: Oxford University Press.

Jami (1980), *Yusuf and Zulaikha*, trans. D. Pendlebury, London: Octagon Press.

Al-Jawzi (2006), *The Attributes of God: Ibn al-Jawzi's daf' shubah al-tashbih bi-akaff al-tanzih*, trans. 'A. b. H. 'Ali, Bristol: Amal Press.

Kessler, H. (2000), *Spiritual Seeing: Picturing God's Invisibility in Medieval Art*, Philadelphia: University of Pennsylvania Press.

Kessler, H. (2005), '"Hoc visibile imaginatum figurat illud invisibile verum": Imagining God in Pictures of Christ', in G. de Nie et al. (eds), *Seeing the Invisible in Late Antiquity and the Early Middle Ages: Papers from 'Verbal and Pictorial Imaging: Representing and Accessing Experience of the Invisible, 400–1000'* (Utrecht, 11–13 December 2003), 291–325, Turnhout: Brepols.

Kessler, H. (2006), 'Turning a Blind Eye: Medieval Art and the Dynamics of Contemplation', in J. Hamburger and A.-M. Bouché (eds), *The Mind's Eye: Art and Theological Argument in the Middle Ages*, 413–39, Princeton: Princeton University Press.

Nizami (1945), *Makhzanol Asrar, the Treasury of Mysteries of Nezami of Ganjeh*, trans. G. H. Darab, London: Arthur Probsthain.

Nizami (1995), *The Haft Paykar: A Medieval Persian Romance*, trans. J. S. Meisami, Oxford and New York: Oxford University Press.

Paret, R. (1930), *Die legendäre Maghazi-Literatur: Arabische Dichtungen über die muslimische Kriegszüge zu Mohammeds Zeit*, Tübingen: J.C.B. Mohr.

Porter, Y. (1992), *Peinture et arts du livre: Essai sur la littérature technique indo-persane*, Paris and Tehran: Institut français de recherche en Iran.

Ranjabar, A. (1952), *Chand Mi'rajnama*, Tehran: Amir Kabir.

Rice, D. (1976), *The Illustrations to the 'World History' of Rashid al-Din*, Edinburgh: Edinburgh University Press.

Robinson, B., ed. (1976), *Islamic Painting and the Arts of the Book: The Keir Collection*, London: Faber and Faber.

Schoen, E. (1990), 'Anthropomorphic Concepts of God', *Religious Studies*, 26: 123–39.

Séguy, M.-R. (1977), *The Miraculous Journey of Mahomet: Miraj Nameh, BN, Paris sup turc 190*, trans. R. Pevear, New York: G. Braziller.

Steingass, F. (2000), *A Comprehensive Persian-English Dictionary*, New Delhi: Manohar Publishers.

Al-Tabari (2002), *La Chronique de Tabarî: Histoire des envoyés de Dieu et des rois*, ed. M. Hamadé, trans. H. Zotenberg, Paris: Al-Bustane.

Van Ess, J. (1989), *The Youthful God: Anthropomorphism in Early Islam*, Tempe: Arizona State University.

Van Ess, J. (1996), 'Le *mi'raj* et la vision de Dieu dans les premières spéculations théologiques en Islam', in M. A. Amir-Moezzi (ed.), *Le voyage initiatique en terre d'Islam: Ascensions célestes et itinéraires spirituels*, 27–56, Louvain: Peeters.

Van Ess, J. (1999), 'Vision and Ascension: *Surat al-najm* and its Relationship with Muhammad's *mi'raj*', *Journal of Qur'anic Studies*, 1 (1): 47–62.
Van Ess, J. (2000), 'Tashbih wa-tanzih', in P. J. Bearman et al. (eds), *The Encyclopaedia of Islam*, 2nd edn, 341–4, Leiden: Brill. Available online: http://dx.doi.org/10.1163/1573-3912_islam_COM_1190 (accessed 6 November 2017).
Al-Waqidi (1882), *Muhammed in Medina: Das ist Vakidi's Kitab alMaghazi*, trans. J. Wellhausen, Berlin: G. Reimer.
Al-Waqidi (2011), *The Life of Muhammad: Al-Waqidi's Kitab al-Maghazi*, ed. and trans. R. Faizer, London and New York: Routledge.
Watt, M. (1990), 'Some Muslim Discussions of Anthropomorphism', in M. Watt (ed.), *Early Islam: Collected Articles*, 86–93, Edinburgh: Edinburgh University Press.
Williams, W. (2002), 'Aspects of the Creed of Imam Ahmad Ibn Hanbal: A Study of Anthropomorphism in Early Islamic Discourse', *International Journal of Middle East Studies*, 34: 441–63.
Williams, W. (2008), '*Tajalli wa-ru'ya:* A Study of Anthropomorphic Theophany and *Visio Dei* in the Hebrew Bible, the Qur'an and Early Sunni Islam', PhD diss., University of Michigan, Ann Arbor.
Al-Yahsubi (1991), *Muhammad, Messenger of Allah: Ash-Sifa of Qadi 'Iyad*, trans. A. A. Bewley, Inverness: Madinah Press.

Chapter 8

Apostolos-Cappadona, D. (2005), 'Discerning the Hand of Fatima: An Iconological Investigation of the Role of Gender in Religious Art', in A. Sonbol (ed.), *Beyond the Exotic: Women's Histories in Islamic Societies*, 347–64, Syracuse: Syracuse University Press.
Aubin-Boltanski, E. (2014), 'Uncertainty at the Heart of a Ritual in Lebanon 2011', *Social Compass*, 61 (4): 511–23.
Bacci, M. (2004), 'A Sacred Space for a Holy Icon: The Shrine of Our Lady of Saydnaya', in A. Lidov (ed.), *Hierotopy: Studies in the Making of Sacred Spaces: Material from the International Symposium*, 373–87, Moskow: Indrik.
Bacci, M. (2005), 'The Legacy of the Hodegetria: Holy Icons and Legends between East and West', in M. Vasilakē (ed.), *Images of the Mother of God: Perceptions of the Theotokos in Byzantium*, 321–36, Burlington: Ashgate.
Bandak, A. (2013), 'Our Lady of Soufanieh: On Knowledge, Ignorance and Indifference among the Christians of Damascus', in A. Bandak and M. Bille (eds), *Politics of Worship in the Contemporary Middle East: Sainthood in Fragile States*, 129–53, Leiden and Boston: Brill.
Barasch, M. (1993), *Icon: Studies in the History of an Idea*, New York: New York University Press.
Belting, H. (1990), *The Image and Its Public: Form and Function of Early Passion Paintings*, trans. M. Bartusis and R. Meyer, New Rochelle: Aristide D. Caratzas Publications.
Belting, H. (1994), *Likeness and Presence: A History of the Image before the Era of Art*, trans. E. Jephcott, Chicago: University of Chicago Press.
Breu, M. and R. Marchese (2005), 'Protecting the Populace: Blue Beads and Other Amulets', in R. Marchese (ed.), *The Fabric of Life: Cultural Transformations in Turkish Society*, 99–126, Binghamton: Global Academic Publishing.

Can, Ş. (2017), 'The Syrian Civil War, Sectarianism and Political Change at the Turkish-Syrian Border', *Social Anthropology*, 25 (2): 174–89.

Dağtaş, S. (2017), 'Whose Mısafırs? Negotiating Difference along the Turkish-Syrian Border', *International Journal of Middle East Studies*, 49 (4): 661–79.

Dalrymple, W. (1998), *From the Holy Mountain: A Journey among the Christians of the East*, New York: Henry Holt and Company.

Doğruel, F. (2009), 'Multiple Identities on the Border: Christian and Muslim Arab Minority Communities in Turkey', in C. Timmerman (ed.), *In-between Spaces: Christian and Muslim Minorities in Transition in Europe and the Middle East*, 79–100, Brussels: Peter Lang.

Doğruel, F. (2013), 'An Authentic Experience of Multiculturalism at the Border City of Antakya', *Çağdaş Türkiye Tarihi Araştırmaları Dergisi* (Journal of Modern Turkish History Studies), 13 (26): 273–95.

Eriksen, A. (2005), 'Our Lady of Perpetual Help: Invented Tradition and Devotional Success', *Journal of Folklore Research*, 42 (3): 295–321.

Ferrero, F. (2001), *The Story of an Icon: The Full History, Tradition, and Spirituality of the Popular Icon of Our Mother of Perpetual Help*, Hampshire: Redemptorist Publications.

Friedman, Y. (2010), *The Nuṣayrī-'Alawīs: An Introduction to the Religion, History, and Identity of the Leading Minority in Syria*, Leiden: Brill.

Garosi, E. (2015), 'The Incarnated Icon of Ṣaydnāyā: Light and Shade', *Islam and Christian-Muslim Relations*, 26 (3): 339–58.

Glover, R. (2009), '"Luke the Antiochene" and Acts', *New Testament Studies*, 11 (1): 97–106.

Grieser, A. and J. Johnston (2017), 'What Is an Aesthetics of Religion? From the Senses to Meaning – And Back Again', in A. Grieser and J. Johnston (eds), *Aesthetics of Religion: A Connective Concept*, 1–49, Berlin and New York: Walter de Gruyter.

Heo, A. (2018), 'Imagining Holy Personhood: Anthropological Thresholds of the Icon', in S. Luehrmann (ed.), *Praying with the Senses: Contemporary Orthodox Christian Spirituality in Practice*, 83–102, Bloomington: Indiana University Press.

Immerzeel, M. (2007), 'The Monastery of Our Lady of Saydnaya and Its Icon', *Eastern Christian Art*, 4 (1): 13–26.

Jansen, W. (2005), 'Visions of Mary in the Middle East: Gender and the Power of a Symbol', in I. M. Okkenhaug and I. Flaskerud (eds), *Gender, Religion and Change in the Middle East: Two Hundred Years of History*, 137–54, New York: Berg.

Jansen, W. and C. Notermans (2010), 'From Vision to Cult Site: A Comparative Perspective', *Archives de Sciences Sociales des Religions*, 55 (151): 71–90.

Kedar, B. (2001), 'Convergences of Oriental Christian, Muslim, and Frankish Worshippers: The Case of Saydnaya', in Y. Hen (ed.), *De Sion Exibit Lex et Verbum Domini de Hierusalem: Essays on Medieval Law, Liturgy, and Literature in Honour of Amnon Linder*, 59–69, Turnhout: Brepols.

Keriakos, S. (2012), 'Apparitions of the Virgin in Egypt: Improving Relations between Copts and Muslims?', in D. Albera and M. Couroucli (eds), *Sharing Sacred Spaces in the Mediterranean: Christians, Muslims, and Jews at Shrines and Sanctuaries*, 174–201, Bloomington: Indiana University Press.

Kreinath, J. (2014), 'Virtual Encounters with Hızır and Other Muslim Saints: Dreaming and Healing at Local Pilgrimage Sites in Hatay, Turkey', *Anthropology of the Contemporary Middle East and Central Eurasia*, 2 (1): 25–66.

Kreinath, J. (2015), 'The Seductiveness of Saints: Interreligious Pilgrimage Sites in Hatay and the Ritual Transformations of Agency', in M. A. Di Giovine and D. Picard (eds),

The Seductions of Pilgrimage: Sacred Journeys Afar and Astray in the Western Religious Tradition, 121–43, Farnham: Ashgate.

Kreinath, J. (2016), 'Intertextualität und Interritualität als Mimesis', *Zeitschrift für Religionswissenschaft*, 24 (2): 153–85.

Kreinath, J. (2017a), 'Aesthetic Dimensions and Transformative Dynamics of Mimetic Acts: The Veneration of Habib-i Neccar among Muslims and Christians in Antakya, Turkey', in A. Grieser and J. Johnston (eds), *Aesthetics of Religion: A Connective Concept*, 271–99, Berlin: Walter de Gruyter.

Kreinath, J. (2017b), 'Interrituality as a New Approach for Studying Interreligious Relations and Ritual Dynamics at Shared Pilgrimage Sites in Hatay', *Interreligious Studies and Intercultural Theology*, 1 (2): 257–84.

Kreinath, J. (2018), 'Implications of Micro-Scale Comparisons for the Study of Entangled Religious Traditions: Reflecting on the Comparative Method in the Study of the Dynamics of Christian-Muslim Relations at a Shared Sacred Site', *Religions*, 9 (2): 45.

Loosley, E. (2004), 'La Communauté d'Al-Khalil: Une vie Monastique au Service du Dialogue Islamo-Chrétien', *Proche-Orient Chrétien*, 54 (1/2): 117–28.

Meyer, B. and J. Verrips (2008), 'Aesthetics', in D. Morgan (ed.), *Key Words in Religion, Media and Culture*, 20–30, New York: Routledge.

Meyer, B. (2009a), 'From Imagined Communities to Aesthetic Formations: Religious Mediations, Sensational Forms, and Styles of Binding', in B. Meyer (ed.), *Aesthetic Formations: Media, Region and the Senses*, 1–18, New York: Palgrave Macmillan.

Meyer, B. (2009b), 'Religious Sensations: Why Media, Aesthetics and Power Matter in the Study of Contemporary Religion', in H. De Vries (ed.), *Religion: Beyond a Concept*, 704–23, Fordham University Press.

Nes, S. (2005), *The Mystical Language of Icons*, Grand Rapids: William B. Eerdmans Publishing Company.

Pénicaud, M. (2016), 'Le père Paolo Dall'Oglio', *Ethnologie française*, 163 (3): 447–58.

Pentcheva, B. V. (2006), 'The Performative Icon', *Art Bulletin*, 88 (4): 631–55. http://dx.doi.org/10.1080/00043079.2006.10786312

Pentcheva, B. (2016), 'Miraculous Icons: Medium, Imagination and Presence', in L. Brubaker and M. Cunningham (eds), *The Cult of the Mother of God in Byzantium: Texts and Images*, 363–77, London: Taylor & Francis.

Poujeau, A. (2012), 'Sharing the Baraka of the Saints: Pluridenominational Visits to Christian Monasteries in Syria', in D. Albera and M. Couroucli (eds), *Sharing Sacred Spaces in the Mediterranean: Christians, Muslims, and Jews at Shrines and Sanctuaries*, 202–18, Bloomington: Indiana University Press.

Prager, L. (2013), 'Alawi Ziyāra Tradition and Its Interreligious Dimensions: Sacred Places and Their Contested Meanings among Christians, Alawi and Sunni Muslims in Contemporary Hatay (Turkey)', *The Muslim World*, 103 (1): 41–61.

Procházka-Eisl, G. and S. Procházka (2010), *The Plain of Saints and Prophets: The Nusayri-Alawi Community of Cilicia (Southern Turkey) and Its Sacred Places*, Wiesbaden: Otto Harrassowitz Verlag.

Pülz, A. (2010), *Ephesos als christliches Pilgerzentrum*, Wien: Verlag der Österreichischen Akademie der Wissenschaften.

Rancière, J. (2004), *The Politics of Aesthetics: The Distribution of the Sensible*, trans. G. Rockhill, London: Continuum.

Rancière, J. (2010a), *Dissensus: On Politics and Aesthetics*, trans. S. Corcoran, London: Continuum.

Rancière, J. (2010b), 'The Aesthetic Heterotopia', *Philosophy Today*, 54: 15–25.

Scouteris, C. (1984), '"Never as Gods": Icons and Their Veneration', *Sobornost*, 6 (1): 6–18.
Scranton, P. (2012), 'Evil Eye', in M. DeMello (ed.), *Faces around the World: A Cultural Encyclopedia of the Human Face: A Cultural Encyclopedia of the Human Face*, 86–91, Santa Barbara: ABC Clio.
Shields, S. (2011), *Fezzes in the River: Identity Politics and European Diplomacy in the Middle East on the Eve of World War II*, New York: Oxford University Press.
Tanke, J. (2011), 'What Is the Aesthetic Regime?' *Parrhesia*, 12: 71–81.
Tradigo, A. (2004), *Icons and Saints of the Eastern Orthodox Church*, trans. S. Sartarelli, Los Angeles: J. Paul Getty Museum.
Türk, H. (2009), *Kültürlerin bin Yıllık Hoşgörüsü: Evliyalar Diyarı Hatay* (The Millennial Tolerance of Cultures: Hatay the Land of Saints), Adana: Karahan Kitabevi.
Usluoğlu, T. (2012), *Arap Hıristiyanlar: Değişim ve Etkileşim Boyutuyla Hıristiyan Kültürü* (Arab Christians: Change and Interaction in Christian Culture), Ankara: Ütopya Yayınları.
Winter, S. (2016), *A History of the 'Alawis: From Medieval Aleppo to the Turkish Republic*, Princeton: Princeton University Press.

Chapter 9

Amir-Moezzi, M. A. (2015), *The Spirituality of Shi'i Islam: Belief and Practices*, London: I.B. Tauris in Association With The Institute Of Ismaili Studies.
Amir-Moezzi, M. A. (2012), 'Icon and Meditation: Between Popular Art and Sufism in Imami Shi'ism', in P. Khosronejad (ed.), *The Art and Material Culture of Iranian Shi'ism: Iconography and Religious Devotion in Shi'i Islam*, 24–45, London: I.B. Tauris and British Institute for Persian Studies.
Arnold, W. T. (1965), *Painting in Islam: A Study of the Place of Pictorial Art in Muslim Culture*, New York: Dover Publication.
Calmard, J. (1996), 'Shi'i Rituals and Power: The Consolidation of Safavid Shi'ism: Folklore and Popular Religion', in C. Melville (ed.), *Safavid Persia*, 141–66, London: I.B. Tauris.
Ekhtiyar, M. (2014), 'Infused with Shi'ism: Representations of the Prophet in Qajar Iran', in C. Gruber and A. Shalem (eds), *The Image of the Prophet between Ideal and Ideology*, 98–112, Boston and Berlin: de Gruyter.
Ekhtiyar, M. (2015), 'Exploring *Ahl al-bayt* imagery in Qajar Iran (1785–1925)', in F. Suleman (ed.), *People of the Prophet's House: Artistic and Ritual Expressions of Shi'i Islam*, 146–54, London: Azimuth Editions.
Flaskerud, I. (2010), *Visualizing Belief and Piety in Iranian Shiism*, 1–20, New York: Bloomsbury Academic.
Gray, B. (1979), 'The Tradition of Wall Painting in Iran', in R. Ettinghousen and E. Yarshater (eds), *Highlights of Persian Art*, 313–29, Boulder, CO: Westview Press.
Gruber, C. (2008), *The Timurid Book of Ascension (Mi'rajnama): Study of Text and Image in a Pan-Asian Context*, Valencia, Spain: Patrimonio Ediciones.
Gruber, C. (2016), 'Prophetic Products: Muhammad in Contemporary Iranian Visual Culture', *Material Religion*, 12 (3): 259–93.
Khosronejad, P. (2012a), 'Introduction: Unburied Memories', in P. Khosronejad (ed.), *Unburied Memories: The Politics of Bodies, and the Material Culture of Sacred Defence Martyrs in Iran*, 1–34, London: Routledge.
Khosronejad, P. (2012b), 'Anthropology, Islam and Sainthood', in P. Khosronejad (ed.), *Saints and Their Pilgrims in Iran and Neighbouring Countries*, 3–20, Oxford: Sean Kingston Publishing.

Khosronejad, P. (2012c), 'Shiite Material Religion and Sacred Art', in P. Khosronejad (ed.), *The Art and Material Culture of Iranian Shi'ism: Iconography and Religious Devotion in Shi'i Islam*, 1–22, London: I.B. Tauris and British Institute for Persian Studies.
Khosronejad, P. (2015a), 'Le Coran n'Interdit pas la Représentation du Prophète', *Le Figaro*, 18 January. Available online: http://www.lefigaro.fr/international/2015/01/20/01003-2 0150120ARTFIG00429-le-coran-n-interdit-pas-la-representation-du-prophete.php (accessed 11 June 2018).
Khosronejad, P. (2015b), 'Le Prophète a un Visage', *Thinkovery*, 3: 4–7.
Khosronejad, P. (2015c), 'Le Coran n'Interdit pas la Représentations du Prophète', *Le Soir*, 21–22 January.
Khosronejad, P. (2018), *Curtains of Heaven: Celestial and Devotional Mural Paintings of Iranian Pilgrimage*, Visual Studies of Modern Iran, vol. 3, New York: Iranian and Persian Gulf Studies.
Landau, A. (2012), 'Adaptation of Religious Iconography in Seventeenth-Century Iran: The Case of Bethlehem Church', in W. Floor and E. Herzig (eds), *Iran and the World in the Safavid Age*, 425–46, London: I.B. Tauris.
Landau, A. and T. M. van Lint (2015), 'Armenian Merchant Patronage of New Julfa's Sacred Spaces', in M. Gharipour (ed.), *Sacred Precincts: Non-Muslim Sites in Islamic Territories*, 308–33. Leiden: Brill.
Lentz, T. W. (1993), 'Dynastic Imagery in Early Timurid Wall Painting', in G. Necipoglu (ed.), *Muqarnas: Essays in Honor of Oleg Grabar*, vol. 10, 253–65, Leiden: Brill.
Lentz, T. W. and G. D. Lowry (1989), *Timur and the Princely Vision: Persian Art and Culture in the Fifteenth Century*, Los Angeles: Los Angeles County Museum of Art.
Mahmoudi, F. and Tawossi, M. (2011), 'The Religious Role of Ashura and Taziyeh in Pictorial Art of Mazandaran', *National Research Journal*, 12/4 (48): 67–92.
Mahmoudinejad, A. (2009), *The Murals of the Tombs in Guilan*. Rasht: Iliya.
Massé, H. (1938), *Croyances et Coutumes Persanes, suivies de Contes et Chansons populaires*. Paris: Librairie Oriental et Américaine.
Membre, M. (1993), *Mission to the Lord Sophy of Persia* (1539–1542), trans. A. H. Morton, reprinted edn, London: School of Oriental and African Studies, University of London.
Mirzaee Mehr, A. A. (2007), *The Paintings of the Iranian Holy Shrines*, Tehran: Farhagnestan Honar.
Peterson, S. R. (1979), 'The Ta'ziyeh and Related Arts', in P. Chelkowski (ed.), *Ta'ziyeh: Ritual and Drama in Iran*, 64–87, New York: New York University Press.
Ruhrdanz, K. (2000), 'The Illustrated Manuscripts of Athar al-Muzaffar: A History of the Prophet', in R. Hillenbrand (ed.), *Persian Painting from the Mongols to the Qajars: Studies in Honour of Basil W. Robinson*, 201–16, London: I.B. Tauris.
Shad Qazvini, P. (2010), Religious Popular Paintings of Licha Saint Shrine of Gilan. *Visual Art Journal*, 41: 13–22.
Stchoukine, I. (1954), *Les Peintures des Manuscrits Timurides*, Paris: P. Geuthner.
Suleman, F., ed. (2015), *People of the Prophet's House: Artistic and Ritual Expressions of Shi'i Islam*, London: Azimuth Editions.
Torab, A. (2006), *Performing Islam: Gender and Ritual in Iran* (Women and Gender: The Middle East and the Islamic World), Leiden: Brill.
Welch, A. (2000), 'Worldly and Otherworldly Love in Safavid Painting', in R. Hillenbrand (ed.), *Persian Painting from the Mongols to the Qajars: Studies in Honour of Basil W. Robinson*, 301–18, London: I.B. Tauris.
Wilber, D. N. (1969), *Architecture of Islamic Iran: The Il Khanid Period*, Westport: Greenwood Press.

Chapter 10

Ahmed, L. (1992), *Women and Gender in Islam: Historical Roots of a Modern Debate*, New Haven and London: Yale University Press.

Ahmed, L. (2011), *The Quiet Revolution: The Veils Resurgence from the Middle East to America*, New Haven, CT: Yale University Press.

Behrend, H. (2012), 'The Terror of the Feast': Photography, Textiles and Memory in Weddings along the East African Coast, in R. Vokes (ed.), *Photography in Africa: Ethnographic Perspectives*, 229–40, Oxford: James Currey.

Behrend, H. (2013), *Contesting Visibility: Photographic Practices on the East African Coast*, Bielefeld: Transcript.

Belting, H. (2008), *Florenz und Bagdad: Eine westöstliche Geschichte des Blicks*, Munich: C.H. Beck.

Boehm, G. (2015), *Wie Bilder Sinn erzeugen: Die Macht des Zeigens*, Berlin: Berlin University Press.

Brielmaier, I. (2003), '"Picture Taking" and the Production of Urban Identities on the Kenyan Coast', PhD diss., Columbia University.

Brown, H. W. (1993), 'Coins of East Africa: An Introductory Survey', *Yarmouk Numismatics*, 5: 9–16.

Dudley, S. (2011), 'Material Visions: Dress and Textiles', in M. Banks and J. Ruby (eds), *Perspectives on the History of Visual Anthropology*, 45–73, Chicago: University of Chicago Press.

Fair, L. (1998), 'Dressing Up: Clothing, Class and Gender in Post-Abolition Zanzibar', *Journal of African History*, 39 (1): 63–94.

Glassman, J. (1995), *Feasts and Riots: Revelry, Rebellion and Popular Consciousness on the Swahili Coast 1856–1888*, London, Nairobi: Heinemann, James Currey.

Goody, J. (1997), *Representations and Contradictions: Ambivalences towards Images, Theatre, Fiction, Relics and Sexuality*, Oxford: Blackwell.

Grabar, O. (1977), *Die Entstehung der Islamischen Kunst*, Cologne: Dumont.

Koerner, J. (2002), 'The Icon as Iconoclash', in B. Latour and P. Weibel (eds), *Iconoclash: Beyond the Image: Wars in Science, Religion and Art*, 164–213, Karlsruhe and Cambridge, MA: MIT Press.

Kramer, F. (2001), 'Praktiken der Imagination', in G. von Graevenitz, S. Rieger and F. Thürlemann (eds), *Die Unvermeidlichkeit der Bilder*, 17–29, Tübingen: Gunther Narr Verlag.

Krapf, J. L. ([1860] 1968), *Travels, Researches, and Missionary Labours: During an Eighteen Years' Residence in Eastern Africa*, London: Frank Cass.

Middleton, J. (1992), *The World of the Swahili: An African Mercantile Civilization*, New Haven and London: Yale University Press, 198–216.

Parkin, D. (1995), 'Blank banners and Islamic consciousness in Zanzibar', in A. Cohen and N. Rapport (eds), *Questions of Consciousness*, 198–216, London: Routledge.

Seitter, W. (2002), *Physik der Medien*, Weimar: VDG.

Taussig, M. (1999), *Defacement: Public Secrecy and the Labor of the Negative*, Stanford: Stanford University Press.

Wendl, T. and H. Behrend, eds (1998), *Snap Me One! Studiofotografen in Afrika*, Munich: Prestel.

Werner, J.-F. (2001), 'Photography and Individualization in Contemporary Africa: An Ivorian Case-Study', *Visual Anthropology*, 14 (3): 251–68.

Chapter 11

Asad, T. ([1986] 2009), 'The Idea of an Anthropology of Islam', *Qui Parle*, 17 (2): 1–30.
Bandak, A. and T. Boylston (2014), 'The "Orthodoxy" of Orthodoxy: On Moral Imperfection, Correctness, and Deferral in Religious Worlds', *Religion and Society*, 5 (1): 25–46.
Belting, H. (1994), *Likeness and Presence: The History of the Image Before the Age of Art*, Chicago: University of Chicago Press.
Bernstein, A. (2014), 'Caution, Religion! Iconoclasm, Secularism, and Ways of Seeing in Post-Soviet Art Wars', *Public Culture*, 26 (3): 419–48.
Boyer, P. (2001), *Religion Explained: The Evolutionary Origins of Religious Thought*, New York: Basic Books.
Boyer, P. and S. Walker (2000), 'Intuitive Ontology and Cultural Input in the Acquisition of Religious Concepts', in K. S. Rosengren, C. N. Johnson and P. L. Harris (eds), *Imagining the Impossible: The Development of Magical, Scientific, and Religious Thinking in Contemporary Society*, 130–56, Cambridge: Cambridge University Press.
Bremer, T., ed. (2014), '*Verehrt wird er in seinem Bilde [...]*' Quellenbuch zur Geschichte der Ikonentheologie, 'Die Schrift Karls des Großen gegen das Konzil (Opus Caroli Regis Contra Synodum)', 177–204, Dillingen: Paulinus.
Chakovskaya, L. (2014), 'Contemporary Russian Church Art between Tradition and Modernity', in K. Tolstaya (ed.), *Orthodox Paradoxes: Heterogeneities and Complexities in Contemporary Russian Orthodoxy*, 318–39, Leiden: Brill.
Christensen, K. H. (2018), *The Making of the New Martyrs of Russia: Soviet Repression in Orthodox Memory*, London: Routledge.
Dukhanin, V. (2005), *Pravoslavie i mir kino*, Moscow: Drakkar.
Engelhardt, J. (2018), 'Listening and the Sacramental Life: Degrees of Mediation in Greek Orthodox Christianity', in S. Luehrmann (ed.), *Praying with the Senses: Contemporary Orthodox Christian Spirituality in Practice*, 58–79, Bloomington: Indiana University Press.
Engelstein, L. (2003), *Castration and the Heavenly Kingdom: A Russian Folktale*, Ithaca: Cornell University Press.
Evseeva, L. M. (1998), *Afonskaia kniga obrastsov, XV v*, Moscow: Indrik.
Freeze, G. (1983), *The Parish Clergy in Nineteenth-Century Russia: Crisis, Reform, Counter-Reform*, Princeton, NJ: Princeton University Press.
Geertz, C. (1973), *The Interpretation of Cultures*, New York: Basic Books.
Greene, R. (2010), *Bodies Like Bright Stars: Saints and Relics in Orthodox Russia*, DeKalb: Northern Illinois University Press.
Guthrie, S. (1993), *Faces in the Clouds: A New Theory of Religion*, New York: Oxford University Press.
Haeri, N. (2017), 'Unbundling Sincerity: Language, Mediation, and Interiority in Comparative Perspective', *HAU: Journal of Ethnographic Theory*, 7 (1): 123–38.
Hanganu, G. (2010), 'Eastern Christians and Religious Objects: Personal and Material Biographies Entangled', in C. M. Hann and H. Goltz (eds), *Eastern Christians in Anthropological Perspective*, 35–55, Berkeley: University of California Press.
Hann, C. (2003), 'Creeds, Cultures and the Witchery of Music', *Journal of the Royal Anthropological Institute*, 9 (2): 223–39.
Hann, C. (2014), 'The Heart of the Matter: Christianity, Materiality, and Modernity', *Current Anthropology*, 55 (Supp 10): S182–92.
Heo, A. (2012), 'The Virgin Made Visible: Intercessory Images of Church Territory in Egypt,' *Comparative Studies in Society and History*, 54 (2): 361–91.

Hirschkind, C. (2006), *The Ethical Soundscape: Cassette Sermons and Islamic Counterpublics*, New York: Columbia University Press.
Huntington, S. (1996), *Clash of Civilizations and the Remaking of World Order*, New York: Simon and Schuster.
John of Damascus, Saint (2003), *Three Treatises on the Divine Images*, ed. A. Louth, Crestwood, NY: St Vladimir's Seminary Press.
Kelemen, D. (2004), 'Intuitive Theists? Reasoning about Purpose and Design in Nature', *Psychological Science*, 15 (5): 295–301.
Kivelson, V. and J. Neuberger (2008), 'Seeing into Being: An Introduction', in V. Kivelson and J. Neuberger (eds), *Picturing Russia: Explorations in Visual Culture*, 1–11, New Haven: Yale University Press.
Levin, E. (2003), 'From Corpse to Cult in Early Modern Russia', in V. Kivelson and R. Greene (eds), *Orthodox Russia: Belief and Practice under the Tsars*, 81–103, University Park: University of Pennsylvania Press.
Luehrmann, S. (2010), 'A Dual Quarrel of Images on the Middle Volga: Icon Veneration in the Face of Protestant and Pagan Critique', in C. M. Hann and H. Goltz (eds), *Eastern Christians in Anthropological Perspective*, 56–78, Berkeley: University of California Press.
Luehrmann, S. (2016), 'Iconographic Historicism: Being Contemporary and Orthodox at the Same Time', *Material Religion*, 12 (2): 238–40.
Luehrmann, S. (2018a), 'Introduction: The Senses of Prayer in Orthodox Christianity', in S. Luehrmann (ed.), *Praying with the Senses: Orthodox Christian Spirituality in Practice*, 1–26, Bloomington: Indiana University Press.
Luehrmann, S. (2018b), 'Beyond Life Itself: The Embedded Fetuses of Russian Orthodox Anti-Abortion Activism', in S. Han, T. Betsinger and A. Scott (eds), *The Anthropology of the Fetus: Biology, Culture, Society*, 227–51, New York: Berghahn.
Luhrmann, T. (2012), *When God Talks Back: Understanding the American Evangelical Relationship with God*, New York: Vintage.
Mahieu, S. (2010), 'Icons and/or Statues? The Greek Catholic Divine Liturgy in Hungary and Romania, between Renewal and Purification', in C. M. Hann and H. Goltz (eds), *Eastern Christians in Anthropological Perspective*, 79–100, Berkeley: University of California Press.
Meyer, B. (2015), *Sensational Movies: Video, Vision, and Christianity in Ghana*, Oakland: University of California Press.
Mitchell, W. J. T. (1994), *Picture Theory*, Chicago: University of Chicago Press.
Mittermaier, A. (2011), *Dreams That Matter: Egyptian Landscapes of the Imagination*, Berkeley: University of California Press.
Noble, I. (2005), 'Religious Experience – Reality or Illusion: Insights from Symeon the New Theologian and Ignatius of Loyola', in L. Boeve, H. Geybels and S. van den Bossche (eds), *Encountering Transcendence: Contributions to a Theology of Christian Religious Experience*, 375–93, Leuven: Peeters.
Osipov, A. I. (2001), 'Sviatitel' Ignatii ob osnovakh dukhovnoi zhizni', in A. I. Osipov, *Pravoslavnoe ponimanie smysli zhizni*, 97–126, Kiev: Izdatel'stvo imeni sviatitelia L'va, Papy Rimskogo.
Pelikan, J. (1974), *The Spirit of Eastern Christendom (600–1700)*, Cambridge, MA: Harvard University Press.
Rolland, P. (2017), 'Guard Your Sight and Curb Your Tongue: Two Moralistic Poems from the Archive of Simeaon Polatski (1629–1680)', *Canadian Slavonic Papers*, 59 (1–2): 101–13.

Shevzov, V. (2004), *Russian Orthodoxy on the Eve of Revolution*, New York: Oxford University Press.
Taves, A. (2016), *Revelatory Events: Three Case Studies of the Emergence of New Spiritual Paths*, Princeton: Princeton University Press.
Taylor, M. and S. M. Carlson (2000), 'The Influence of Religious Belief on Parental Attitudes About Children's Fantasy Behavior', in *Imagining the Impossible: Magic, Scientific and Religious Thinking in Children*, eds. K. S. Rosengren, C. Johnson and P. Harris, 247–68, Cambridge: Cambridge University Press.
Wiesing, L. (2005), 'Virtuelle Realität: Die Angleichung des Bildes an die Imagination', in L. Wiesing, *Artifizielle Präsenz: Studien zur Philosophie des Bildes*, 107–24, Frankfurt: Suhrkamp.
Wolff, L. (1994), *Inventing Eastern Europe: The Map of Civilization on the Mind of the Enlightenment*, Stanford: Stanford University Press.
Yazykova, I. (2010), *Hidden and Triumphant: The Underground Struggle to Save Russian Iconography*, Brewster, MA: Paraclete Press.

Chapter 12

Avery, C. (2006), *Bernini: Genius of the Baroque*, London: Thames & Hudson.
Bernini, D. (2011), *The Life of Gian Lorenzo Bernini*, trans. F. Mormando, University Park, PA: Pennsylvania State University Press.
Bukdahl, E. M. (1999), 'Nybrud i barokkens kirkekunst: Det guddommelige lys i en ustabil og foranderlig verden', in *Transfiguration. Nordisk tidsskrift for kunst & kristendom*, 1: 43–68.
Bukdahl, E. M. (2017), *The Recurrent Actuality of the Baroque*, København: Controluce.
Cole, M. W. (2009), 'Perpetual Exorcism in Sistine Rome', in M. Wayne Cole and R. Zorach (eds), *The Idol in the Age of Art: Objects, Devotions and the Early Modern World*, 57–76, Farnham: Ashgate.
Cooper, L. H. and A. Denny-Brown, eds (2013), *The Arma Christi in Medieval and Early Modern Material Culture: With a Critical Edition of 'O Vernicle'*, Farnham: Ashgate.
Fortunatus, Venantius. 'Vexilla Regis Prodeunt', in *Analecta Hymnica*. Available online: http://www.preceslatinae.org/thesaurus/Hymni/Vexilla.html (accessed 12 February 2018).
Francia, E. (1975), 'Die neue Petersbasilika', in G.-M. Garonne (ed.), *Der Vatikan und das christliche Rom*, 59–93, Vatican City: Libreria editrice Vaticana.
Gadamer, H.-G. (1990), *Wahrheit und Methode*, Tübingen: Mohr.
Gardner, H. (2001), *Gardner's Art through the Ages*, Fort Worth, TX: Harcourt Brace College Publishers.
Hibbard, H. (1965), *Bernini*, London: Penguin Books.
Jensen, E., ed. (n.d.), *The Spiritual Exercises of Saint Ignatius Loyola*, Study edn, Guelph, Ontario: Ignatius Jesuit Center. Available online: https://ignatiusguelph.ca/wp-content/uploads/2017/03/The_Spiritual_Exercises_Eric_Jensen_SJ.pdf (accessed 12 February 2018).
Kostof, S. (1995), *A History of Architecture: Settings and Rituals*, Oxford: Oxford University Press.
Kuhn, R. (1970), 'Gian Lorenzo Bernini und Ignatius von Loyola', in M. Gosebruch and L. Dittmann (eds), *Festschrift für Kurt Badt*, Cologne: Argo-Verlag.
Largier, N. (2009), 'Medieval Mysticism', in J. Corrigan (ed.), *The Oxford Handbook of Religion and Emotion*, Oxford: Oxford University Press. Available online: http://dx.doi.org/10.1093/oxfordhb/9780195170214.003.0021 (accessed 12 February 2018).

Lees-Milne, J. (1967), *Saint Peter's: The Story of Saint Peter's Basilica in Rome*, London: Hamish Hamilton.
Levy, E. (2004), *Propaganda and the Jesuit Baroque*, Berkeley and Los Angeles: University of California Press.
Maggioni, G. P., ed. (1998), *Iacopo da Varazze: Legenda aurea*, Florence: SISMEL-Edizioni del Galluzzo.
Marder, T. A. (1998), *Bernini and the Art of Architecture*, New York: Abbeville Press.
Mitchell, D. (1980), *The Jesuits: A History*, London: Macdonald Futura Publishers.
Mormando, F. (2011), *Bernini: His Life and His Rome*, Chicago: University of Chicago Press.
Nykjær, M. (1999), *Peterskirken: Historie og betydning*, Copenhagen: Gyldendal.
Nykjær, M. (2004), *I pavernes Rom: Bybilleder, kunst og historie 1420–1870*, Copenhagen: Gyldendal.
O'Malley, J. W. (1993), *The First* Jesuits, Cambridge, MA: Harvard University Press.
Perniola, M. (2001), 'Icons, Visions, Simulacra', in M. Perniola (ed.), *Ritual Thinking: Sexuality, Death, World*, 158–71, New York: Humanity Books, 2001.
Sedlmayr, H. (1985), 'Der Bilderkreis von Neu St. Peter in Rom', in H. Sedlmayr (ed.), *Epochen und Werke: Gesammelte Schriften zur Kunstgeschichte II*, Vienna: Verlag Herold.
Waterworth, J., ed. and trans. (1848), 'The Council of Trent: The Twenty-Fifth Session', in *The Canons and Decrees of the Sacred and Oecumenical Council of Trent*, 232–89, London: Dolman. Available online: https://history.hanover.edu/texts/trent/ct25.html (accessed 15 January 2017).
Weibel, W. (1909), *Jesuitismus und Barockskulptur in Rom*, Strasbourg: Heitz & Mündel.
Weil, M. S. (1974), *The History and Decoration of the Ponte S. Angelo*, University Park, PA: Pennsylvania State University Press.
Wittkower, R. (1955), *Gian Lorenzo Bernini: The Sculptor of the Roman Baroque*, London: Phaidon Press.
Wölfflin, H. (1966), *Renaissance and Baroque*, trans. K. Simon, Ithaca: Cornell University Press.
Woodrow, A. (1995), *The Jesuits: A Story of Power*, London: Geoffrey Chapman. (English translation: Father Brian McNeil C.R.V.)

Chapter 13

Andersen, B. (1989), '"Rummets betydning" (Interview with Hein Heinsen on the Significance of the Interior)', *Kritisk Forum for Praktisk Teologi*, 23: 61–2.
Banning, K. (1980), 'Biblia Pauperum and the Wall Paintings in the Church of Bellinge: The Book and the Church Wall', in F. G. Andersen (ed.), *Medieval Iconography and Narrative: A Symposium*, 124–34, Odense: Odense University Press.
Bukdahl, E. M. (2005), *Caspar David Friedrich's Study Years at the Royal Danish Academy of Fine Arts and His Importance for Danish Art, Particularly for the Painters of the Golden Age and of the Present Day*, Copenhagen: The Royal Danish Academy of Fine Art's Schools of Visual Arts.
Bukdahl, E. M. (2016), 'Lyotard between Philosophy and Art', in M. Bolt, P. Borum, E. M. Bukdahl and E. Rocca (eds), *Hospitality in Art and Politics*, Copenhagen: Basilisk.
Bukdahl, E. M. (2017), *The Recurrent Actuality of the Baroque*, Copenhagen: Controluce.

Burke, E. ([1757] 1967), *A Philosophical Enquiry into the Origin of Our Ideas of the Sublime and Beautiful*, ed. J. T. Boulton, London: Routledge and Kegan Paul.

Deleuze, G. (1990), *Pourparlers 1972-1990*, Paris: Les Editions de Minuit.

Freise, E. (1981), 'Roger von Helmarshausen in seiner monastischen Umwelt', Frühmittelalterliche Studien, 15: 180-293.

Glucksmann, C. (1996), 'L'Invisible en ses formes' in the catalogue of the exhibition, *Formes de l'invisible*, Paris: Mairie de Paris.

Hellstein, V. (2014), 'Barnett Newman, The Stations of the Cross: Lema Sabachtani', *Conversations: An Online Journal of the Center for the Study of Material and Visual Cultures of Religion*. Available online: http://dx.doi.org/10.22332/con.obj.2014.16 (accessed 25 May 2018).

Holt, E., ed. (1957), 'Theophilus, *Diversarum Artium Schedula* (ca. 1125) Preface to Book III', in *A Documentary History of Art*, New York: Doubleday Anchor Books.

Juhl, C. (1986), 'Det sublimes kultur', *Den blå Port*, 4: 77.

Juhl, C., ed. (1988), *Kunstens og filosofiens værker efter emancipationen* (The Works of Art and Philosophy after the Emancipation), Copenhagen: The Royal Danish Academy of Fine Arts.

Kant, I. (1979), *Kritik der Urteilskraft*, Werkausgabe. Band X, ed. W. Weischedel, Frankfurt aM: Suhrkamp.

Kant, I. (1986), *The Critique of Judgement*, trans. James Creed Meredith, Oxford: Clarendon Press.

Kant, I. ([1790] 2000), *Critique of the Power of Judgement*, ed. P. Guyer, trans. E. Matthews, New York: Cambridge University Press.

Keenan, D. K. (2005), *The Question of Sacrifice*, Bloomington: Indiana University Press.

Lee, R. W. (1967), *Ut Pictura Poesis: The Humanistic Theory of Painting*, New York: The Norton Library.

Løgstrup, K. E. (1965), *Kants æstetik (Kant's Aesthetics)*, Copenhagen: Gyldendal.

Lyotard, J.-F. (1984), 'The Sublime and the Avant-Garde', *Artforum*, 22 (8): 36-43.

Lyotard, J.-F., ed. (1986), 'Answering the Question: What Is Postmodernism?' in *The Postmodern Condition: A Report on Knowledge*, 71-82, Manchester: Manchester University Press.

Lyotard, J.-F. (1992), *Gestus* [trans. Kasper Nefer Olsen from a then unpublished French manuscript. A new version published in 2009 in French in *Jean-François Lyotard, Writings on Contemporary Art and Artists*, Leuven: Leuven University Press, vol. 1.], Copenhagen: The Royal Danish Academy of Fine Arts.

Merleau-Ponty, M. (1964), *The Primacy of Perception*, Evanston, IL: Northwestern University Press.

Monty, Ib., trans. (1953), *Leonardo da Vinci: Optegnelser (Notebooks)*, Copenhagen: Hasselbalch.

O'Neill, P., ed. (1990), *Barnett Newman: Selected Writings and Interviews*, New York: Alfred A. Knopf. Including i.a. these original pieces:

— Newman, B. (1948), 'The Sublime Is Now', *The Tiger's Eye*, 1 (6): 51-3.

— Newman, B. (1966), 'The Fourteen Stations of the Cross', *ARTnews*, 3.

— Newman, B. (1966), 'Catalogue statement for *Barnett Newman: The Stations of the Cross, Lema Sabachtani*'

— Newman, B. (1965),'Interview with David Sylvester'.

Perniola, M. (1995), 'Aesthetics and Theology', *Estetica News*, 22. Available online: http://www.marioperniola.it/site/dettagliotext.asp?idtexts=32 (accessed 4 December 2017).

The New Shorter Oxford English Dictionary (1993), 4th edn, Oxford: Oxford University Press.
Wecker, M. (2012), 'His Cross to Bear: Barnett Newman Dealt with Suffering in Zips', *The Jewish Daily: Forward*. Available online: https://forward.com/culture/159912/his-cross-to-bear/?p=all&p=all (accessed 24 May 2018).
Wittkower, R. (1980), *Art and Architecture in Italy 1600–1750*, London: Pelican History of Art.

Chapter 14

Assman, J. (n.d.), *Die Mosaische Unterscheidung in Arnold Schönberg's Oper Moses und Aaron*. Available online: http://www.aroumah.net/agora/assmann03-schoenbergEF.pdf (accessed 2 January 2018).
Baert, B. (2014), 'The Dancing Daughter and the Head of John the Baptist (Mark 6:14–29) Revisited: An Interdisciplinary Approach', *Louvain Studies*, 38: 5–29.
Becker-Leckrone, M. (1995), 'Salome: The Fetishization of a Textual Corpus', *New Literary History*, 26 (2): 239–60.
Belting, H. (2014), *An Anthropology of Images: Picture, Medium, Body*, Princeton: Princeton University Press. (First publication date 2001; then 2011.)
Blumberg, H. (1985), *Work on Myth*, Cambridge, MA: MIT Press.
Boyarin, D. (1990), *Intertextuality and the Reading of Midrash*, Bloomington: Indiana University Press.
Brunotte, U. (2012), 'Unveiling Salome 1900 – Entschleierungen zwischen Sexualität, Pathosformel und Oriental Dance', in B. Dennerlein, E. Frietsch and T. Steffen (eds), *Verschleierter Orient – Entschleierter Okzident?* 93–116, Munich: Fink Verlag.
Brunotte, U. (2013), 'Salome and the Head of John the Baptist', in U. Brunotte (ed.), *Dämonen des Wissens: Gender, Performativity und materielle Kultur im Werk von Jane Ellen Harrison*, 217–44, Würzburg: Ergon.
Brunotte, U. (2015), '"All Jews Are Womanly, But No Woman Is a Jew". The "Femininity" Game of Deception: Female Jew, Femme Fatale Orientale, and Belle Jew', in U. Brunotte, A. D. Ludewig and A. Stähler (eds), *Orientalism, Gender and the Jews*, 195–220, Oldenburg: de Gruyter.
Bucknell, B. (1993), 'On, "Seeing" Salome', *ELH: English Literary History*, 60 (2): 503–26.
Ceramaeus, T. ([12.Jh.] 2000), 'Über die Enthauptung des ehrwürdigen Künders', in T. Rohde (ed.), *Mythos Salome: Vom Markusevangelium bis Djuna Barnes*, 70–2, Leipzig: Reclam.
Chrysostomos, J. ([350–407] 2000), 'Wo eben ein Tanz ist […]', in T. Rohde (ed.), *Mythos Salome: Vom Markusevangelium bis Djuna Barnes*, 68–70, Leipzig: Reclam.
De Bruyn, B. (2012), *Wolfgang Iser: A Companion*, Boston and Berlin: de Gruyter.
Dierkes-Thrun, P. (2011), *Salome's Modernity: Oscar Wilde and the Aesthetics of Transgression*, Ann Arbor: University of Michigan Press.
Ellmann, R. (1988), *Oscar Wilde*, New York: Knopf.
Garber, M. (1993), *Vested Interests: Cross-Dressing and Cultural Anxiety*, New York: Harper Perennial.
Hägg, T. (2012), *The Art of Biography in Antiquity*, New York: Cambridge University Press.
Heffernan, J. (1993), *The Museum of Words: The Poetics of Ekphrasis from Homer to Ashbery*, Chicago: University of Chicago Press.

Heinrich, K. (1995), *Floß der Medusa. 3 Studien zur Faszinationsgeschichte*, Frankfurt/M.: Stroemfeld.
Høgasen-Hallesby, H. (2014), 'Performing the Icon: The Body on Stage and the Staged Body in Salome's "Dance of the Seven Veils"', in H. Lee and N. D. Segal (eds), *Opera, Exoticism and Visual Culture*, 179–202, Bern: Peter Lang.
Høgasen-Hallesby, H. (2015), 'Salome's Silent Spaces: Canonicity, Creativity, and Critique', *The Opera Quaterly*, 31 (4): 223–41.
Hoven-Buchholz, K. (2008), 'Was verschleiert Salmes Tanz? Eine psychoanalytische Interpretation jenseits des Femme-fatale Klischees', *Psyche – Zeitschrift für Psychoanalyse*, 62 (2008): 356–80.
Hutcheon, L. and M. Hutcheon (1998), '"Here's Lookin' at You, Kid": The Empowering Gaze in "Salome"', *Profession*, 98 (MLA): 11–22.
Hutcheon, L. and M. Hutcheon (2000), 'Staging the Female Body: Richard Strauss's Salome', in M. A. Smart (ed.), *Siren Songs: Representations of Gender and Sexuality in Opera*, 204–21, Princeton: Princeton University Press.
Huysmans, J. K. ([1884] 2008), *Against Nature*, trans. B. King, Cambs: Dedalus.
Inowlocki, S. (2016), 'Josephus and Patristic Literature', in H. Howell Chapman and Z. Rodgers (eds), *A Compagnion to Josephus*, 356–67, Oxford: Wiley-Blackwell.
Iser, W. (1978), *The Act of Reading: A Theory of Aesthetic Respons*, Baltimore and London: Johns Hopkins University Press.
Iser, W. (1989), *Prospecting: From Reader Response to Literary Anthropology*, Baltimore: Johns Hopkins University Press.
Iser, W. (1993), *The Fictive and the Imaginary: Charting Literary Anthropology*, Baltimore: Johns Hopkins University Press.
Iser, W. (1994), *Der Akt des Lesens: Theorie ästhetischer Wirkung*, Munich: W. Fink.
Koritz, A. (1996), 'Dancing the Orient for England: Maus Allan's "Vision of Salome"', *Theatre Journal*, 46 (1): 63–78.
Kramer, L. (1990), 'Culture and Musical Hermeneutics: The Salome Complex', *Cambridge Opera Journal*, 2 (3): 269–94.
Kruse, C. (2003), *Wozu Menschen malen: Historische Begründungen des Bildmediums*, Munich: Fink Verlag.
Levine, A. J., ed. (2008), *A Feminist Companion to Patristic Literature*, London: T&T Clark International.
Lohmeyer, E. (1967), *Kirchlich-exegetischer Kommentar über das neue Testament, Das Evangelium des Markus, übersetzt und erklärt von Ernst Lohmeyer*, Göttingen: Vandenhoeck & Ruprecht.
Ludewig, A. D. (2014), 'Between Orientalization and Self-Orientalization: Remarks on the Image of the "Beautiful Jewess" in Nineteenth- and Early-Twentieth-Century European Literature', in U. Brunotte, A. D. Ludewig and A. Stähler (eds), *Orientalism, Gender, and the Jews: Literary and Artistic Transformations of European National Discourses*, 221–9, Oldenburg: de Gruyter.
Meyer, B. (2015a), *Sensational Movies: Video, Vision, and Christianity in Ghana*, California: University of California Press.
Meyer, B. (2015b), 'Picturing the Invisible: Visual Culture and the Study of Religion', *Method and Theory in the Study of Religion*, 27 (4–5): 333–60.
Mulvey, L. ([1975] 1999), 'Visual Pleasure and Narrative Cinema', in L. Braudy and M. Cohen (eds), *Film Theory and Criticism: Introductory Readings*, 833–44, New York: Oxford University Press.
Neginsky, R. (2013), *Salome: The Image of a Woman Who Never Was*, Cambridge: Cambridge Scholarly Publishing.

Nezhinskaia, R. (2010), *Symbolism, Its Origins and Its Consequences*, Newcastle upon Tyne: Cambridge Scholarly Press.
Nietzsche, F. ([1872] 1993), *The Birth of Tragedy*, trans. S. Whiteside, London: Penguin Books.
Pesch, R. (1976), *Das Markus Evangelium: Einführung und Kommentar*, Freiburg and Basel: Herder.
Pfeiffer, H. (2006), 'Salome im Fin de Siècle: Ästhetisierung des Sakralen, Sakralisierung des Ästhetischen', in S. Martus and A. Polaschegg (eds), *Das Buch der Bücher – Gelesen: Lesarten der Bibel in den Wissenschaften und Künsten*, 303–36, Bern: Peter Lang.
Rohde, T., ed. (2000), *Mythos Salome: Vom Markusevangelium bis Djuna Barnes*, Leipzig: Reclam Verlag.
Seshadri, A. L. (2006), 'The Taste of Love: Salome's Transfiguration', *Women and Music: A Journal of Gender and Culture*, 10: 24–44.
Steiner, W. (2004), 'Pictorial Narrativity', in M. L. Ryan (ed.), *Narrative across Media: The Language of Storytelling*, 145–74, Lincoln and London: University of Nebraska Press.
Strauss, R. (1949), *Betrachtungen und Erinnerungen, hg. v. Willi Schuh*, Mainz: Schott.
The NRSV (1998), Bible New Standard Version. Available online: http://www.devotions.net/bible/00bible.htm (accessed 2 January 2018).
Tolbert, M. A. (1978), *Sowing the Gospel: Mark's World in Literary-Historical Perspective*, Minneapolis: Fortress Press.
Tooke, A. (2000), *Flaubert and the Pictorial Arts: From Image to Text*, Oxford: Oxford University Press.
Uehlinger, C. (2005), '"Medien" in der Lebenswelt des Antiken Palästina?', in C. Frevel (ed.), *Medien im antiken Palästina: Materielle Kommunikation und Medialität als Thema der Palästinaarchäologie*, 31–61, Tübingen: Mohr Siebeck.
Valman, N. (2007), *The Jewess in Nineteenth-Century British Literary Culture*, Cambridge: Cambridge University Press.
Wallen, J. (1992), 'Illustrating *Salome*: Perverting the Text?' *Word & Image*, 8 (2): 124–32.
Warburg, A. (2010), 'Mnemosyne Eileitung', in M. Treml, S. Weigel and P. Ladwig (eds), *Aby Warburg: Werke in einem Band*, 629–39, Berlin: Suhrkamp.
Wellhausen, J. ([1923] 2010), *Das Evangelium Marci*, United States: Nabu Press.

Chapter 15

Benthien, C. (2002), *Haut: Literaturgeschichte – Körperbilder – Grenzdiskurse*, Reinbek bei Hamburg: Rowohlt.
Bohde, D. (2007), 'Le Tinte delle Carni: Zur Begrifflichkeit für Haut und Fleisch in italienischen Kunsttraktaten des 15. bis 17. Jahrhunderts.', in D. Bohde and M. Fend (eds), *Weder Haut noch Fleisch: Das Inkarnat in der Kunstgeschichte*, 41–63, Berlin: Deutscher Kunstverlag.
Bohde, D. and M. Fend, eds (2007), *Weder Haut noch Fleisch: Das Inkarnat in der Kunstgeschichte*, Berlin: Deutscher Kunstverlag.
Cennini, C. (2015), *Cennino Cennini's Il Libro dell'arte: A New English Translation and Commentary with Italian Transcription*, London: Archetype.
Démoris, R. (2006), 'Boucher, Diderot, Rousseau', in M. Hyde and M. Ledbury (eds), *Rethinking Boucher*, 201–28, Los Angeles: Getty Research Institute.
De Piles, R. (1677), *Divers Conversations sur la Peinture*, Paris: Nicolas Langlois.
Diderot, D. (1995), *Diderot on Art, Vol. 1: The Salon of 1765 and Notes on Painting*, trans. J. Goodman, New Haven and London: Yale University Press.

Fend, M. (2007), 'Die Substanz der Oberfläche: Haut und Fleisch in der französischen Kunsttheorie des 17. bis 19. Jahrhunderts', in D. Bohde and M. Fend (eds), *Weder Haut noch Fleisch: Das Inkarnat in der Kunstgeschichte*, 87–104, Berlin: Deutscher Kunstverlag.

Hecht, C. (2012), *Katholische Bildertheologie der frühen Neuzeit: Studien zu Traktaten von Johannes Molanus, Gabriele Paleotti und anderen Autoren*, Berlin: Deutscher Kunstverlag.

Houellebecq, M. (2015), *Submission: A Novel*, trans. L. Stein, New York: Farrar, Straus and Giroux.

Huysmans, J.-K. ([1883] 1969), *L'art Moderne*, Farnborough: Gregg. Available online: https://archive.org/details/lartmoderne01huysgoog (accessed 23 May 2018).

Huysmans, J.-K. ([1884] 2003), *Against Nature (A Rebours)*, trans. R. Baldick, London, New York: Penguin.

Hyde, M. and M. Ledbury, eds (2006), *Rethinking Boucher*, Los Angeles: Getty Research Institute.

Koos, M. (2007), 'Haut als mediale Metapher in der Malerei von Caravaggio', in D. Bohde and M. Fend (eds), *Weder Haut noch Fleisch: Das Inkarnat in der Kunstgeschichte*, 65–85, Berlin: Deutscher Kunstverlag.

Koos, M. (2014), *Haut, Farbe und Medialität. Oberfläche im Werk Jean-Étienne Liotard*, Munich: Fink Verlag.

Krüger, M. (2007), 'Das Fleisch der Malerei. Physilologische Kunstkritik im 19. Jahrhundert', in D. Bohde and M. Fend (eds), *Weder Haut noch Fleisch: Das Inkarnat in der Kunstgeschichte*, Berlin: Deutscher Kunstverlag.

Kruse, C. (2003), *Wozu Menschen malen: Historische Begründungen der Malerei*, Munich: Fink Verlag.

Kruse, V. (2008), *Geschichte der Soziologie*, Konstanz: UVK Verlag.

Lanczkowski, G. (1982), 'Inkarnation', in K. Gründer and J. Ritter (eds), *Historisches Wörterbuch der Philosophie*, vol. 4, 368–82, Basel and Stuttgart: Schwabe.

Lepenies, W. (2010), *Auguste Comte: Die Macht der Zeichen*, Munich: Carl Hanser Verlag.

Michel, A. (1923), 'Incarnation', *Dictionnaire de Théologie Catholique*, vol. 7, 1446–87, Paris: Letouzey et Ané.

Schieder, M. (1997), *Jenseits der Aufklärung: Die Religiöse Malerei im ausgehenden Ancien Regime*, Berlin: Gebrüder Mann Verlag.

Schieder, M. (2006), 'Between *Grace* and *Volupté*: Boucher and Religious Painting', in M. Hyde and M. Ledbury (eds), *Rethinking Boucher*, 61–87, Los Angeles: Getty Research Institute.

Vasari, G. (1903), *The Life of Leonardo da Vinci by Giorgio Vasari*, ed. L. Bin-Yon, trans. H. P. Horne, New York: Longmans, Green and Co. Available online: http://digital.library.yale.edu/cdm/ref/collection/rebooks/id/24652 (accessed 27 October 2017).

Wine, H. (2002), 'Madame de Pompadour im "Salon"', in X. Salmon and J. G. von Hohenzollern (eds), *Madame Pompadour und die Künste*, 19–27, Munich: Hirmer.

Zola, É. (1959), *Salons, recueillis*, ed. F. W. J. Hemings and Robert J. Nies, Geneva and Paris: Minard.

Zola, É. ([1867] 1979), *Thérèse Raquin*, Paris: Gallimard.

Zola, É. (1979a), 'Réponse de Zola à Ferragus (1868)', in *Thérèse Raquin*, 324–8, Paris: Gallimard.

Zola, É. (1993), *The Masterpiece*, trans. T. Walton, New York: Oxford University Press.

Afterword

Barthes, R. (1993), *Camera Lucida: Reflections on Photography*, trans. Richard Howard, New York: Hill and Wang.

Bynum, C. W. (1995), *The Resurrection of the Body in Western Christianity, 200–1336*, New York: Columbia University Press.

Calvin, J. (1989), *Institutes of the Christian Religion*, trans. H. Beveridge, Grand Rapids: Wm. B. Eerdmans.

Kurth, W. (1963), *The Complete Woodcuts of Albrecht Dürer*, New York: Dover.

Luther, M. (1969), 'A Mediation on Christ's Passion', *Luther's Works*, ed. Martin O. Dietrich, vol. 42, Philadelphia: Fortress Press.

Meyer, B. (2006), *Religious Sensations: Why Media, Aesthetics and Power Matter in the Study of Contemporary Religion*, Amsterdam: Vrije Universiteit.

Morgan, D. (2012), *The Embodied Eye: Religious Visual Culture and the Social Life of Feeling*, Berkeley: University of California Press.

Morgan, D. (2015), *The Forge of Vision: A Visual History of Modern Christianity*, Berkeley: University of California Press.

Index

Page numbers in bold refer to primary passages to the theme in question.

aesthetics
  aesthetic regime(s) 2, 9, 15, 16, 33, 34, 115, **156-8**, 166-7, 169, 170, 171
  aesthetics of music 4, 11, 37, 42, 43, 55
  aesthetics of religion 62, 104, 115, 123, 157, 158, 209, 216
  aesthetics of the non-representable 4, 11, 17, 21, **33-5**
  aesthetics of the sublime 4, 10, 12, 17, 33-4, 62, 82, 229, **234-7**, **240-4**, 276
  aesthetics of the unseen 4-6, 77, 78, 84-8, 91, 93, 95, 157, 170, 172, 183, 184
  aesthetics of withdrawal 4, 15-16, 33, **185-6, 188**, 194
Africa 55, 78, 79, 88-95, 130, 185-7, 193, 195, 210
Akoto, Kwame (alias Almighty God) 96
altar 28, 30, 71, 72, 91, 158, 214, 223-7, 241, 242, *see also* sites for veneration
aniconism 1, **2-4**, 9, 10, **21-5**, 31, 36, 60, 62, 63, 69, 70, 77-84, 94, **99-104**, 110-15, 116, 117, 119, 120-3, 187, 190, 192, 195, 196, 197, 198, 236, 242, 243
anthropology 4, 14, 15, 83, 85, 87, 119, 122, 202, 253, 255, 274
anthropomorphism 2, 54, 65, 69, 75, 90, 100, 108-10, 115, 132, 133
antiquity 23, 37, 39, 42, 55, 88, 99, 101, 102, 103, 118, 120, 121, 232
archaeology 3, 13, 23, 24, 71, 105, 106, 110, 111, 117, 119, 123, 187
art history 4, 12, 43, 45, 79, 81, 84, 85, 88, 94, 124, 129, 253

Bakor, Omar Said 194-7
baroque 8, 16, 17, 86, 213, 214, 215, 223, 228, 230, 232, 233, 245, 248, *see also* images, in Christianity

Becker-Leckrone, Megan 246, 255
Belting, Hans 5, 7, 58, 66, 85, 86, 87, 88, 91, 94, 124, 160, 161, 166, 171, 195, 199, 200, 253, 255
Bernini, Gian Lorenzo 17, 213-28, 232, 233
biblical studies 4, 10, 21, 23, 35, 62, 82, 84, 116, 117, 118, 119, 122
blank 8, 17, **245-7**, **253-5**, 256, 279, 286 n.9
body 18, 22, 34, 45, 51, 53-5, 75-6, 91, 123, 135, 136, 143, 145, 147, 183, 186, 188, 215, 220, 229, 230, 233, 246-7, 250-6, **256-9**, 266, 269-70, **270-2**, 275-82
Boehm, Gottfried 5, 23, **84-5**, 88, 94, 96, 185
Boucher, François 267, 268
Brethren of Purity 45, 47, 48, 50, 51, 53, 54, 124, 127, 128
Burke, Edmund 17, 234, 236

Cabanel, Alexandre 270, 271
Caravaggio, Michelangelo Merisi da 232, 233, 234, 237, 248, 265
Catholic traditions 2, 3, 6, 63, 64, 70, 80, 82, 86, 89, 91, 102, 118, 167, 200, 201, 204, 205, 214, 215, 220, 223-8, 237, 262, 267, 273, 282
Cennini, Cennino 17, 261-3, 265
Christianity, *see* Catholic traditions, Eastern Orthodox traditions, Protestant traditions, Reformed traditions
Church 45, 130, 158, 176, 203, 214, 215, 216, 217, 221, 222, 223-8, 230, 231, 239, 240, 241, 242, *see also* sites for veneration
Comte, Auguste 269, 270, 272
Counter-Reformation, *see* reformation

desires 2, 5, 7, **9–12**, 16, 33, 46, 48, 51, 57, 58, 63, 69, 74, 81, 93, 130, 158, 171, 186, 188, 193, 204, 215, 222, 235, 245, 246, 247, 248, 251, 255, 268, 273
  contested desire(s) 5, **9–10**, 57, 64, 69, 79, 81
devil 7, 46, 78, 89, 91–2, 95, 96, 127, 250, see also Satan
Diderot, Denis 266, 267, 268, 274
al-Din, Rashid 134, 135, 136, 137, 139
Duran, Profiat 14, 129
Dürer, Albrecht 278, 279, 280, 281, 282

Eastern Orthodox traditions 2, 3, 6, 8, 9, 55, 64, 82, 118, **156–71**, **198–210**, 225
enlightenment 78, 82, 89, 118, 201, 233, 234, 237, 243, 260, 267, 269, 273
Europe 10, 12, 16, 17, 37, 38, 39, 41, 42, 45, 52–6, 70, 79, 83, 85, 88, 90, 91, 101, 118, 131, 134, 137, 145, 176, 190, 210, 237, 247, 251, 254, 260, 263, 274, 278, 280, 282

face 58, 75, 86, 143, 145, 182, 186, 188–9, 192–4, 261–4
al-Farabi 44, 45, 50, 52, 55
fetish, fetishism 66, 74, 78, **88–90**, 186, 246, 251, **256–9**
figuration(s) 1, 4, 6–9, 10, 76, 77, 78, 79, 81, 87, 93, 95, 96, 103, 110, 112, 120, 122, 157, 170, 176, 183, 186, 187, 194, 238, 243, 275, 276, 277
Foucault, Michel 10, 185
Freud, Sigmund 12, 67–71
Friedrich, Caspar David 230, 237, 276

Gaifman, Milette 2, 22, 99, 122
al-Ghazali, Ahmad 46, 48, 50, 51, 141, 143
Giotto 262, 263
golden calf 10, 12, **57–76**, 78, 83, 84, 112, 117, 250, see also aniconism
Guth, Claus 246, 257, 258

Hadith 39, 40, 43, 48, 138, 143
al-Ḥarizi, Yehudah 14, 130
Heinsen, Hein 241, 242, 243

heritage 61, 78, 88, 92, 118, 155, 158, 173, 208, 290
Houellebecq, Michel 7, 17, **260–1**, **272–4**
Huysmans, Joris-Karl 7, 18, 254–6, 260, 270, 272, 273

iconic difference 84, 96
iconic presence 5, 87, 265
iconoclash 9, 60, 79, 80, 82, 85, 87, 197
iconoclasm 13, 26, 27, 39, 41, 55, 59, 60, 70, 75, 79, 80, 81, 82, 84, 85, 88, 95, 196, 198–201, 216, 230
icon(s) 4, 6, 8, 9, 12, 15, 16, 57, 58, 77, 81, 86, 101, 128, 129, 131, **155–71**, 186, 196–7, **198–200**, 203, 204, **205–8**, 209, 263
idolatry 3, 4, 5, 6, 16, 39, 62, 66, 73, 74, 77–9, 80, 81, 86, 87, **88–96**, 101, 102, 103, 114, 117–20, 128, 129, 182, 187, 191, 199, 208, 209, 210, 229, 230, 235, 243, 276
idol(s) 2, 10, 21, 24, 41, 57, 60, 64, 66, 67, 68, 74, **77–9**, 80, **85–96**, 102, 103, 187, 191, 192, 198, 199, 209–10, 276
Ignatius of Loyola 8, 9, 16, 17, 204, 213, 215, 216, 218–20, 222, 226–8
illuminations 14, 125, 127, 128, 129, 131
image (in general, as in theory of) 4, 7–8, 41, 57, 58, 66, 77, 80, 84–8, 185, 186, 201, 203, 229, 234–6, 252–3, 261–72, 275
image ban 3, 4, 6, 11, 23, 33, 35, 99, 102, 104, 108, 110, 111, 112, 120, 122, 123, 230, see also aniconism
images and art
  in ancient Hebrew religion 21–36, 57–76, 99–123
  in Christianity 57–76, 77–96, 155–71, 198–210, 213–28, 229–44, 245–59, 260–74
  in Islam 37–56, 132–51, 155–71, 172–84, 185–97
  in Judaism 57–76, 99–123, 124–31
imagination 2, **6–9**, 21, 28, 31, 32–3, 78, 79, 86, 87, 91, 93, 105, 108, 110, 117, 123, 124, 133, 141, 145, 149, 198, 200, 201–3, 204, 205, 208, 209,

210, 215, 222, 229, 234, 235, 245,
247, 250, 251, 252, 253, 254, 255,
256, 275, 276, 282
incarnation 7, 22, 75, 86, 87, 118, 269, 278
incarnazione **260-6**
Iran 4, 8, 15, 134, 136, 139, 141-3, 146,
172-84
Iser, Wolfgang 247, 252, 253, 255
Islam 7, 11, 14, 37-56, 61, 77, 88, 99,
101, 102, 103, 111, 127, 130, 131,
132-51, 172-84, 185-96, 260, 261,
273, 274, 276
Islamic State (IS) 88

Jerusalem 24, 26, 27, 28, 71, 103, 104,
105, 106, 107, 108, 109, 110, 111,
112, 113, 116, 119, 122, 245, 276
Jesuits 5, 16, **214-15**, 220, 222, 228, 267,
see also Ignatius of Loyola
Judaism 14, 23, 61, 63, 64, 69, 70, 78,
82, 99, 101, 102, 103, 111, 115, 120,
128, 130, 131
Judaism, Christianity and Islam 1, 2,
3, 4, 5, 6, 13, 61, 77, 111, 127, 132,
275, 276

Kafka, Franz 14, 124, 125, 127, 128
Kant, Immanuel 10, 12, 17, 42, 62, 69,
70, 71, 82, 89, 234-6, 240, 242
Karlstadt 95, 96
Keel, Othmar 23, 107, 108, 109, 112
Khazanad, Madhu 37, 38
Klages, Ludwig 21
Koran 274, *see also* Qur'an

Largier, Niklaus 7, 9, **213**, 251
Latour, Bruno 3, 12, 60, 65, 66, 73,
79-84, 85, 94
light 4, 5, 6, 8, 10, 14, 17, 34, 36, 47, 70,
93, 96, 133, 138, **143-**7, 215, 227,
230-3, 238, 241, 242, 278
Lippi, Fillipino (follower of) 59, 72, 73
logocentrism **21-2**, 32-3, 58, 80, 115,
229
Lyotard, Jean-François 230, 240-1

Maderno, Carlo 214, 221, 222, 223, 224
Maimonides, (Moses ben Maimon) 14,
129

Manet, Edouard 271, 272
Mary 15, 86, 88, 93, **155-**7, 164-5,
167-8, 199, 200, 203, 209, 231, 262,
267, 282, *see also* Meryem Ana
Masuzawa, Tomoko 66, 74
material culture 2, 3, 10, 13, 89, 95, 110,
117-20, 187, 120-3, 187
materiality, materialize 2-3, 6-9, 9-12,
22, 24-6, 32-5, 51-2, 57-9, 61-76,
78-80, 87-90, 103, 113-16, 122-3,
128, 157, 167, 184, 198-201, 205,
209, 227, 255, 264-5, 267, 277
mental imagery 7-8, 16, 35, 78-9, 86-7,
149, 183, 198, 201-4, 208, 216, 240,
246, 252-3, 255, 259
Meryem Ana 155-71, *see also* Mary
Mettinger, Tryggve 31, 32, 99, 110
Middle Ages 5, 17, 86, 101, 124,
128, 213, 217, 230, 231, 233,
274, 279
Mitchell, W. J. T., 3, 7, 12, 57, 58, 59, 63,
64, 65, 66, 67, 69, 71, 79, 83, 84,
200
modernism 12, 42, 55, 58, 60, 61, 62, 63,
65, 66, 67, 68, 79, 80, 82, 83, 84, 85,
88, 94, 101, 115, 119, 124, 127, 236,
238, 240, 245, 249, 253, 254, 256,
265, 268, 273
modernity 12, 60, 62, **65-8**, 79, **82-4**,
119, 190, 240, 249, 253
monotheism 1, 10, 12, 41, 49, 61, 62,
63, 64, 68, 69, 70, 71, 77, 82, 89, 99,
100, 101, 103, 127, 131, 132, 186,
191
Moses 12, 24, 25, 26, 30, 31, 32, 33, 34,
57, 58, 59, 65, 68, 69, 70, 71, 72, 75,
102, 103, 111, 112, 115, 118, 129,
145, 210, 250
Mosque 45, 46, 174, 193, *see also* sites
for veneration
Muhammad (Prophet) 3, 4, 7, 39,
134-50, 172-8, 182, 183-4, 202
mural paintings 8, 15, **172-84**

al-Nawawi 40, 55, 276
Newman, Barnett 237-41
Nizami of Ganj 11, 37, 38, 49, 50, 52, 54,
55, 141, 142, 145, 148
Nolde, Emil 59, 60, 71, 236, 237

object(s)   2, 10, 12, 40–2, 44–5, 49, 58, 65, 66–7, 69, 72, 74, 77–8, 80–2, 85, 87–9, 90, 95, 113, 117, 122–3, 131, 166, 173, 186, 192, 199–200, 240, 256, 258, 263, 273, 275, *see also* body; golden calf; icon(s); idol(s); tablets of the law

Perniola, Mario   216, 235, 236
photography   10, 15, 16, 59, 125, 172, **185, 186, 187, 190–6**, 203, 205, 207, 254, 261
pilgrimage   16, 17, 170, 183, 184, 193, 194, 213, 217, 218, 219, 228, 266, 273
Plato   11, 37, 38, 42, 45, 49, 50, 51, 52, 53, 54, 57, 62, 64, 127
Ponte Sant'Angelo   16, 213, 214, 216–17, 221, 225, 226, 228
Poussin, Nicholas   59, 60, 71
practice/s (religious, aesthetic)   **1–18**, 23–6, 34, 36, 38–40, 42–3, 45, 53, 55, **77–82**, 89–91, 99–102, 105, 115, **117–20**, 133, 147, 149, 157–9, 174, 182–4, 187, 198–204, 209, 261, 269, 277–8
Protestant Chrsitian traditions   6, 7, 12, 13, 39, 58, 63, 78, 80, 81, 89, 90, 102, 118, 187, 209, 215, 221, 237

Qur'an   5, 39, 41, 43, 47, 48, 52, 58, 61, 73, 127, 134, 137, 138, 140, 143, 147, 167, 182, 194, 284 n.1, 288 n.2

Rabbi Meir of Rothenburg   14, 128, 129
Raphael   59, 264
reformation   82, 86, 88, 118, 125, 131, 215, 221, 224
   Counter-Reformation   214, 215, 217, 220, 221, 227, 266, 283, *see also* Jesuits
Reformed Christian traditions   2, 6, 12, 21, 78, 79, 80, 81, 82, 83, 84, 88, 95, 101, 102, 118, 276
religion   4–6, 77–9, 99–102, 272–3
religious studies   4, 78, 83, 85, 87, 88, 101, 116, 117, 119, 120, 123, 201, 276
Renaissance   17, 64, 65, 215, 223, 230, 231, 233, 234, 237, 245, 263

representations of the divine   1, 2, 3, 5, 6, 7, 8, 9, 10, 21, 22, 24, 26, 31, 32, 35, 36, 46, 66, 69, 72, 75, 77, 79, 80, 84, 86, 87, 92, 100, 101, 104, 106, 108, 110, 112, 113, 115, 122, 132, 133, 135, 137, 138, 139, 141, 145, 149, 199, 201, 229, 230, 234, 276
Rumi, Jelal ad-Din   47, 55
Russia   16, 198, 200–6, 209–10

sacred (the sacred, the sacred story, place, etc.)   11, 16–17, 32, 33–5, 39, 67, 80, 88–9, 96, 110, 125, 131, 149, 177–8, 180, 183–4, 209, 225, 228–30, 235, 241–2, 247, 251, 275
The Sacred Heart of Jesus   203
Saint Peter   213–14, 217, 220–5, 228
Sarajevo Haggadah   14, 125, 126, 128
Satan   89, 92, 95–6, 250, *see also* devil
scripturalism   10, 13, 100, 104, 118
scripture   39, 57, 58, 75, 100, 101, 102, 115, 116, 118, 127, **134–8**, 140, 166, 187, 199, 230, 232, 282
Second Commandment   2, 3, 21, 22, 24, 31, 62, 63, 64, 77–89, 94, 96, 103, 110, 112, 199, 203, 210
sensation(s)   1, 3, 4, **6–9**, 33, 36, 75, 77, 79, 85, 156, 157, 158, 169, 170, 171, 173, 174, 184, 213, 214, 219, 226, 234, 275, 276, 277
senses
   hearing   11, 33, 46, 48, 50, 51, 53, 55, 114, 115, 165, 188, 190, 245, 251, 258, 259
   seeing   3, 8, 11, 37, 51, 53, 55, 62, 125, 127, 174, 183, 184, 186, 199, 201, 203, 245, 251, 281
   smelling   11, 33, 135, 168
   touch   32, 45, 70, 75, 134, 163, 165, 180, 203, 213, 274
shrine   15, 26, 71, 92, 104, 110, 113, 119, 173, 177, 178, 179, 180, 181, 182, 183, 184, 201, *see also* sites for veneration
sites for veneration   41, 45, 71, 130, 155, 158–9, 165, 166, 169, 171, 176, 204

soul   7, 18, 44–8, 49, 51, 53, 129–30, 183, 213, 219, 228, 229, 256, **265–7, 269–70**, 272, 274
space (room)   31, 34, 36, 59, 116, 122–3, 133, 141, 145, 183, 184, 187, 190, 192, 199, 215–16, 222, 224, 225, 228, 231–6, 238, 240, 245–6, 252–3, 277, 280, 282
spirit, spiritual, spiratualization   92–3, 127, 140, 148, 149, 151, 167, 168, 174, 183–4, 187, 201–2, **204–5**, 213–18, 227–8, **250–4**, 269, 272–4, 280
Strauss, Richard   10, 17, 245, 246, 250, 252, 256–9
symbolism   14, 28, 30, 31, 32, 33, 46, 74, 108, 112, 133, 138, 143–50, 207, 225, 227, 231, 236, 251, 255, 256
synagogue   117, 121, *see also* sites for veneration

tablets of the law   31–35, 58, 72, 75, 110
temple   24, 26, 45, 71, 72, 75, 111, 116, 117, 119, 120, 121, 122, 127, 129, 272
  Solomonic Temple   4, 11, 24, **26–36**, 104, 108, 112, 116, 119, 225, *see also* sites for veneration
theory
  aesthetic theory   43–9, 130, 131, 157–8, 185, 186, 245, 247, 252–3
  art theory   7, 129, 130, 231, 234–6, 240, 261–6, 267, 269, 272
  religio-historical theory   13, 103, 105–6, 121
Torah   24, 25, 26, 31, 32, 58, 75, 82, 102, 103, 104, 111, 112, 115, 117, 118
transcedence   9, 10, 14, 23, 31, 34–5, 58–9, 62, 67, 87, 99–101, 122, 124, 132–3, 140–1, 147, 157, 199, 201, 235–6, 275–7, 281–2
transfiguration   8, 93, 231, 250, 253
tree   28, 63, 64, 65, 127, 135, 231, 266
  wish tree   158, 159, *see also* sites for veneration
Turkey   9, 14, 15, 143, 145, 148–50, 155–6, 158, 163, 165, 169
Twelver Shiism   15, 172, 174, 175, 178, 183

Vasari, Giorgio   64, 65, 264
Vatican   213, 214, 216, 217, 218, 220, 223, 228
Veil, unveil   14, 15, 16, 17, 47, 70, 133, 135, **140–3**, 145, 185, 186, **187–94**, 219–20, 245–6, 251, 254–7, 276, 280
Vinci, Leonardo da   8, 45, 229, 231, 232, 264

Wilde, Oscar   9, 17, 245–7, 250–2, 254–8

Zola, Émile   18, **270–3**

www.ingramcontent.com/pod-product-compliance
Lightning Source LLC
Chambersburg PA
CBHW070012010526
44117CB00011B/1537